LINOCUT

HERBERT PRESS
Bloomsbury Publishing Plc
50 Bedford Square, London, WC1B 3DP, UK
Bloomsbury Publishing Ireland Limited,
29 Earlsfort Terrace, Dublin 2, D02 AY28, Ireland

BLOOMSBURY, HERBERT PRESS and the Herbert Press logo are trademarks of
Bloomsbury Publishing Plc

First published in Great Britain in 2023

A catalogue record for this book is available from the British Library
Library of Congress Cataloguing-in-Publication data has been applied for

ISBN: 978-1-78994-070-1; eBook: 978-1-78994-068-8

8 10 9

Designed and typeset by Laura Woussen
Printed and bound in China by C&C Offset Printing Co., Ltd.

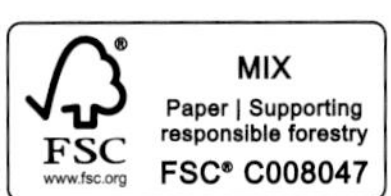

To find out more about our authors and books visit www.bloomsbury.com and sign up
for our newsletters
For product safety related questions contact productsafety@bloomsbury.com

LINOCUT

A Creative Guide to Making Beautiful Prints

Sam Marshall

HERBERT PRESS

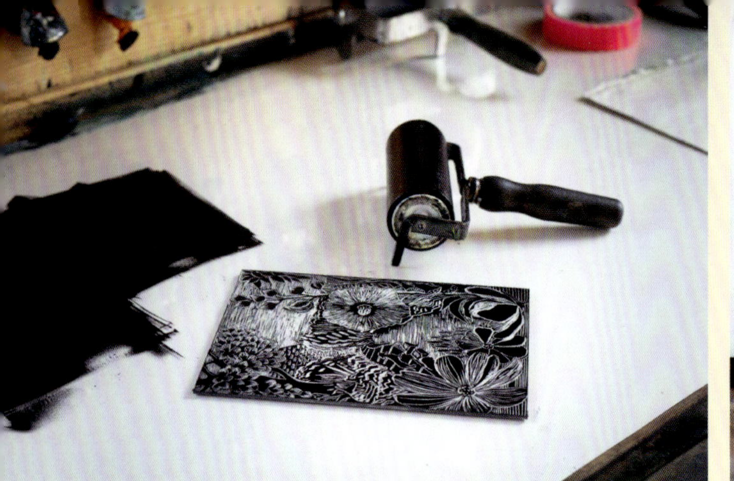
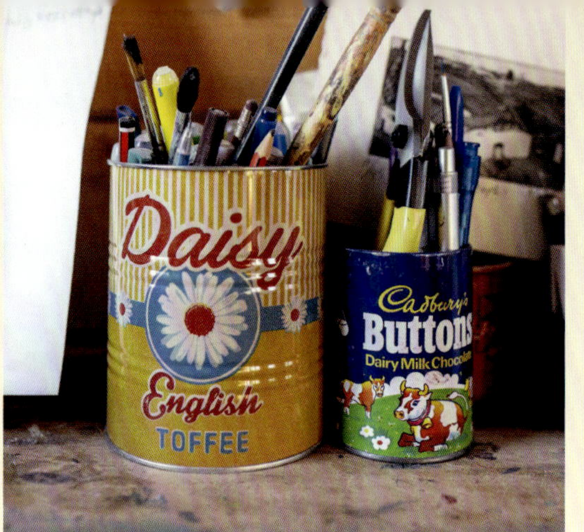
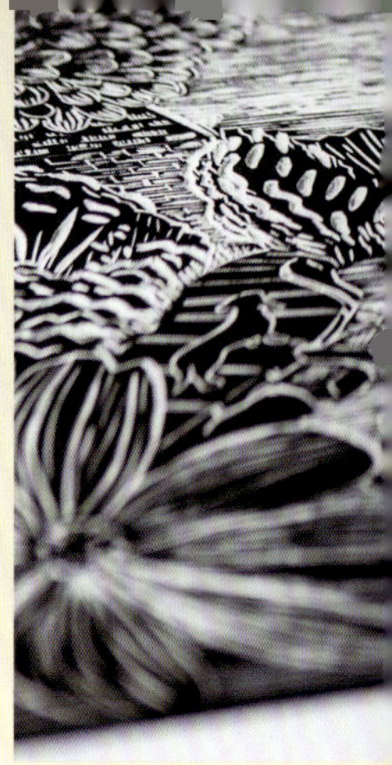

CONTENTS

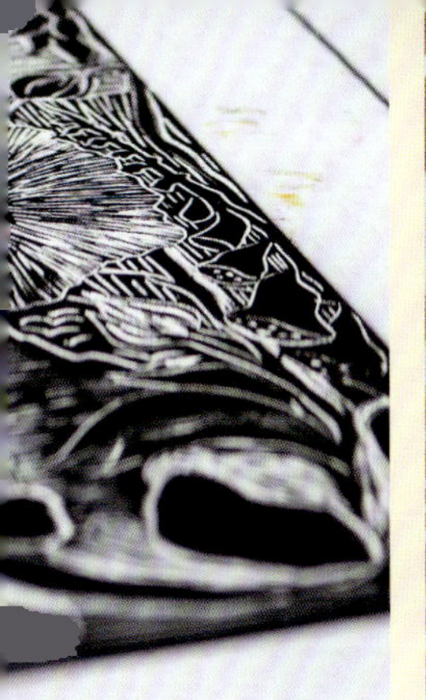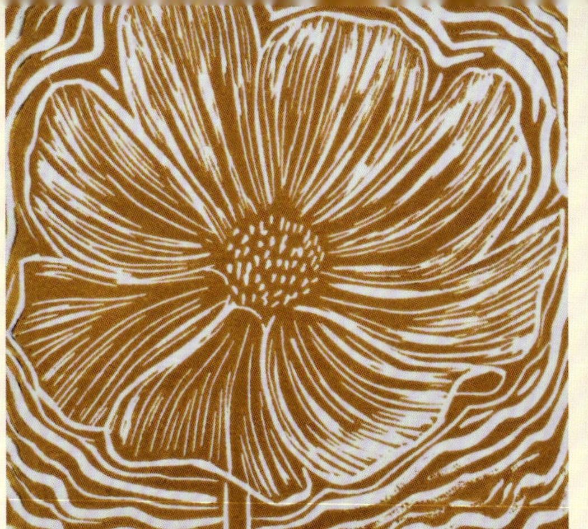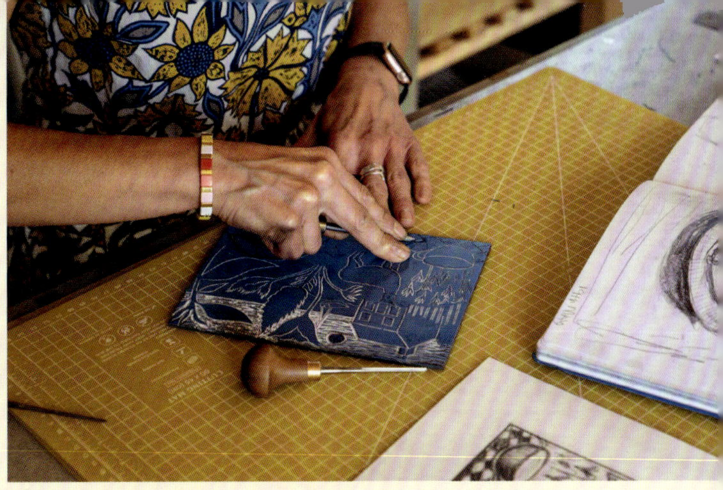

INTRODUCTION

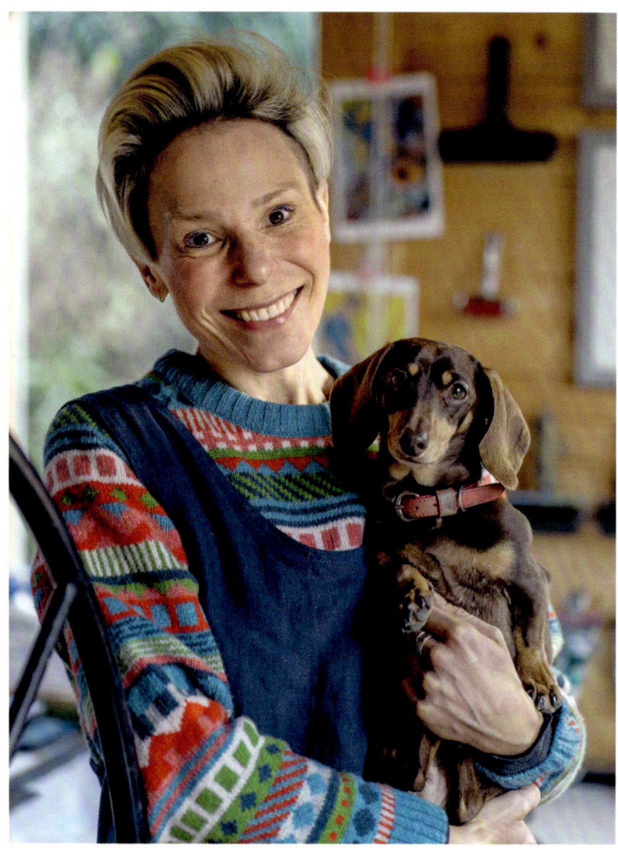

Hi, I'm Sam. I'm a printmaker, living in rural Northamptonshire with my miniature dachshund, Miss Marple. I have a print studio in my garden where I make all my work and run my workshops, both in person and online. I've been printmaking for over twenty years now. I started with etching and spent a good few years concentrating solely on this. However, over time, I wanted to vary my practice and include more dynamic colours in my work, so linocut seemed to be the obvious next step.

At first, I must confess, I really struggled with linocut. I was teaching myself using blunt tools and old lino. I just couldn't understand how so many people could achieve such amazing results with what seemed, to me, to be an unwieldy technique. However, I'm stubborn and don't like to be defeated, so I battled on.

I did a lot of research, bought better tools and, most importantly, kept practising… and very soon I was hooked. At this point I was living in London; I didn't have a studio or a lot of space so I made do with what I had and repurposed a corner of my bedroom into my 'studio' – it served as my drawing space as well as a carving, inking and printing area. I was amazed by how much I could achieve with so few tools and equipment.

The fact that linocut can be carried out at home, on your kitchen table, is just one of the things that attracted me to it. I love the spontaneity of the marks you can make with the tools, the quality of lines that can be produced and how varied they can be. I find the whole process really helpful for my busy mind; the fact that there are so many different stages of producing a print has taught me to be much more patient. The physical act of carving can also be really meditative. I hear this from my students, too; they often end a three-hour session by saying how much calmer they feel. Concentrating solely on one task for a couple of hours can have a transformative effect.

I have been teaching linocut for over ten years now and I've noticed that students often struggle with subject matter; they frequently tell me that they don't know where to start or what to base their work on. It's easy to understand why – linocut can be so daunting! The marks are very definite and you can't easily erase your mistakes.

Another thing I hear so often is 'I can't draw', which makes me feel sad, as I truly believe we can all make our own unique marks. Drawing is at the heart of my practice – I always start off with a sketch – and although this book does not contain drawing exercises as such, every project begins with a drawing. I encourage you to just give it a go and see what you come up with. This book is designed to help you build up your confidence with drawing, to be inspired to discover your subject matter and to improve your printmaking skills. I want you to really enjoy the whole process of linocut – from the drawing to the carving, from the inking to the printing – and then showing them off at the end. I will support you to make mistakes, to take risks and to turn things upside down and see what happens.

My own work is autobiographical. I make prints about my life and the stories it contains. I use my everyday surroundings as inspiration, drawing all the time and always looking for a way to include what I see in my prints. During the first lockdown, I made a series of linocuts that documented my life in the garden that summer, which included mowing the lawn

incessantly as I found it soothed my anxious mind! In April 2019, I visited Japan for fifteen days. While I was there I sketched, made notes and took photographs to record every day of my trip, then when I got back to the studio I turned them into a series of fifteen linocuts that told my daily stories.

I aim to use my own practice as a guide to help inspire your own ideas. Throughout this book, you will work through a series of projects that will not only develop your practical skills but will also help you to build up the confidence to make work that is personal to you and tells your stories. I am hopeful (and quietly confident!) that as you progress through the book you will find your own unique style which highlights just how you see and experience the world. It will be a lovely record of your own life and journey.

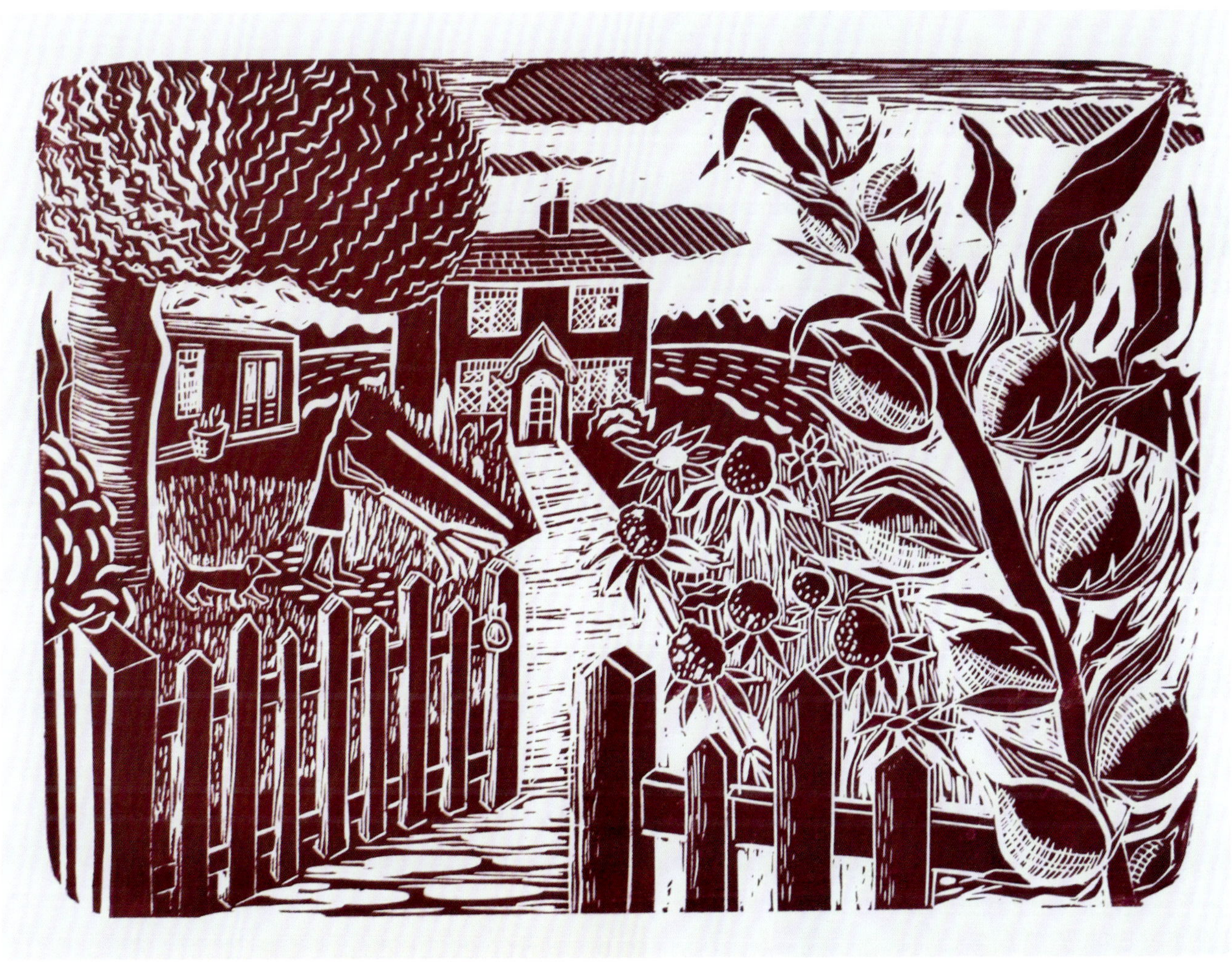

ABOUT THIS BOOK

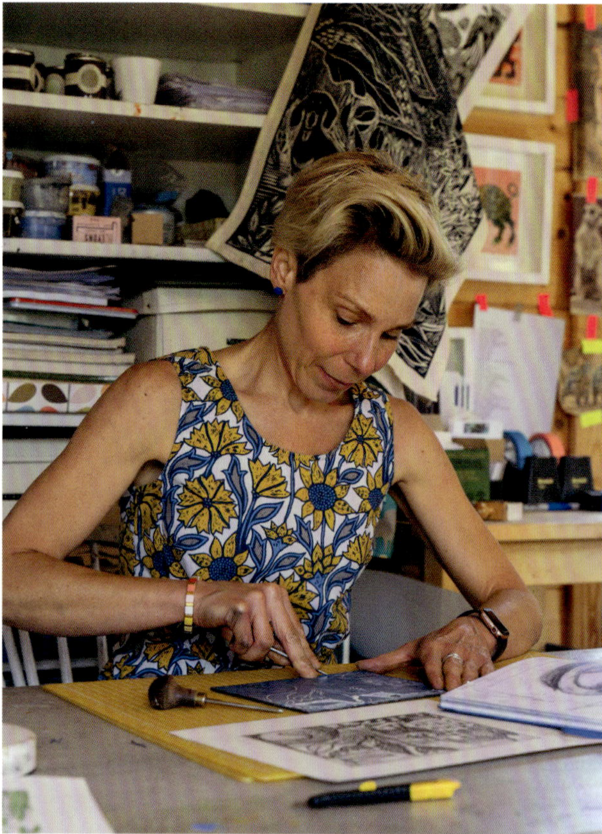

This book is suitable for complete beginners as well as those of you who have some experience and want to expand upon and enhance your skills. I have structured the projects so they build up in complexity and allow your skills to develop, however, feel free to dip in and out of the book as you like.

For each project I go through exactly what is entailed, providing step-by-step instructions and sharing my own progress as I work through the tasks. I'm keen to get you drawing, so each project starts off with a sketch – just give it a go and remember it's all about having fun and enjoying what you are doing. By all means, take photos to remind you of what it is you are drawing, but remember that nothing beats a drawing done on the spot – with your hand and eye responding directly to what is in front of you – making your own unique marks.

For each project I will give you a specific task to help you narrow down your choices and become more selective about what you choose to draw. In my experience, beginners often respond best when there are clear boundaries that point them towards a subject to base their work on – it helps to prevent overwhelm. But don't worry if you can't find anything suitable; read through the projects and think about what object or subject matter could work for you.

Throughout the book, I talk you through everything to do with linocut and answer many of the questions I am asked in my workshops. I discuss which tools and materials to buy and how to set up your workspace, so you are all set up to start your journey. I demonstrate practical methods such as how to draw and transfer images onto your block, to hold and use your tools safely and to clean up your inks. I then explain the basics of registration and how to use or reduce noise in your prints, and I give advice on how to edition your prints, including tips on edition size, pricing, and numbering and signing your work.

I will start you off – as I always do in my workshops – with a mark-making warm-up block (see page 39), where you will make a really quick drawing, using lots of different marks, and translate it to linocut. This will encourage you to see what marks are possible to make using your tools, providing a handy reference for the rest of the projects. We will then build on this to show you how carving the same image in four different ways (see page 49) can really affect the look of your print.

Starting at home, the simple black-and-white linocut (see page 63) is inspired by a familiar object that is important to you – I chose an antique rocking horse. I then ask you to move outside to your garden (or any green space) to complete a nature study (see page 72), working your sketches up into larger designs to be carved into your linocut and printed using a single colour. We then move further afield, where I encourage you to take your sketchbook on a weekend away with you to document your trip by combining drawings on location to make a lovely holiday memory print (see page 86).

Next, we will explore colour. First, I will show you how to create a reduction linocut, which will require you to hunt around your house for a practical object to serve as your subject matter (see page 92) – I used simple Japanese secateurs. We then create two different multi-block prints: a stunning fennec fox (see page 102) which uses key block, and a memento of my treasured Japanese Kokeshi doll (see page 108) without key block. And, after all your sketching practice, I'm sure you will be keen to discover how to showcase a series of prints on a similar theme, so I demonstrate how to create a spectacular concertina book (see page 119).

We then move on to more experimental techniques, including combining monoprint and linocut (see page 131), repurposing old blocks (see page 134), discovering chine collé (see page 138), cutting up old linocut blocks to create new and exciting jigsaw prints (see page 143) and exploring the rainbow roll technique (see page 149). These will expand on your skill set to create some unique and impressive prints.

When you near the end of the book, you will have a sketchbook bursting with drawings of special moments, interesting characters and memories, and making linocut cards is such a great way to share these designs with others. I include two projects to show you how to create cards from your sketches: a single-block design featuring Miss Marple (see page 154) and a lovely two-block cat card (see page 157).

The grand finale is a linocut countryside scene (see page 162), whereby you bring together everything that you have learnt, combining some of the images and drawings you have worked on throughout the book to turn them into one large print. By the end of the book, you should feel confident in the technicalities of the printing process and in making and developing your own work, and you will have a wonderful selection of prints that record our time together.

One last thing: I'm going to show you my way of printmaking – how I do things. My practice is a culmination of many years of learning from lots of different people. You will find other printmakers do things differently. There is a right and wrong way for many things, but other times I encourage you to find your own way of printmaking – to make it unique to you.

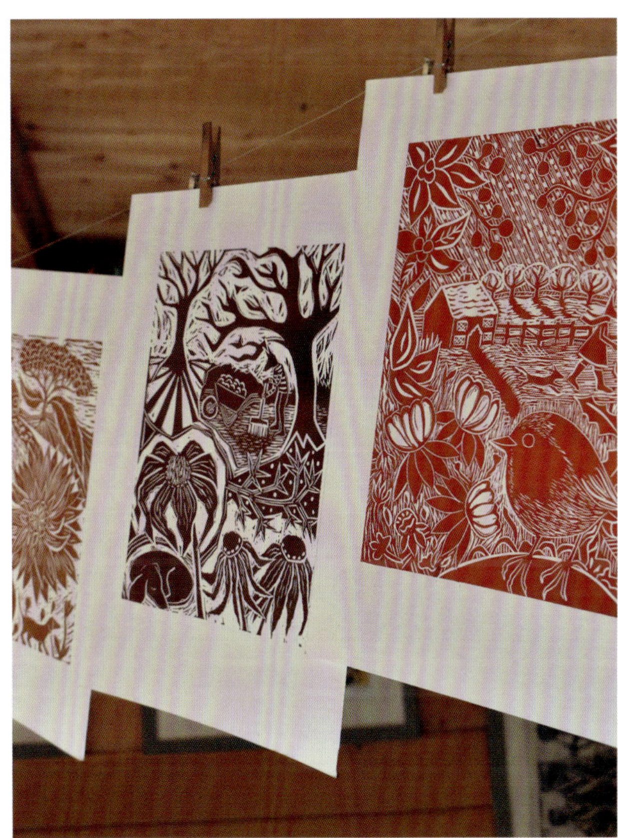

1 WHAT IS LINOCUT?

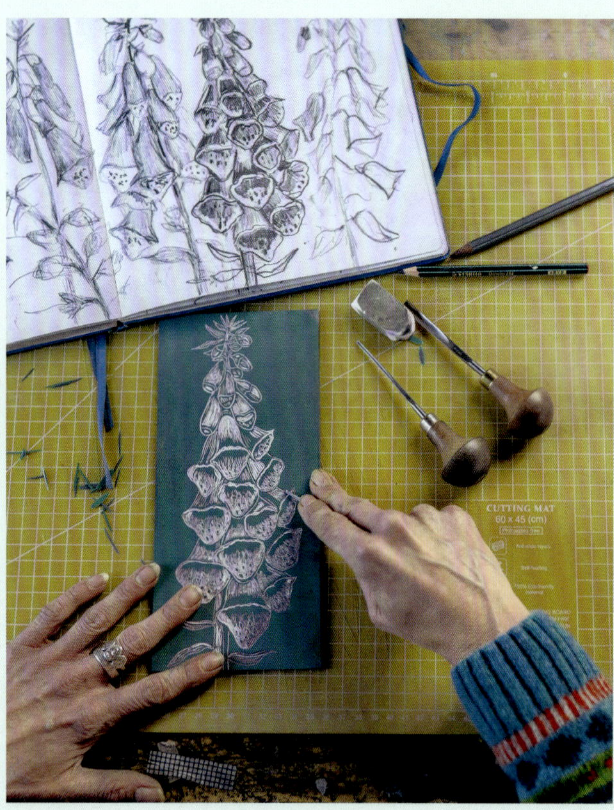

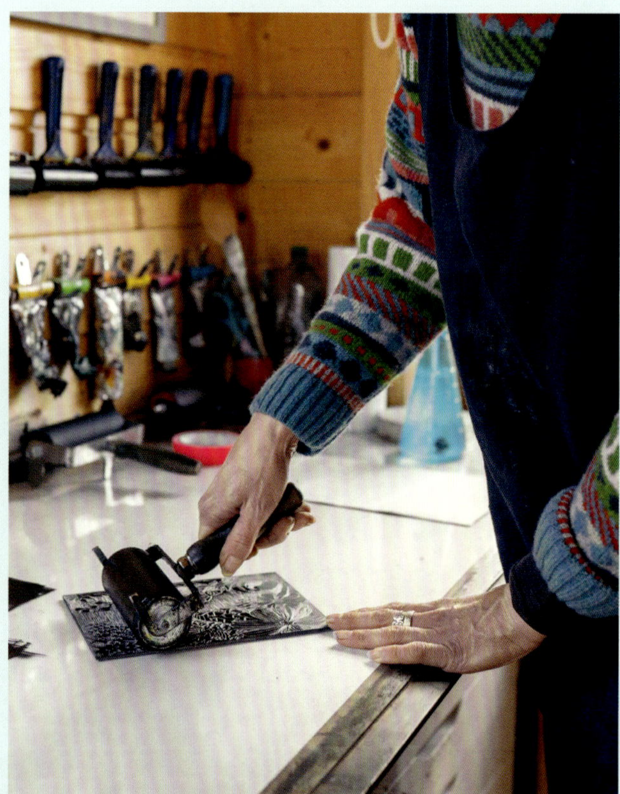

Many of us can recollect trying out linocut at school – maybe you have memories of rock-hard lino and blunt tools; perhaps there was even an injury or two. When some of my students reminisce about their first memories of linocut, which so often involve cuts and blood, I'm amazed they want to try again!

Simply put, linocut is a type of relief printmaking, meaning that the ink remains on the surface and everything you carve away remains white. It is a negative mark-making technique, in that you are removing rather than adding, and what you leave behind gives you your image.

First of all, a design is created and then transferred to lino, either by tracing or drawing directly. Linocutting tools are then used to carve away at the design, removing the areas you want to print white and leaving those you want to print in relief. It's important to remember that whatever you carve will be the reverse or mirror image; so, if you want to print your name, you will need to carve it in reverse so you are able to read it the right way round.

Once the block has been carved, the lino is inked up using a roller (or brayer) and paper is placed on top. Printing can be done by hand using a burnishing tool, such as a wooden spoon or a baren, which is used to rub the back of the paper and the ink is then transferred to the paper. If not done by hand, a press can be used, but for the purpose of this book, we will be printing by hand using your chosen burnishing tool.

What I love about linocut is its versatility and the endless possibilities it offers. Once you get the hang of creating simple prints, you can really begin to experiment. You can use multiple blocks with different colours, create jigsaw prints and combine with other techniques such as monoprint and collage – all of which we are going to explore in this book. While the results are quite bold and dramatic, linocutting can be really sensitive, too – I love the fact that you can create such a variety of marks to produce dynamic and visually exciting prints.

THE HISTORY OF LINOCUTTING

Linoleum – a mixture of cork and linseed oil on a canvas backing – was invented in the 1860s as a hardwearing, cheap and easily cleaned floor covering. By 1900 it had been incorporated into relief printmaking as a suitable material for cutting into, and it was often used by amateurs or as a teaching product in schools. Frank Cisek, an art teacher in Vienna, encouraged his students to make linocuts in the early twentieth century. His students' work was much admired, and its cheapness and comparable ease of handling led to its extensive use in schools.

Around the same time, linocutting became a popular way of working among the German expressionist and Russian constructivist movements. The first major artist to adopt linocut as a medium was Erich Heckel, whose earliest linocut is dated 1903. He was also the founding member of the group Die Brücke (The Bridge) – artists from this group regularly used linocut instead of woodcut from 1905 to the 1920s.

In the early 1920s, the British artist Claude Flight had started to experiment with linocut, wanting to create a new form of art that celebrated the movement, speed, and hustle and bustle of the new post-war world. He began teaching at the Grosvenor School of Modern Art in 1926 and it was here that he was able to share his passion for the technique with his pupils, helping to establish and popularise it as an important and powerful new art form. The first ever linocut exhibition, organised by Flight and featuring work by his students Cyril Power, Sybil Andrews and Dorrit Black, took place at the Redfern Gallery in 1929 and was a great success. The students became known collectively as the 'Grosvenor School' and their work was characterised by multiple blocks of colour with a sense of dynamic movement and design, with urban transport and sport featuring as popular subjects.

However, it was really when artists such as Henri Matisse and Pablo Picasso started using linoleum that its popularity grew. Picasso began experimenting with linocuts in 1939 and continued until the early 1960s. He is also credited for inventing the 'reduction' method, where a piece of lino in each colour layer is taken from the same block. We will be using this technique later in the book (see page 92).

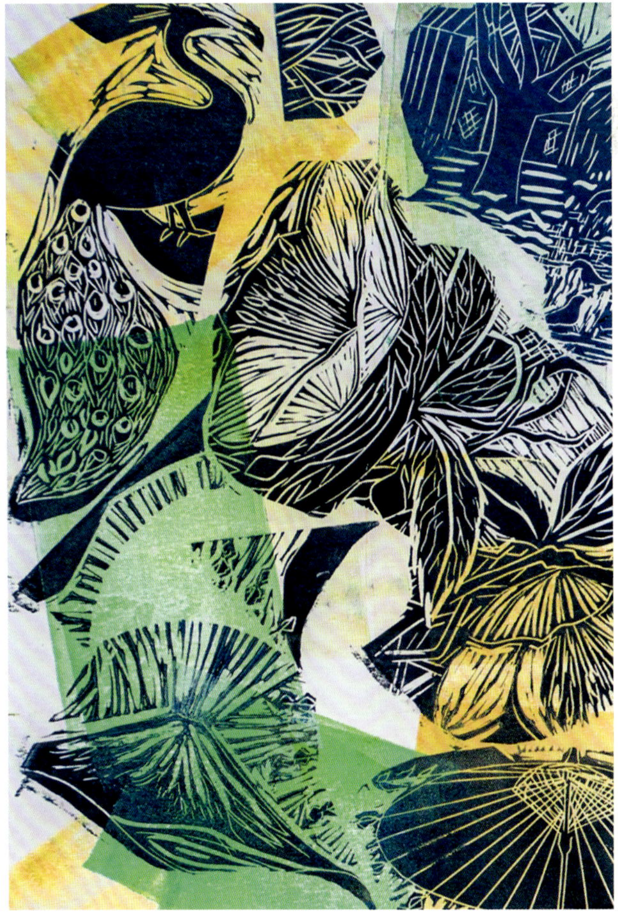

HOW IT IS USED TODAY

When I started linocutting over fifteen years ago it certainly wasn't as popular as it is now. I struggled to get decent materials and equipment, and finding courses on how to learn were few and far between. However, I've seen a real resurgence over the past few years – my studio workshops have always sold out and my online classes have been phenomenally successful. It's easy to see why – the fact that you need so few tools and equipment and that there are no harsh chemicals involved means that people are curious to try it out.

During the pandemic, there was a huge surge in interest in linocutting. Suppliers were running out of materials as people found themselves stuck at home, eager to get creative. So many people have told me they found solace in linocutting, helping them to focus their emotions and channel them into something concrete. As a consequence, I'm seeing many more crafters setting up online shops and selling their prints, using printmaking both as a hobby and a side hustle.

For people who use screens every day in their work, such as illustrators and graphic artists, linocut is a great way to step away from the computer and do something hands-on. Many of them use a computer to design their image, carve it by hand, then return to the computer to add any extras. Book covers, posters and other graphics often feature linocuts; their bold lines can be a great way to convey a message.

I also have a couple of textile designer friends who use linocut for printing onto fabric. They design and carve their block and repeat print the design onto cushions, clothing, home furnishing and more. The fact that designs can be so easily repeated makes linocut so attractive.

As the last few years have demonstrated, people are eager to explore their creativity, especially with techniques that can be done from the comfort of their own homes. As the popularity of linocut increases, I have no doubt we will be seeing new ways of it being used in the future.

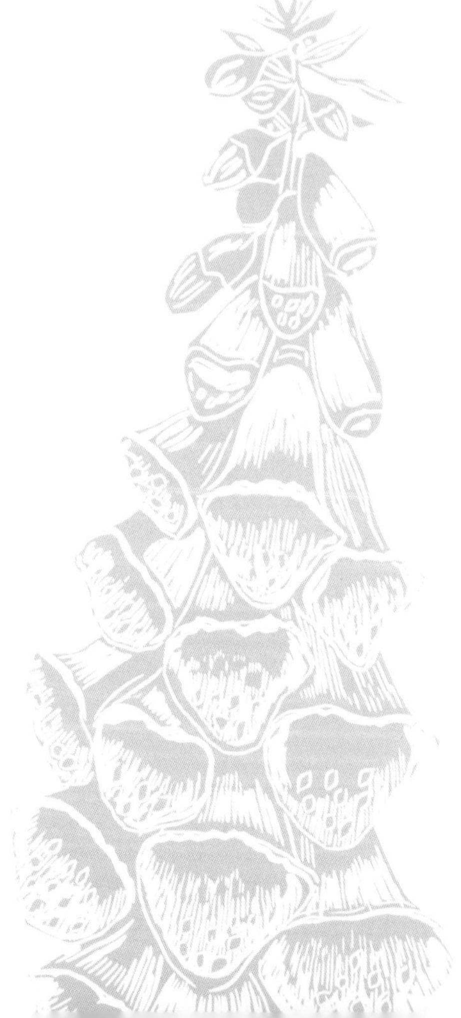

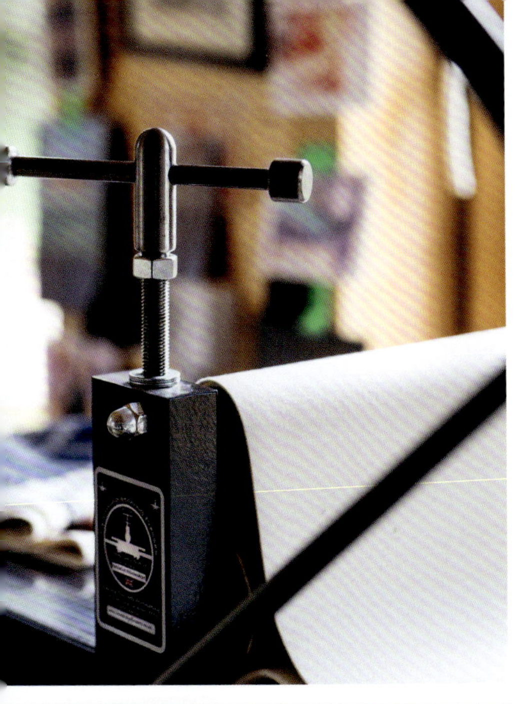
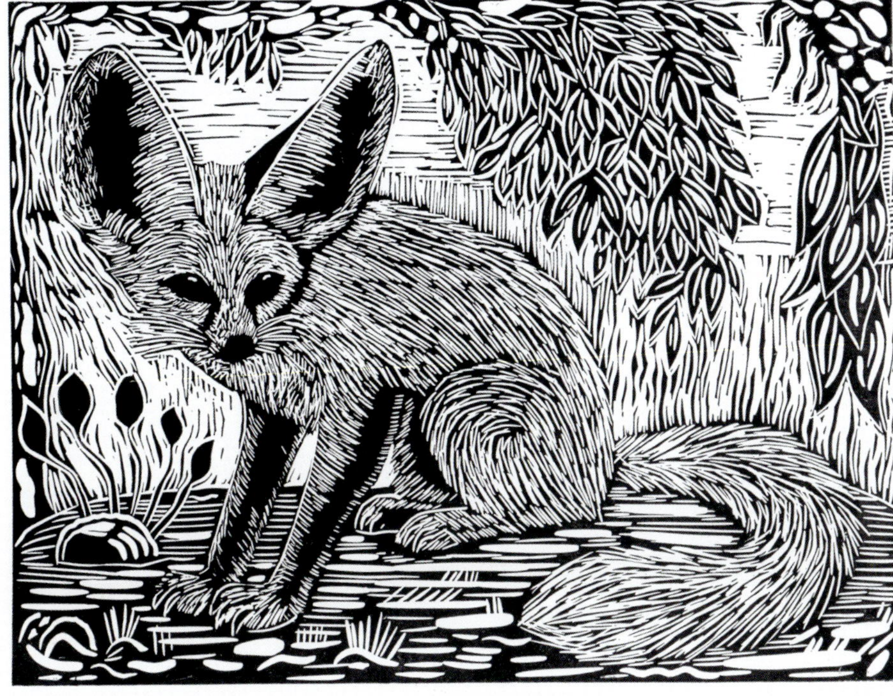
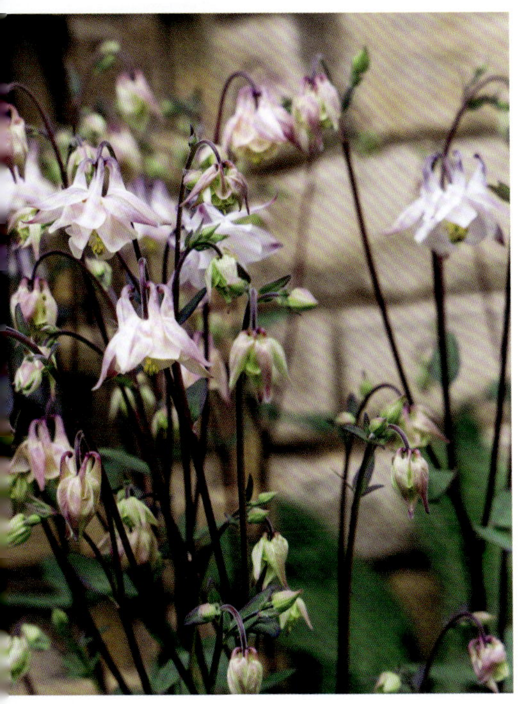
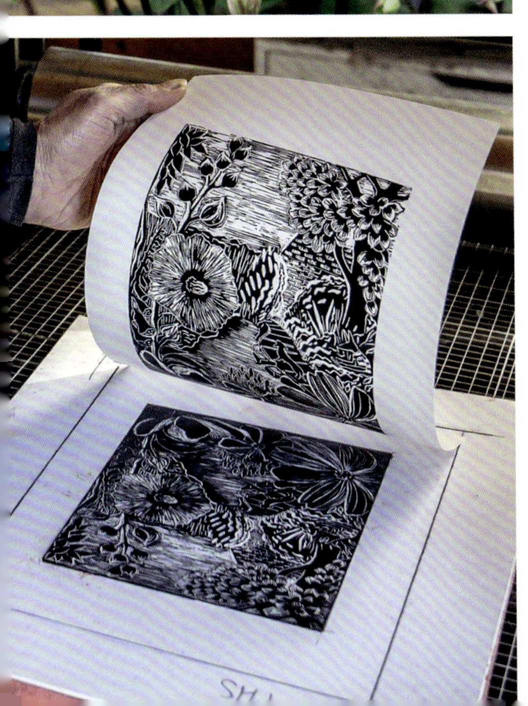

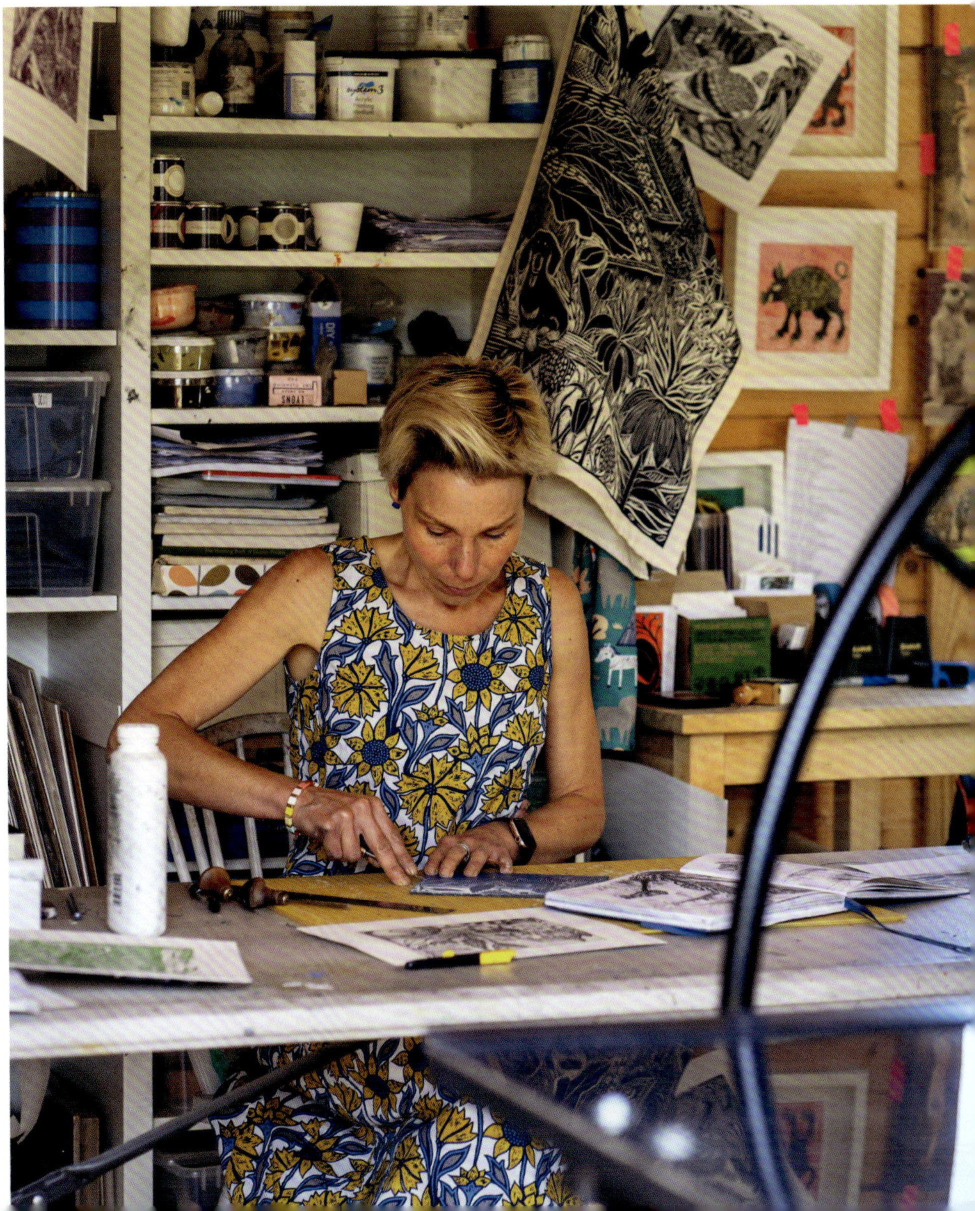

2 TOOLS AND MATERIALS

One of the main things that attracted me to linocut was the fact that you need very little equipment to get started. As my online workshops over the past few years have shown, brilliant results can be achieved at home with limited space. There is something so magical about the whole process, and seeing your image turned into a print is really exciting. Once you are all set up with your kit and have sorted out your working area, you will have access to this magic at any time. When it comes to equipment, personal preference and budget play a big part in selecting printmaking tools and my advice at the start is to buy the best you can afford. If possible, steer clear of the cheapest options and gradually build up your kit as your practice develops. In this chapter, I will talk you through my recommendations and advise you on the tools you will need to get started. I also list suppliers at the end of the book.

Here are the essentials you will need:

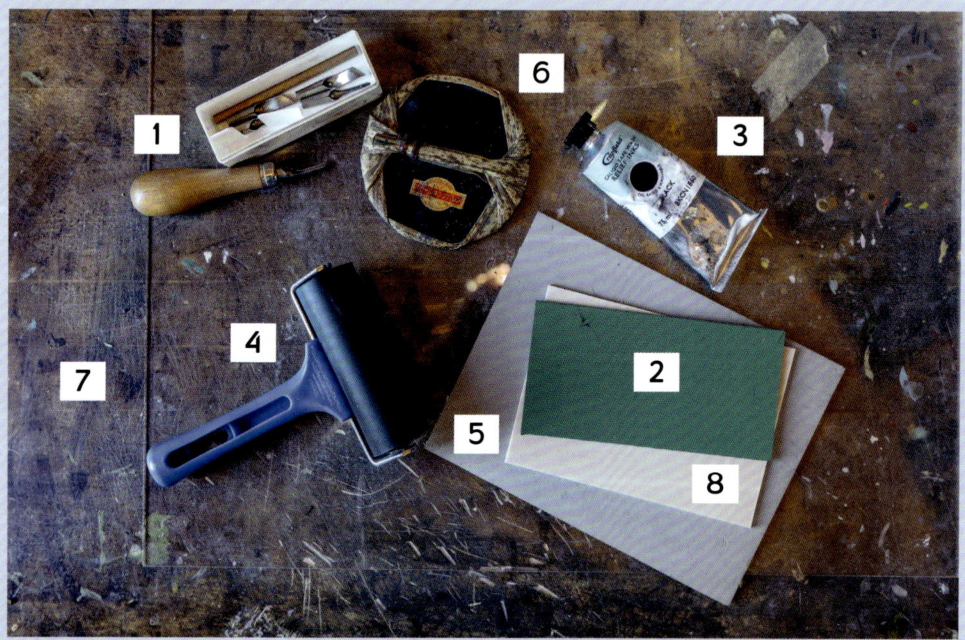

1. Linocut tools
2. Lino
3. Printing ink
4. Rollers (or brayers)
5. Paper
6. Hand printing tools/ small press
7. Inking slab/surface (something to roll your ink onto)
8. A small portable sketchbook

LINOCUT TOOLS

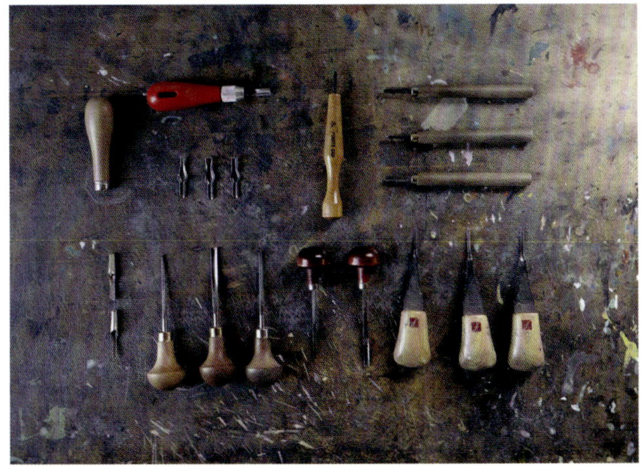

There are many types of linocutting tools available of varying quality. In my studio workshops I have a whole range, from the cheapest to the most expensive. This enables my students to try them all out and see which one works for them. Often, it's about how they fit in your hand, how comfortable they feel and how your hand feels after a lot of carving.

I always recommend going for a mid-range-priced set to start off with; I like the German brand ABIG with their wooden handles or the longer pencil-like Japanese woodcarving tools. If possible, I would avoid buying the cheapest sets on the market – they will probably end up frustrating you and may even put you off continuing. I would then recommend adding better-quality tools as your practice develops.

V AND U TOOLS

The most common linocut tools are V and U tools. (There are other shapes but these are less common, so for the purpose of this book we will just be working with V and U shapes.)

V tools can give you a variety of line widths by simply angling the tool differently. They are good for outlines, accurate edges, textures and corners. Lines cut with V tools will have a sharp pointed end. You may find you use a V tool the most because of its versatility.

U tools carve more of a consistent line width and have a curved end point. They are great for making circles and creating dots and round shapes. Large, wide U tools are used for clearing out big areas of lino – they can leave behind 'noise' or 'chatter', which I will explain in Chapter 10.

SWISS PFEIL TOOLS

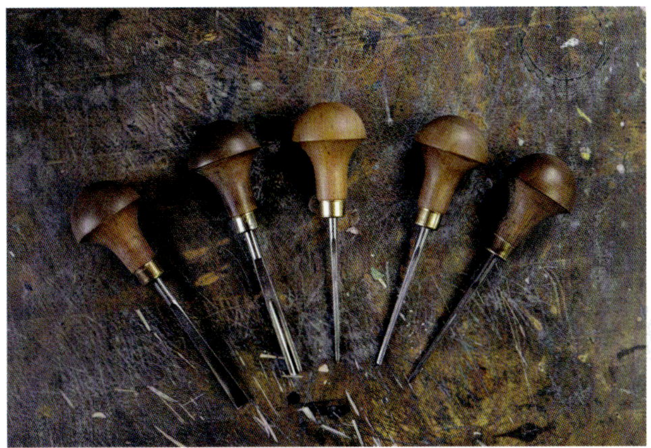

Many linocut artists, myself included, use Swiss Pfeil tools. They have a mushroom-shaped handle, which fits in your hand beautifully. They are made from high-quality steel with hardwood handles sourced from ecologically managed Swiss forests. They are pricey, though, so take your time building up your collection. I would steer clear of buying sets, as often they contain tools that you might not need or use.

I started with three tools and have built my collection up to contain most sizes, however I only really use five frequently. Each tool is categorised by a number, e.g. 11/0.5, which refers to the curvature and width of the blade in millimetres. It can be confusing, so here are the tools I use the most:

- **L 12/1** – smallest V tool
- **L 11/0.5** – very small U tool
- **L 11/3** – medium U tool
- **L 9/5** – large U tool
- **L 7/10** – large flat U tool, used for clearing.

Looking After Your Tools

If you decide to invest in more expensive tools, you will want to make sure you protect them properly. The fine blades are easily damaged and, if dropped, can be hard to sharpen correctly. It's important to keep an eye on them while you are working with them too – I was teaching recently when one of my students' cats jumped onto the table, sending all her expensive tools flying onto the floor and damaging some of the blades! I advise keeping them together in a solid box or tin and protecting the ends by pushing them into corks.

Sharpening Your Tools

This is something I get asked a lot about, as your tools inevitably lose their sharpness when you have been working with them for a while. While this is important with more expensive tools, don't bother sharpening cheaper tools with changeable blades – it's not worth the effort.

To maintain their sharpness, I use a Flexcut SlipStrop to 'hone' my tools while I'm carving. The SlipStrop is a block of wood with two strips of leather on either side: one side is flat while the other has a selection of profiles to remove the burr. It comes with a yellow polishing compound that actually does the work – it's like the grit on sandpaper, the leather is just what is holding it. The idea of stropping is simply to maintain and refine the already efficiently sharpened edges of your tools. I tend to keep my strop by my side when I'm carving and hone the tool I'm using every hour or so. If you keep up this routine, you will reduce the number of times you need to properly sharpen your tools.

1   To hone the outside of a U tool, take your yellow compound and coat the flat surface of the strop generously.

2   It's important to hone the bevel of the tool at the correct angle – not too high or low. A good way to check you are doing this correctly is to apply black marker pen to the bevel.

3   Gently pull your U tool towards you, carefully rotating as you do so to ensure you are sharpening evenly. Check the marker pen on the bevel – if you are sharpening correctly, it will all be removed. If you see any black areas, return the tool to strop and adjust your angle until all the black has been removed.

4   Flip the strop over and find the profile that fits your tool. Rub the compound over the profile, place your tool on the profile and pull it towards you. This removes the burr that might have collected on the inside when honing the outside. Just a couple of pulls should be adequate.

5   With the V tools there are three different profiles: the two edges and the middle. There are differing opinions on how to sharpen the middle; I tend to just sharpen the two outside edges as I feel this then takes care of the middle – if you sharpen the middle incorrectly, you might end up turning it into a U instead of a V, so I would advise caution.

6   To hone the edges, apply more compound to the flat leather and then place one side of the tool flat to the surface and pull towards you.

7   Repeat for the other side. Hone both sides around fifteen to twenty times.

8   Flip the profile over and choose the right profile for your V tool. Apply compound, lay your tool on the profile and pull towards you to remove the burr.

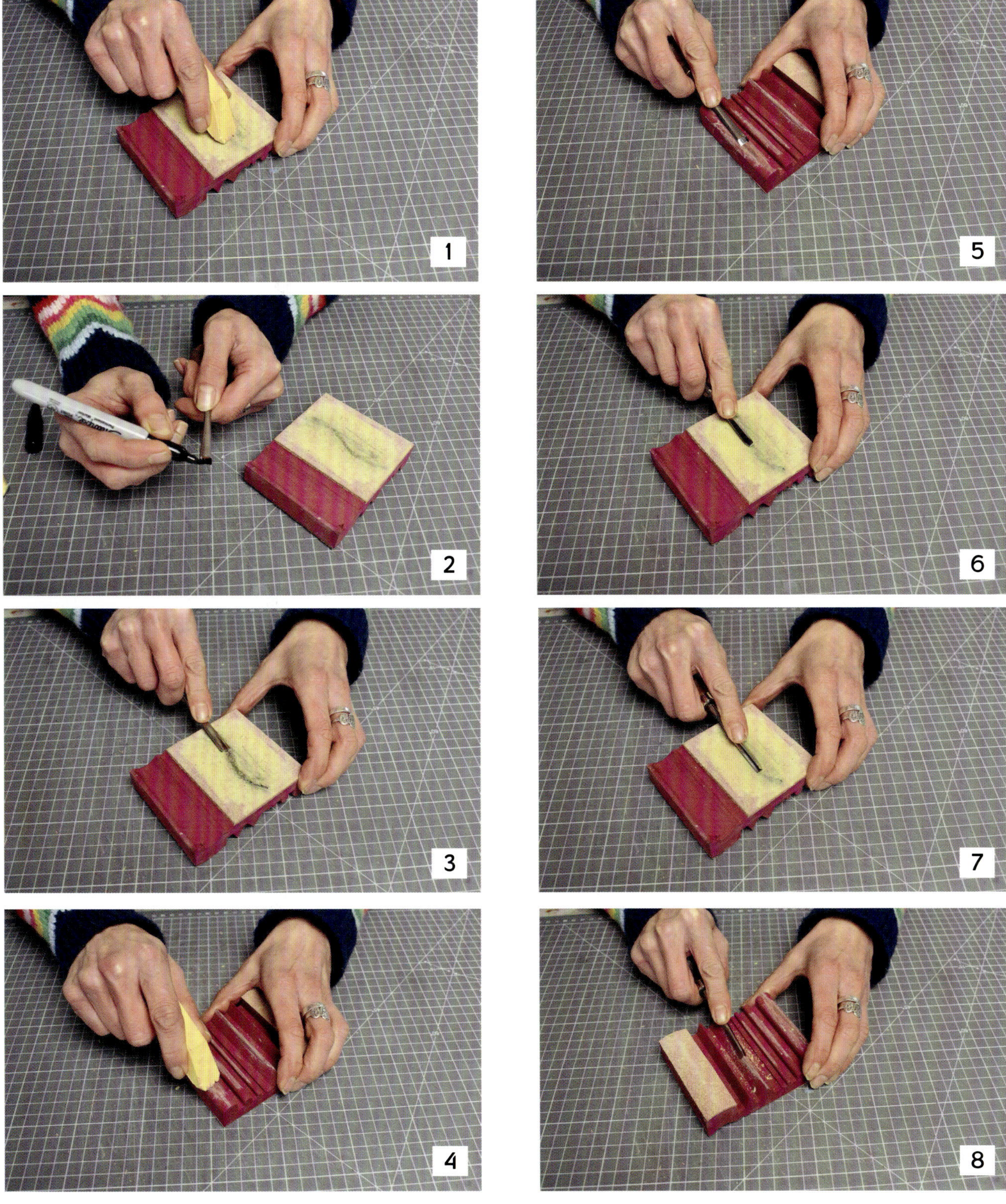

You will need to sharpen your tools regularly, too. This is an art in itself and requires patience and practice. I recommend getting either an oil or water stone (I use a water stone). As their name suggests, water acts as a lubricant for the water stones and oil lubricates the oil stones. There are many helpful videos on the internet that show you how to sharpen your tools. It also might be worth sending them away to be professionally sharpened from time to time. I dropped one of my favourite tools, and as hard as I tried I couldn't get it sharp again, so I sent it off and it came back as good as new.

LINO

I use Japanese Vinyl throughout the book, but will refer to it as 'lino' for ease. As with all tools and materials, lino choice is a matter of personal preference – experiment and see what works for you.

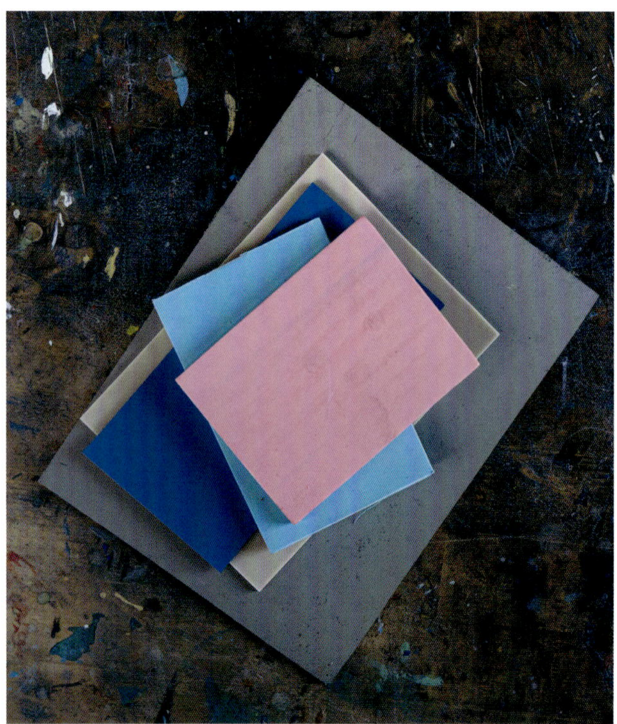

BATTLESHIP GREY

The lino you may have used at school is the grey sort – known as 'battleship grey' – with a hessian back. This is also the kind most found in art shops. It has a smooth surface and a fine grade. (It also comes in brown; this tends to be harder and coarser.)

Battleship grey is great when it's warm and fresh as it's easy to cut – however, when it's old and cold it's the opposite. When using this lino it is best to warm it up, either by using a hairdryer or sitting on it for a little while. When it is fresh and good to use it should bend easily and smell of linseed. It loses moisture as it gets old, so it's best not to hoard this type of lino – just buy it when you need it. If it remains hard when you have warmed it and is difficult to cut, then it is unusable and is not worth persevering with.

Many printmakers prefer this type of lino as its brittleness makes cutting really pleasurable. One of the really satisfying things is its ability to flick and break at the end of the line – something that isn't as easy with other alternatives.

SOFTCUT

Another common readily available option is SoftCut or easy-cut lino. It is creamy beige in colour and has a smooth surface with a textured reverse. This is great for children, beginners or people with hand problems; my mum uses it as she has arthritis in her hands and finds it easier to use. It can be difficult to get sharp, clean lines with SoftCut and the edges can look a little raggedy.

SPEEDY CARVE/
SPEEDY-CUT EASY

Speedy Carve is a pink rubberlike block which is very easy to cut (like the SoftCut). It has a spongy surface which isn't suitable for small detail but is great if you want to produce something quick, loose and spontaneous.

Speedy-Cut Easy is a blue block, similar to Speedy Carve but even softer, and is great for using for stamps.

JAPANESE VINYL

Another alternative – and one that is becoming more common – is Japanese vinyl, which is the type I use. Japanese vinyl is slightly softer than traditional lino but harder than SoftCut or Speedy Carve. It is a double-sided synthetic rubber, which is green on one side, blue on the other and has a black centre (you can use both sides and it doesn't matter which you use).

Japanese vinyl is a relatively new material on the UK printmaking scene, even though it has been used in Japan for a long time. What I love about it is that you can get really fine details and I find it really satisfying to carve. Another advantage, for me, is that it's easy to clean off – I'm a printmaker who likes to do many proofs as I move along, therefore speed and ease of clean-up is important to me. However, it only goes up to A3 size so if you want to work larger than this, traditional lino is your only option.

ECO-FRIENDLY NOTE

Although I'm sure you will keep your linocuts and make prints from them for years to come, the offcuts accumulate and are destined for the bin. I feel it's important to point out that battleship grey lino is the only fully biodegradable linocut block. The other blocks are made from PVC and can be recycled, but finding places to recycle them can be difficult (I've found a place near me after much searching). It's something to be conscious about and I will be transitioning to working with traditional lino in the future.

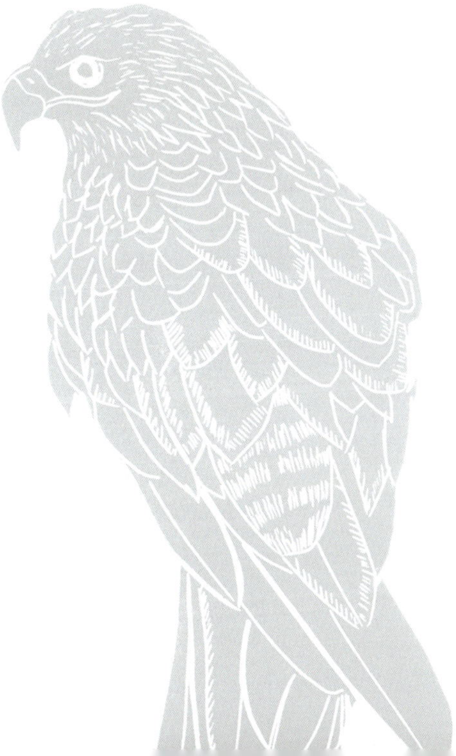

INK

I get asked a lot about inks, and it comes as no surprise that the ink you use will make a real difference to the quality of your prints. Inks are either water-based or oil-based and there are advantages and disadvantages to both. Again, it comes down to what works for you, your budget and the project you are working on. One important must, however, is to always use inks that are labelled 'relief ink' as these are specifically designed for block printing; other inks such as etching inks will be too thick and tacky to roll.

WATER-BASED INKS

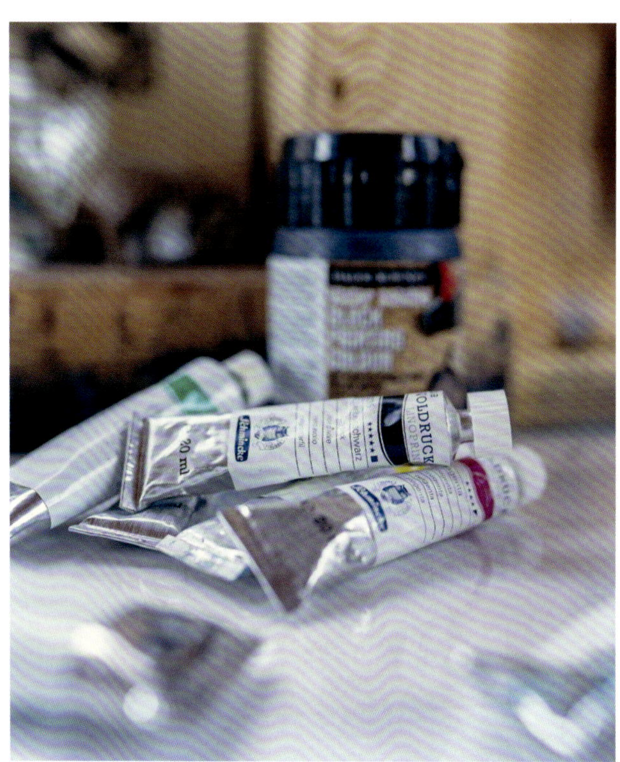

Most beginners start off with water-based inks. These are soluble in water and easy to clean up. They dry quickly, so your prints will be ready within ten minutes, which can be helpful if you are block printing cards or want a layer to dry quickly. However, this can be a disadvantage if you are working on a longer project; they dry up on your printing surface and on your roller, so can prevent you from working fluidly. They also don't have great coverage and can appear blotchy and dry with a matt finish. The shelf life of water-based inks is short – over time they dry out and become clumpy.

OIL-BASED INKS

Traditional oil-based inks are the inks of choice for many printmakers. They are highly pigmented and come in a wide range of colours. Unlike water-based inks, they dry slowly, remaining 'open' so you can work on a longer project. They give crisp, clean results on detailed work and dry with a lovely rich finish. You don't have to use harsh solvents when cleaning up oil-based inks; using vegetable oil and a rag and finishing off with a plant-based solvent like Zest-It works really well.

WATER-SOLUBLE OIL-BASED INKS

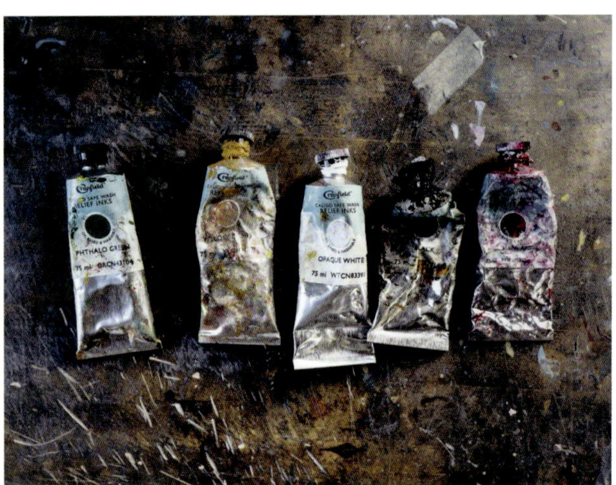

I use the oil-based but water-soluble Caligo Safe Wash inks, which are vegetable oil-based inks that wash off in soap and water. I've tried lots of different inks and these are the ones I always return to. They have all the benefits of traditional oil-based inks but their special formulation means you can clean them up with soapy water and there's no need to use any chemicals. I love the quality of the inks; they are easy to mix and the finish is velvety and luxurious. Like traditional oil inks, they are highly pigmented, which means that you can print layers on top of one another without too much visual mixing.

The inks come in many different colours, and it's tempting to go wild and buy lots. However, moderation is key here, especially when you are beginning. I would recommend starting off with black, white and their process colours – red, blue and yellow. With this simple palette you can mix up an amazing variety of tones. I would always go for the tubes too, as the tubs can get a skin on top, which can be tricky to remove.

Unlike water-based inks, oil-based inks take longer to dry, and Caligo is no exception. However, I find that they usually dry in a couple of days or so. Several things affect drying times: the temperature and humidity of your room, the paper used, the thickness of the inks and how many layers you have. In general, I always wait at least seven to ten days before I put my prints into my shop.

ADDITIONAL PRODUCTS TO ADD TO YOUR INKS

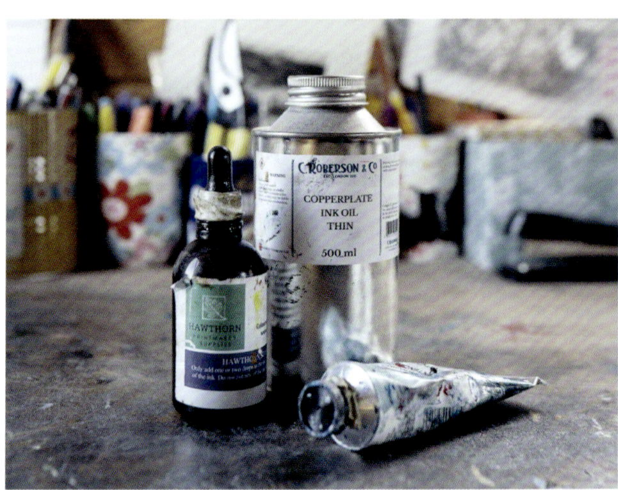

There are a few other products that can make your inking life easier, all of which do different things. Here, I've listed the ones I use the most:

Cobalt Drier

Cobalt Drier is a purple liquid that speeds up drying time from a few days to a few hours. It's important to use a pipette when using the drier, as adding too much can affect the consistency of the ink – you only need one or two drops.

Extender

Another useful product is extender – a colourless medium designed to make your inks more transparent. It adds bulk and literally 'extends' the colour. The more extender you use, the stickier the ink will get, and it can then be difficult to roll out; I would always advise adding a little at a time and testing it out. It's worth remembering that adding extender will prolong the drying time of your prints.

Drying Retarder

If you are using water–based inks and want to keep the ink 'open' for longer, it's useful to have some drying retarder in your kit. This does exactly what it suggests – it prevents the ink from drying out so you can keep working for longer.

Copperplate Oil

Copperplate oils are the base carrier for traditional printing inks to which pigment is added before grinding to the appropriate consistency for the various printmaking techniques. It comes in three different strengths: thin, medium and thick. I use the medium strength occasionally to loosen up my inks if I feel they are too thick.

Magnesium Carbonate

I use this mostly when I'm etching, but I have used it successfully when relief printmaking. Adding a sprinkling of magnesium carbonate to your inks can help stiffen them if they are too runny.

INK ROLLERS

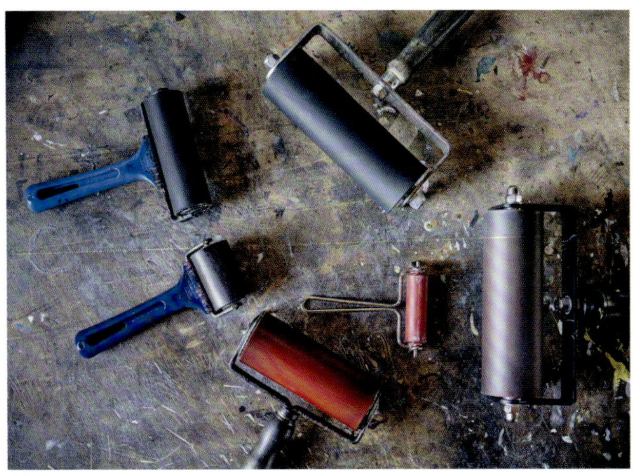

To transfer the ink to your block, you will need a roller (otherwise known as a brayer). Choosing the right roller can be confusing as there are so many options. When you are starting out, one roller is enough, but as your practice expands and you begin to use multiple colours, you will want to get a few. In general, rollers want to be slightly wider than your linocut so you can get good coverage. Once again, I would advise not going for the cheapest options.

Ink rollers can be soft or hard – hard rollers will ink up less of the noise but can leave roller marks; soft ones can deposit more ink into the grooves. I prefer using a softer roller as I feel it's more sympathetic to the surface of the lino, picking up the ink easily and depositing a nice, even layer. Rollers almost always have a stand; do use this, as it prevents the rubber from getting damaged.

It's important to ensure your rollers get a good clean after every session as dry ink can be really difficult to clean up. Pay attention to the ends of the roller too, as this is where ink gets banked up. I hang my rollers up on a nail once I've cleaned them.

PAPER

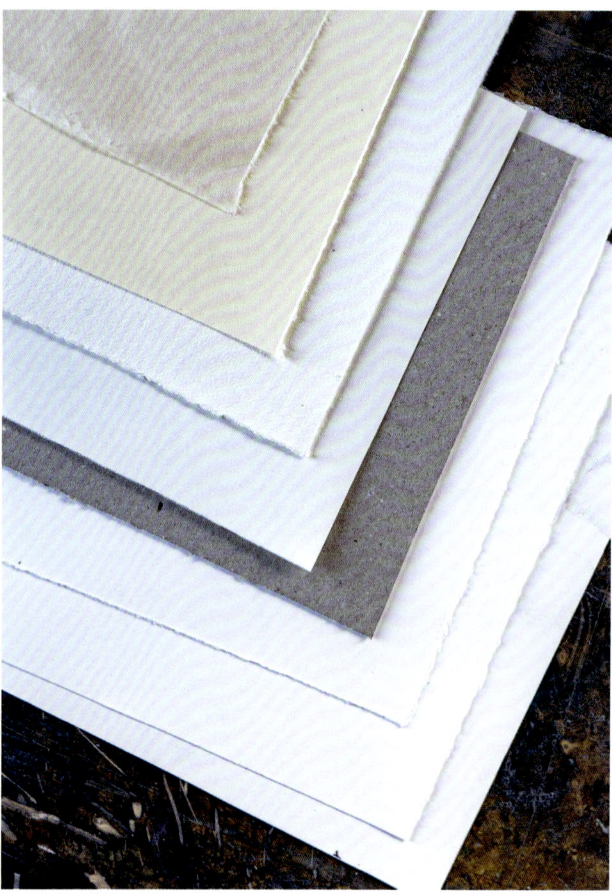

The type of paper you use for your prints is important and there are many different kinds to choose from, which can be confusing. As with many printmaking materials, it often comes down to personal preference – ask any printmaker and they will have a preferred paper type.

There are important considerations to think about when choosing your paper. The weight and texture of the paper will affect the quality of the print that you produce. As most of you will be hand burnishing your prints, you will need to ensure your paper is smooth and lightweight. The heavier and coarser the paper, the more difficult it will be to achieve a consistent quality of print. Similarly, a paper that is too shiny will repel the ink. I would suggest you look for paper that

is between 80 and 160 gsm for hand printing (gsm stands for grams per square metre and is a measure of a paper's weight: the higher the gsm, the heavier the paper).

My two favourites for hand printing are Strathmore lightweight printing paper and Zerkall, a smooth German paper that picks up detail well. Japanese washi papers are also wonderful to use for hand printing as they are smooth, lightweight and strong; I particularly like Kitakata and Kozo papers. Another paper to try is Simili, a Japanese-style printing paper, made in the Netherlands. It's dark cream, very smooth and works really well with linocut. My suggestion is to try out a few different types, see what works for you and keep experimenting.

Unless you are specifically seeking a textured effect then textured papers such as watercolour paper should be avoided as they do not pick up ink evenly. For proofing and testing your prints, I would just use newsprint, cartridge paper or even photocopy paper, which will enable you to experiment freely without worrying about the expense. It's always good to have a stack of newsprint in the studio as it has a multitude of uses. I go to my local paper company and buy their offcuts – they are so pleased to get rid of it and I get it at a bargain price.

HAND PRINTING TOOLS

As most of you will be printing by hand, it's important to choose a tool that will enable you to 'burnish' (rubbing the back of your paper to transfer the ink).

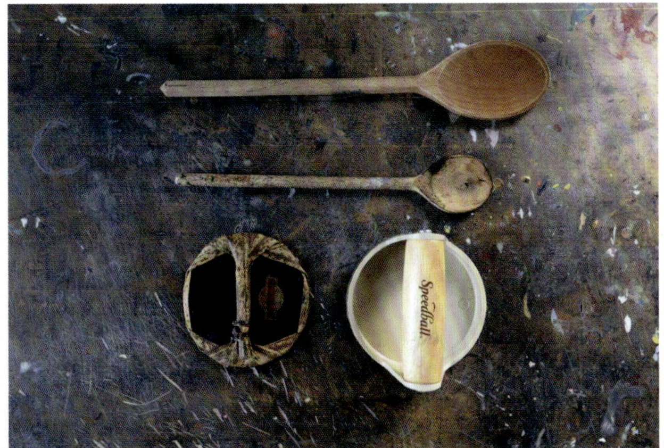

WOODEN SPOON

Many printmakers just use a wooden spoon, and they become very attached to it. One of my friends still uses the spoon she started printmaking with over twenty years ago! The smooth, flat surface of the wooden spoon puts a nice, even pressure on the paper.

BAREN

For my hand-burnished prints, I use a baren to apply pressure. A baren is a smooth, flat, hand-held disc with a handle across the back so you can grip it. It is used to apply even pressure to a printing surface. I use a simple Japanese bamboo baren, which is a disc that is covered in a bamboo leaf. It's cheap and effective, but they do need replacing over time. You can buy more expensive barens, but I find the bamboo baren to be as effective.

SMALL PRESSES

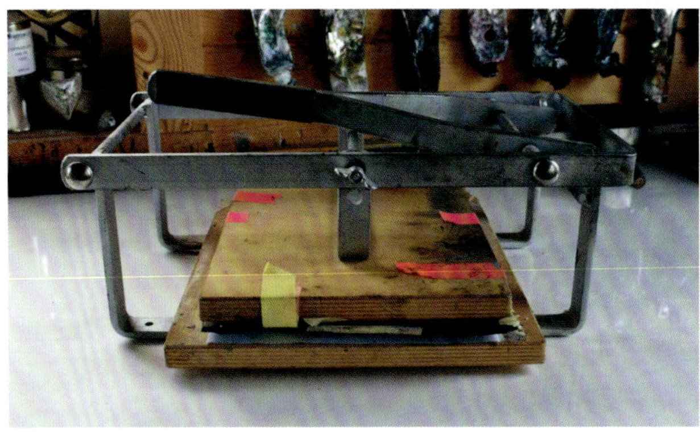

As your practice expands, you might want to invest in a printing press. A huge array of presses are available and, for linocut, some work better than others. After I had been hand printing for a year or so, I invested in a small hand lever press (shown above). They are much more readily available now and there is a great range of choice, both in size and price. They are very simple to use – you lift the lever, place your inked-up lino on the press and then lower the lever down firmly.

I used my printing press happily for many years until I bought my etching press (you can buy a tabletop etching press that can be used for both etching and linocutting). Other small presses that can be used are book presses (also known as nipping presses) and Adana presses, which were designed for making letter press prints at home – one of my students has one of these and her small linocuts are a delight! If you are lucky, you might be able to source a second-hand nipping or Adana press.

If necessary, improvise! To burnish your prints anything that has a smooth, flat surface is OK to use.

INKING SLAB

You will need a smooth surface to roll your ink out onto, which you can clean up easily after your printing session. I have a large piece of Perspex (plexiglass) in my studio which covers my inking table; you can get this cut to size. Other options are a large sheet of glass (be mindful with the edges!), a glass chopping board, an old mirror, a large tray or a messy mat (something that children use in school).

SKETCHBOOKS

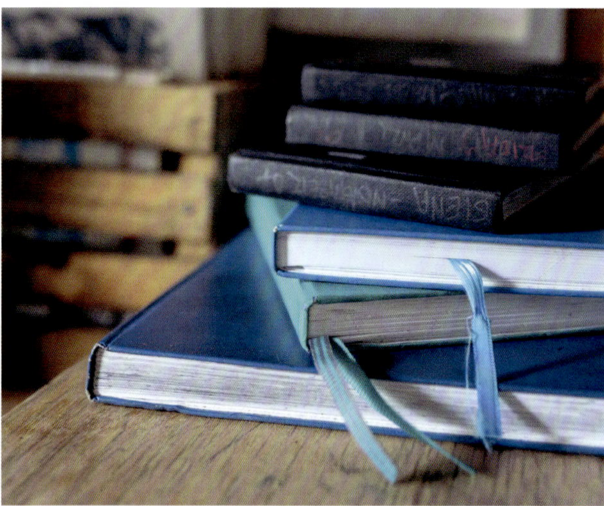

For most of the projects in this book, you will need a small portable sketchbook that you can take with you on your trips. Make sure you choose one that you really like. It's important that you enjoy the feel of it and that the paper feels good to draw on (it may sound daft, but all these things are important – I know I'm much more motivated to pick up my sketchbook when I like the look of it and I enjoy drawing in it).

OTHER BITS AND BOBS

Along with everything I've listed, you will also need a few other things to complete your printmaking kit:

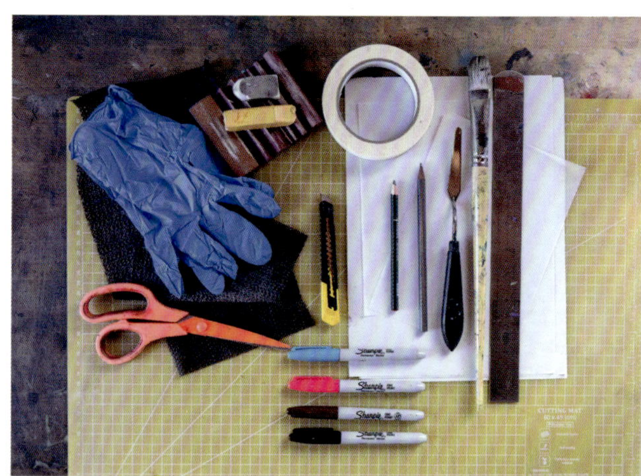

- Pencils, pens, rubbers/erasers
- Cutting mat
- Craft knife
- Non-slip mat
- Permanent marker pens
- Steel ruler
- Newsprint/scrap paper/newspapers
- Tracing/carbon paper
- Greyboard/mountboard (for registration boards)
- Palette knives
- Masking tape
- Stiff brush for removing bits of lino
- Paintbrushes
- Scissors
- Apron and gloves
- Rags (for cleaning up)
- Vegetable oil
- Talcum powder
- Spray bottle with water and washing-up liquid

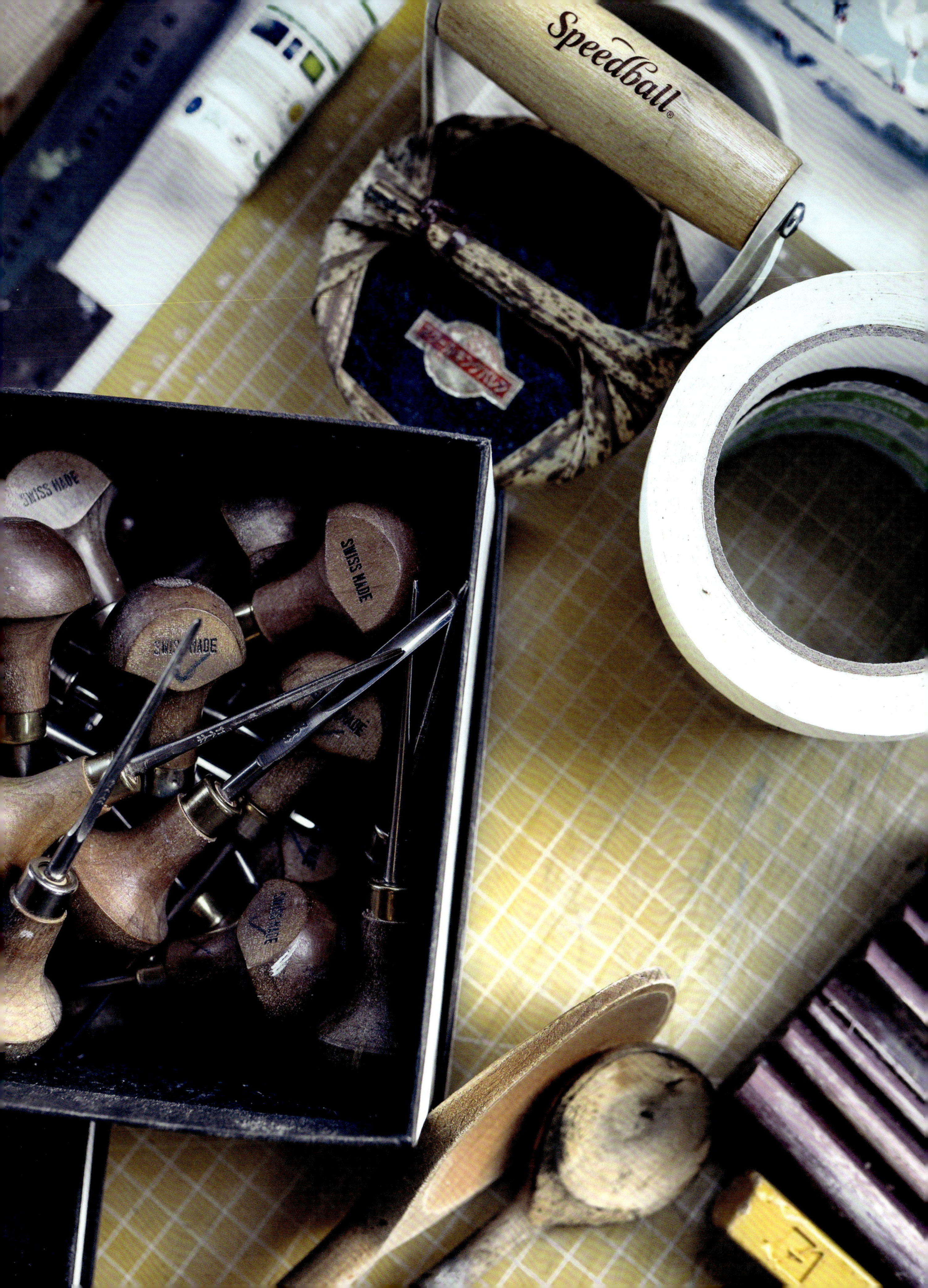
Speedball
SWISS MADE
SWISS MADE
SWISS MADE
SWISS MADE

3 PREPARING YOUR WORKSPACE

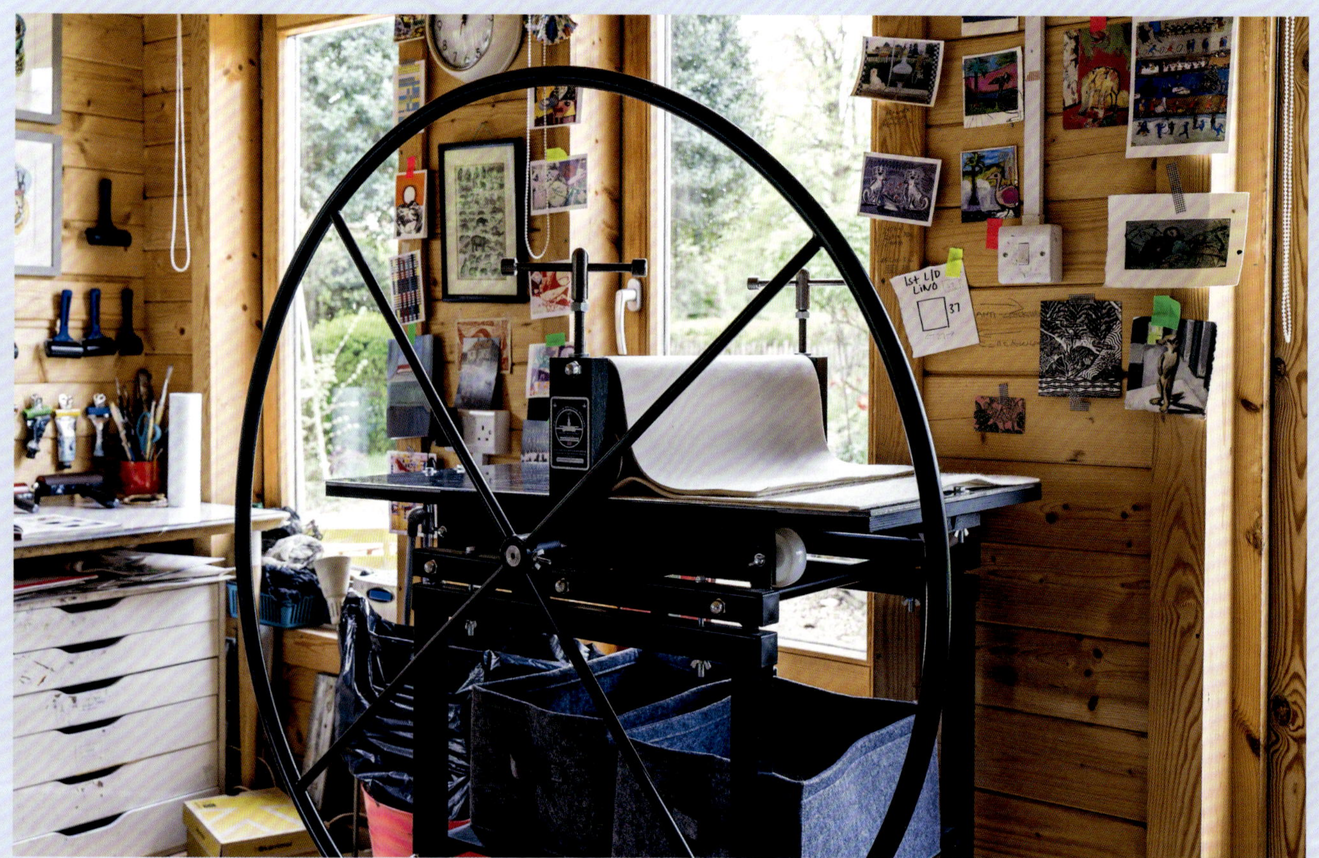

When I first started practising linocut, I allocated a corner of my bedroom to printmaking. I had a table that had to function for everything – drawing, carving, inking and printing. Your own working space might be a spare room or a table in your kitchen or you might have your own studio. The general requirements remain the same: you will need a drawing and cutting area, a printing area (this can be the same space), a drying area and a place to store your work.

DRAWING AND CUTTING AREA

You will need a dry drawing and cutting area where you can draw and transfer your designs then carve your blocks. It could be a large kitchen or dining table – and, obviously, the larger the space, the better. This can be the same space as your inking area; you will just need to move everything once you are ready to ink up.

If you are using your kitchen table, make sure you clear away as much clutter as you can, giving yourself as large a working space as possible. Make sure everything is clean and your surface is stable (there's nothing more frustrating than trying to carve on a wobbly table). Equip yourself with a comfy chair and make sure it's at the correct height so you don't have to reach too high or too low. It goes without saying that it's important to have good lighting so you don't strain your eyes.

You will also need a cutting mat to protect the surface of the table, as gauging out a large chunk of your family table isn't ideal! Covering the table with a sheet or blanket is a good idea, too.

PRINTING AREA

Once you have carved your linocut or you want to take a proof, you will need to set up your printing space. Ideally, this should be separate from your drawing space, but if this isn't possible, you will need to clear up your carving stuff and transform it into your printing space. Make sure that you are meticulous about clearing away the carved bits of linocut when you are cleaning up your space, as these can easily get into your ink and roller and transfer onto the print (go to page 45 to see what this looks like).

DRYING AREA

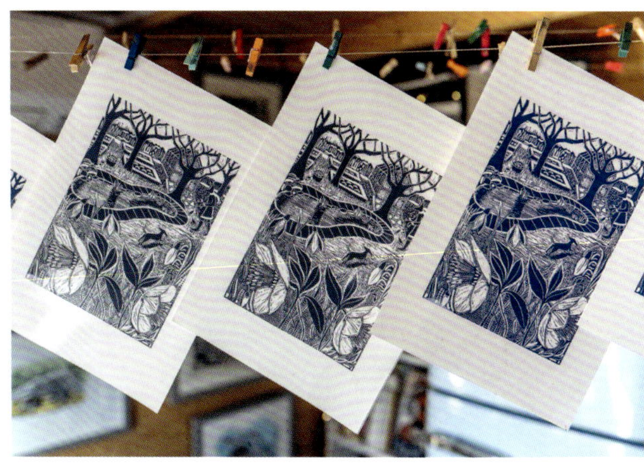

The nature of printmaking means that you produce multiple works and then have to find a way to allow these numerous pieces to dry. This is especially important when using oil-based inks and not so relevant when using water-based inks, as they dry so quickly.

There are various ways to dry prints, and I've tried out many in my years of printmaking. There are expensive and not-so-expensive methods, and luckily the one I'm going to recommend is very economical – I call it the 'wire and peg method'. It's literally just fishing wire, stretched from one corner of my studio to the other, on which I use small wooden pegs to hang my prints. I find this the most space-efficient method.

If you don't have room to hang a washing line then store your prints on a flat surface that is warm, dry and dust-free, making sure that the prints are separated so they don't stick together. If you are making larger prints, you could consider a print rack, although these do take up a lot of space.

Do make sure you check carefully that your prints are dry before storing them. Gently touch an area with your finger; if there is any tackiness, they will need to be left to dry for longer.

STORAGE AREA FOR MATERIALS AND PRINTS

You will need a storage area for all your materials and prints. When I worked in my bedroom, I had a large box where I stored all my materials. I kept it under my bed and made sure that everything was stored correctly to prevent any damage. Now that I have my own studio, I hang my inks up using bulldog clips and I hang my rollers on hooks. This allows me to work quickly and efficiently – it also means that they are kept clean and out of the way.

When your prints are fully dry, they can be stored away. I now have a plan chest in my studio but for many years I kept all my prints in an A3 display folder. Wherever you store your prints, make sure they are kept clean, dry, dust-free and out of direct sunlight.

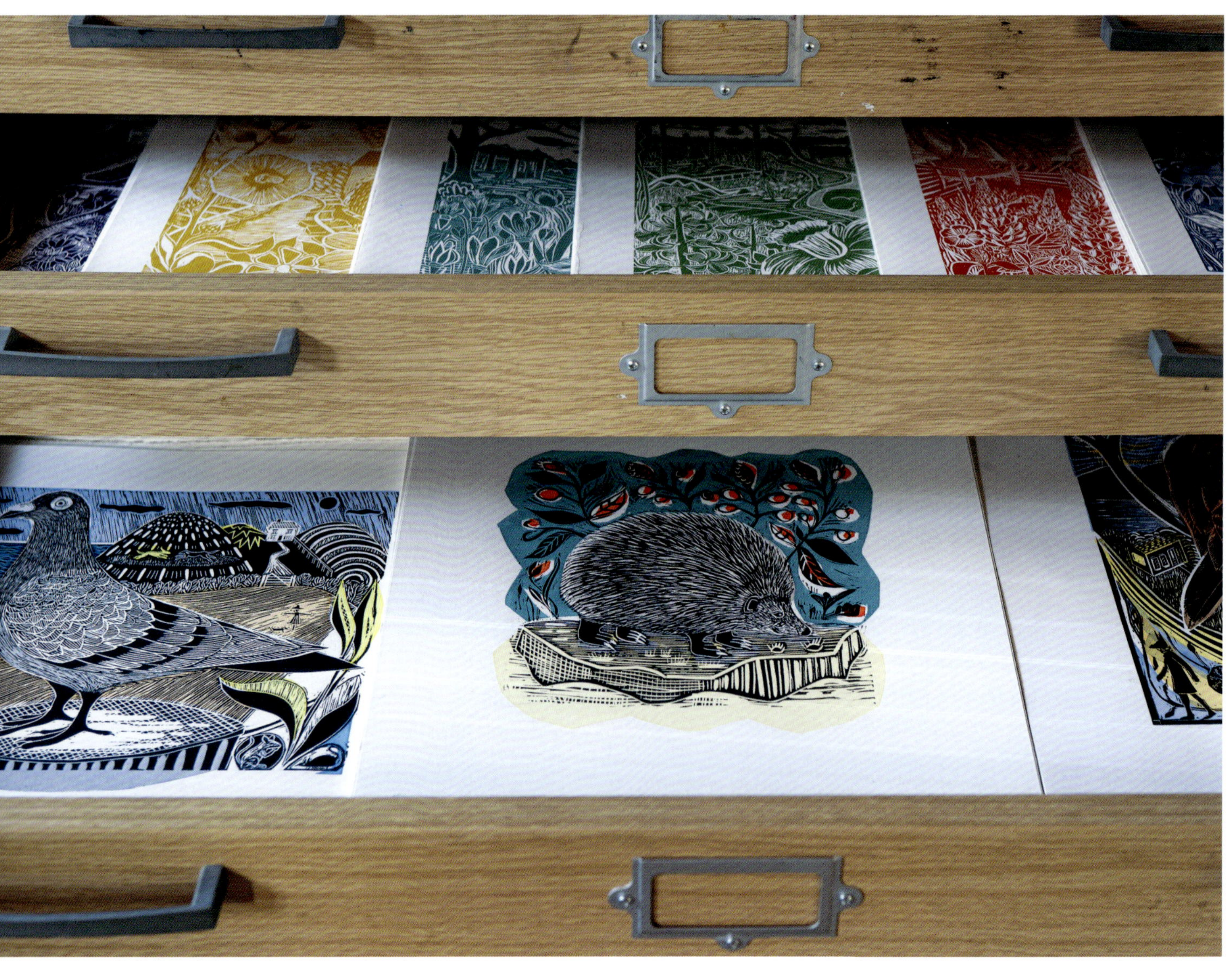

4 FROM IMAGE TO BLOCK

Once you have completed your drawing, you will want to transfer it to your linocut block. There are a number of ways of doing this, and in this chapter I am going to show you the four methods I use: drawing directly onto the block, tracing your drawing the traditional way, using tracing paper to work directly from the drawing, and using carbon paper to transfer your drawing.

The method you choose really depends on which way of working suits you best. Let's say you are using text or you want an image to print the same way round as your drawing – if you're working on a print of your house, for example – it's important to use tracing paper to reverse the image so it comes out the right way. You can, of course, scan and reverse your drawing and work from it that way, but for me it still doesn't work – there is something about how I draw that means this is important. Like with all these methods, just have a go and see what works for you – that's the joy.

DRAWING DIRECTLY ONTO THE BLOCK

This is the most direct method of transfer – it saves you the time spent tracing your image, and can be a lovely way of keeping your lines spontaneous and your drawing fresh. If you use this method, remember that your final print will be the reverse of your drawing.

A nice sharp HB pencil does the job on traditional lino, but a softer pencil such as a 2B or 4B is easier to use on Japanese vinyl or other linos. It's always a good idea to reinforce your lines with a permanent marker to ensure they remain in place while you print and proof your linocut.

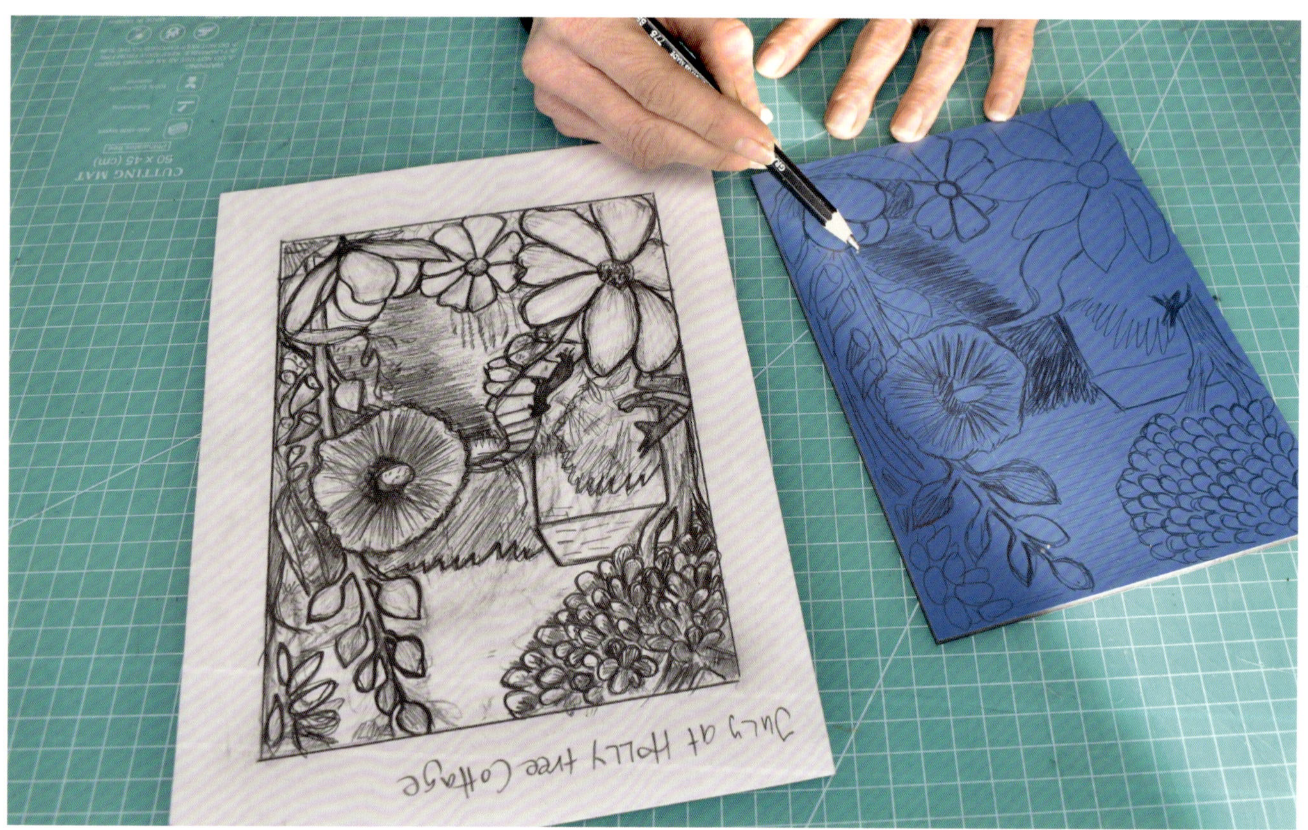

TRACING YOUR DRAWING THE TRADITIONAL WAY

Using this method will mean that the image on your block will be the reverse of your drawing, but your final print will be the same way round as your drawing.

1 Place your tracing paper over your drawing and trace the image using a soft pencil.

2 Turn the tracing paper over onto the block so that the drawing is on the underside of the tracing paper. Go over the lines so the carbon of the pencil transfers to the block.

3 Go over the pencil lines with permanent marker to make them stronger. This enables you to proof your lino as you go, without the lines rubbing off. Don't forget that this is a reverse image of your drawing, but this means that when it is printed it will be same way round as your drawing.

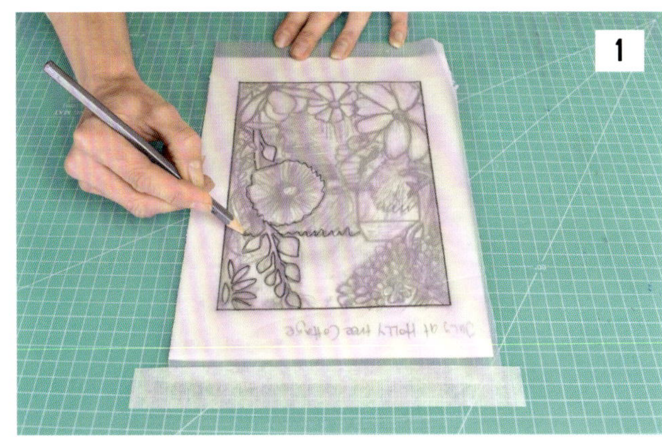

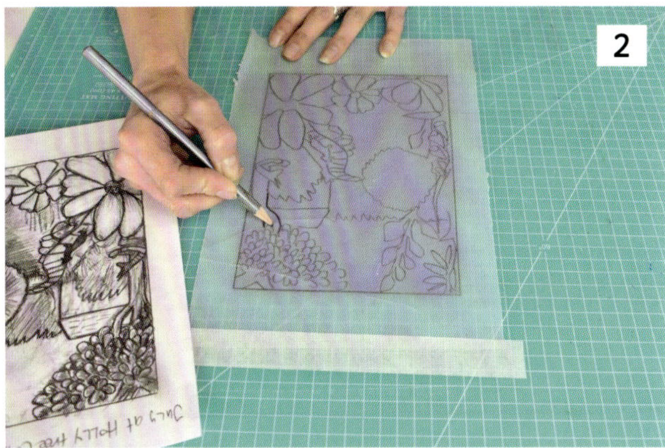

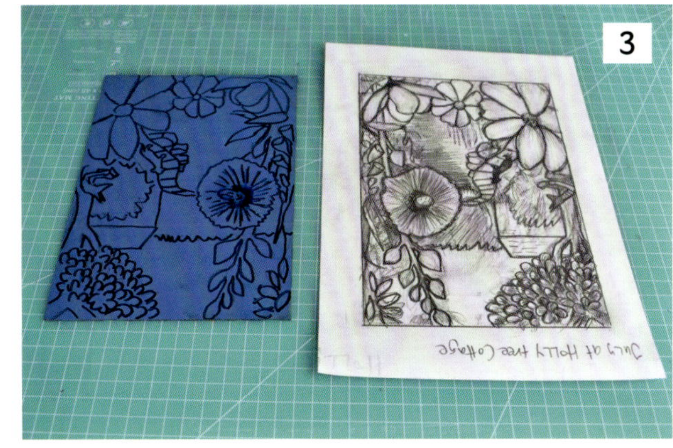

TRACING DIRECTLY FROM THE DRAWING

If, like me, you prefer to work directly from your drawing and carve it the same way, you can trace the image, turn the trace over, go over the lines again, then turn it over again and trace this onto the block.

The image on the block will be the same as the drawing, but the print will come out in reverse. I don't mind this at all; in fact, I find this really exciting and, for me, it means that the print has an entirely different character to the drawing.

1   Trace the linocut as you did in the above section, then turn the tracing paper over and place it on a sheet of plain paper. Go over the lines again so there is carbon on both sides of the trace.

2   Place your trace on top of your lino block and draw over the lines again.

3   Reinforce the lines with permanent marker. Here you will see that the drawing on the linocut is the same way round as your original drawing. I find it easier to carve directly from the drawing, so this is the method I use most. The print, however, will be the reverse of the drawing.

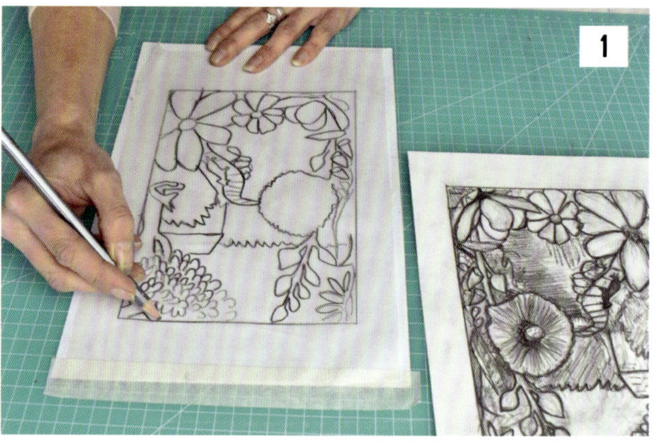

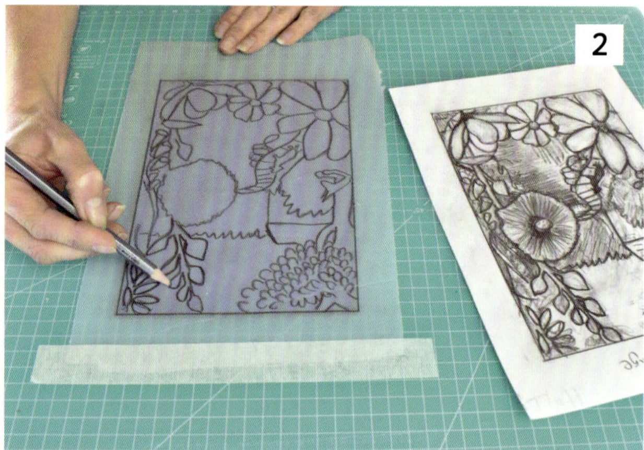

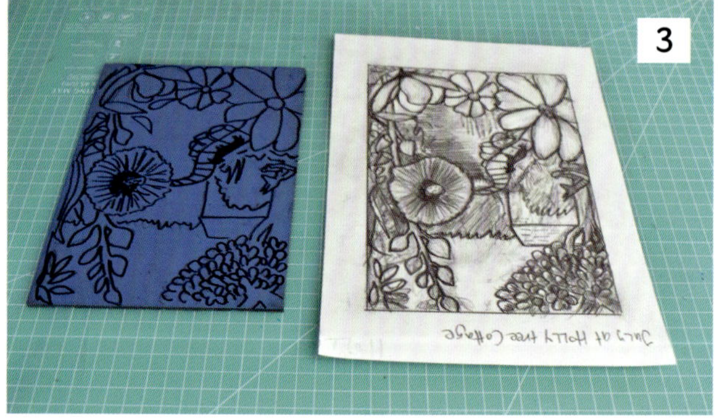

USING CARBON PAPER TO TRANSFER YOUR DRAWING

Carbon paper is another alternative for transferring your image onto your block. Again, the image will transfer the same way round as your drawing but will print out in reverse. I'm using white carbon paper here as it transfers well onto the blue vinyl.

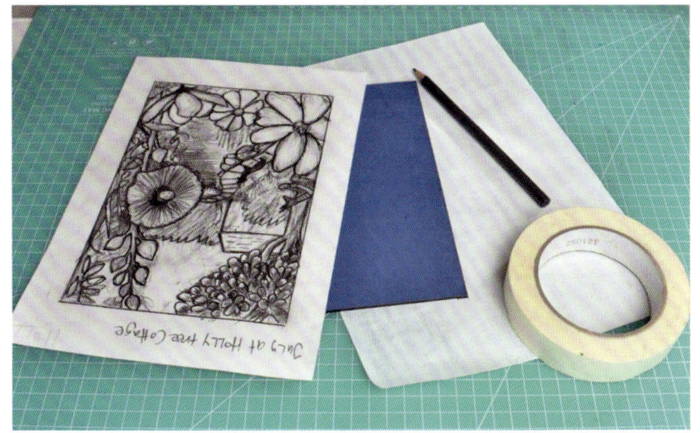

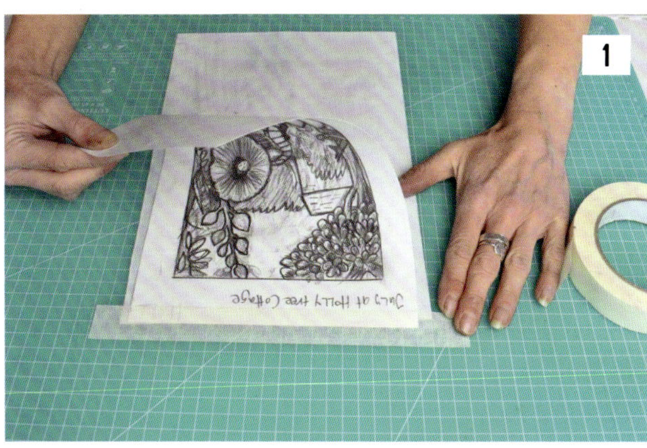

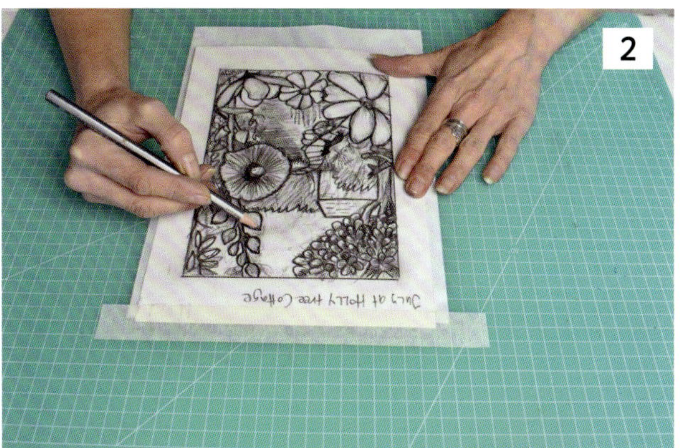

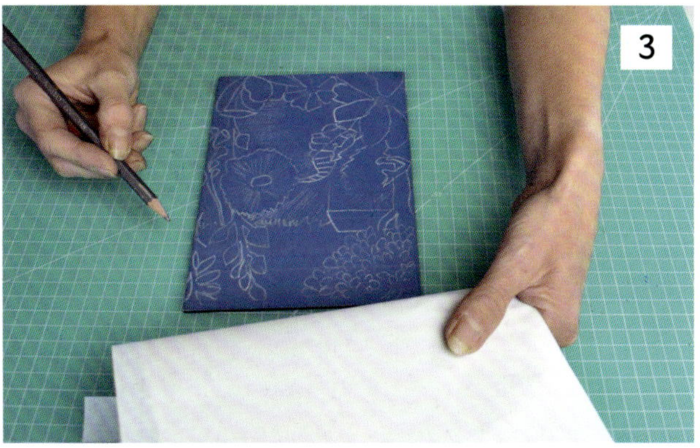

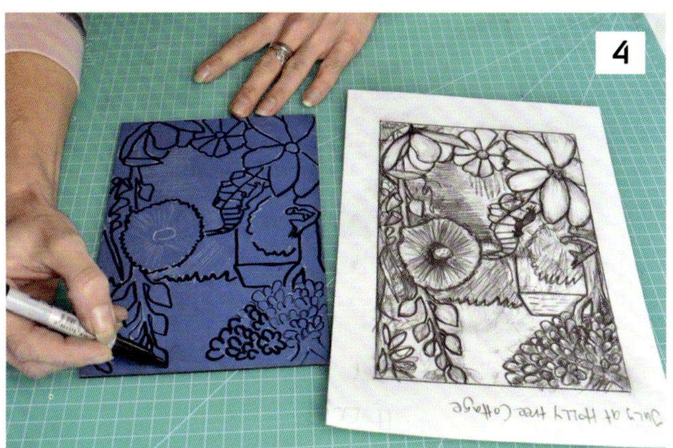

1   Lay a sheet of carbon paper on top of your linocut block, making sure it's carbon-side down. It can be tricky to see which is the right side of white carbon paper, so always test it out first. Place your drawing over the top and use masking tape to hold it in place.

2   Using a hard pencil, such as a 2H, go over the drawing, thus transferring the carbon to the lino block.

3   Lift the paper off to check your progress.

4   Use a marker pen to go over and strengthen your lines before cutting. Like the previous method, the image on the block will be the same way round as your drawing, but it will print up in reverse.

AN INTERVIEW WITH CALLY CONWAY

What first attracted you to printmaking?

Printmaking seemed like a form of magic when I discovered it in the first year of my degree course. You created something on a surface, pushed it through a press and an image appeared on paper – amazing!

I was studying painting but ended up in the print room one day after seeing these beautiful jewel-like tiny etchings made by a visiting printmaker. I was instantly hooked.

I think I fell in love with the whole process of creating a print because of the process; I knew I had to do certain things to make the image happen, but there was also the surprise at the end of never knowing exactly how it might turn out. I also loved the atmosphere in the print room, and although it was a bit scary (in case you got ink on the press blankets and were told off by the technician!), there was a real comradery.

Your work is so intricate and detailed. What are your main sources of inspiration behind this style of working?

I've always been a bit obsessed with intricate pattern and decoration, be it an engraved piece of jewellery, a William De Morgan ceramic design, fine embroidery on a historical dress or an illuminated manuscript. I can spend hours in the Victoria and Albert Museum in London studying these and gathering ideas. I do enjoy the fact that these are all from very different historical eras but are beautiful objects made by artisans with a real understanding of their craft.

I'm also fascinated by tiny details and the idea of 'little worlds' in nature: the way a minute spleenwort fern grows – twisting, curled and unnoticed from a wall, for example – or how a fiddlehead fern unfurls. I love the intricacy of overlapping forms in nature, so I suppose that really inspires the way in which I create linocuts. .

Could you tell us a little more about your process? How do you start and how do you know when the print is finished?

I do a lot of reading and research before I start the process of sketching out an idea. Sometimes I'll draw on paper and occasionally I'll draw directly onto the block, which has been stained with red ink so that I can see the lines that I'm carving.

I am quite old school in that I draw everything by hand and use tracing paper to transfer my image to the block. I might then go over this with permanent marker or ink and dip pen; at this stage, the design can change again as I make adjustments.

I'm notoriously bad at taking proof prints to check the image while I'm carving, so I usually spend a lot of time looking to see what I think it needs. I'm always trying to aim for a balance to the composition, so even at this stage things might change slightly.

Because of the detailed way in which I work, I can often keep going with the carving process and need to force myself to stop! I try to remind myself of the ratio between light and dark areas to give me an idea as to when it's complete. That's usually when I print the block, and if something needs changing I've hopefully not left it too late to do so!

@callyconwayprints
www.callyconwayprints.com

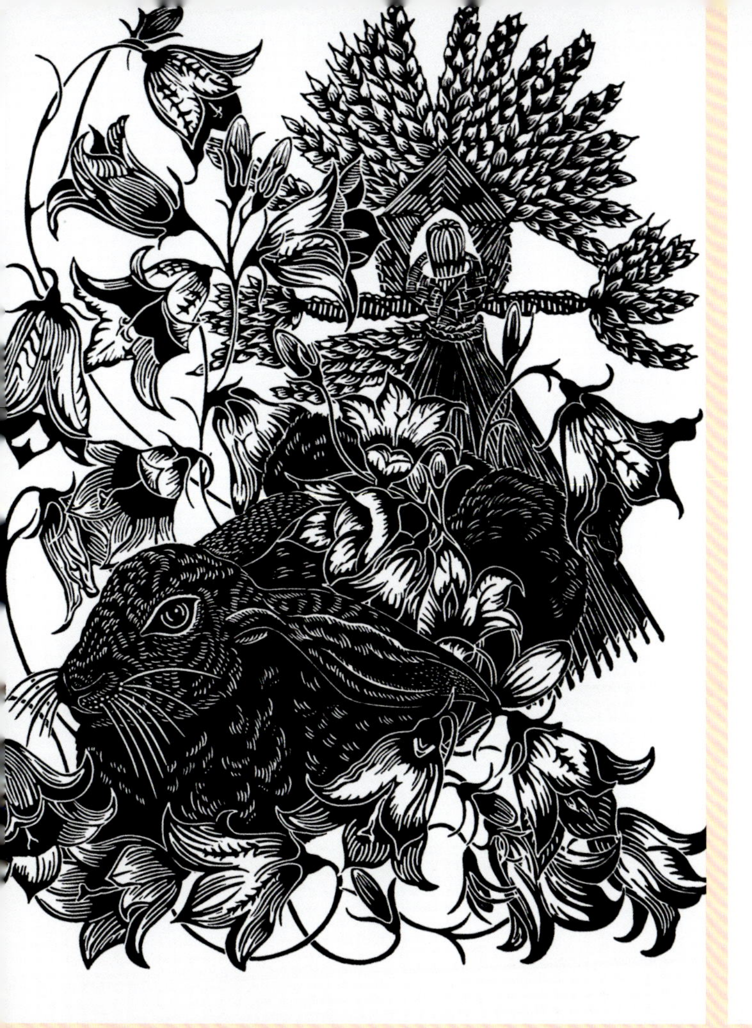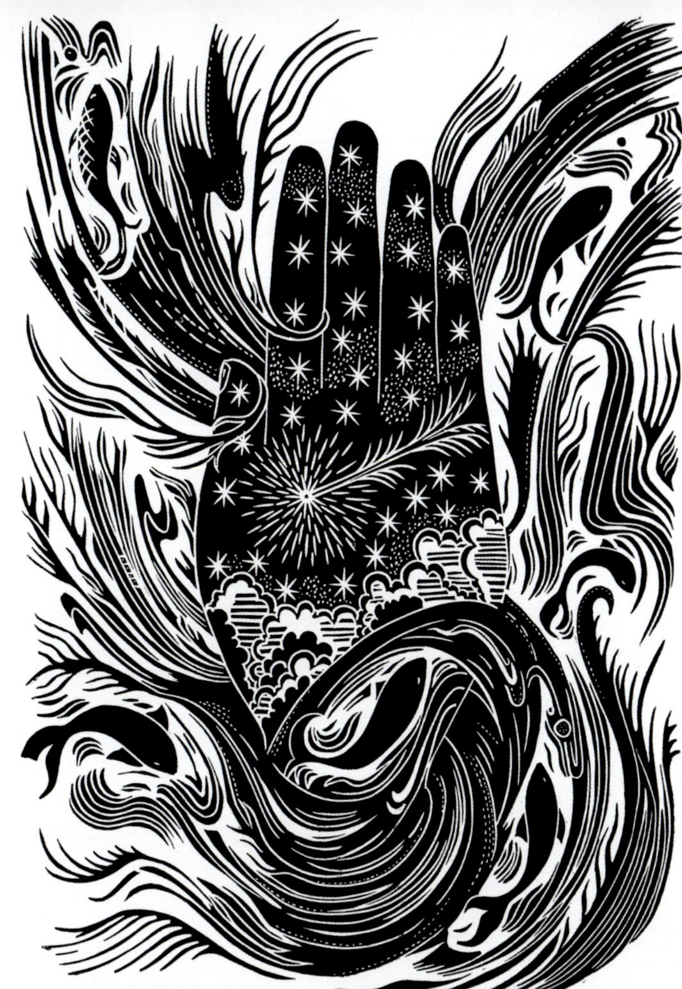

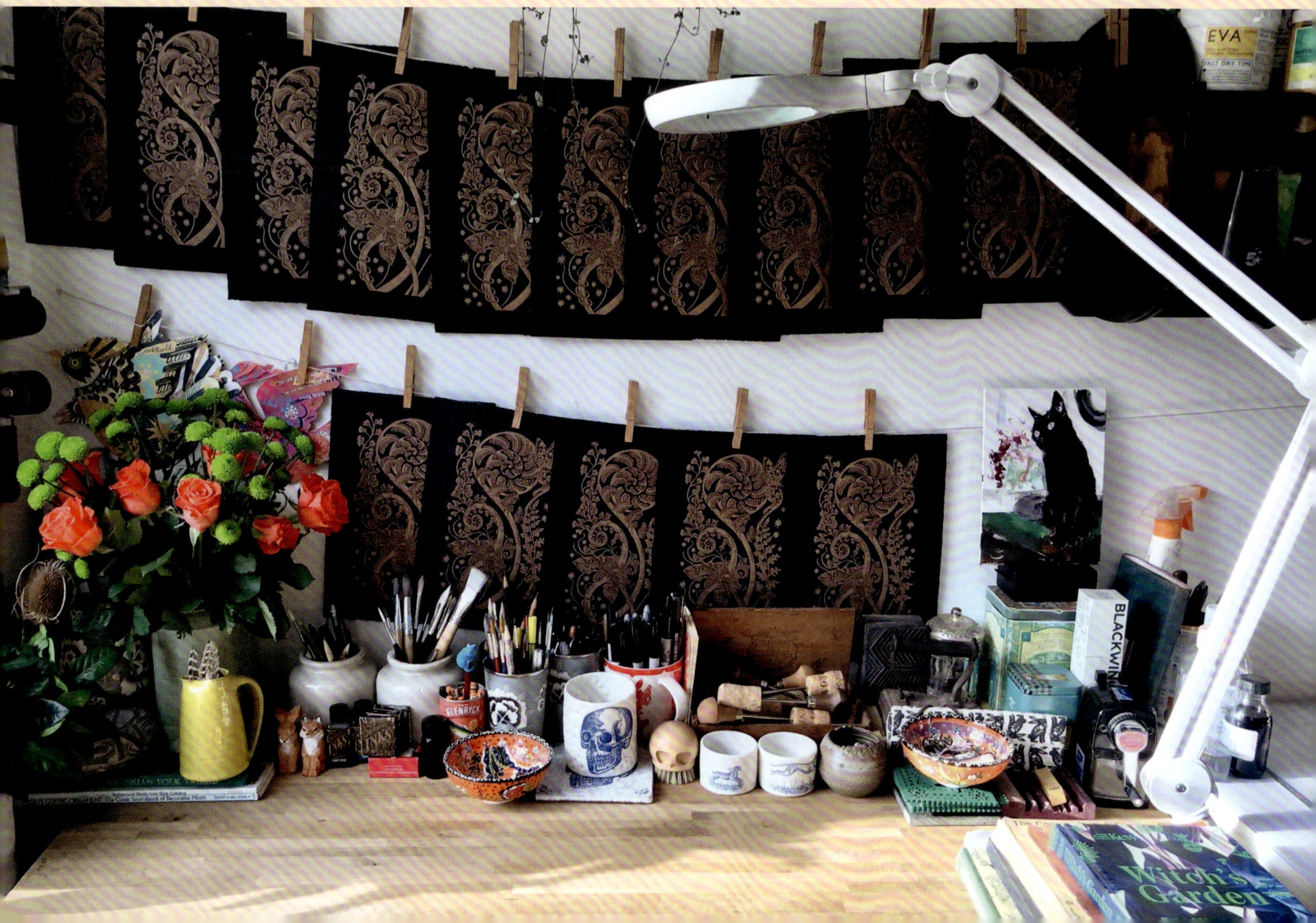

5 MARK MAKING

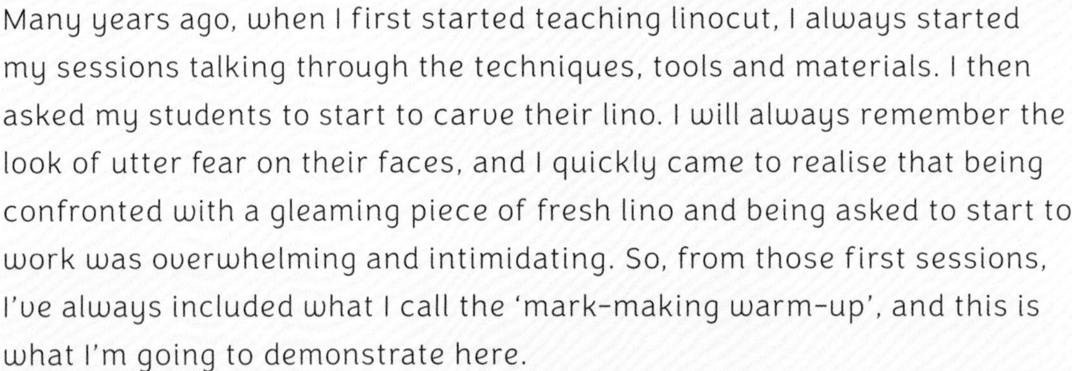

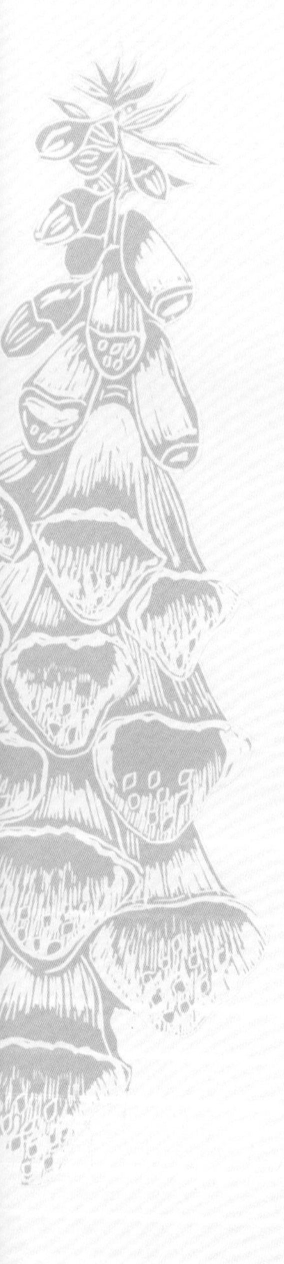

Many years ago, when I first started teaching linocut, I always started my sessions talking through the techniques, tools and materials. I then asked my students to start to carve their lino. I will always remember the look of utter fear on their faces, and I quickly came to realise that being confronted with a gleaming piece of fresh lino and being asked to start to work was overwhelming and intimidating. So, from those first sessions, I've always included what I call the 'mark-making warm-up', and this is what I'm going to demonstrate here.

The mark-making warm-up is simply an opportunity for you to get to know your tools, how they feel in your hands, and to start to develop your own mark-making language. Have fun with this and be as inventive as possible. Try to make as many different marks as you can – this will then provide a handy reference for what is possible in terms of mark-making for all the other projects.

HOLDING YOUR TOOLS

It's important when carving to make sure that you are holding your tools correctly and they feel comfortable in your hands. Place the handle of your cutter in the palm of your hand and wrap your fingers around it. Position your index finger near the end of the blade to ensure you have good control (I use my middle finger to stabilise my hand, but this is just personal preference). Try not to grip your tool too hard. Your arm and hand should be relaxed to prevent you from forcing too much.

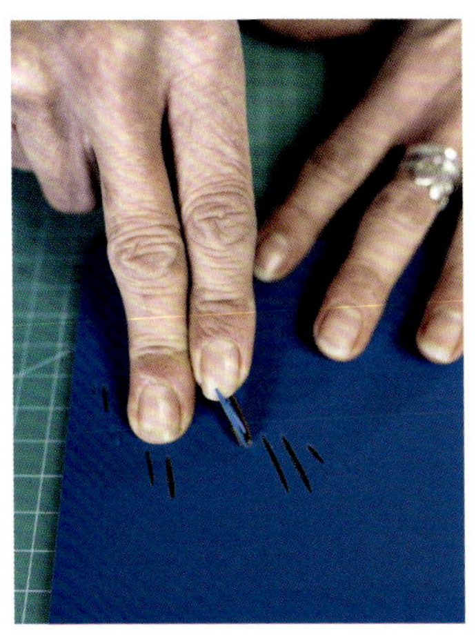

Ideally you should hold the tool at a forty-five degree angle and it should glide across the surface, cutting effortlessly. You should be carving away up to half the thickness of the lino.

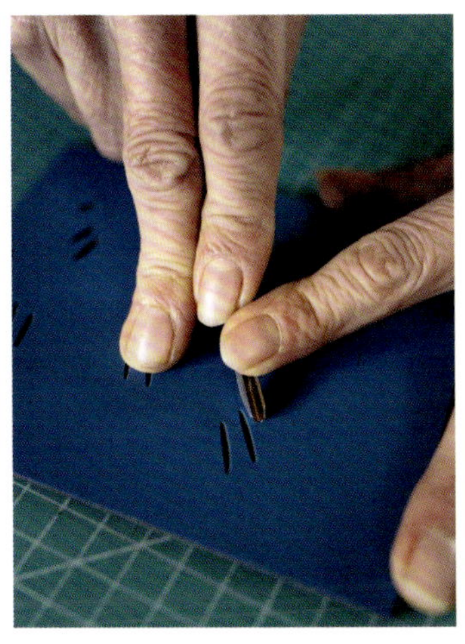

For extra control when cutting something really detailed, I like to use the index finger from my other hand to provide additional support.

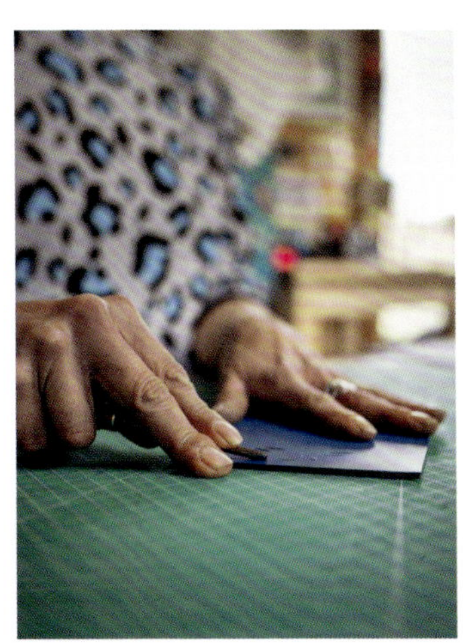

If you carve at too shallow an angle, the tool will slip and slide across the surface and could plunge into your hand.

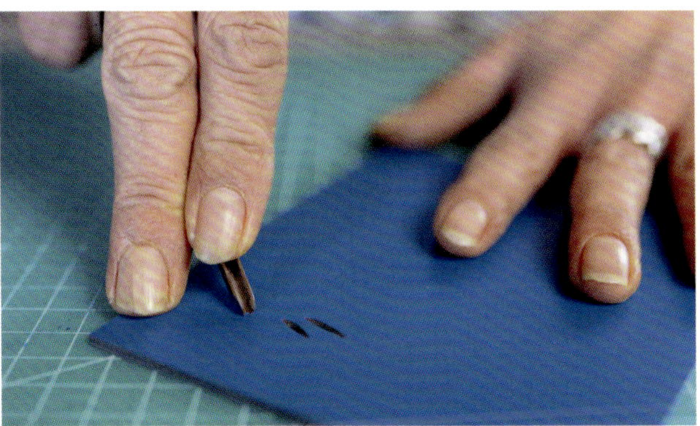

It's important to maintain the correct angle. If you plunge your tool too deep into the lino, it can get stuck, rip and damage the surface.

USING YOUR TOOLS SAFELY

Always carve away from yourself – it's very easy to slip and for the tool to pierce your fingers or hand. If you have cut yourself while linocutting, you will know how painful it can be. When I'm running my workshops from my studio, I always make sure I have a big box of plasters in case of any emergencies. Inevitably, people get chatting and one of their tools slips – it's so easy to do.

For extra safety, you can use a bench hook – a piece of wood with ledges on opposite sides. This holds your linocut in place while you are carving and prevents slipping. Another alternative is a non-slip mat, which you can get from any hardware store.

One of the worse injuries I've suffered was when I was cutting a piece of lino with a craft knife. I got momentarily distracted and my hand slipped and sliced off a sliver of my finger. To avoid similar pain, here's how to cut Japanese vinyl safely:

WORKING HEIGHT

It's important to work at a comfortable height, ideally keeping your back nice and straight and avoiding slouching. An ongoing back issue means I find it uncomfortable to sit for too long, so I've invested in an adjustable standing desk that I just pop on top of my normal desk, allowing me to carve at a height that suits me. I've noticed that when my students carve, they concentrate so hard that their breathing becomes shallow and their shoulders come up to their ears, which brings me on to my next point...

TAKE BREAKS

It's so important to rest your eyes, hands and brain. To avoid carving stiffness, get up at regular intervals – have a stretch, a snack and a sip of something. This also gives you space away from your work; often, when working for long stretches, we lose the ability to 'see' the work as we are so involved and invested in it.

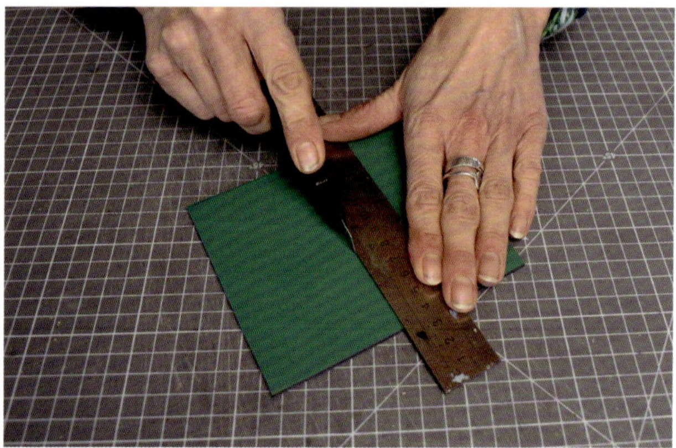

Your craft knife should be sharp; it's worth testing it out if you are unsure. Place your lino on your cutting mat and, using a metal ruler (plastic and wood rulers are easily damaged), make a light score where you want to cut. Keep reinforcing the cut, building up depth until you go right through the lino.

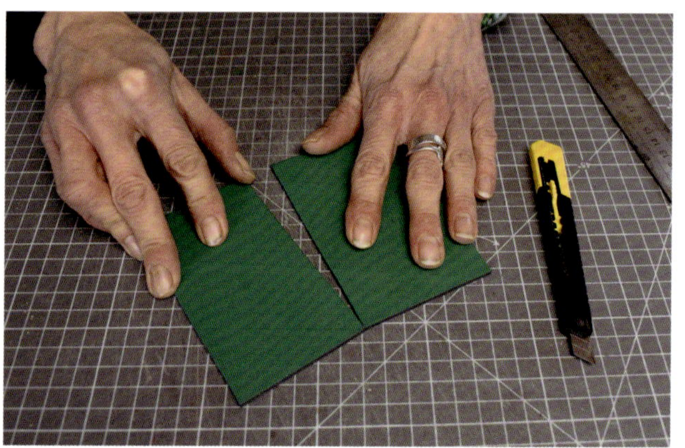

Once you have gone through the lino, gently pull it apart to separate. For traditional lino, score lightly several times then bend it along the scored line. It will snap.

MARK–MAKING WARM–UP

You Will Need

- Cutting mat
- Selection of pencils, e.g. HB/2B/4B
- Rubber/eraser
- A5 or A6 lino
- Thin paper for printing and drawing (photocopy paper is fine)
- Cutting tools
- Stiff brush
- Relief printing ink (just one colour is needed)
- Inking slab
- Roller
- Baren or wooden spoon
- Cleaning materials

1   Gather a good selection of different grades of pencils and a piece of paper. Draw around your lino block onto your paper.

2   Take five to ten minutes to make as many different marks as you can using the different grades of pencils. Be playful and just have fun drawing whatever comes to mind. Here are some ideas:

- Straight lines – fine and thick
- Cross-hatching – parallel lines close to one another
- Circles – some that are filled in, others just outlined
- Patterns – look around you: what patterns can you see?
- Fur-like marks – have a look at your pet and try and draw their fur
- Wiggles
- Symbols
- Dots and dashes.

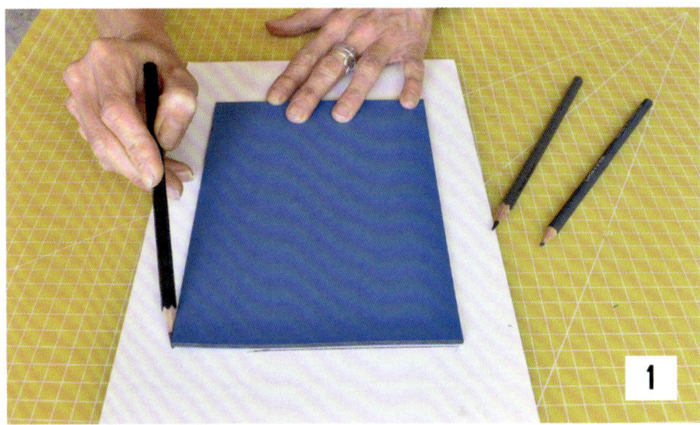

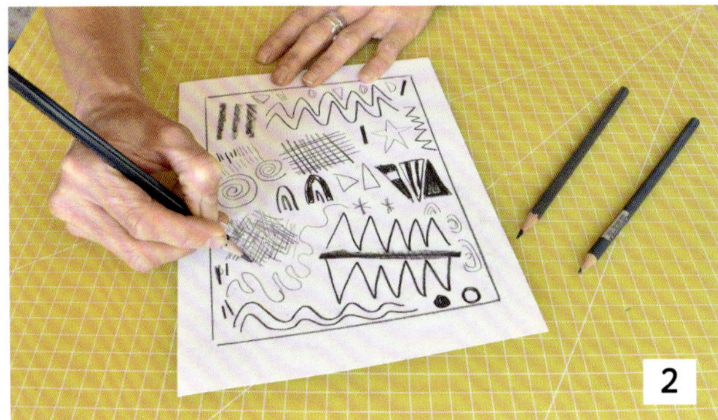

3 Try to translate your drawn marks into linocut marks. The challenge is to aim to replicate the drawn lines as best you can. Be firm and confident, and enjoy yourself – the tools will let you know what marks they want to make. You might want to make a note of which tools you have used to make which marks. Always remember to carve away from yourself to avoid slipping and cutting your fingers. I'm going to translate all the black lines as white lines for ease in this project.

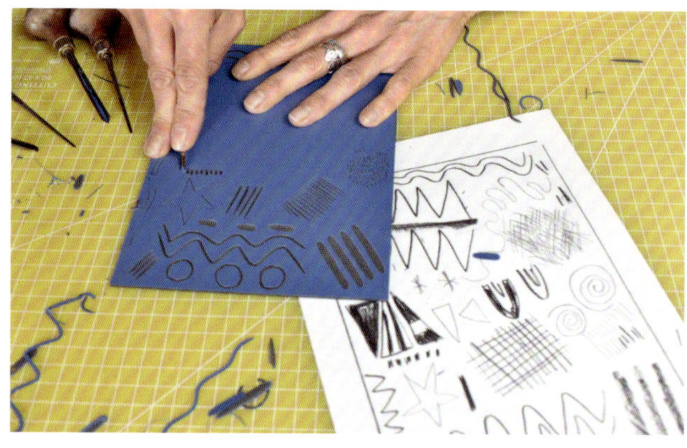

Using a small/medium U tool to create dashes.

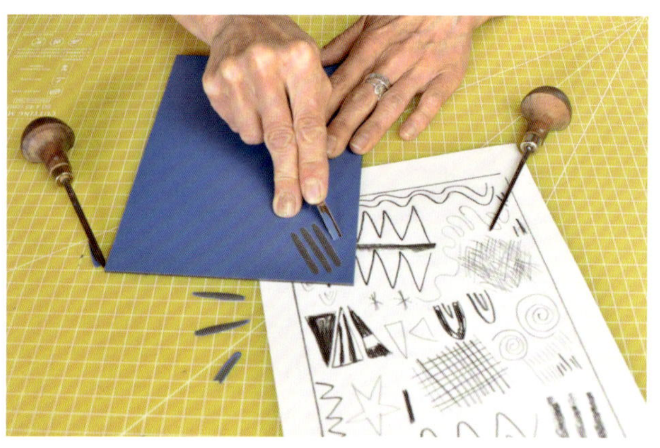

Using a wide U tool to make wide gouge marks.

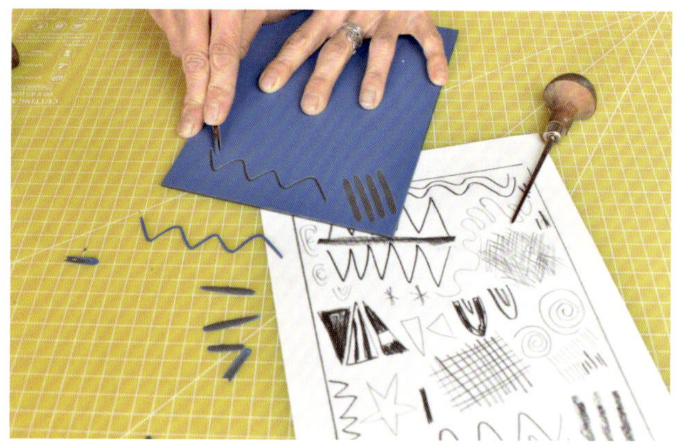

Using a medium U tool to create a squiggly line.

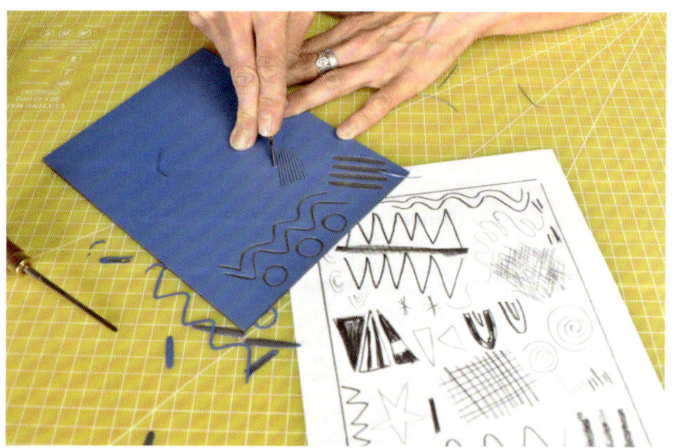

Using a very fine V tool to create fine lines that are close together.

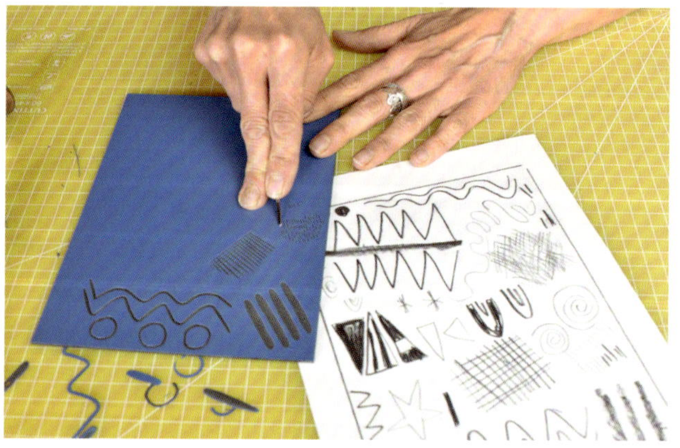

Using a very fine U tool to create fur-like marks.

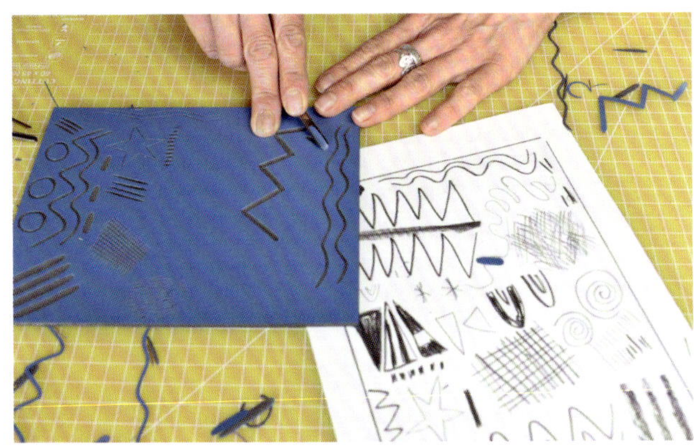

Using a wide V tool to create thick lines with a sharp edge at the corners.

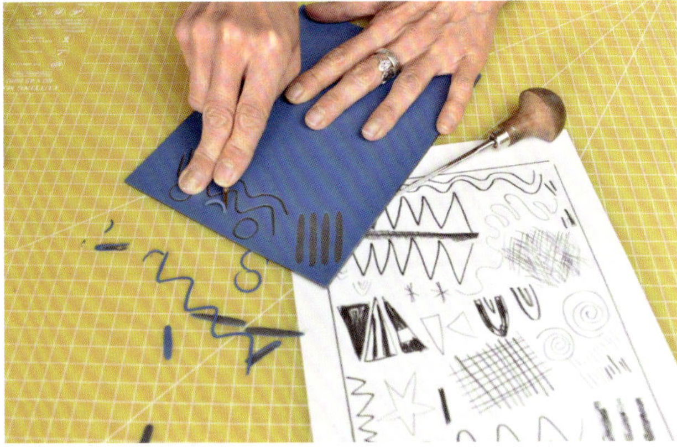

Using a medium U tool to create a circle. To do this, make contact with the lino and then rotate the block around, keeping the tool steady. The movement of the block will carve the circle.

4   Once you have finished carving, you are ready to take a print. To check how your print is coming along, you can always take a rubbing by placing a piece of paper on top of your lino and gently rubbing a soft pencil across the surface. This will pick up the marks.

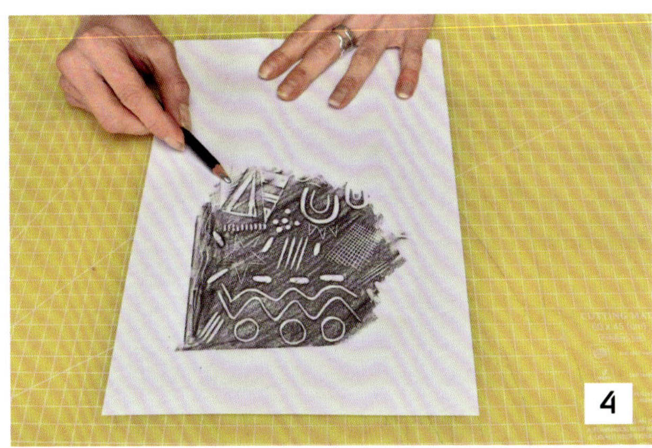

NOTE

Taking a rubbing is always an option throughout the book if you don't want to ink up and proof your print. I will always encourage you to take an actual print but this is, of course, entirely up to you.

5   Once you have finished carving, run a stiff brush across the surface to make sure you have cleared off any little bits of lino debris that might be stuck on.

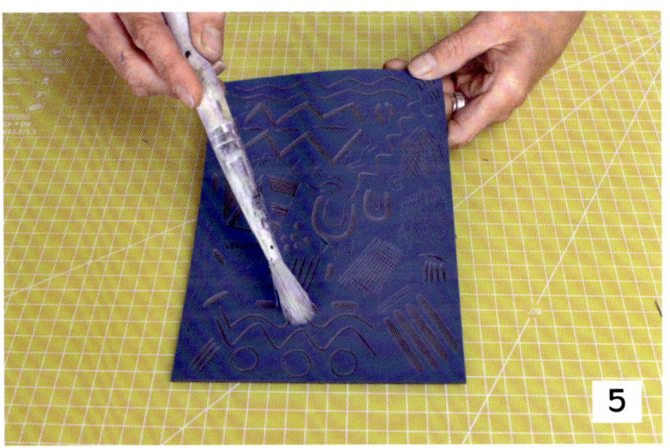

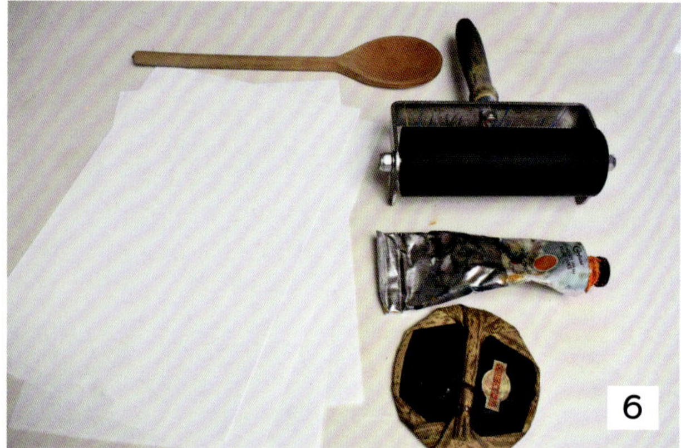

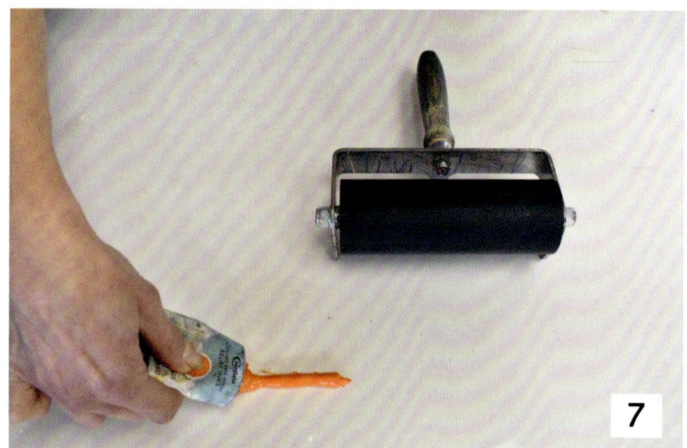

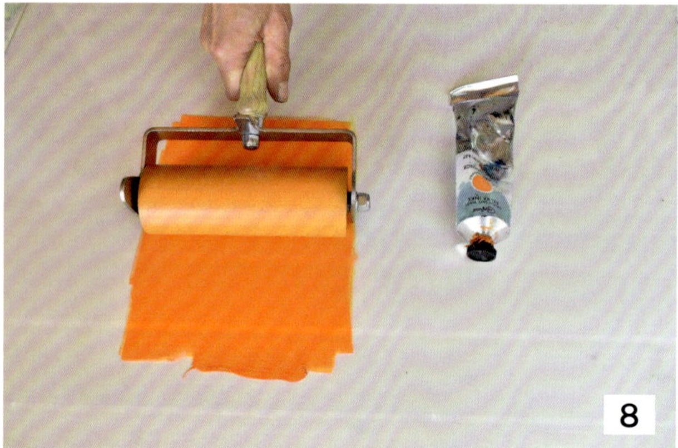

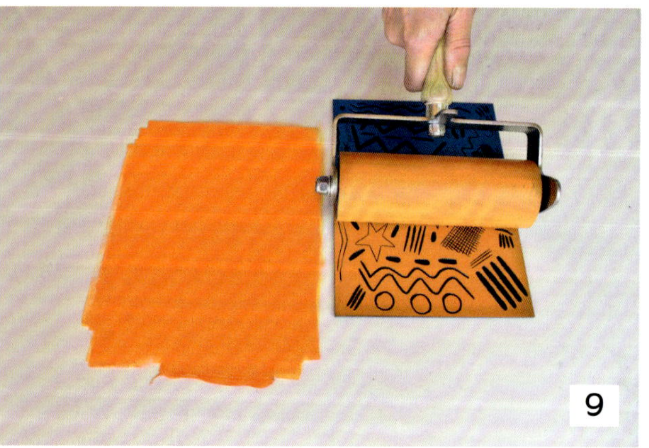

6 It's important now to clean up your carving space and make sure it's ready for inking. Ensure you clear away any pieces of linocut debris that might be liable to get into the ink. Gather your ink, paper, roller and baren (or wooden spoon).

7 Squeeze ink onto your inking slab.

8 Take your roller and roll out the ink onto your slab until it is spread evenly into a thin layer – giving the roller a nice, even coverage. The ink shouldn't be too thick and sound squelchy; it should make a gentle hissing noise, like the sound of the sea. If you have too much ink on your roller, just roll the excess onto a piece of newsprint.

9 Take the roller and roll onto the block slowly, making sure all the raised areas are coated in ink. Try not to roll back and forth, which means you are rolling the ink on and then off.

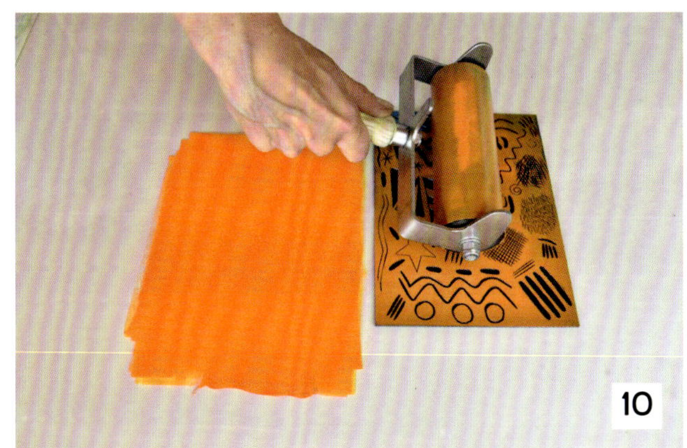

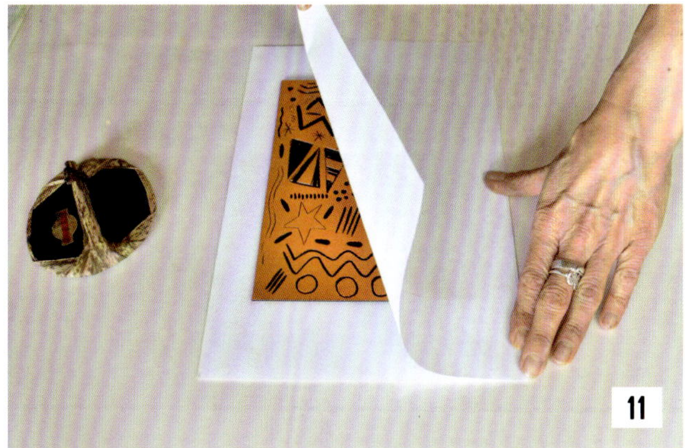

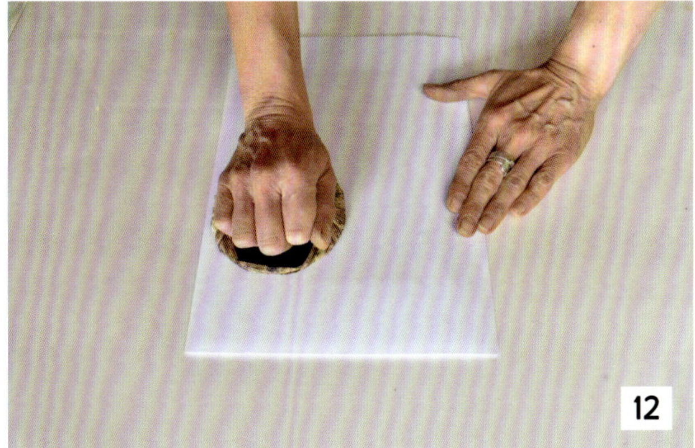

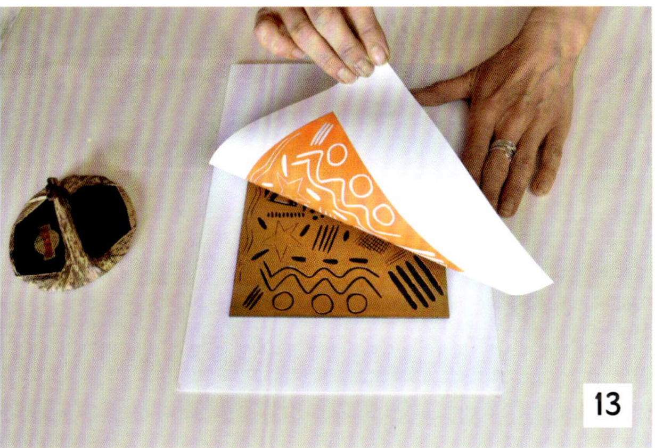

10 Roll in different directions to make sure the linocut is covered. As you get more experienced, you will be able to tell if you have inked your block up properly – it takes practice. A good tip is to hold it up to eye level: if the surface looks textured, there is too much ink – use a piece of newsprint to blot it and remove the excess.

11 Once your plate is inked, move it to your clean printing area. Take a piece of paper of the same size and place your linocut on top, ink side up. Try and place it as evenly within the paper as you can. Then take another piece of paper and carefully place it on top of the print. Using a piece of paper underneath as a guide ensures that the paper is registered nicely (see Chapter 8). Roll the paper down with care and gently rub your hand across the paper to smooth the surface.

12 Now we need to burnish the print using either a baren or wooden spoon. If you are using a baren, insert your fingers through into the handle and clasp them around, making a fist. Keeping your arm straight, use your body weight to push down (I find it easier and more effective to stand when hand burnishing). Gently move the baren around the back of the paper, using the edge to focus pressure on smaller areas. You will start to see the image emerge through the paper. Continue until you are confident you have burnished the whole area completely.

Using a spoon has the same principle as using a baren. Try and keep the spoon as flat as you can to ensure you get a nice, even, flat pressure.

13 Check your progress by peeling back the print. If it looks too light, place the paper down and continue burnishing.

14 Once you have pulled back your print, it's time to have a look at it. Inevitably, the first print won't be perfect – it might be over-inked, under-inked, moved slightly or have a tiny bit of lino attached to it.

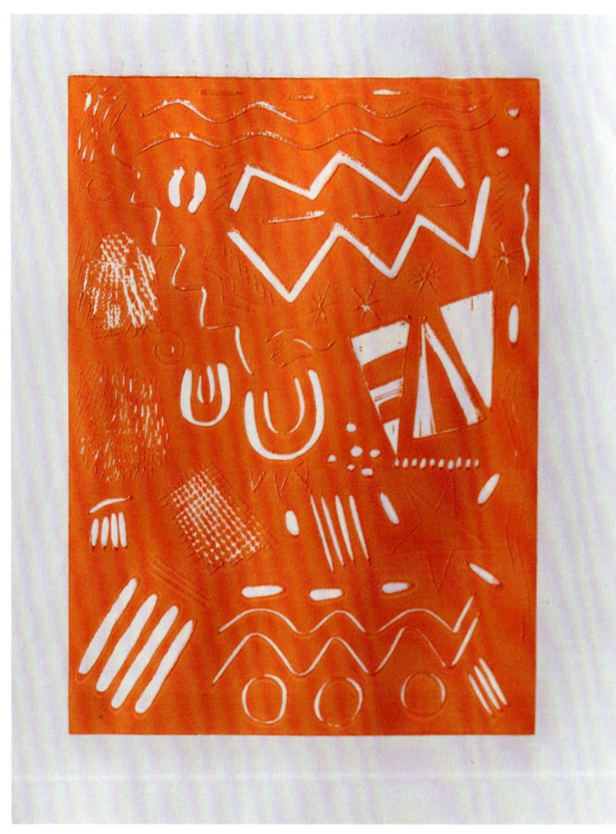

This print is over-inked; you can see the ink collecting in the cuts, causing a loss of detail.

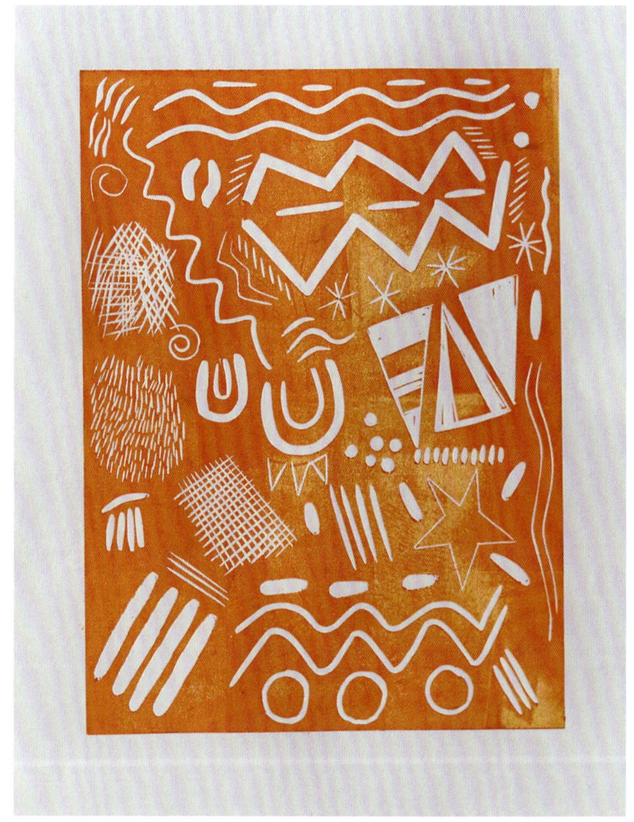

This print is under-inked, meaning there isn't enough ink on the surface to cover the lino, causing a patchy print.

15 Keep trying until you get a print you are happy
with. There is no need to clean the lino between
prints; simply apply more ink and print again.
However, if you want to print the block in another
colour, you must ensure you clean up the block
and roller before you start again.

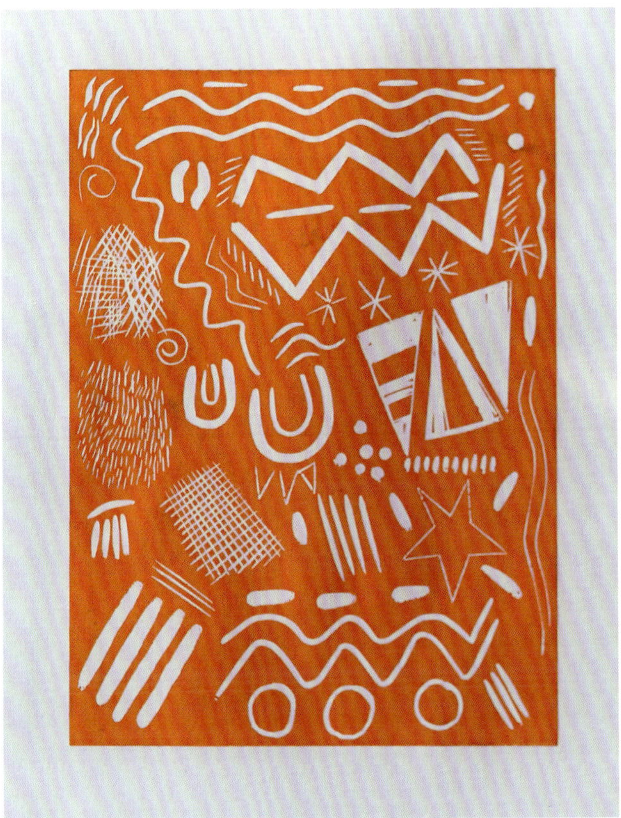

*This is a good print; the ink
coverage is even and there is a
consistency of quality throughout.*

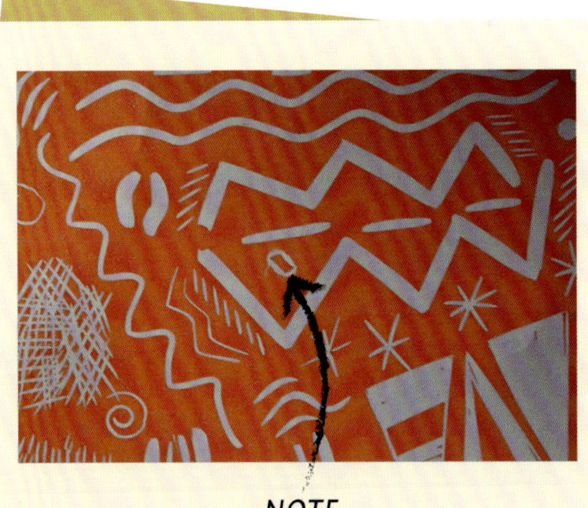

NOTE

*This print detail shows what happens when
a tiny bit of lino gets into the ink, sticks to
the lino and then prints. The result is a little
halo – you can see it in the middle of the
zigzag lines. The best way to avoid this is
to give your lino a good brush after carving
and before printing.*

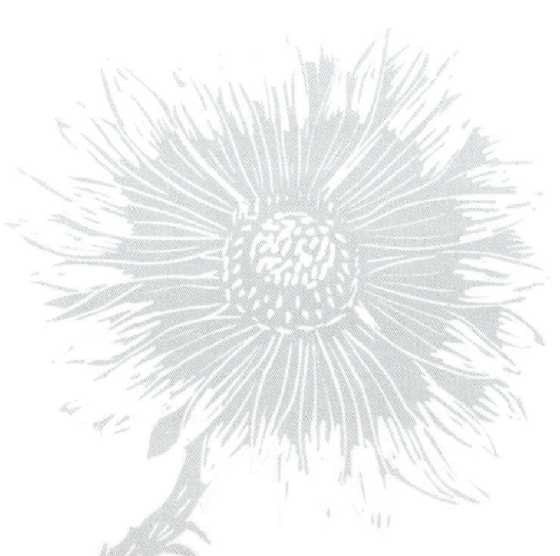

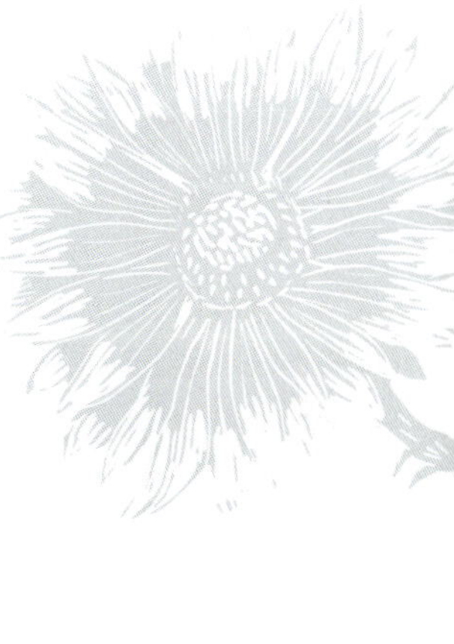

6 CLEANING UP

I love cleaning up at the end of a printing session; I see it like the cool-down part of an exercise class. It can be such a useful time to reflect on what has worked, what hasn't and what can be achieved next. Regardless of whether you enjoy it or see it as a chore, it's an important part of printmaking and when executed well will make your next session more pleasurable. I also love coming into a nice clean studio in the morning; I find it sets the day off well.

Make sure you have the right cleaning agent for the inks you have used and wear gloves to protect your hands while cleaning up. I use oil-based but water-soluble inks and I find the best way to clean them is with a spray bottle filled with water, a good squirt of washing-up liquid and elbow grease. Normal oil-based inks are traditionally cleaned off with white spirit or turpentine – these are highly toxic, though, so a good non-toxic alternative is to use vegetable oil and finish off with a non-toxic solvent such as Zest-It. As ink is harder to clean off when it has dried, it's always advisable to clean up as soon as you have finished printing.

OIL-BASED WATER-SOLUBLE INKS

You Will Need

- Gloves
- Spray bottle filled with diluted washing-up liquid
- Rags (e.g. old t-shirts)
- Newspaper
- Vegetable oil (optional)
- Spatula
- Tracing/tissue paper

1   Wearing gloves, clean off your block using diluted washing-up liquid from a spray bottle and an old rag.

2   Roll any excess ink from your roller onto newspaper.

3   Clean your roller using the diluted washing-up liquid and a rag. Pay attention to the edges, as ink tends to congregate there. You might then want to use vegetable oil to give it a final going over to ensure all the ink has been removed.

4   If you have a quantity of ink left that's worth saving, scrape it up using a spatula and place it in a piece of tracing or tissue paper.

5   Fold over the tracing paper so that the ink is carefully wrapped up and store it in a tin for future use. (Note: this is only for oil-based inks; water-based ones would just dry out.)

6   Clean off your inking slab with your soapy water and finish with a good wipe over with vegetable oil. Use a clean rag at the end to mop up any excess grease.

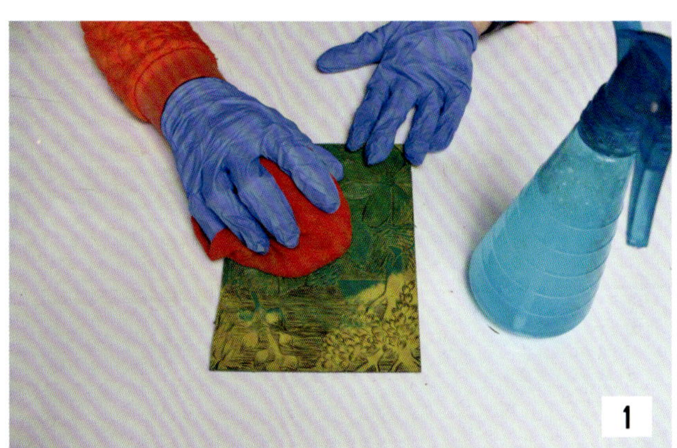

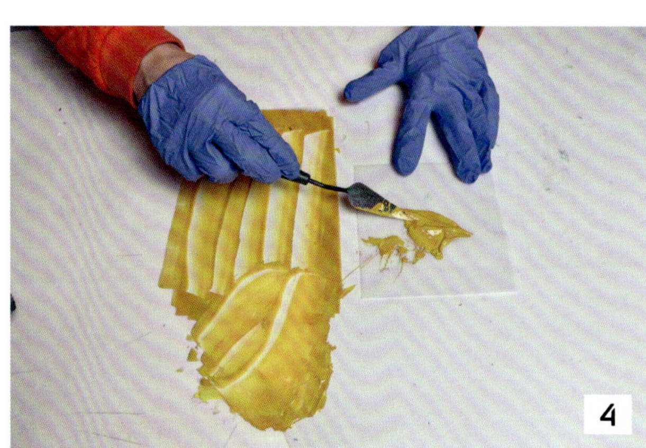

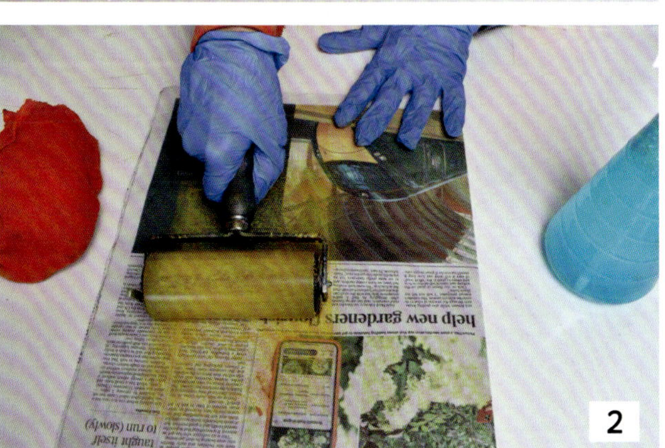

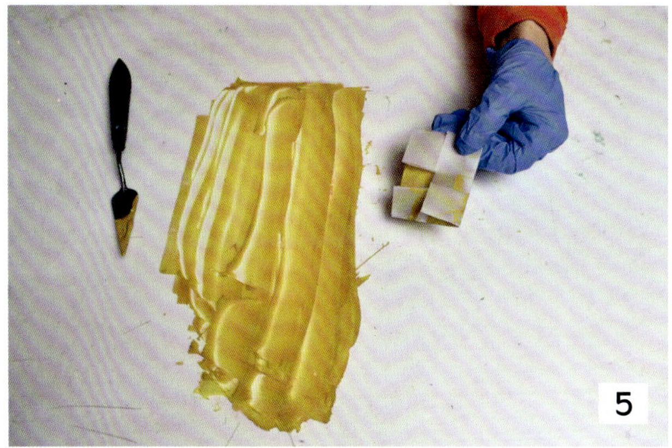

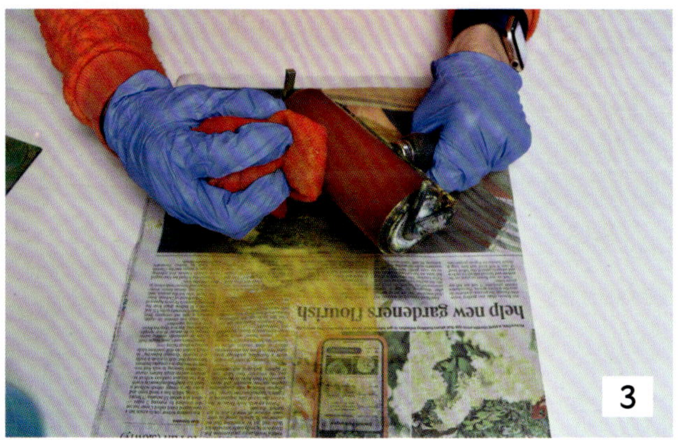

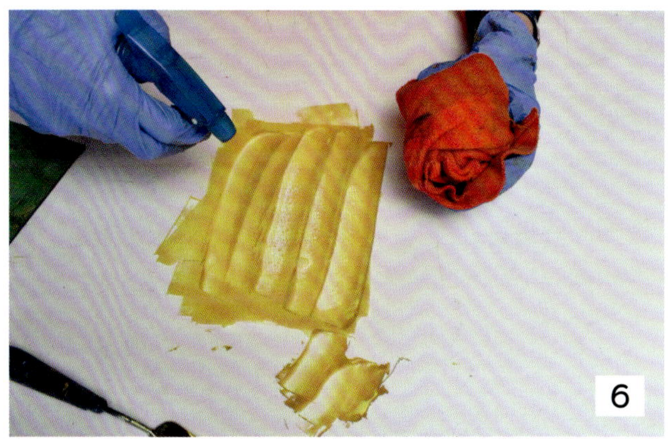

7 CARVING LINO

One of the hardest things to get your head around when you first start practising linocutting is deciding what to carve away and what to leave. In the past, I've had students send me a basic line drawing before a workshop, concerned that it's too simple and they will be finished too quickly. I email back and say it's not too simple; in fact, it could be quite difficult depending on how they approach it.

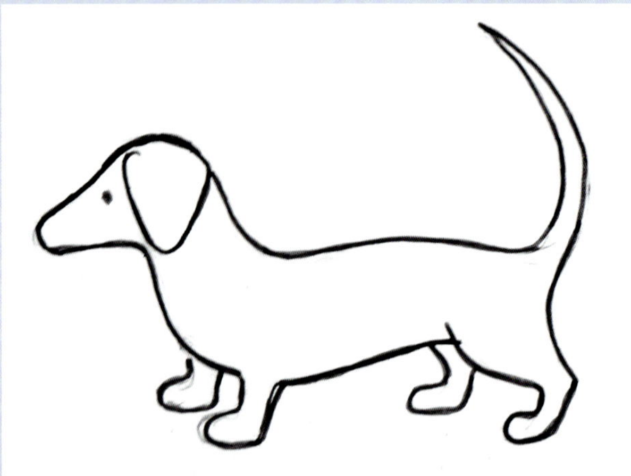

Let's take a simple line drawing of a dog. Can you see why it would be tricky to cut? If you want just a printed background and a white line then yes, it's simple; however, if you want to recreate the outline and have it look exactly like the drawing then it's more complicated. This is because in order to achieve an outline with linocut you must carve out all the background and leave just the line in relief, which makes for a lot of cutting!

In this project we are going to carve four different versions of the same image so that you can understand how carving in these different ways will give you very individual results. This will give you a much clearer understanding of how to approach your work moving forward.

We will be experimenting with:
- **Positive carving**: carving outside your drawn lines; carving away the background to leave a solid shape on a white background
- **Negative carving**: carving inside your drawn lines to create a silhouette
- **White line carving**: carving away the drawn lines themselves
- **Black line carving**: carving away everything apart from the drawn lines, including your background.

ONE IMAGE FOUR WAYS

You Will Need

- Cutting mat
- Large piece of lino – I used A4 cut into 4 sections
- Metal ruler
- Permanent marker pen
- Craft knife
- Thin paper for printing and drawing (photocopy paper is fine)
- Cutting tools
- Inking slab
- Relief printing ink
- Roller
- Baren or wooden spoon
- Stiff brush
- Selection of pencils, e.g. 4B/6B, and a rubber/eraser
- Cleaning materials

CARVING THE BLOCKS

1 Take your piece of lino and use a ruler and marker pen to divide it into four equal blocks.

2 Cut your lino carefully using a craft knife and steel ruler (see page 38).

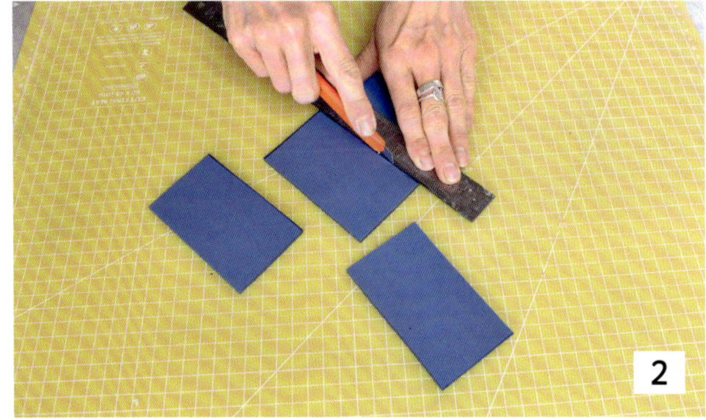

3   Use a pencil to draw round one of the pieces of
    lino onto a piece of paper.

4   Draw a simple line sketch onto your paper, using
    pencil and going over your lines with marker pen.
    Don't overcomplicate your design. I chose to draw
    a dachshund.

5   Transfer the drawing to all four blocks. Go over
    your pencil lines with a permanent marker.

6   Carve away all of the background from one of your
    blocks. Start by going around the outline with a
    small V or U tool, then clear away the background
    using a wide U tool, leaving just the body of the
    image. This is **positive carving.**

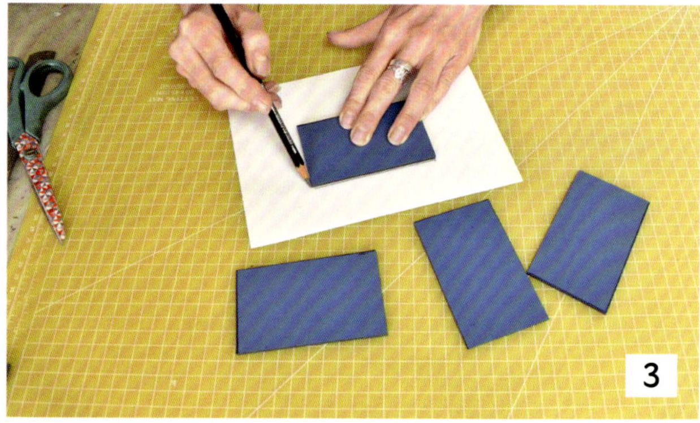

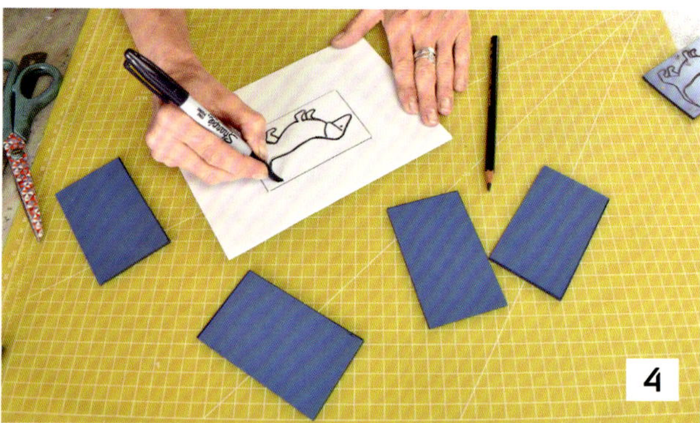

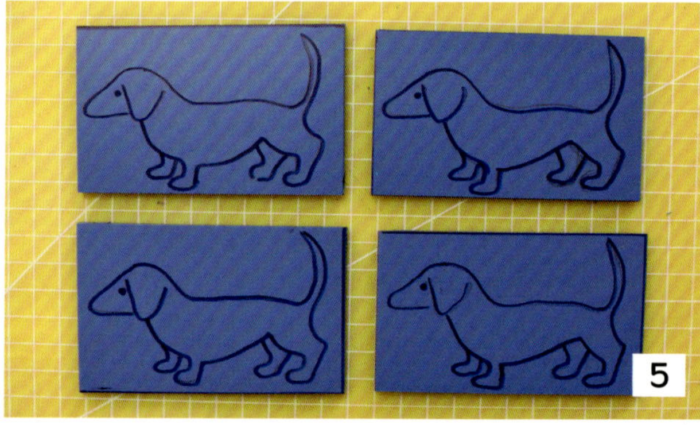

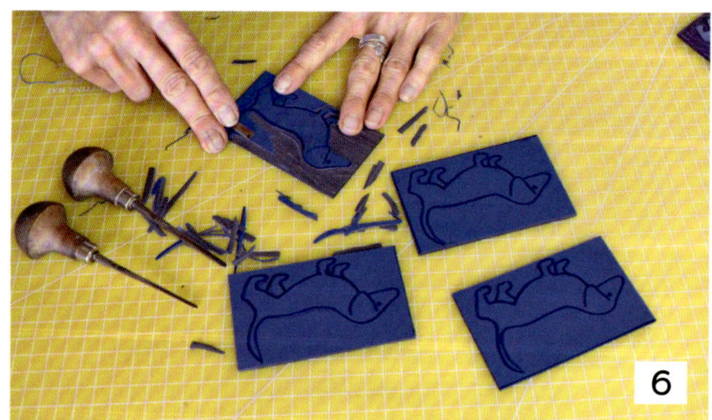

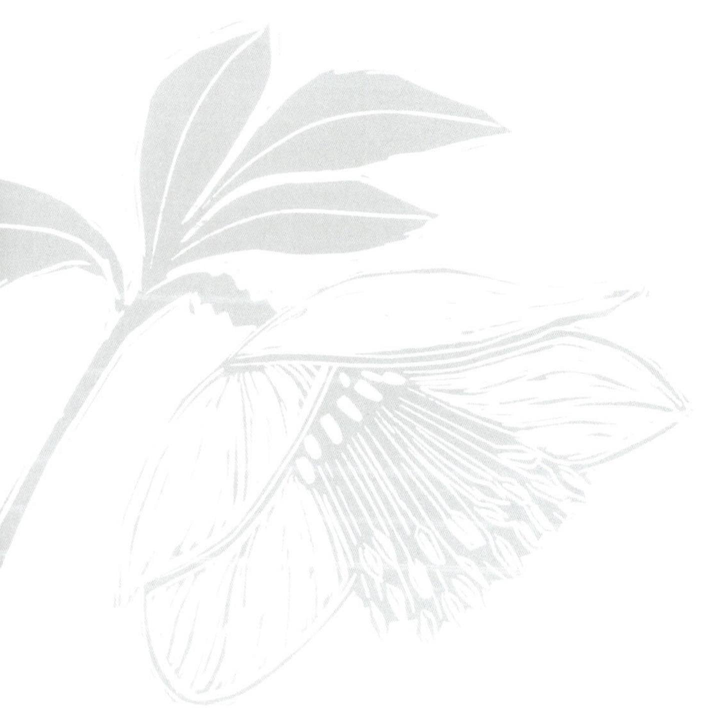

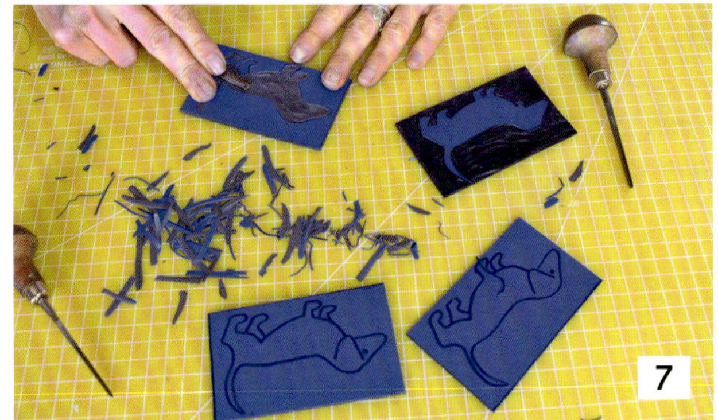

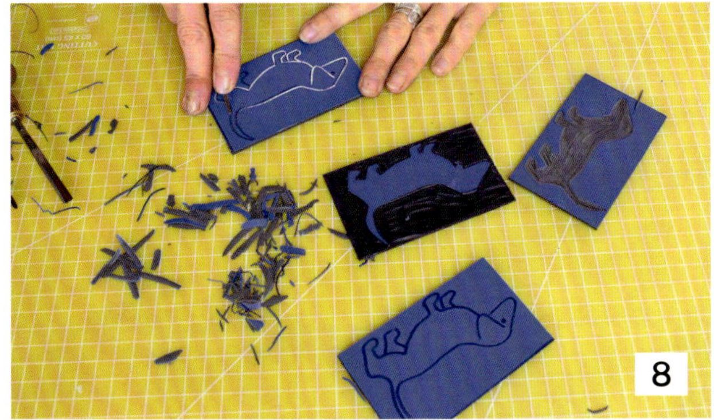

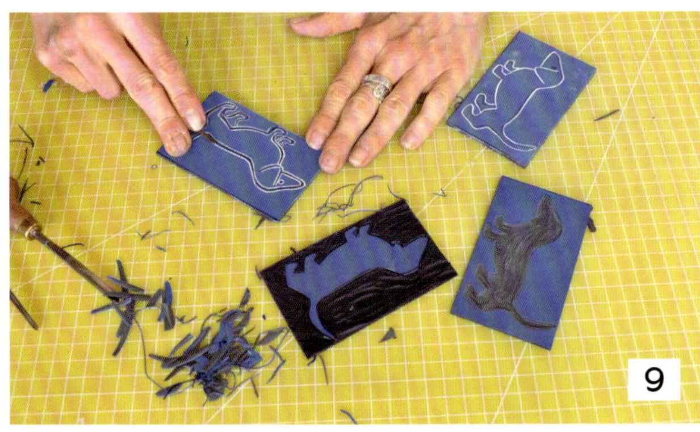

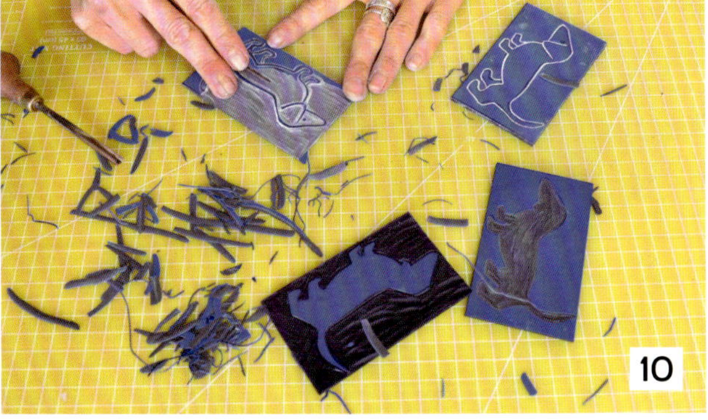

7   Take the second block and carve away the inside of the image. Start by outlining the shape with a fine tool, then use a wider U tool to remove the inside to leave a white shape with a block background. This is **negative carving**.

8   Take your third block and carve just the line itself using a small U tool. This will result in a **white line carving**. (Note: the white you see in this photo is talcum powder, which I will explain the use of in the next chapter, see page 64).

9   The final block is the trickiest to carve – the **solid printed outline**. Here you need to carve either side of your line, leaving the line in relief. I used a small V tool to carve around the outline.

10 I used a medium U tool for the inside of the body and a wider U tool for the background. The outline will print up positive, leaving the background negative.

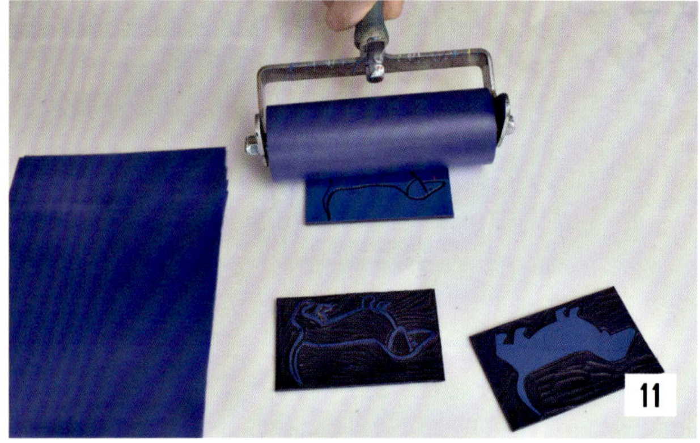

13 Burnish carefully using your wooden spoon or baren.

14 Slowly peel back your print.

15 Print all the blocks up in the same way and place them together so you can evaluate how they have printed up.

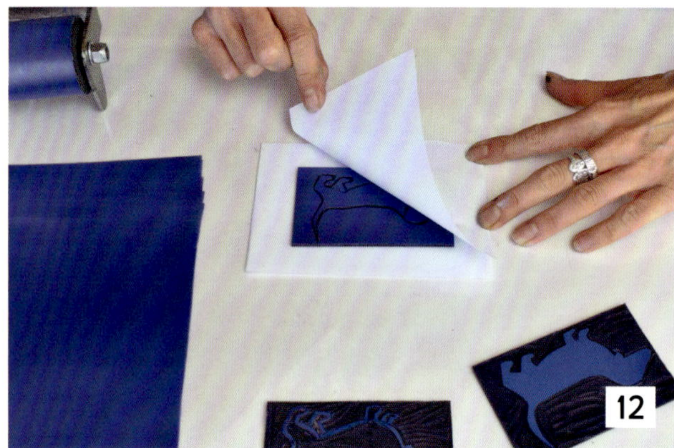

11 Now you are ready to print. Mix up a colour of your choice and carefully ink up one of your blocks.

12 Place a piece of paper down onto your printing surface and position the block in the middle, facing upwards. Then take a piece of paper the same size and place it on top.

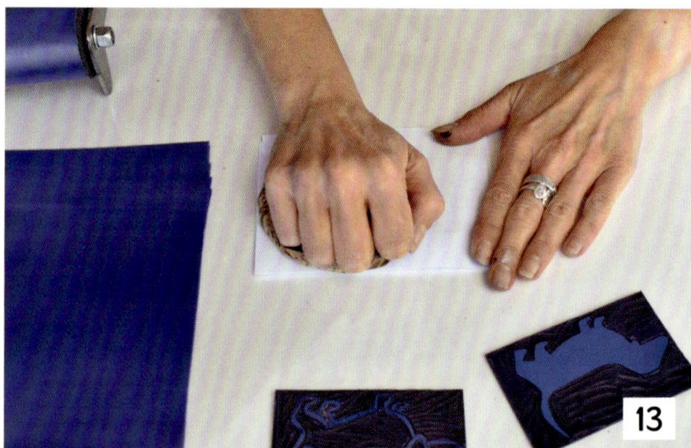

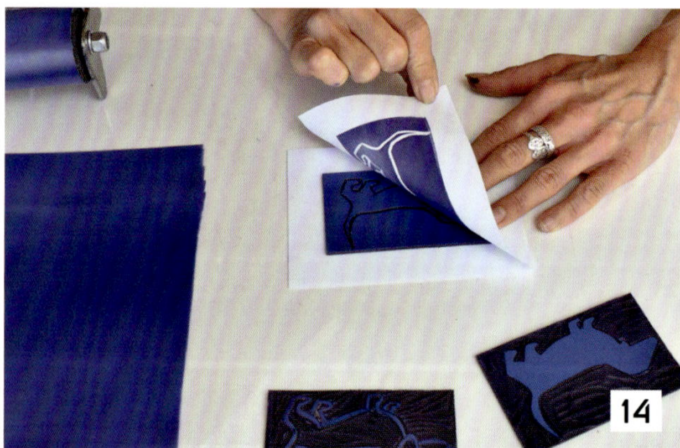

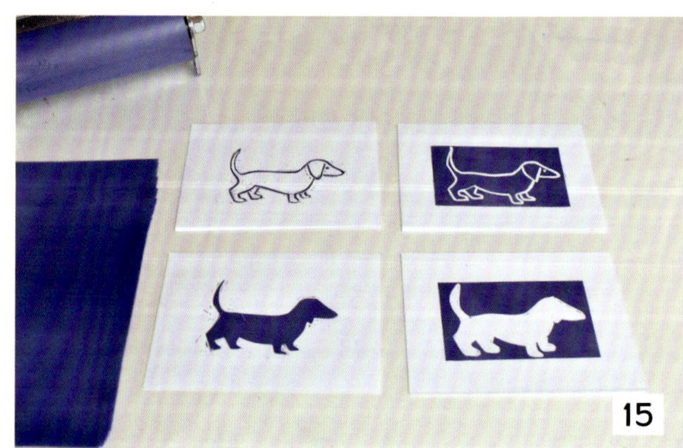

YOUR FOUR PRINTS

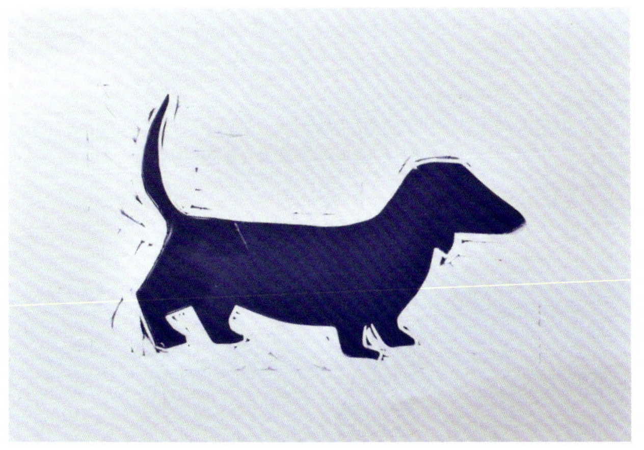

Positive carving *The body has been left in relief, with the background carved away.*

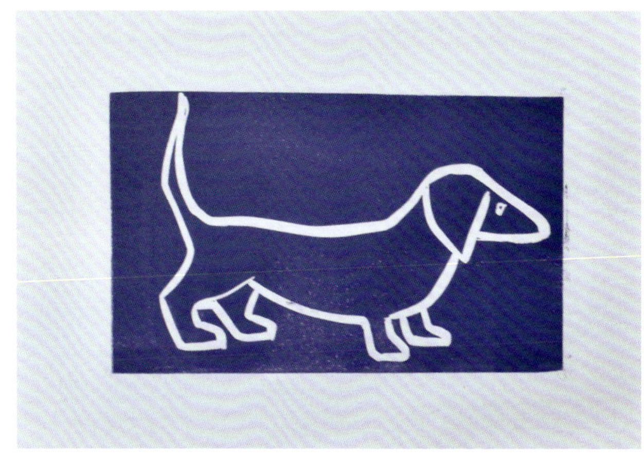

White line carving *The outline has been carved away, leaving a simple white line.*

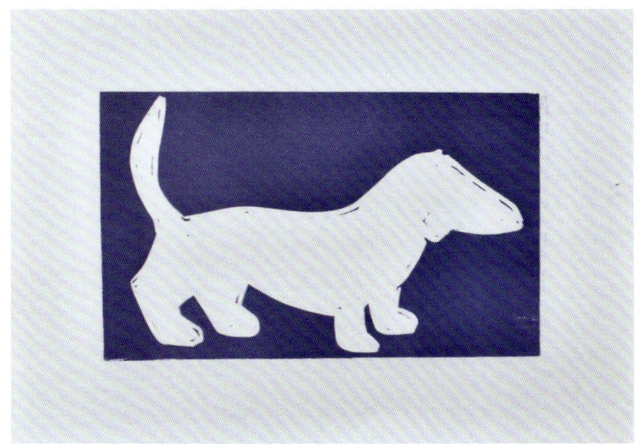

Negative carving *The body of the image has been carved away, leaving the background in relief. It forms a silhouette.*

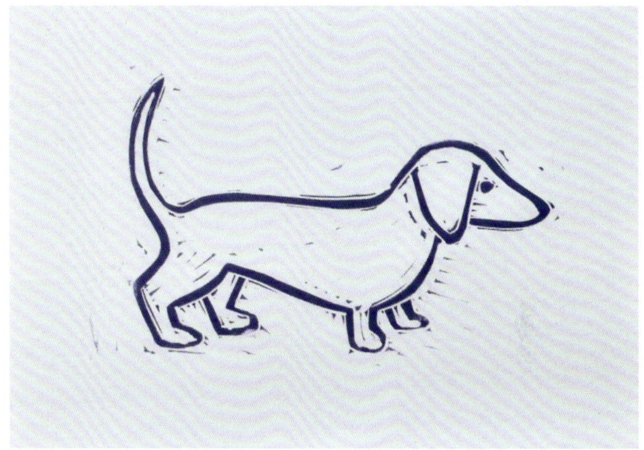

Solid printed outline *The marker pen outline has been cut around, leaving the outline in relief, and the rest of the lino is carved away. This method involves the most carving and is the most difficult.*

AN INTERVIEW WITH HARRIET POPHAM

You have a very unique way of approaching printmaking with your jigsaw style. Could you talk us through this?

I cut my lino into shapes, ink up each piece individually, slot them back together and then print the whole thing as one. I really enjoy this approach as it allows me to work in different colours without needing layers to dry in between. It also suits my linear illustration style, as my blocks tend to be mostly solid colour with white line details. (Note: this method is easier with SoftCut and Japanese vinyl.)

What do you love about printmaking?

I love what a physical process it is and, although it is fairly labour-intensive, I like the commitment of carving into a block of lino; once you're in, you're invested and likely to see it through. As a result of this, I don't overthink my work the way I used to before I got into printmaking. I find the planning exciting, the carving calming and that first ink-up and peel-back super satisfying.

I also really love seeing the joy that this process spreads. I have run workshops where people have arrived with such a lack of confidence about getting creative, but as they've relaxed into the workshop, I've seen them be completely surprised and delighted at what they've created. I definitely believe making with our hands is so beneficial, especially today.

Could you offer some advice to people who are just starting on their printmaking journey?

Let things like your workspace and kit evolve and improve as you develop. I used beginner tools for a long time and printed everything by hand with a Speedball baren (which I still often do). You don't have to have it all to start creating.

Once you get confident with the process, try, where possible, to use your own photographs and personal experiences to inform your work. You will feel more connected to your prints that way and be in a better position to start selling them! It will also add to your experiences as you'll start spotting potential prints all around you.

Don't be afraid to try lots of different ways of working. There is a pressure to have your style nailed down and to be consistent these days, but it is so important to allow yourself time to find the way you love to work. Make room for happy accidents and experimentation and, above all, have fun!

@harrietpopham
www.harrietpopham.com

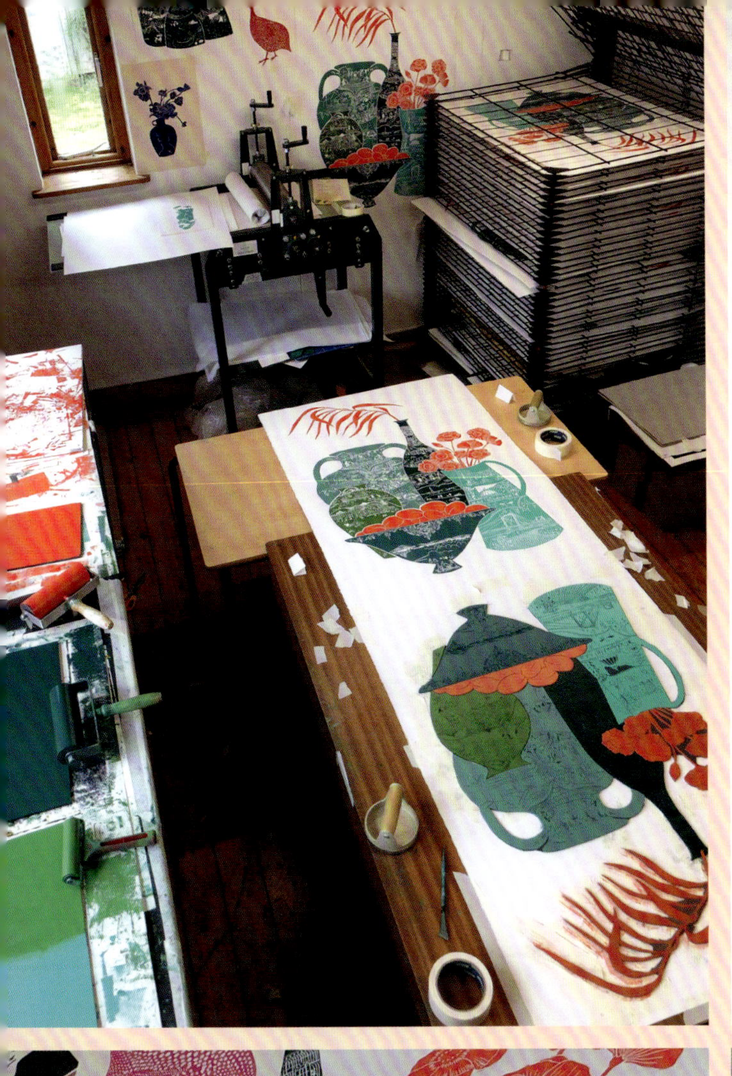
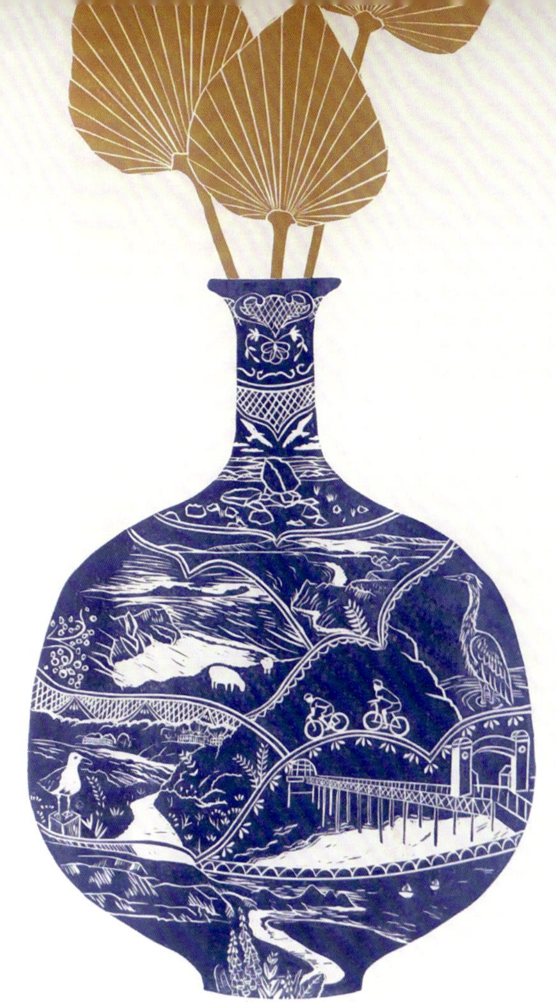
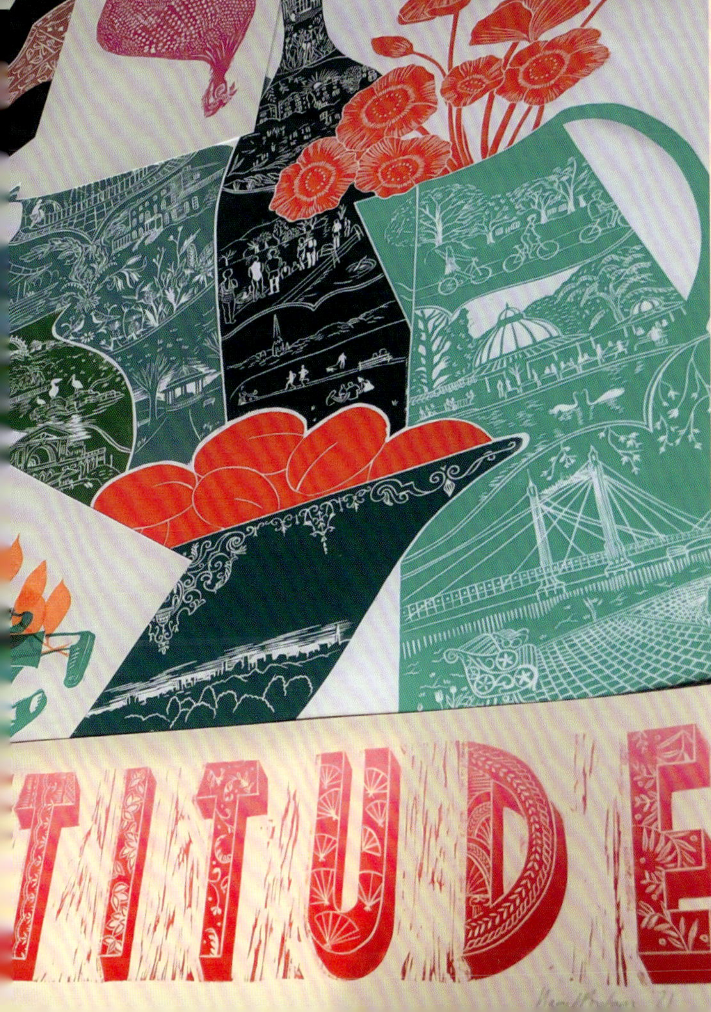TITUDE
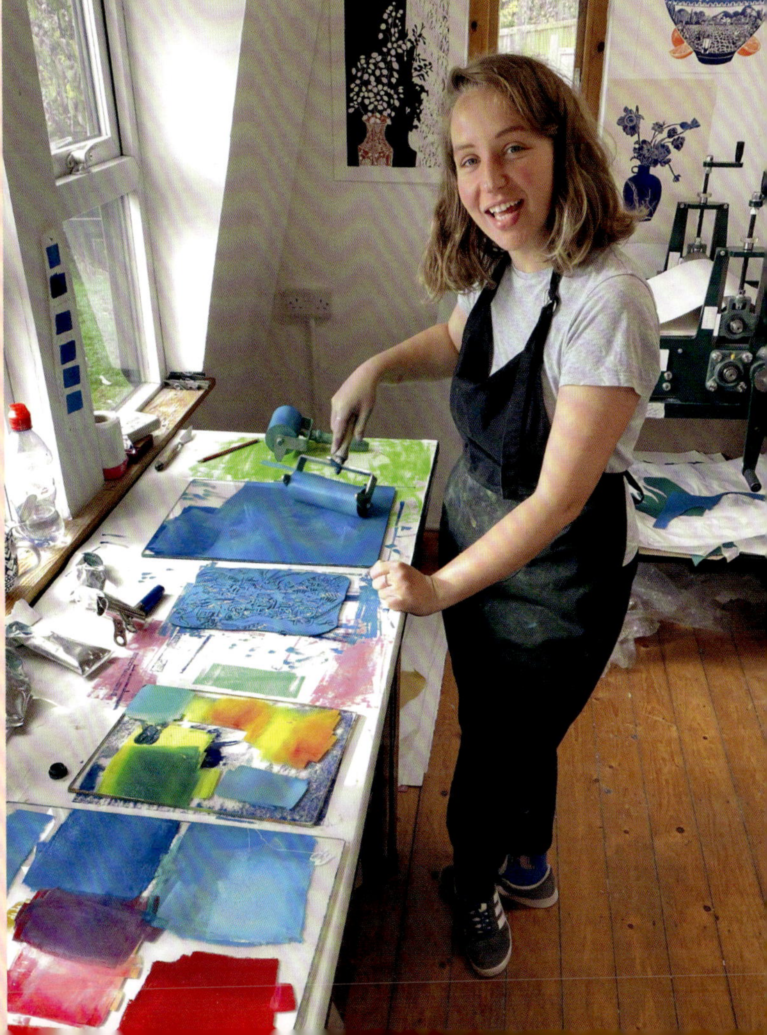

8 REGISTRATION

Registration is one of the most important elements of printmaking. It is the process of lining up the paper in relation to the linocut block to make sure the block is positioned correctly to give the desired border. If you're using multiple colours or plates, registration becomes even more important (see Chapters 15 and 16) as you will need to make sure all the colours register in exactly the same places on top of each other.

There are many methods of registration, and many printers have their own registration systems. In this chapter I'm going to show you the four different methods that I use the most.

SUPER-SIMPLE REGISTRATION

This is a quick and easy way of registering your print.

You Will Need

- **Inked-up pre-carved piece of lino**
- **Two sheets of printing paper, both the same size (photocopy paper is fine)**
- **Pencil**
- **Baren or wooden spoon**

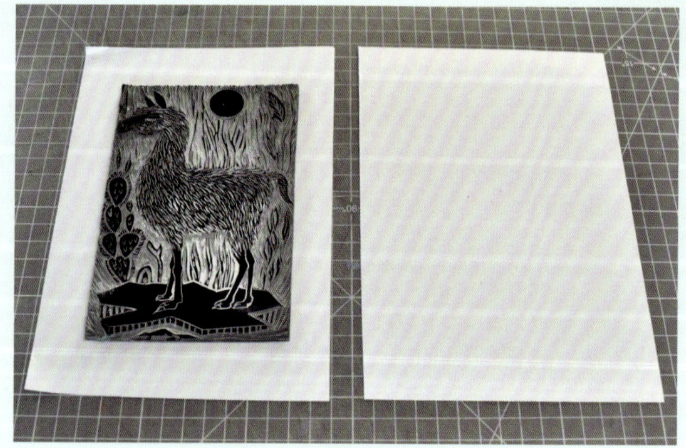

1   Make sure your paper is all the same size.

2   Place one piece of paper down and position your inked-up linocut block on top.

3   Draw around the lino.

4   Then take another piece of paper (which is the same size), match it up and place it down.

5   Burnish as usual.

PAPER TEMPLATE REGISTRATION

This is one of the registration methods I use the most when I'm proofing my prints. It's really just a slightly more refined version of the super–simple registration method. I don't tend to use it for editioning my prints (see page 79), as I like something more robust such as the registration board method (see next page), but it's great to use when you're in a hurry.

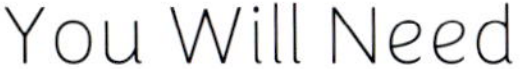

You Will Need

- Two sheets of paper – one piece larger than the other
- Pencil or pen
- Pre-carved piece of lino
- Metal ruler

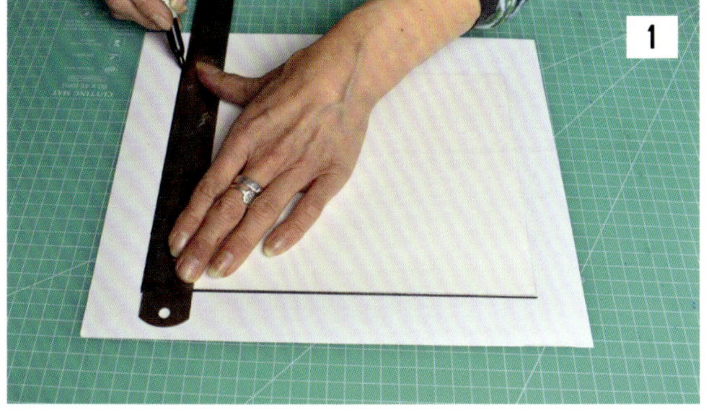

1 Take a piece of paper that is larger than your printing paper – I'm just using photocopy paper here. Place your printing paper in the centre of the paper and draw around the paper with a pencil or pen.

2 Remove the printing paper. Take your lino block and place it in the centre of the printing paper outline. I normally do this by eye, but for greater accuracy, use a ruler. Draw around your block.

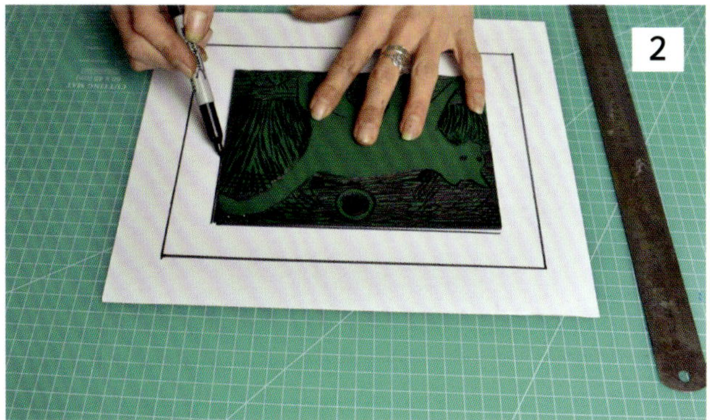

3 Remove your block. You now have two outlines: one for your paper and one for your lino block. Ink up your lino as usual and position it in the lino block outline. Place your printing paper in the paper outline, on top of your lino block. Repeat for the whole edition. Mark on your template which way is up – it's always helpful!

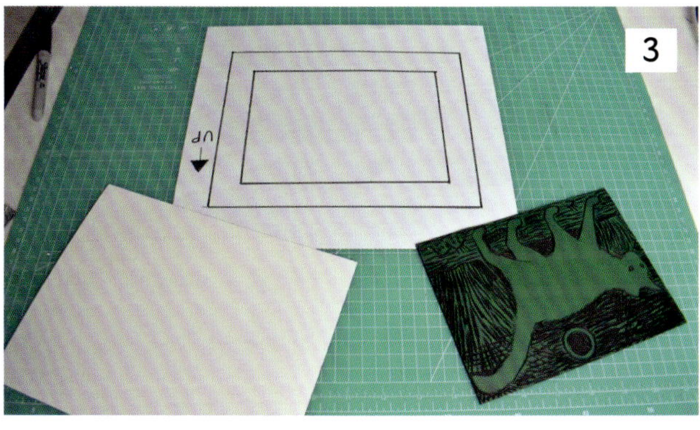

REGISTRATION BOARD

I use greyboard or mountboard for my registration boards. I tend to avoid cardboard as it can be too soft.

You Will Need

- **Piece of greyboard or mountboard, larger than your printing paper**
- **Printing paper**
- **Pencil or pen**
- **Metal ruler**
- **Craft knife**
- **Pre-carved piece of lino**
- **Four small pieces of card**
- **Glue**

1 Take a piece of board that is larger than your printing paper. Place your printing paper in the centre of the board and draw around it. You can use pencil or pen for the outline.

2 Place your linocut inside your paper outline. Draw around the block.

3 Using a craft knife, cut out a hole in the board for the linocut to fit into.

4 Place the linocut inside the hole to make sure it fits.

5 Take four pieces of card and place them at the top of your paper outline – two each side. Glue them onto the board.

6 This will provide an edge for the sides of the paper, so the paper sits snugly inside every time you print. Ink up and burnish as usual.

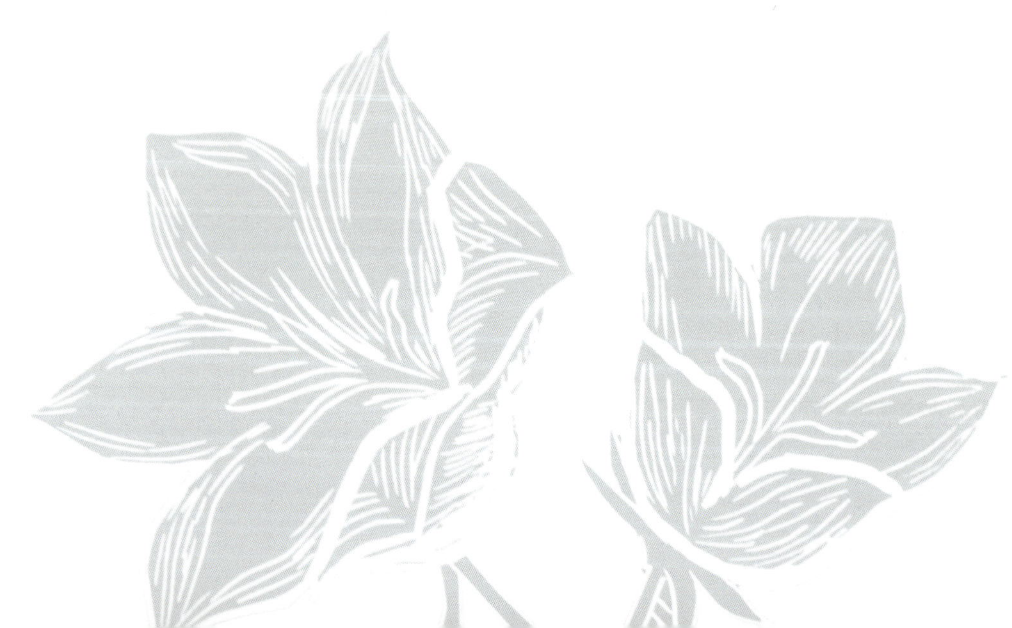

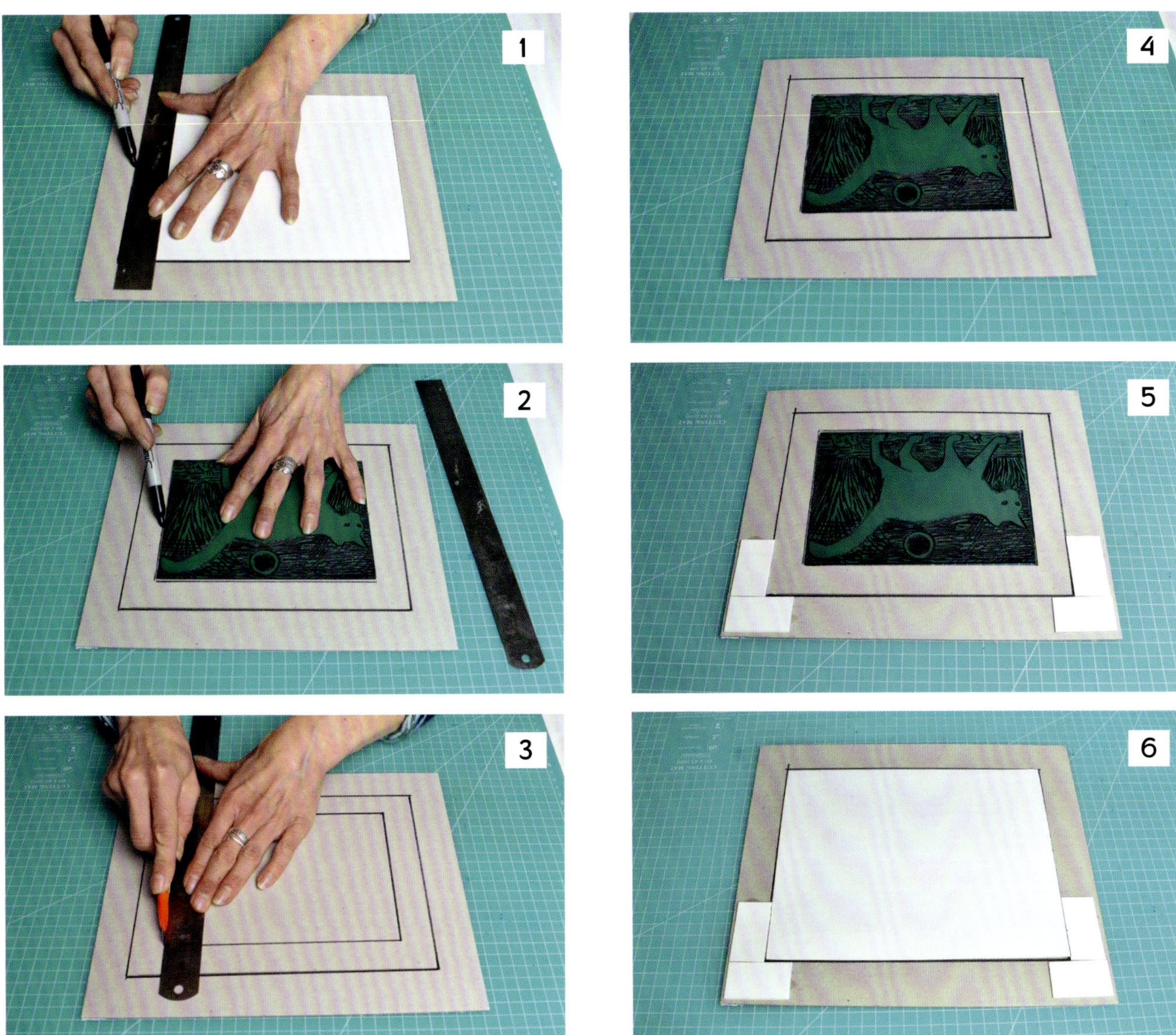

TERNES BURTON CLIPS

Here I am going to show you how to use Ternes Burton clips, which are specifically designed to help you achieve accurate registration. I sometimes use Ternes Burton clips when I'm working on multi-block and reduction prints (see Chapters 15 and 16).

Some printmakers glue the block to the board and ink up on the board. I don't do this as I like to ink up in a separate area, but feel free to experiment to find the way that suits you best.

You Will Need

- Pre-carved piece of lino
- Printing paper
- Cutting mat
- Metal ruler
- Craft knife
- Pencil or pen
- Piece of cardboard (larger than your printing paper)
- Piece of greyboard or mountboard, larger than your printing paper
- Ternes Burton clips
- Masking tape
- Parcel tape

1   Using your linocut block, prepare your printing paper to the size required. Cut all the paper for your edition at this point. Do leave extra paper at the at top, as I have done here, as the masking tape used to attach the tabs can tear the paper, so you will be able to trim any torn paper down.

2   Take a piece of cardboard that is larger than your printing paper and draw around your printing paper onto the board.

3   Place your linocut block evenly on the board, being mindful of the extra paper at the top. Draw around the block using pencil.

4   Cut out the hole so your lino can sit snugly inside the board.

5   Place your block in the hole and then tape the clips at the top of the paper outline using parcel tape.

6   Take your printing paper and place it on top of your lino block, in the paper outline. Place two of your stripping tabs onto the pins so that they overlap the paper. They should make a clicking sound as they go into place. Stick your tabs down with masking tape.

7   Prepare your paper for your whole edition in this way. To see the process in action see Chapter 15, where I demonstrate using this method.

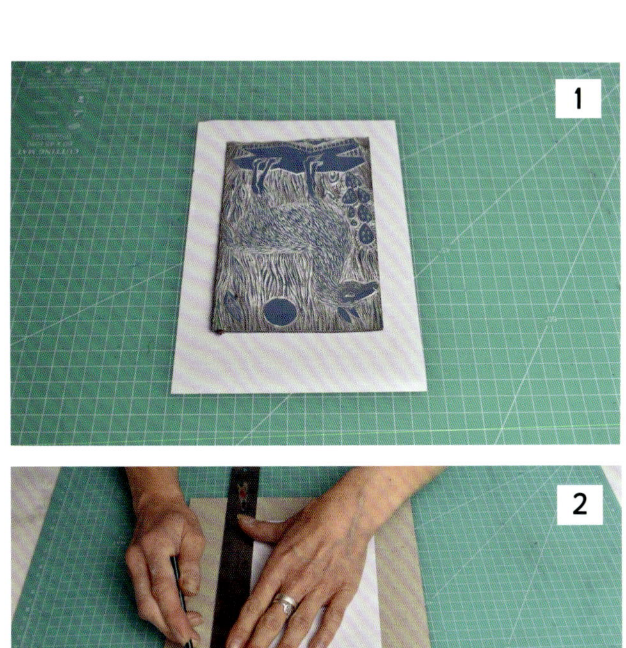

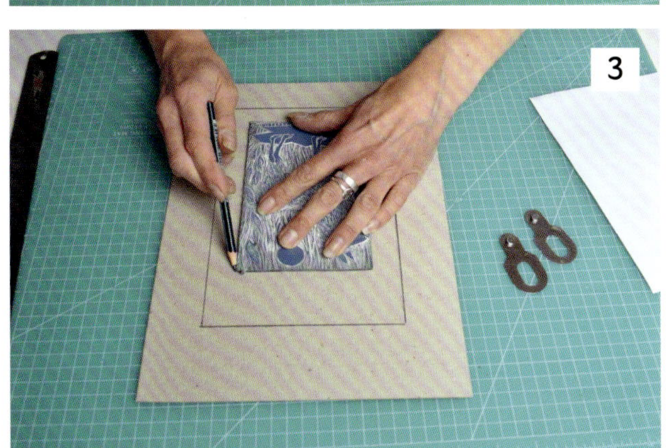

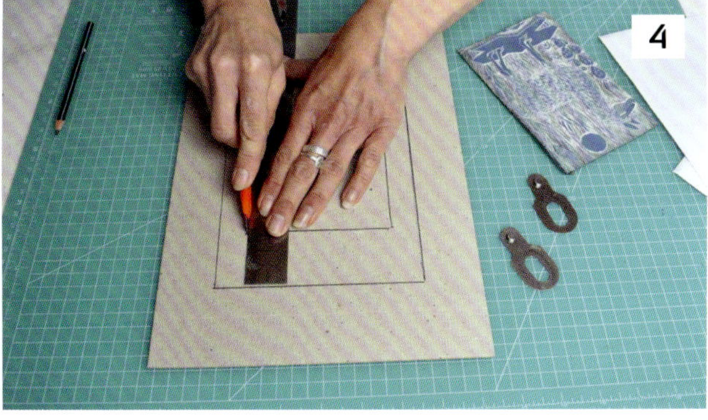

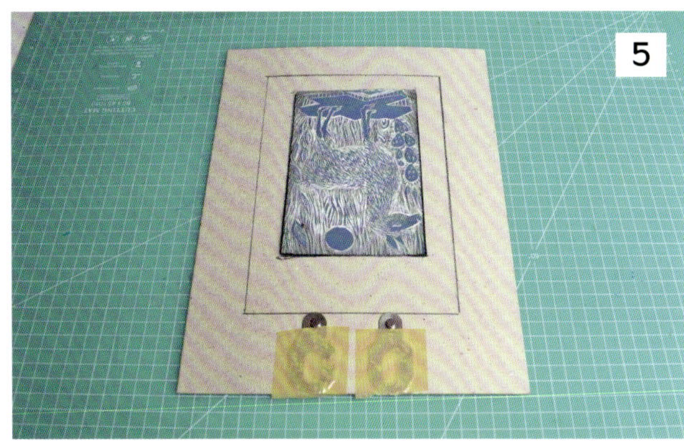

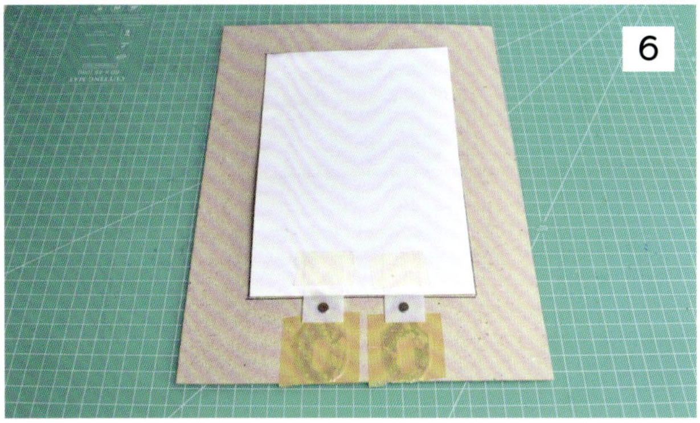

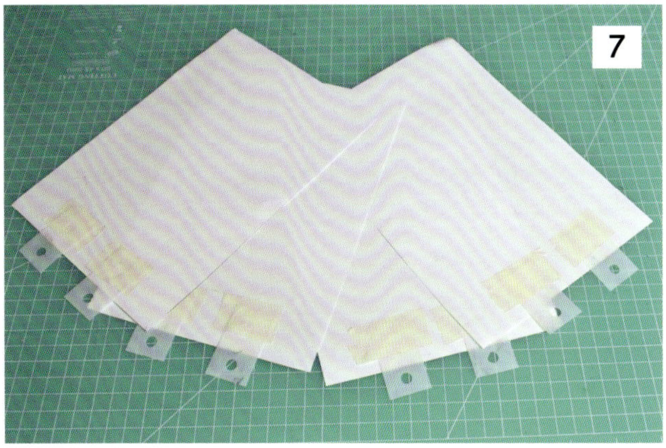

9 SIMPLE LINOCUTS

Now that you've had some time to become familiar with the tools and different ways of carving, you will be ready to start the first project – a simple black-and-white linocut. Start by choosing a simple object in your home that you have a sentimental attachment to – ideally, one that you feel confident to draw and turn into a print. There's no pressure here; try to enjoy the drawing and the whole process of carving, inking and printing.

I have chosen to work with an old rocking horse that I bought from an antique shop in North Norfolk. I've had it for years and I absolutely treasure it. It's a good choice as it has a simple shape and patterned surface.

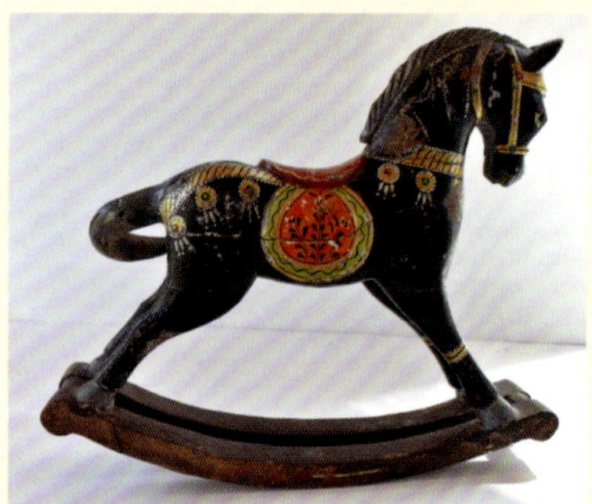

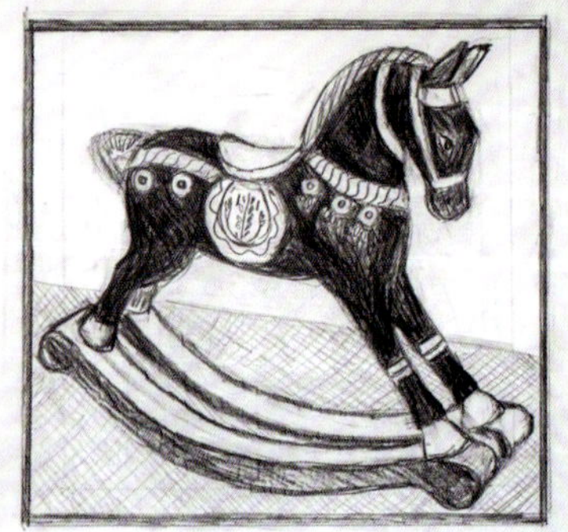

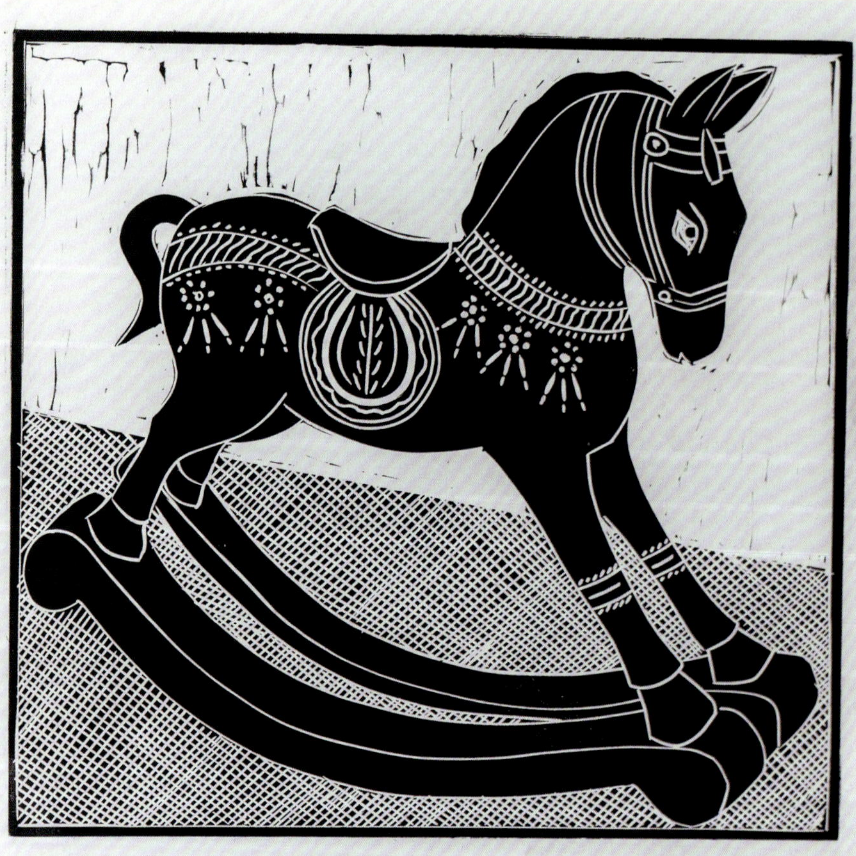

BLACK-AND-WHITE PRINT

You Will Need

- One piece of lino
- Paper for drawing
- Selection of pencils, e.g. HB/2B
- Rubber/eraser
- Metal ruler
- Carbon paper (optional)

- Permanent marker pen
- Cutting mat
- Cutting tools
- Talcum powder (optional)
- Stiff brush
- Photocopy paper
- Relief printing ink – black

- Roller
- Baren or wooden spoon
- Craft knife
- Inking slab
- Cleaning materials

1 Start by drawing around your piece of lino onto paper using a pencil. Your drawing is going to fit inside the box.

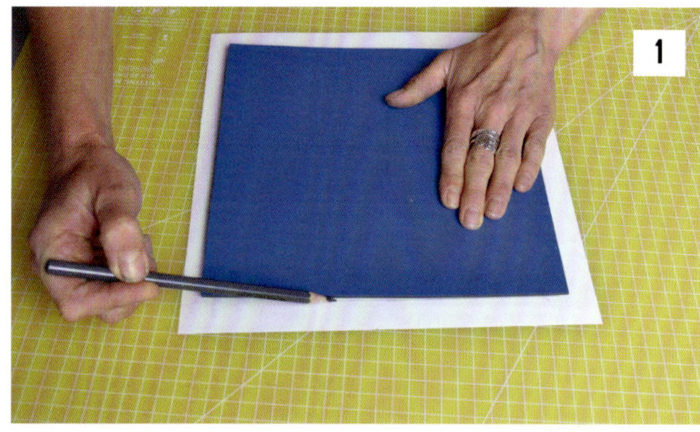

2 Draw your object. Enjoy using the different grades of pencil, considering the light and dark areas. Make as many different marks as you can, remembering that you are exploring your own style. Try not to judge whether it's 'right' or 'wrong' – the drawing will be your own interpretation of your object.

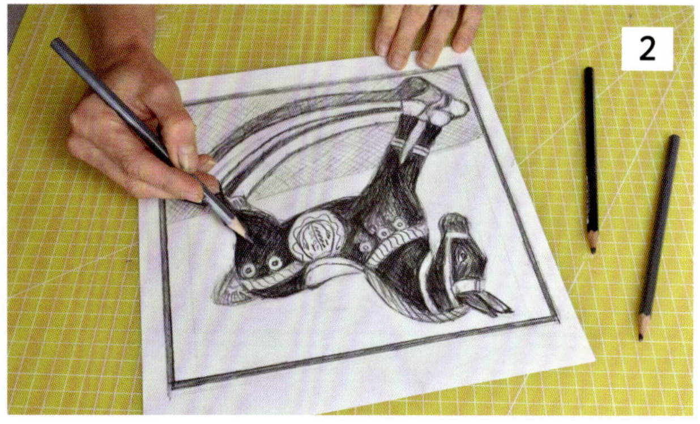

3 Once you are happy with your drawing, you can transfer it to your linocut block. You can either trace it using carbon paper or just draw directly onto the block. I am using my favourite method, whereby I trace the image on both sides so the image on the block is the same way around as my drawing (see Tracing Your Drawing the Traditional Way on page 31).

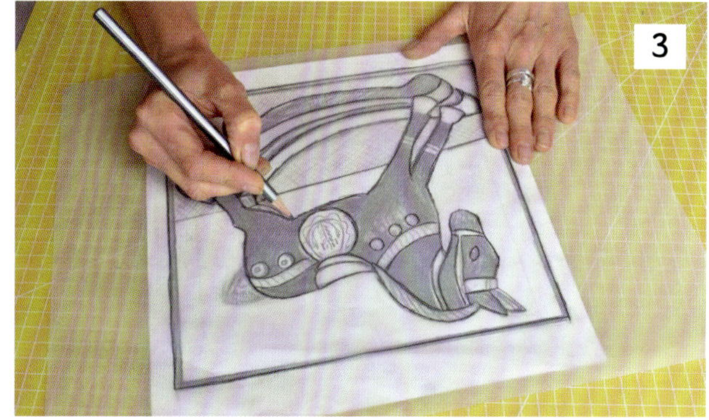

4   Once you have traced your image onto the block, go over the pencil lines with a marker pen. You will want to ink up and print your image as you progress (known as proofing) and you don't want the lines to wipe off.

5   Now you are ready to start carving. Begin by outlining your object with a fine V tool.

6   When I was taught wood engraving, we were shown how to use talcum powder to check the images we were carving. I find this useful with my linocuts too (although it doesn't work so well with traditional lino). Simply sprinkle a small amount of talcum powder onto the block and rub the block with the palm of your hand. The talc sinks into the carved lines, enabling you to see what you have cut.

7   If you have large areas to clear away, it's a good idea to start with this step. I'm using a large flat U tool to clear out the background that I want to be white. Think about the direction in which you are carving, especially when clearing large areas. I will leave some peaks and troughs in the lino, as I want to create some 'noise' or 'chatter' (literally the raised bits in between the cuts – I'll explain this in more detail in Chapter 10). Noise left by these carved areas can help to add movement or texture to an image.

8   When you have been carving for a while and are curious to see how it is going, I recommend taking a proof or rubbing. Brush your linocut to remove any bits of stray lino, clear your space and get ready to take a print. Photocopy paper is ideal for your proofs as it's cheap and lightweight. Follow the inking and printing steps in the mark-making warm-up (see page 39).

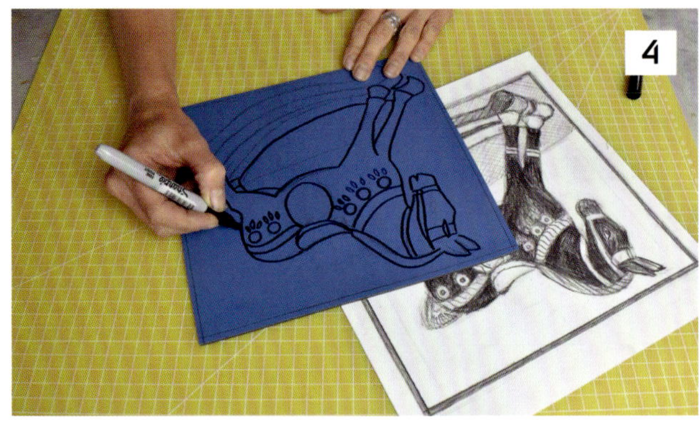

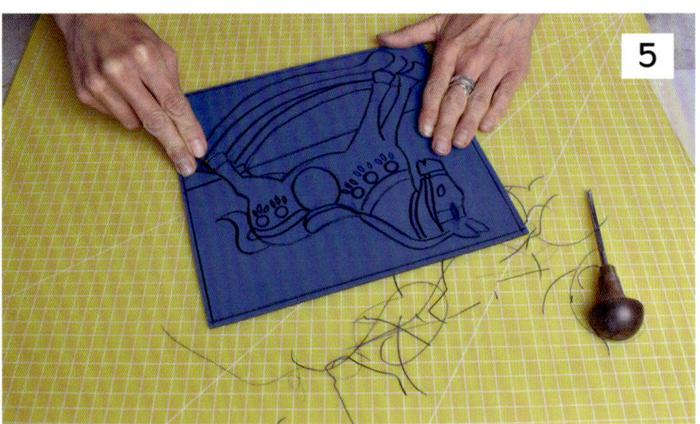

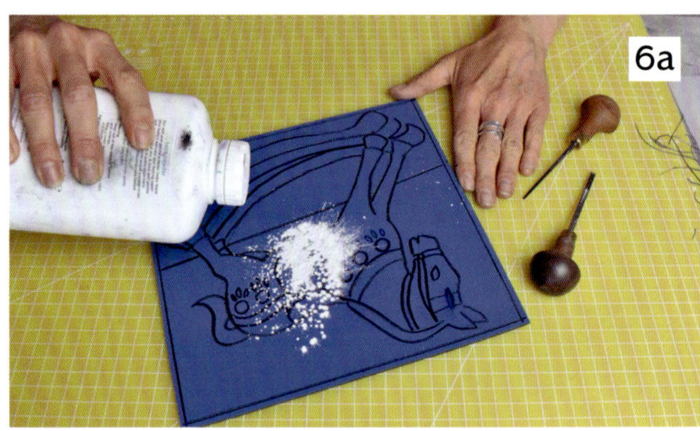

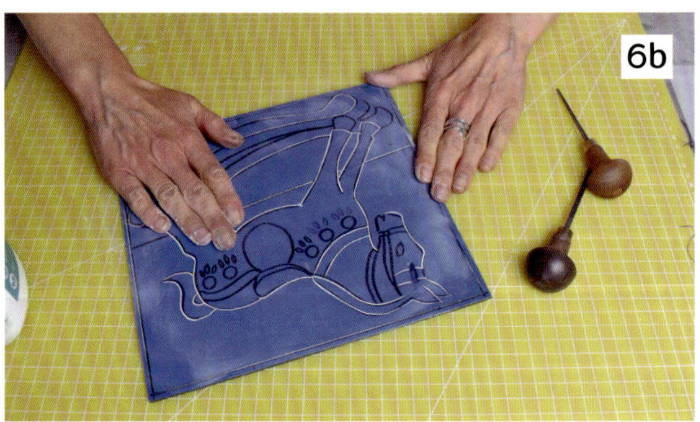

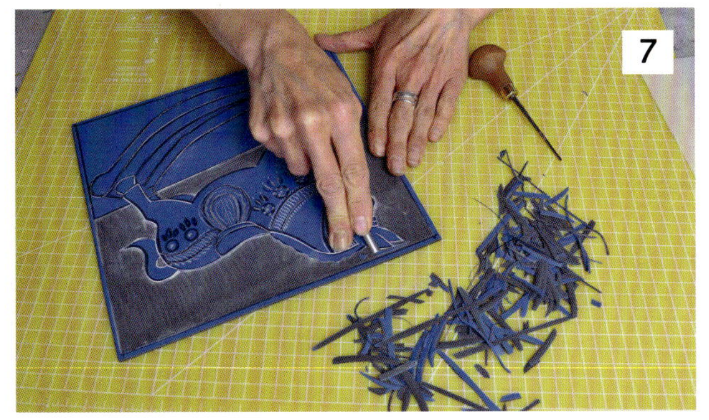

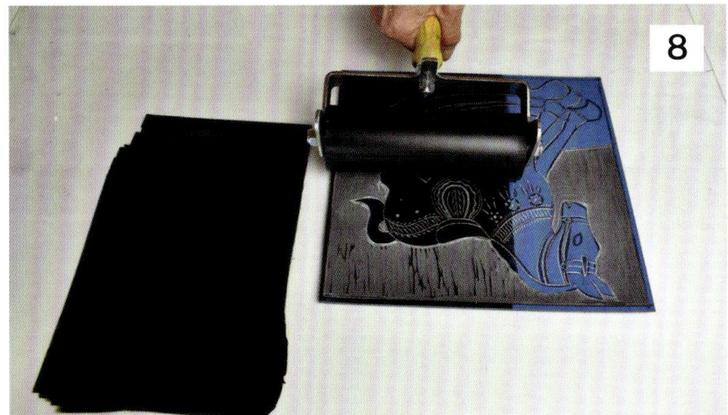

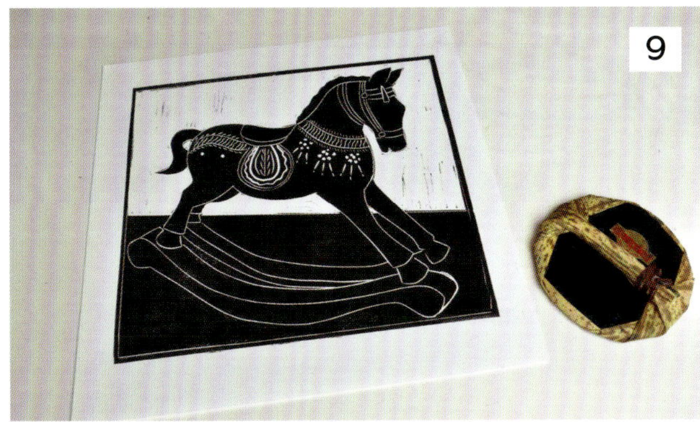

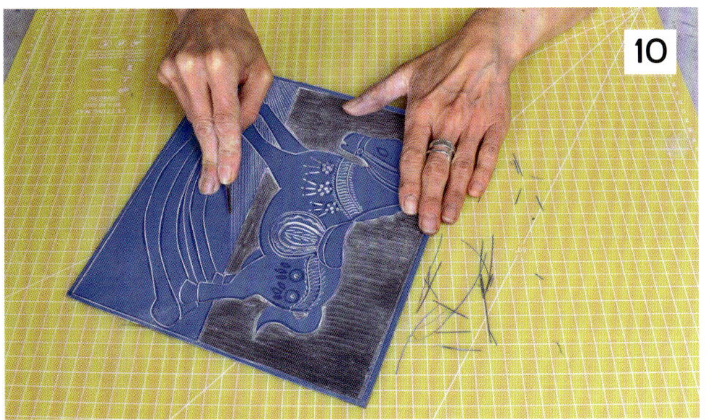

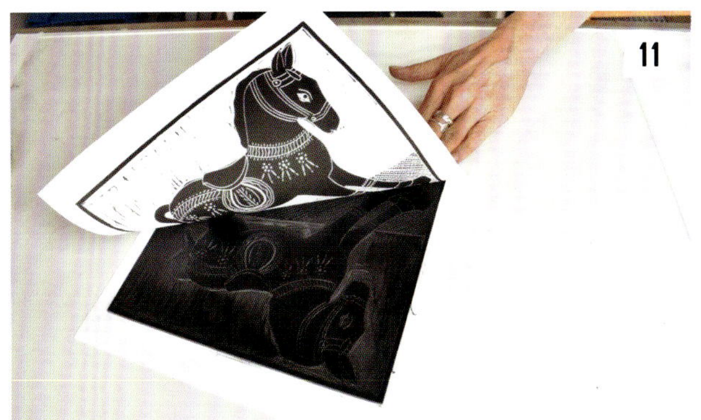

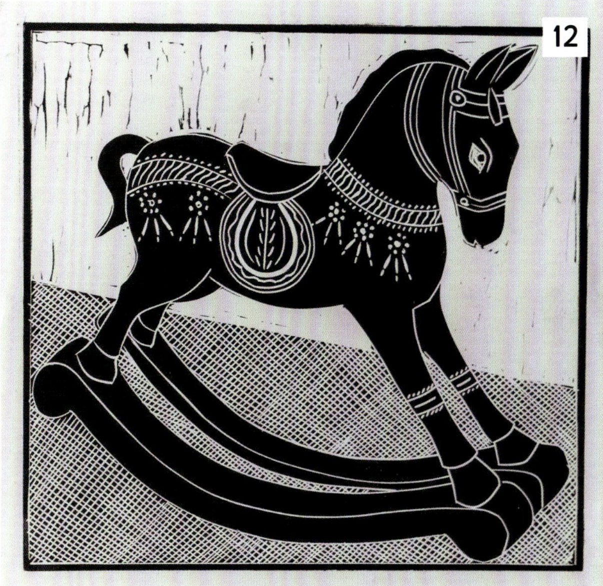

9 Once you have peeled back your first proof, take a few minutes to assess it and see how it's progressing. I have the overall structure here but still need to complete the floor and add more details to the rocking horse's head and body.

10 Clean your linocut and then continue to carve.

11 Keep carving and proofing until you are happy with your print. Remember it's not about perfection – remind yourself about the pleasure you've got from the whole process – this is such an important part of printmaking.

12 This is my finished print. There are still a few more tweaks I could make, but I'm happy with it. I feel it represents my beloved rocking horse well, and that's all that matters.

ADDING COLOUR TO YOUR LINOCUT

A really simple way to add colour to your linocut is to print the main image onto a background of solid colour. If you are using Japanese vinyl, you can simply clean your linocut block, turn it over and use the other side as your background. If you are using other forms of lino, you will need to cut a block the same size as your other block.

You Will Need

- Two lino blocks: one plain and one pre-carved (or one pre-carved Japanese vinyl block)
- Relief printing ink – black and one other colour
- Photocopy paper
- Baren or wooden spoon
- Roller
- Inking slab
- Cleaning materials

1 Ink up your plain block (or the back of your Japanese vinyl block). I chose a light blue for my background colour.

2 Place your paper carefully on top.

3 Burnish as usual.

4 Peel back the print. Don't worry if the colour is a little patchy; your main image will cover most of it.

5 If you are using Japanese vinyl, you will need to clean off the blue ink and then ink the other side with your main image in black. If you are using another block, put your coloured block to the side and ink up your pre-carved block in black.

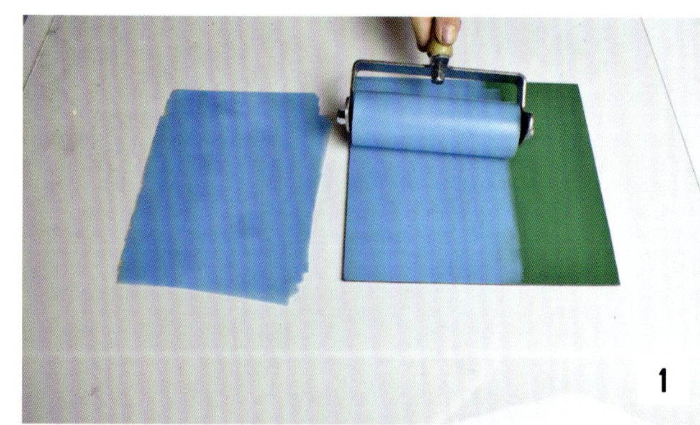

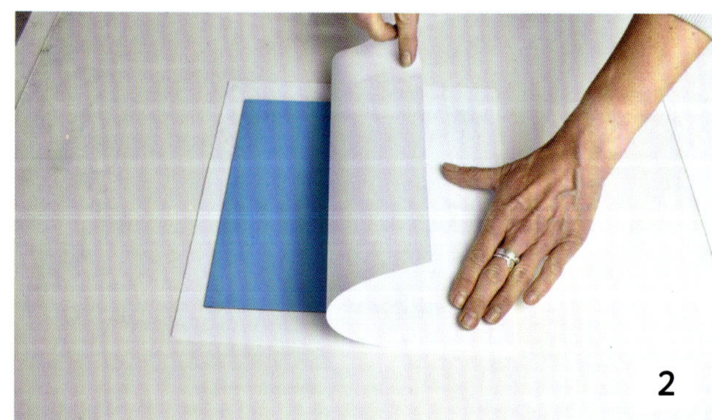

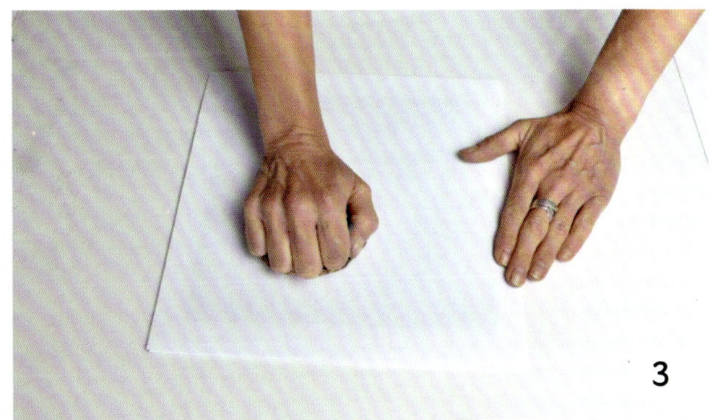

3

4

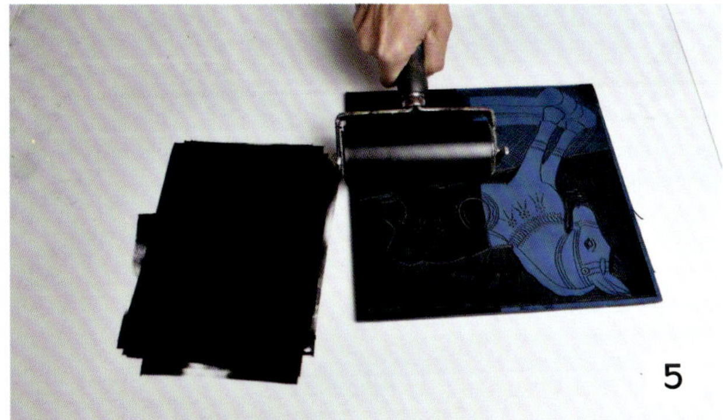

5

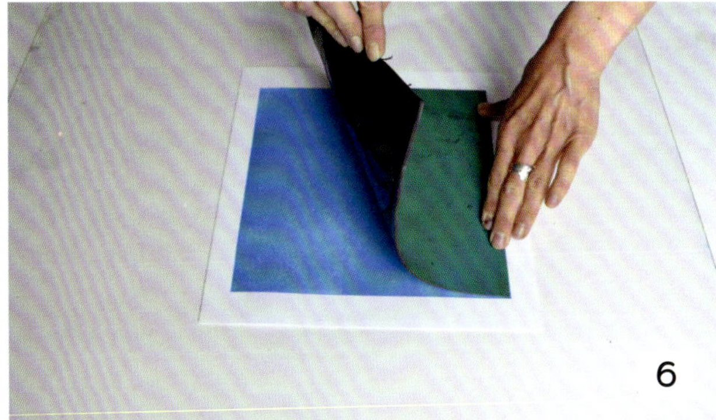

6

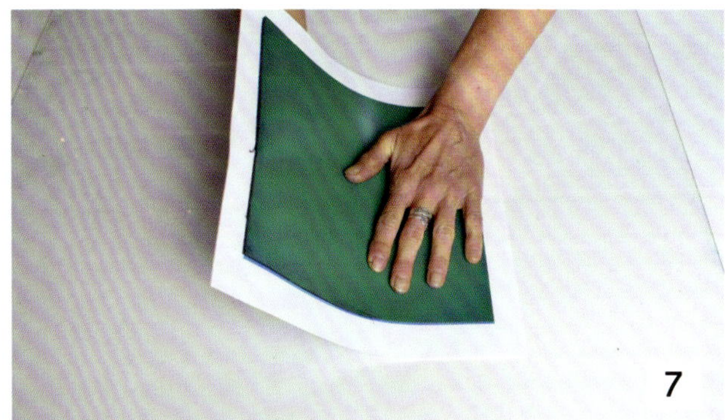

7

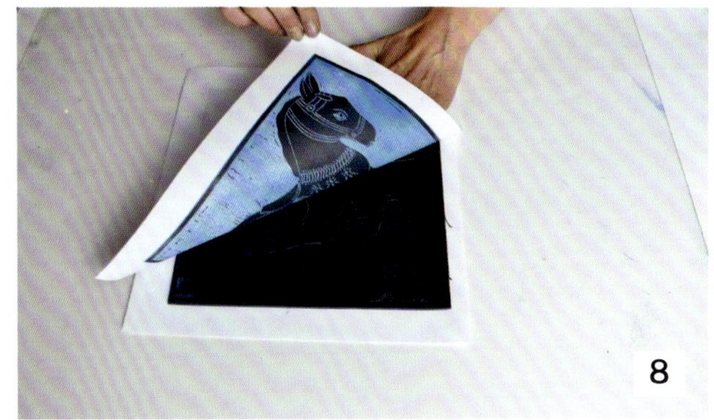

8

6   Place the inked-up block on top of the print.

7   Carefully put your hand on top, pull everything towards you, turn it over and burnish.

8   Carefully peel back your print.

9   Hopefully you will achieve a print you are happy with. If not, keep practising this technique. It can be tricky at first to flip the linocut block over but, once you get the hang of it, it's such an easy way to enhance your simple black block. Try experimenting with different colours too – the options are endless.

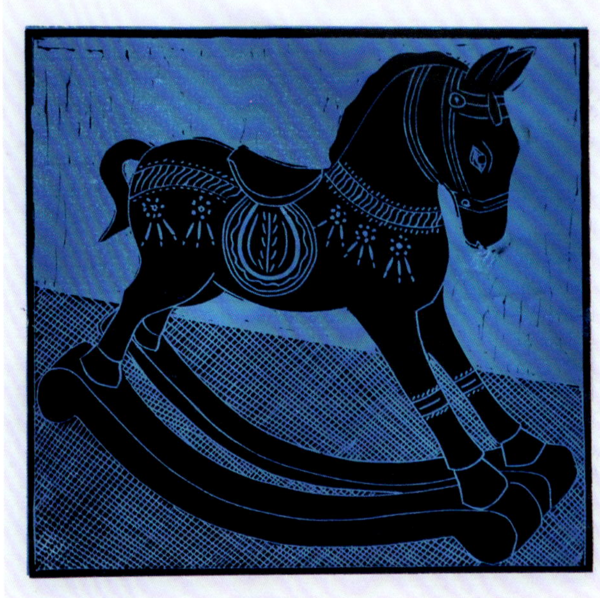

10 NOISE

Noise (or chatter) occurs when ink is picked up on the ridges of the carved-away areas of the block and is transferred onto the paper. Some printmakers see this as a problem and want to avoid it at all cost; others – myself included – use it to add character and interest to their work. I enjoy the handmade quality that noise gives to my prints.

There are times, though, when an image calls for a clean, crisp background.

RED KITES

As you can see from these three prints of a red kite, noise can be used in varying degrees to achieve different outcomes in your prints.

1   Here I have carved the red kite leaving lots of noise in the background. I used a wide U tool to get this effect; a large flat U tool, which is normally used for clearing, would have taken too much away. I deliberately carved in sympathy with the shape of the bird to ensure the noise worked with the image. I like the drama of the noise at this stage as I feel that it complements the energy of the red kite.

2   Still using my U tool, I took just a little more away. I always carve in stages like this, as once you have carved it away you can't put it back. There can be a fine line between enhancing the image to give it energy and adding too many distractions.

3   In this final image I have removed most of the noise with a large flat U tool to achieve a clean background.

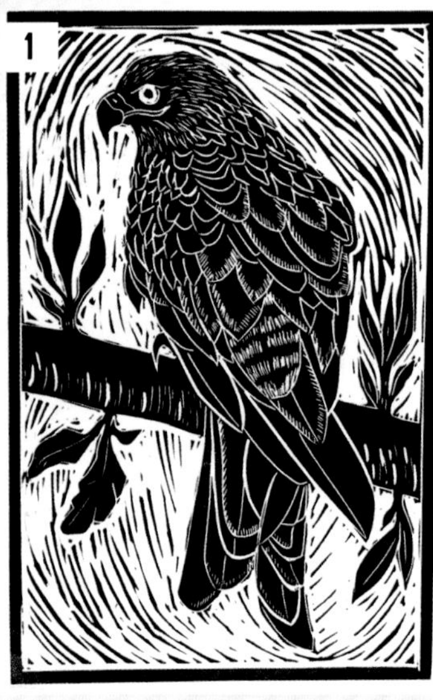
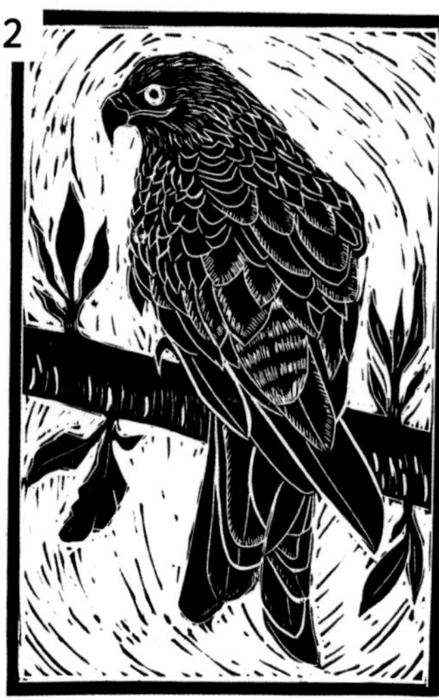
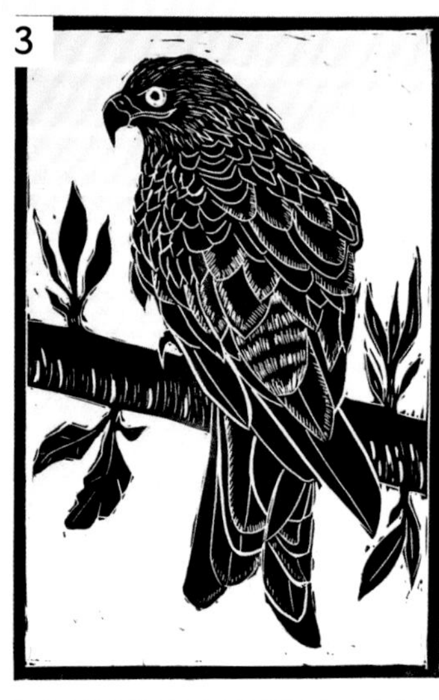

OTHER WAYS
TO REDUCE NOISE

Aside from carving away the noise, as I did in the red kite examples above, there are other options that I use throughout the book to reduce it which I will explore here. You can:

- Use a rag to wipe away any inked-up noise (see Four-block Print on page 108)
- Cut away around the image (see the single block card on page 154)
- Use a mask (see below and Chapters 14 and 15)

Using a Mask to Reduce Chatter

You can create a mask from newsprint, tracing paper or stencil films, such as a Mylar film. I use newsprint throughout the book as it's cheap and effective.

1   Take a print of your linocut. Once it has dried, place tracing paper on top and draw around the area you want to cover with the mask.

2   Turn the trace over and place it on top of a piece of newsprint. Go over the trace with a sharp pencil.

3   Using scissors or a craft knife, cut out your mask (or, in this case, masks).

4   Place your mask onto your linocut to make sure it covers the correct area. Ink up as usual and place your mask on top of the linocut after it has been inked (not before or it will get inky!). You can keep reusing your mask.

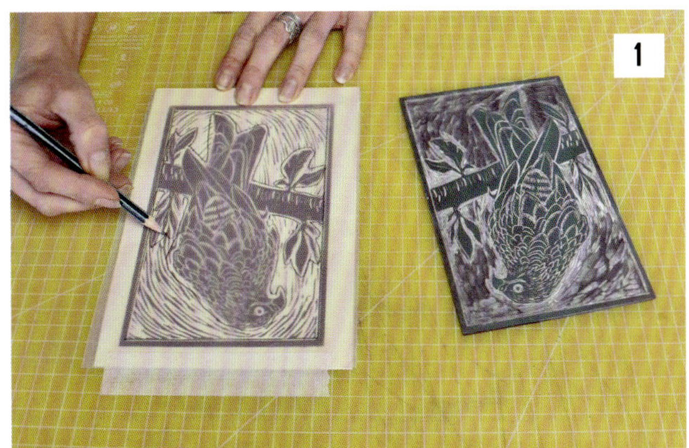

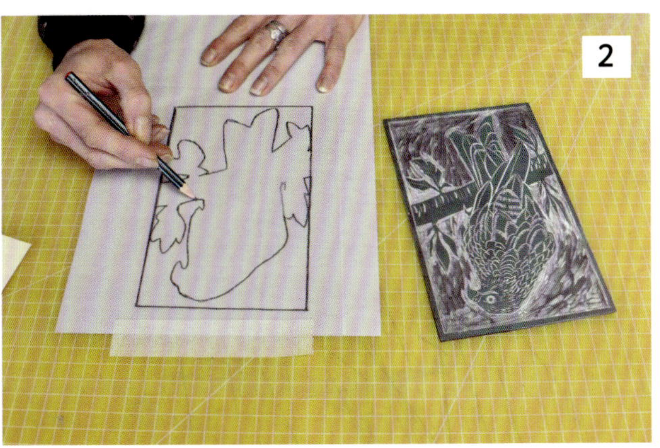

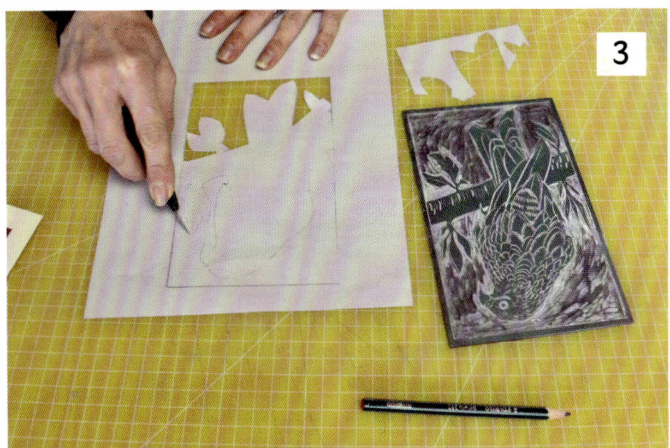

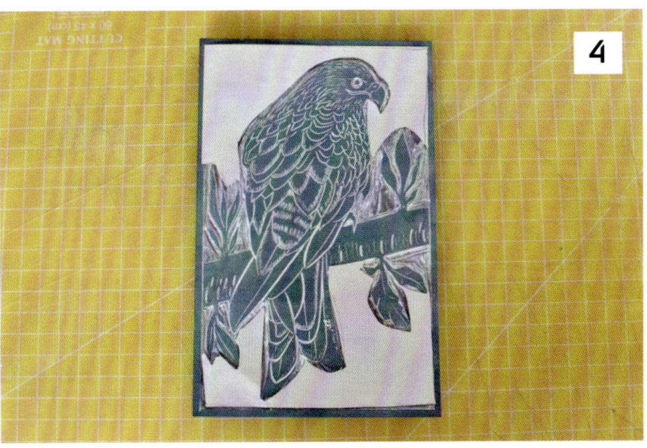

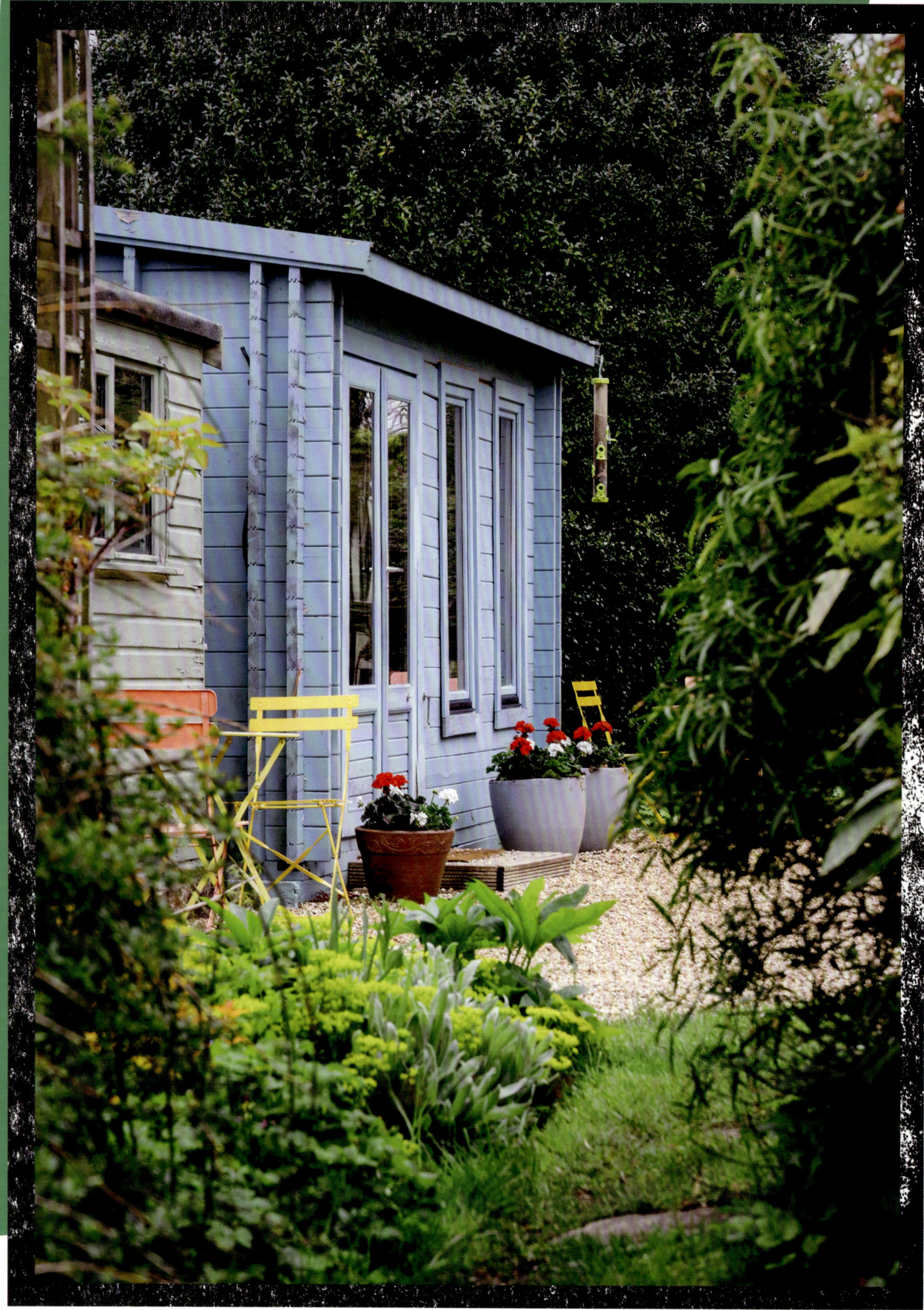

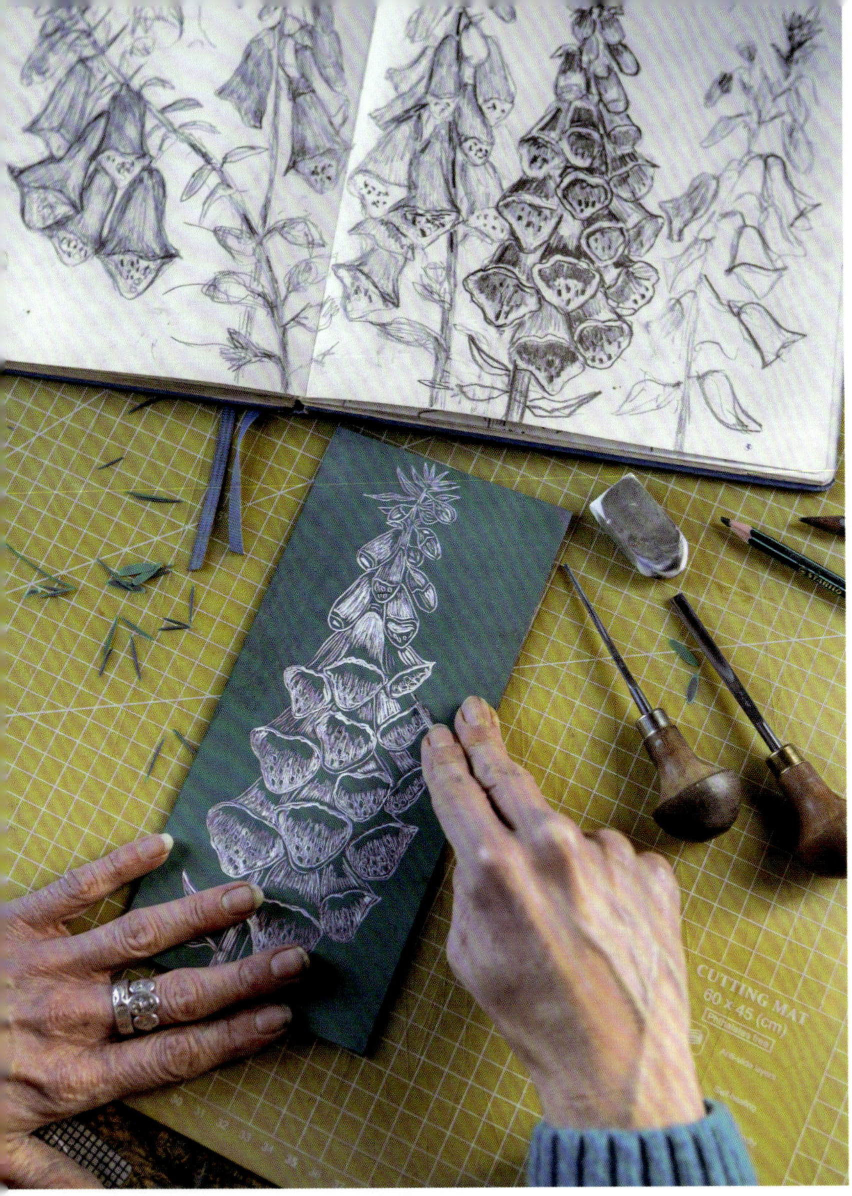

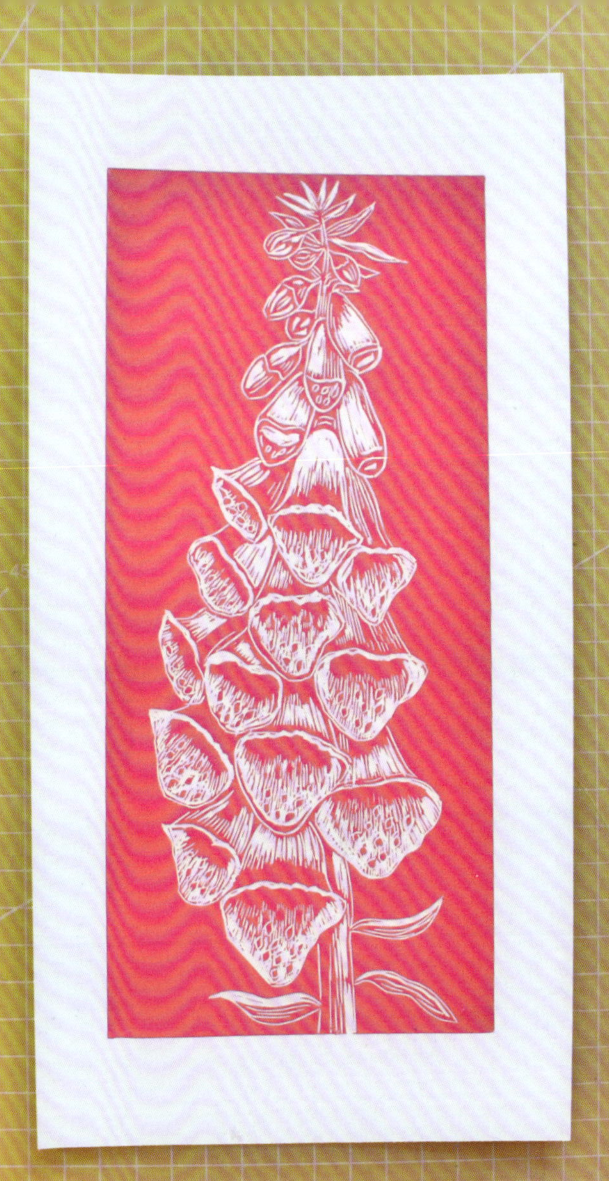

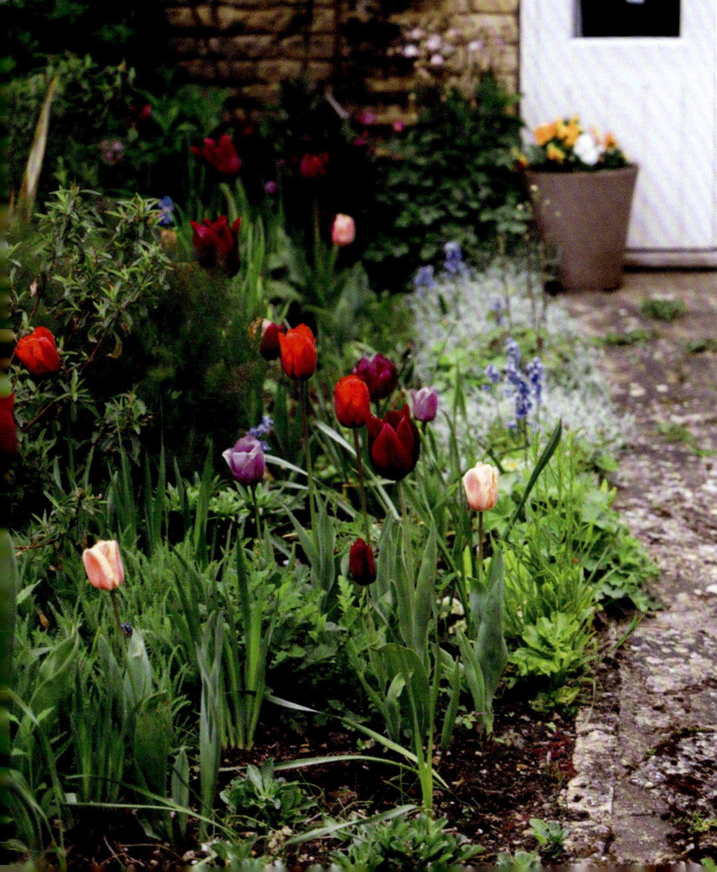

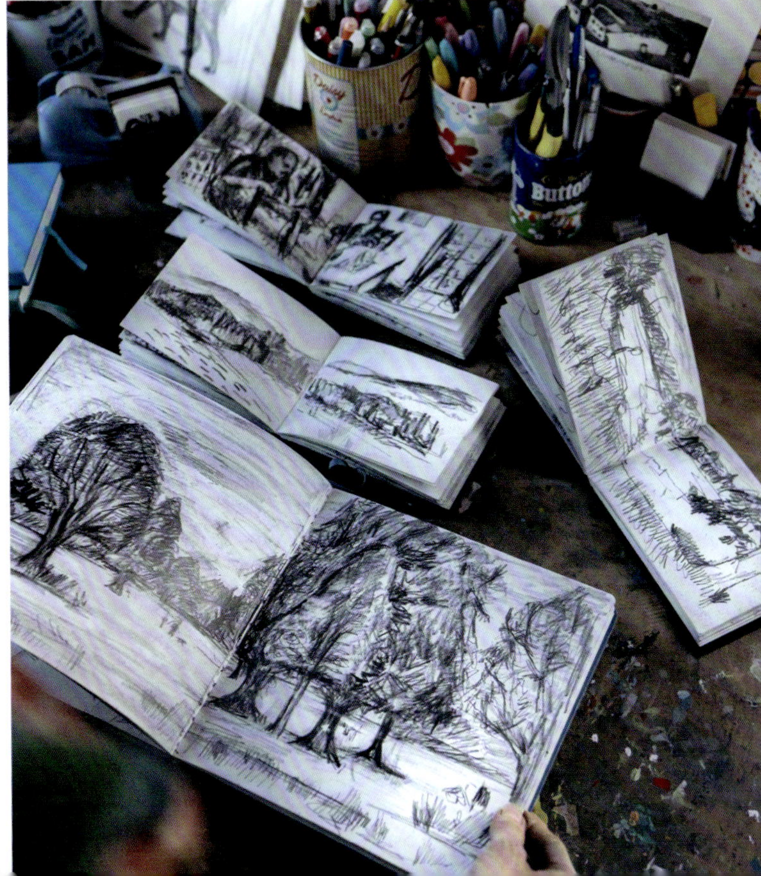

11 OUT IN THE GARDEN

For this project, venture outside to your garden, or any green space, with your sketchbook and pencils. Create a drawing of a flower or plant of your choice that will then be used to make a linocut with a solid colour background. Think about light and dark areas and make sure there is a variety of tones and lines. Enjoy your time outside and reflect on making the print while you are drawing, thinking about the previous projects and what you have learnt about carving different lines.

A NATURE STUDY

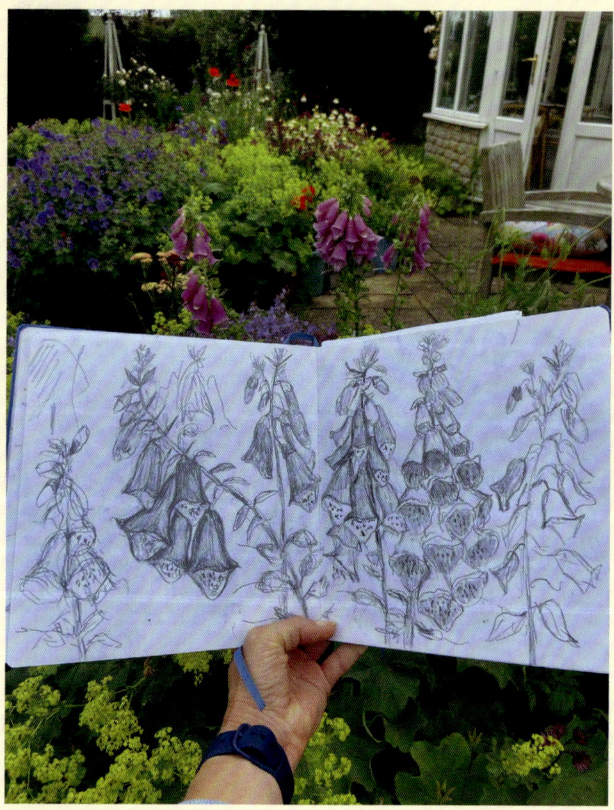

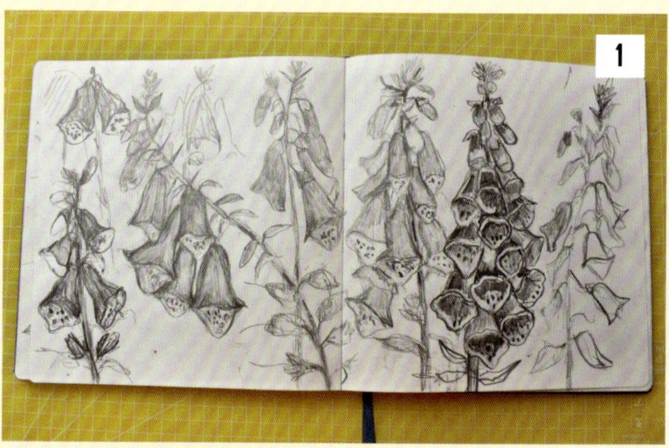

Begin this project by spending some time outside drawing a plant or flower of your choice. Try and include as much detail as you can in your sketch, as you will need all this information for your print.

You Will Need

- Selection of pencils, e.g. HB/2B
- Rubber/eraser
- Drawing paper or sketchbook
- Tracing paper
- One piece of lino
- Craft knife
- Metal ruler
- Biro or permanent marker pen (optional)
- Cutting tools
- Cutting mat
- Stiff brush
- Relief printing ink
- Inking slab
- Roller
- Photocopy paper for proofing (all the same size)
- Baren or wooden spoon
- Paper for making a small edition
- Cleaning materials

1   Spend at least one hour drawing in your green space of choice, gathering as much information in your sketch as you can. Remember to build up the light and dark areas in your drawing as these will be invaluable in your carving. This is my initial drawing, although I later chose to focus on just one of the foxgloves.

2   Back inside, take a good look at your sketch. I chose to work on the foxglove on the right-hand side, making sure I had a good contrast between the light and dark tones. Trace your drawing using a sharp pencil, ensuring you get as much detail as you can.

3   Next cut a piece of lino that is of a sympathetic size to your drawing. Make sure you cut carefully using a sharp craft knife and metal ruler (see page 38). Transfer your image to the linocut using your preferred method (see page 29).

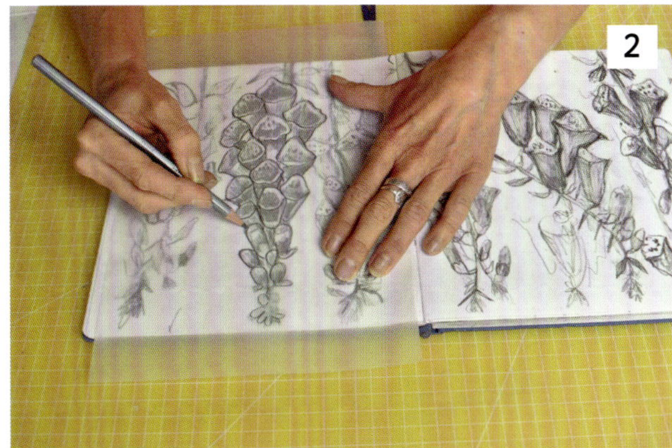

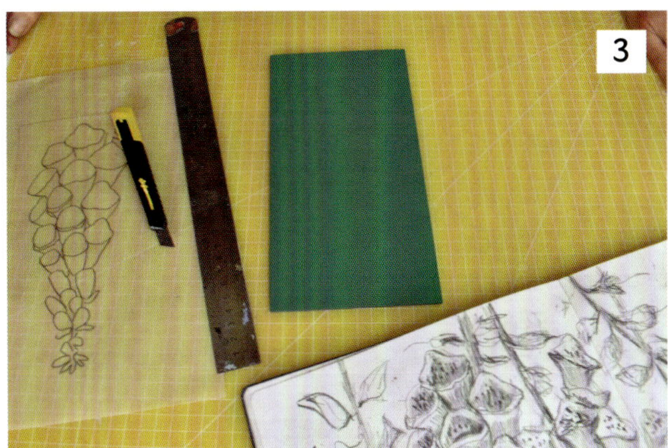

4   Once you have a basic outline, you can work on adding more detail. If you are using Japanese vinyl, biro works nicely, although it does fade after lots of proofing. You can always go around with a permanent marker to be on the safe side.

5   Here you can see my lino, ready to carve. I've shaded the darker tonal areas, which helps me to see what I need to carve away (the areas that are left green – I won't be carving away the background). This is just a rough guide; you don't have to stick faithfully to your drawing – once you start proofing your lino it's inevitable (and encouraged) that you will change your design.

6   Now you can start carving. Carve around the outline using a fine V tool.

7   Continue carving until you are ready to take your first proof. You can take your proof at any stage, but I always recommend taking a proof at least one hour after starting to carve to see how you are progressing. You can prevent mistakes by taking lots of proofs. (If you prefer, you can always take a rubbing instead.)

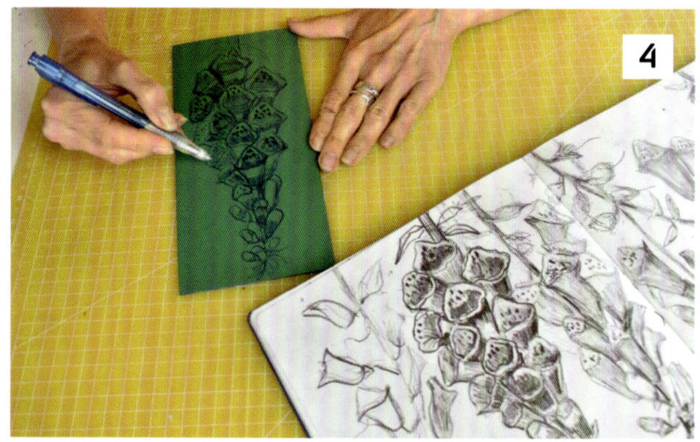

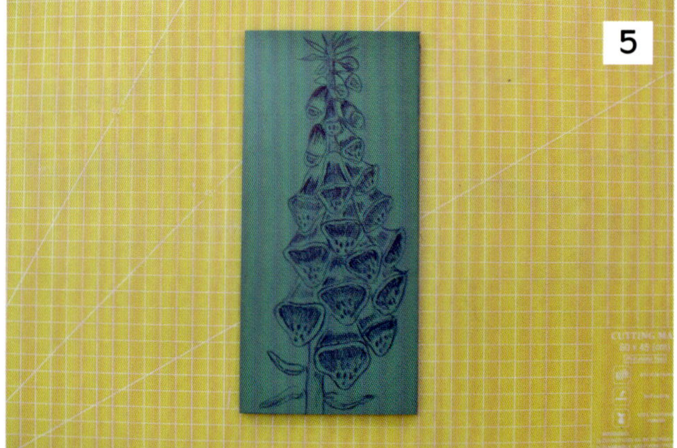

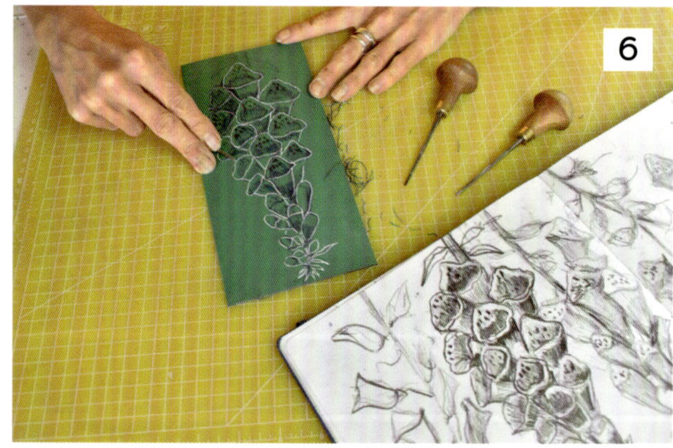

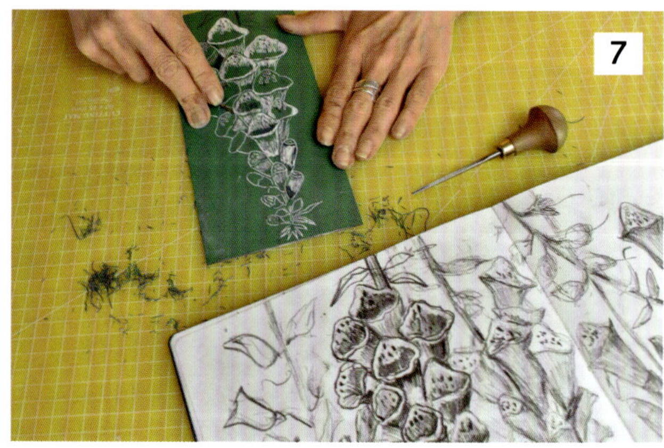

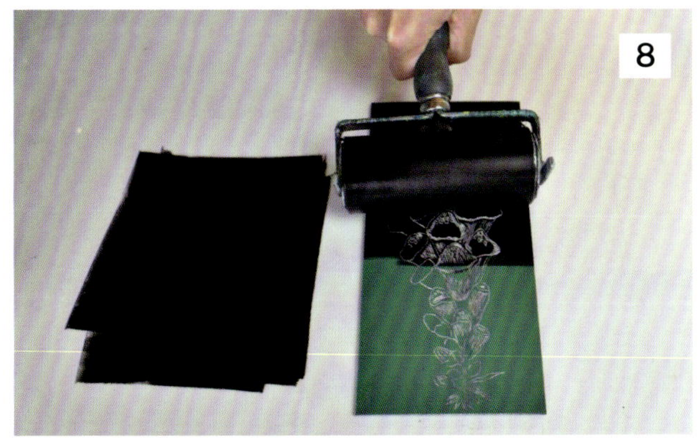

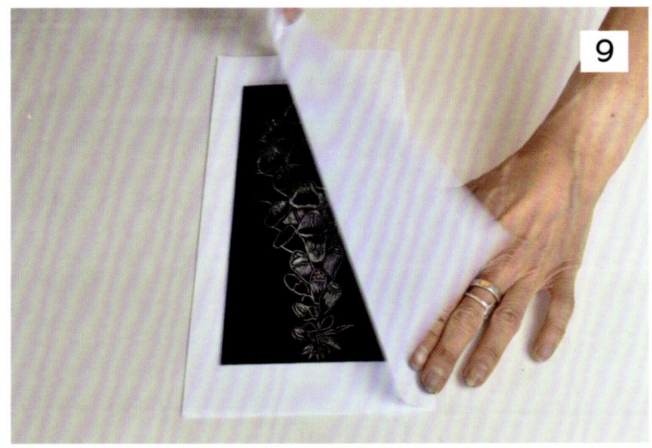

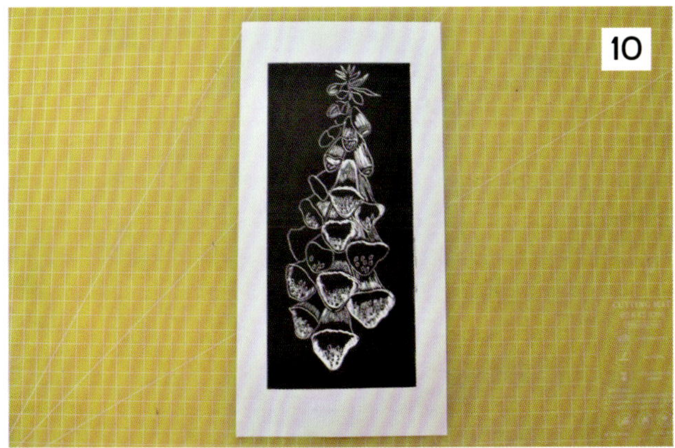

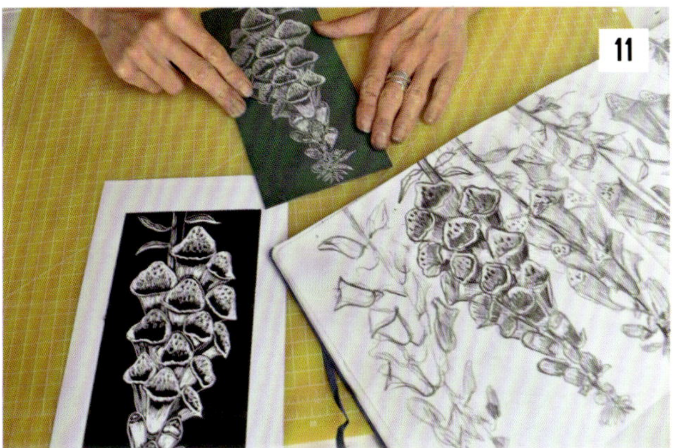

8   Ink up your block, as shown in the mark-making warm-up (see page 39). I always use black when proofing, as I feel it gives the best indication of how your print is shaping up.

9   Place your paper on top. Here I'm using a bottom sheet of paper, the same size as my printing paper, as I did in the mark-making warm-up (see page 39). Burnish as usual.

10 Examine your progress by carefully studying your first proof. Ask yourself: What is working and what isn't? What more needs to be done? Do you need to vary your tools more to add more line interest?

11 Continue carving, using your proof to help you. At this point, it's helpful to let the print guide you, alongside the drawing.

12 Keep carving and proofing until you are happy with the result. Decide on a colour and you're ready to print.

13 Mix up a colour that you feel would best complement your garden image. Here I've mixed up a pink that I feel would work well for my foxglove.

14 Once you are happy with your carving and colour choice, you can make a small edition (see Chapter 12). Hang up your edition to dry.

15 The final print.

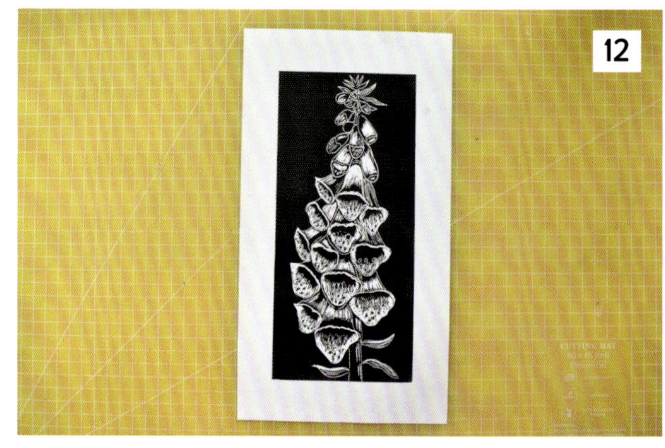

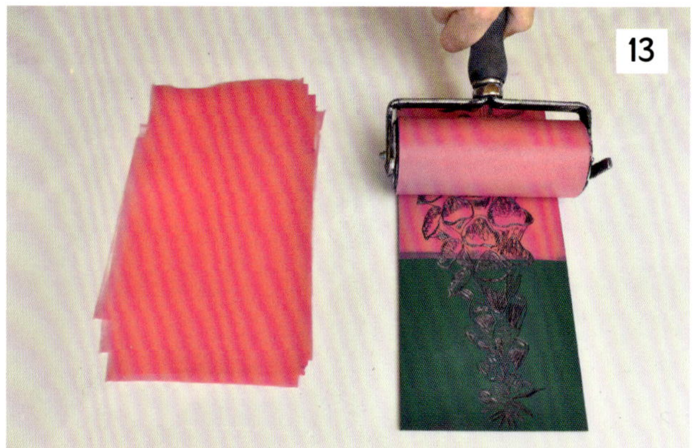

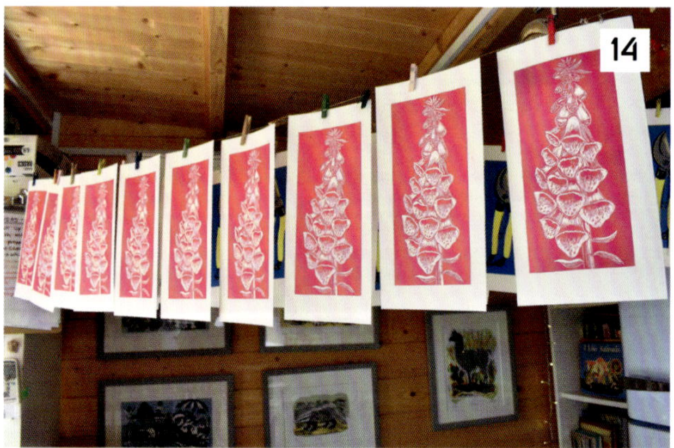

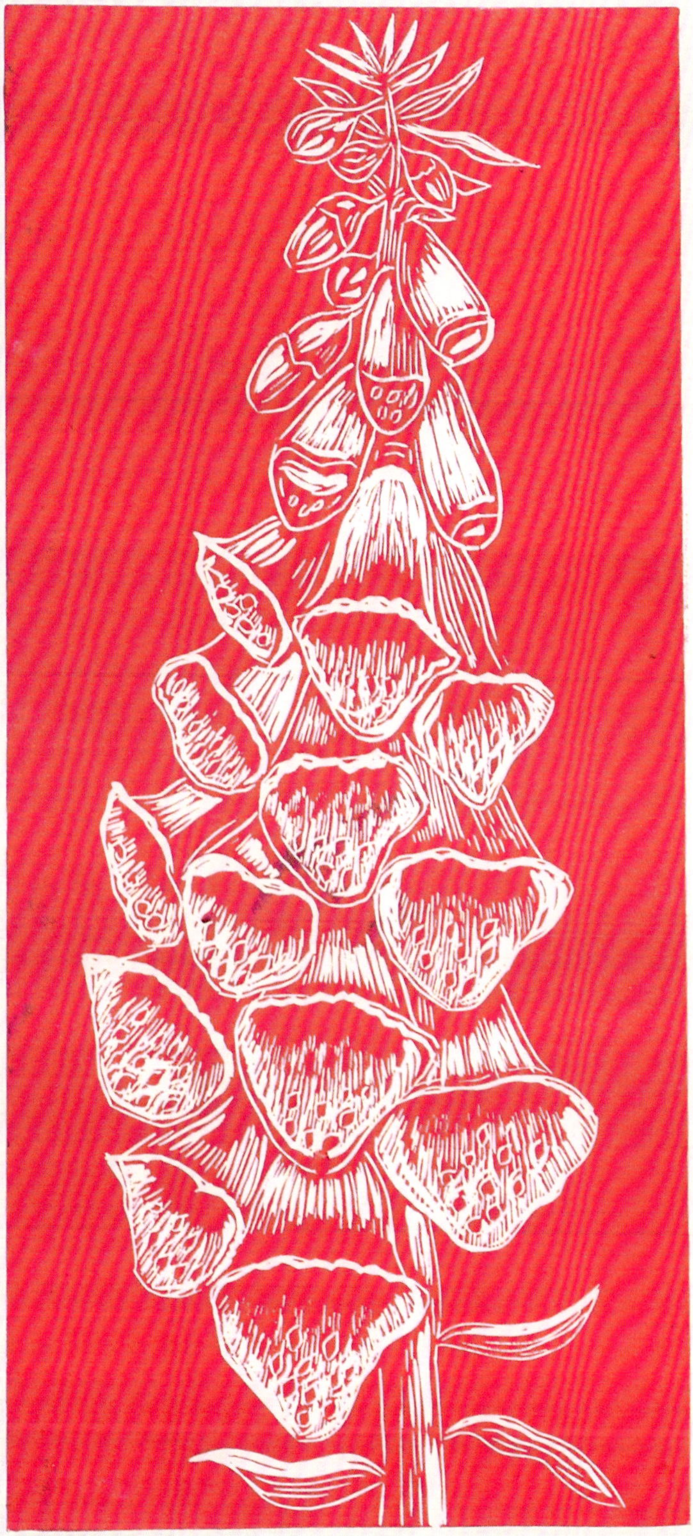

TIPS ON DRAWING OUTSIDE OR IN PUBLIC

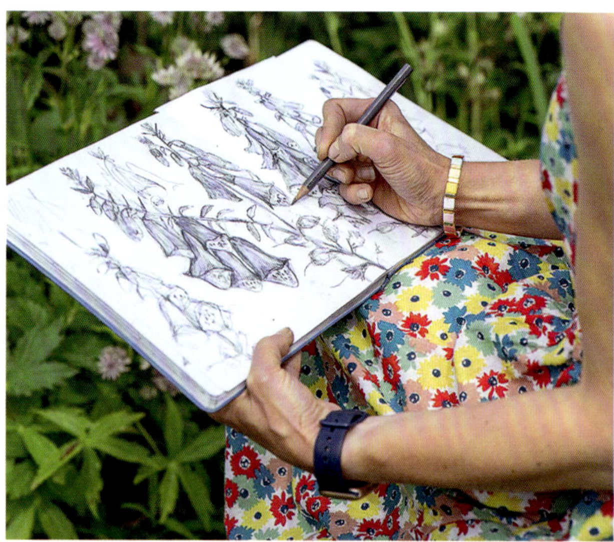

I won't beat around the bush, drawing in public can be awkward and feel uncomfortable – at least at first. When I first started, I had to build up my confidence gradually, using many of the tips below. Now I don't even think about it – I sit myself down, get out my stuff and start drawing – but it has taken me years to get to this stage. So, go slowly, take your time and feel proud of yourself for stepping out of your comfort zone to do something that is ultimately so rewarding. I know you will want to keep on going back for more!

- Wear headphones, sunglasses or a hat
- Sit in the car
- Get someone else to sit with you
- Sit against a wall or tuck yourself away
- Start in a less-crowded setting
- Have all your materials to hand
- Use a small hardbound book or journal – this can look like a diary and most people will respect your privacy
- Draw in small intervals to build up your stamina gradually
- Work small! It's unobtrusive and less likely to draw attention to what you're doing.

These are all helpful tips, but what if someone does come up to you or watches what you are doing or wants to chat about your drawing? The thing to remember here is that people are naturally curious; art is a magnet and they can't help but be drawn to it.

People who approach you generally fall into two categories: those who want to sketch and those who already sketch. I've never had anyone criticise my work, and the majority of people who approach me don't hang around long enough for an extended conversation. They normally take a quick look and say 'nice drawing' or something similar. If they do want to chat, I am always polite but keep my answers short and keep drawing – this is normally enough to discourage more interaction.

Sometimes, though, having a little chat can be really rewarding. While I was in Japan, I was drawing down a little backstreet and a lady kept peering out of her window, watching what I was doing. After an hour or so, she popped out to have a look at my work and we communicated in the best way we could – smiling, nodding and pointing. She then went back into her house and a few minutes later she emerged with a pot of tea for me and a slice of delicious castella cake (a popular Japanese honey sponge cake).

A final note – which relates not just to drawing but to life in general – it's always good to remind yourself that people are busy doing their own thing and you are only a momentary distraction. People aren't thinking about us as much as we believe they are; they are too busy thinking about themselves. Once I had got my head around this, I felt a tremendous sense of liberation – in all aspects of my life!

12 EDITIONING PRINTS

Once you are happy with your print, it's time to make an edition. After all, that's the point of printmaking – to make multiples. It's also one of my favourite parts of the whole process; I put on a good audiobook and enjoy the repetitive act of printing the same thing, time after time. It wasn't always like this, though – when I first began printmaking, I was always impatient to get onto the next piece – but after a while I began to see it as a valuable opportunity to wrap everything up and enjoy a real sense of completion.

An edition of original prints is a set of identical prints taken from the same matrix (printing surface). This is not the same as a reproduction, which is usually digitally printed. Editioning helps printmakers to distinguish their work from reproduction prints. Limited editions mean that no more of the same prints will be made, and they must be identical. If there is a discrepancy in quality or ink colour, or even a change of paper, these prints should not be considered part of the edition. However, as linocut is a handmade process, I always feel there should be a little bit of wiggle room as there will always be some minor variations. When you sign and number your prints, you are guaranteeing that each print is made exactly like the rest in terms of quality and only that number of the print is in existence.

EDITION SIZE

A question I get asked frequently is how to decide how many prints should be in an edition. In all honesty, as the artist, this is entirely up to you. However, there are a number of factors to consider:

- How long did it take you to create it (i.e. how complex is it and how long does it take you to ink up and print)?
- How much does the paper and ink cost?
- How many prints do you think you can sell?
- How much time do you have?

In general, the smaller the edition, the higher the price and the more valuable the print is.

Another important consideration is how strong the printing surface itself is and if it can survive a large edition size. A collagraph or dry point plate, for example, degrades with use and therefore a small edition is always wise. This is not so relevant for linocuts, though.

You can decide to print the whole edition in one run, or print a few and then continue to print the edition as your prints sell. Some methods require you to print the whole edition at once. For example, with the reduction method (see Chapter 14), changes are made to the original block as more layers are carved and printed, making it impossible to go back to print more. I tend to print my editions all in one go as I find the newer the print, the more excited and invested I am in it, so it makes the whole process more enjoyable. However, it's a personal thing and it's important to do what suits you.

Whichever way you print your edition, it's important to keep track of your edition size; of how many you have printed and signed and who has bought them. You could keep a logbook with all the details or use an online database – I do this as I find it really user-friendly and more reliable than my own notekeeping!

PRICING

Another important topic is how to price your work. This, again, is very much up to you. In my experience, beginners always tend to undervalue their work, forgetting how long it has taken them to create their prints. There always seems to be a demon on one shoulder saying it's not good enough, or asking: who would buy it anyway? It's important to try and ignore this voice; take pride in what you have accomplished and price it accordingly. When students ask me for advice on pricing their work, I always ask them what they think and then add on £10–20 extra. Try this – it just might work.

However, instead of just relying on what you think is the right price, it's always helpful to calculate how much money each print costs you to create. To work this out, you must include the time spent making the work and multiply this by your hourly rate, plus all of your materials (adding a small amount for electricity used, etc.), then divide it by the amount of number of prints in the edition. When you have that figure, you can roughly double the cost price to find the right price to sell your work.

So, a simple formula would be:
Hourly rate x number of hours working on the edition
+ cost of materials
+ other costs / number of prints
= cost price of print
Selling price = cost price of print x 2

HOW TO EDITION

Once you are ready to make your edition, it's worth taking the time to get yourself organised, to make the whole process as smooth and enjoyable as possible. These are the steps I follow when editioning my prints:

1   Making sure I have clean hands, I pre-cut my paper, making sure I have enough for the whole edition plus a few extra for misprints.

2   I prepare my registration system to ensure my block is placed in the right position every time.

3   I then give my inking surfaces and rollers a good clean, just to make sure there are no rogue bits of ink or lino that have escaped my notice.

4   It's then time to mix up my inks, ensuring I mix enough for the whole session (you don't want to be trying to get the right colour again halfway through your edition).

5   I then check to make sure I have plenty of rags to keep me going and enough space to hang all my prints to dry.

6   Finally, I line up a good podcast or audiobook, and I'm ready to go.

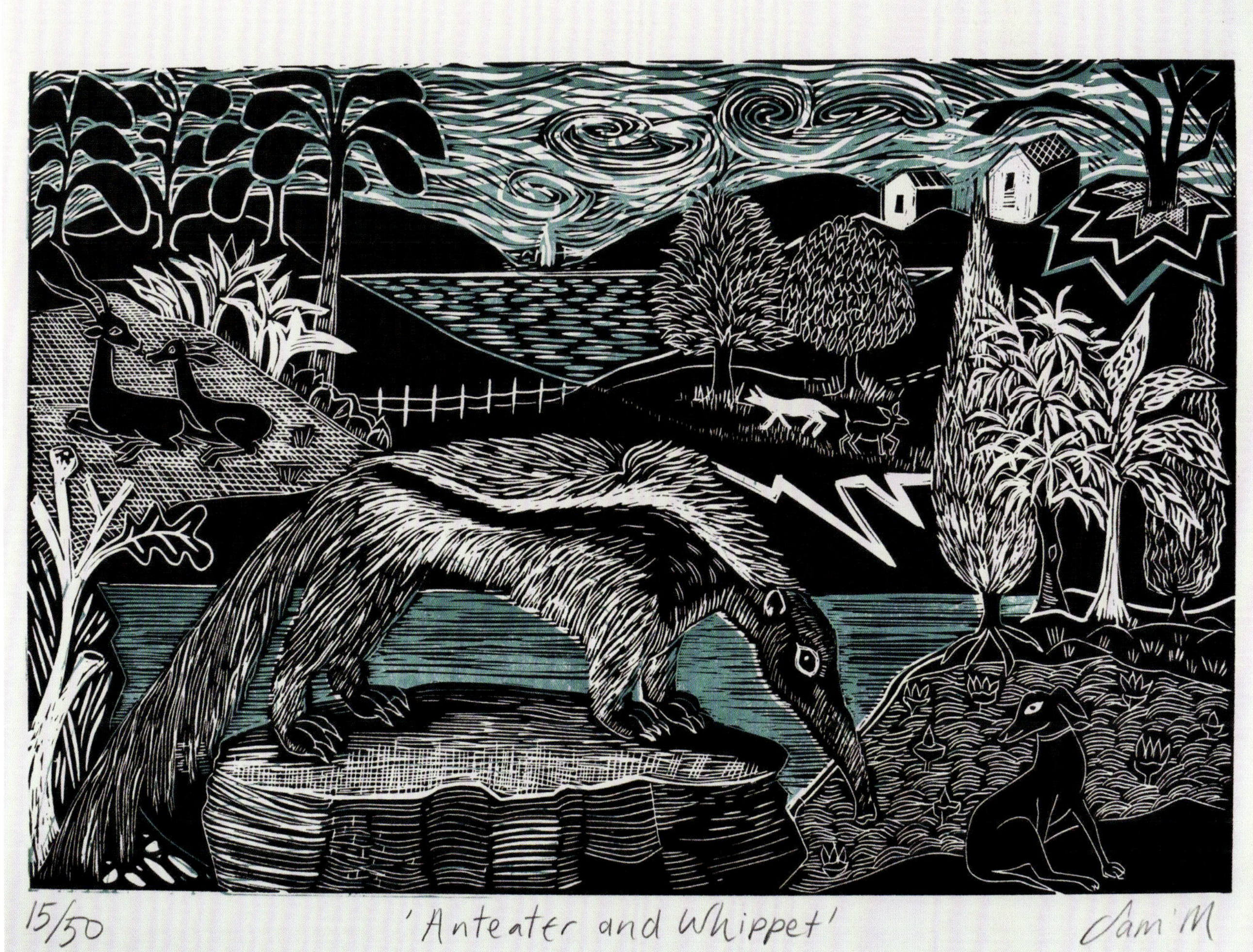

15/50   'Anteater and Whippet'   Sam M

NUMBERING AND SIGNING LIMITED-EDITION PRINTS

Once you have finished your edition and your prints are dry, you can number and sign them. First of all, go through them all thoroughly and remove the ones that haven't quite worked. They might be over-inked, under-inked, or have a blob of ink in the border – anything that makes them not quite perfect in your eyes. Always keep hold of these prints, as they can come in useful for future projects. Always sign your prints with a pencil rather than a pen; ideally a HB that isn't too sharp – otherwise it can damage the paper. Pencil is far more stable than pen and less liable to fade in time.

Sign your name in the bottom right-hand corner of the image. You can use your full name or abbreviate (I just use Sam M, for example), or add your normal signature. The most important thing is to be consistent – don't keep changing it. You might want to practice until you are comfortable with the way you are signing your prints. If you want to date your print, this generally goes after your signature. Dating your print is optional, though (I tend not to).

Number your prints from one upwards, on the left-hand side, using the format X/Y. So, let's say you are numbering the first print in an edition of twenty, you would sign it: 1/20.

Most printmakers title their prints, but, again, this is optional. If you do title your print it should go in the middle between the edition number and the signature. Titles are often written in inverted commas – e.g. 'Title'. If I think one or some prints are less than perfect (for me), then I'll not edition them and will keep them aside to use as, or for, something else (e.g. a collage, book cover, card, etc.). That said, there are some prints I deemed as 'less than perfect' then looked back on them months later and regretted being too hard on myself. The process isn't perfect.

ADDITIONAL EDITION LABELS

Variable Edition (VE or EV)
If prints in your edition vary – either by design or by the nature of the printmaking process you have chosen (chine collé or hand coloured for example) – then they need to be labelled differently. Prints in editions like this can be labelled VE X/Y or EV X/Y. Essentially, each print within the 'edition' is different to the other.

Artist Proofs (A/P)
A proof suggests a work in progress but artist proofs from an edition are usually identical to the edition and are marked A/P. Artist proofs usually shouldn't exceed ten per cent of the overall number in the edition. So, if there is an edition of fifty, there should not be more than five artist proofs.

Historically, the artist was given a portion of the edition to sell as payment for their work, as when an artist was commissioned to execute a print, they were given living expenses and often accommodation, supplies and paper, assistants and a studio.

Trial Proof (T/P)
A trial proof is pulled before the edition to see what the print looks like at a stage of development when you are adjusting and developing the final image, which differs from the edition. There can be any number of trial proofs, but usually it is a small number and each one differs from the others. They can be sold and annotated T/P.

Open Editions (O/E)
Open editions are prints that are not limited to a number, meaning you can print as many as you like, therefore you don't number them. Open editions aren't considered as valuable as numbered prints, though, and collectors often only buy limited editions.

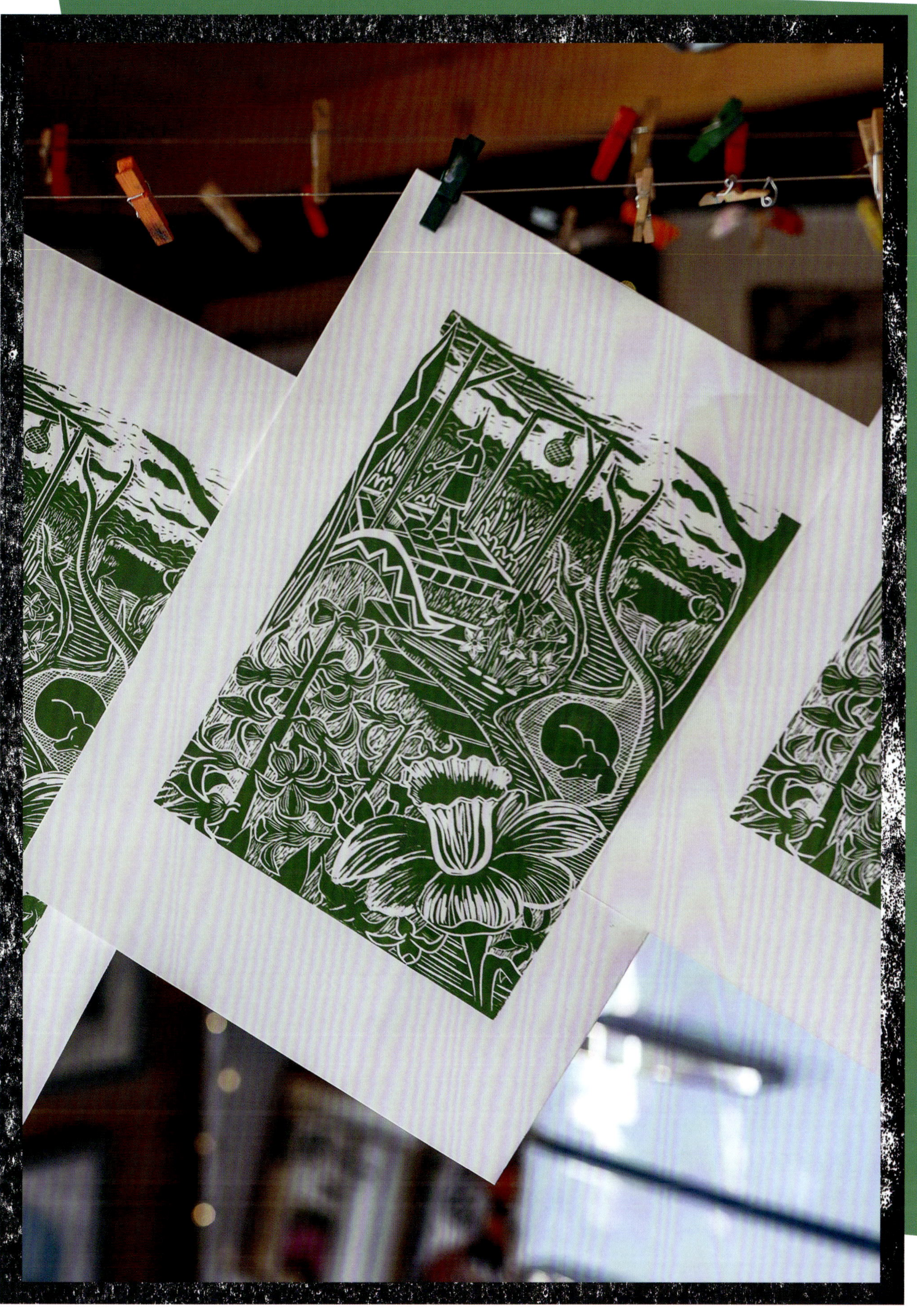

13 A WEEKEND AWAY

This is the perfect project if you have a weekend or a few days away planned soon. Over the course of your break, take your sketchbook with you and compile a selection of drawings of things that interest you. It could be something as simple as your morning coffee or an afternoon snack, or something more challenging such as a landscape that takes your eye. If you are feeling nervous or unconfident (or both!) about drawing outside, look back at my tips on page 78 for how to make this a little easier.

This project really invites you to consider what it is that you find visually exciting and how you would like to document your time away. At the start of writing this book, I had a lovely weekend away in Norfolk where I took the opportunity to collect lots of drawings for my projects. Do take photographs along the way so you can also refer to these when you are working on your drawings and linocuts. This is quite an advanced project but it's a lot of fun, and, once you have finished, you'll have a lovely memory in print of your time away.

Opposite page

A selection of sketches from my weekend away in Norfolk.

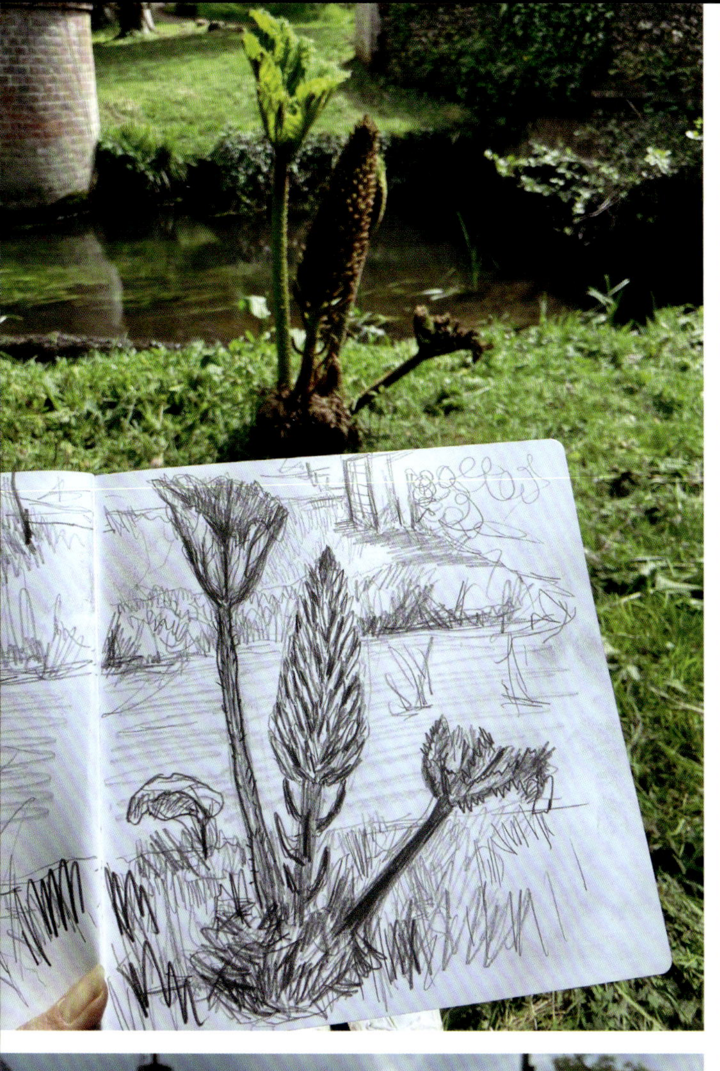

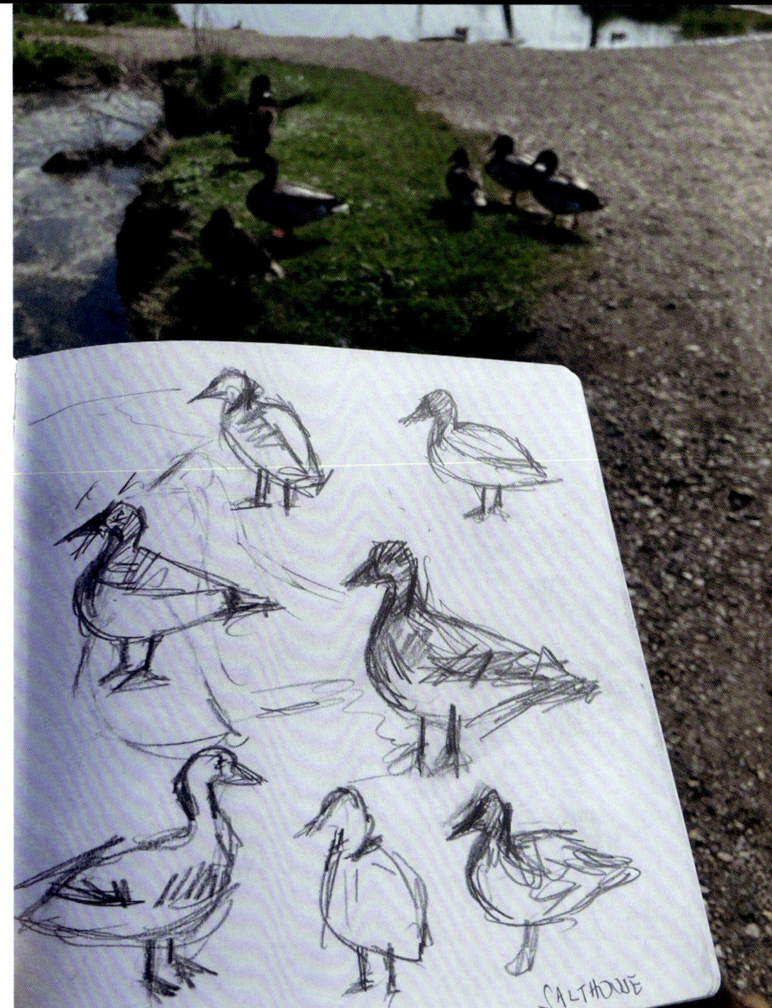
SALTHOUSE

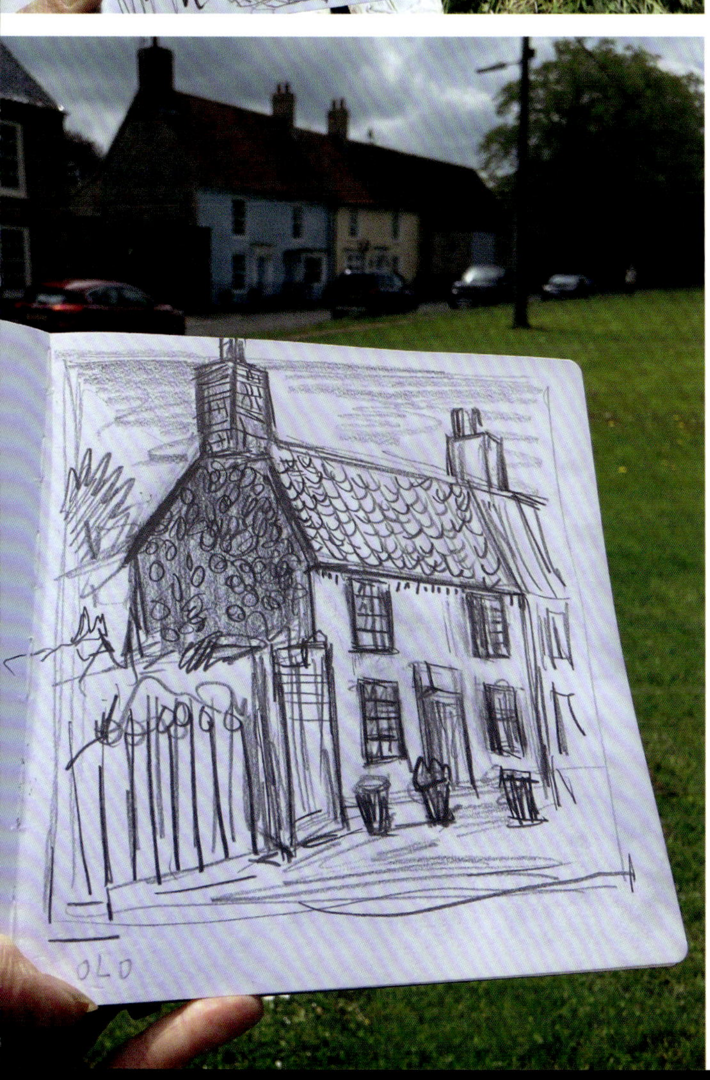
OLD

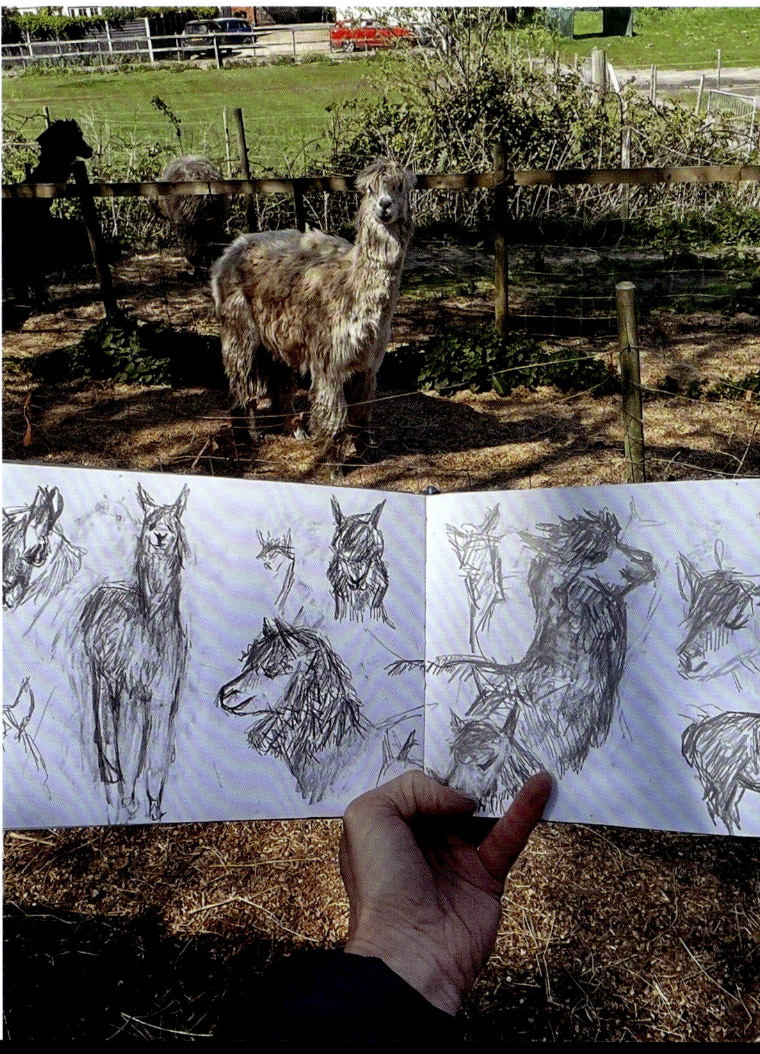

HOLIDAY MEMORY PRINT

You Will Need

- A5 piece of lino
- Photocopy paper for proofing
- Selection of pencils, e.g. HB/2B
- Rubber/eraser
- Tracing paper (optional)

- Masking tape (optional)
- Marker pen or biro
- Cutting mat
- Cutting tools
- Stiff brush
- Talcum powder (optional)
- Relief printing ink

- Inking slab
- Roller
- Baren or wooden spoon
- Good-quality paper for making a small edition
- Cleaning materials

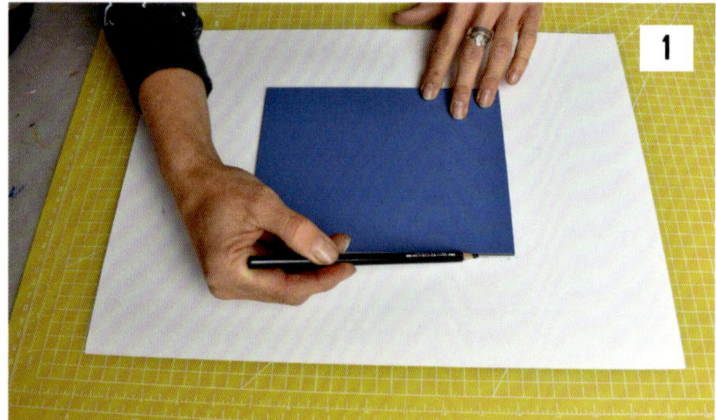

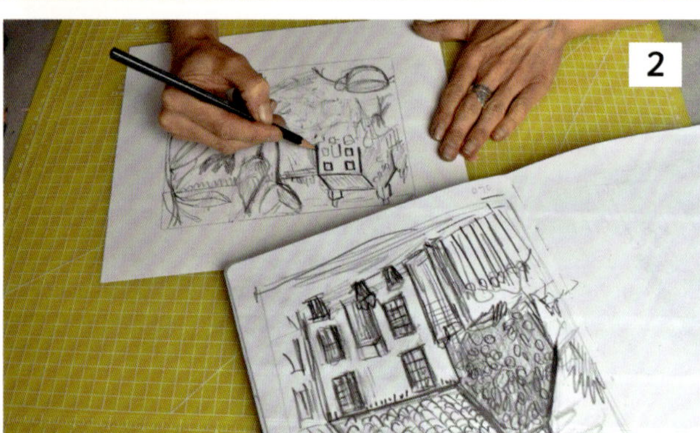

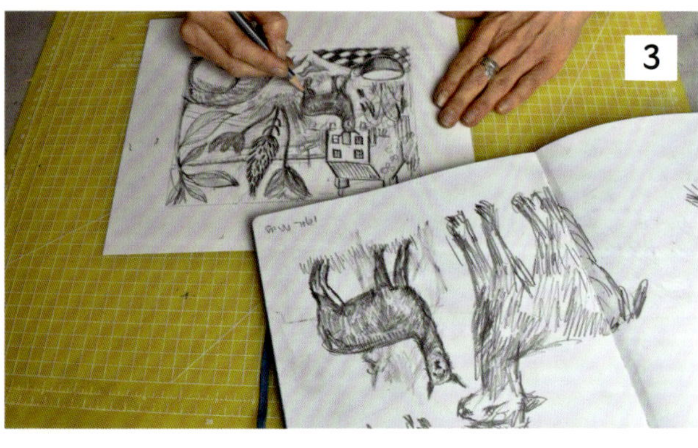

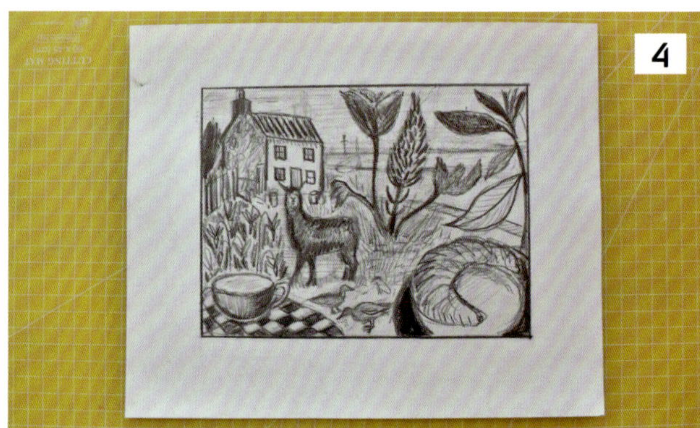

1   Take an A5 piece of lino and draw around it.

2   Spend some time looking at your sketches and start to experiment with redrawing on your paper. Play around with scale and composition and remember you aren't trying to recreate a believable scene – more of an interesting collection of memories all on one page.

3   Keep adding to your drawing – rubbing out, editing, etc. Don't worry too much about what you will carve out and leave yet. Look at the marks you have made in your original sketch and try to incorporate them into your new drawing.

4   Here is my finished drawing. You can see I've got a mixture of scales and a variety of lines and marks.

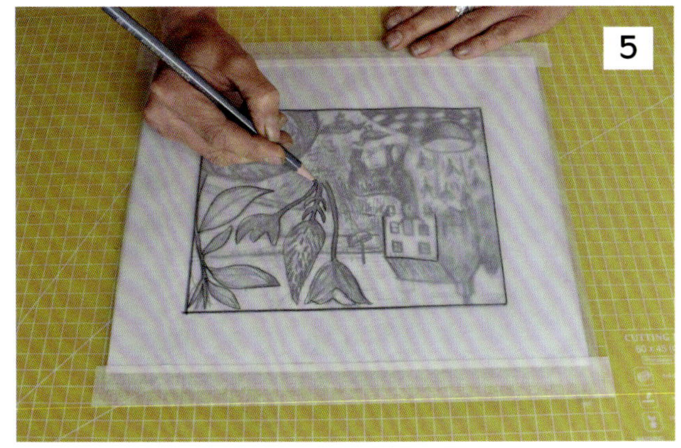

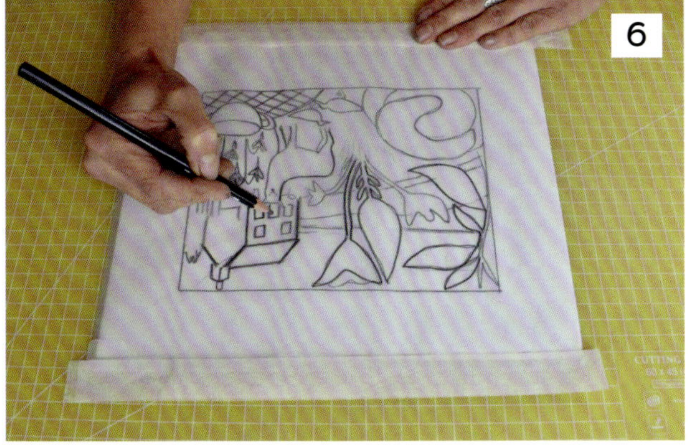

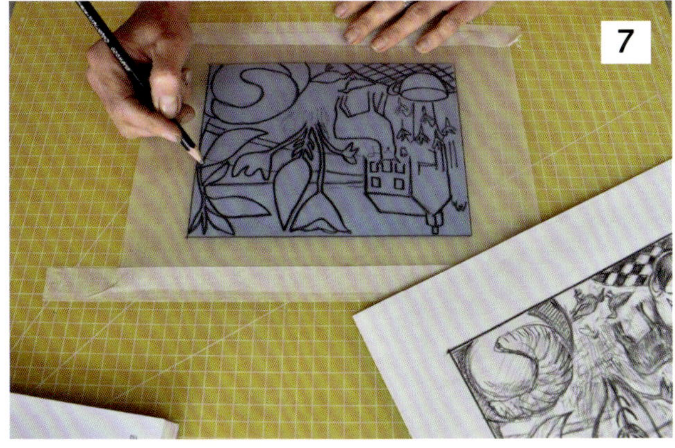

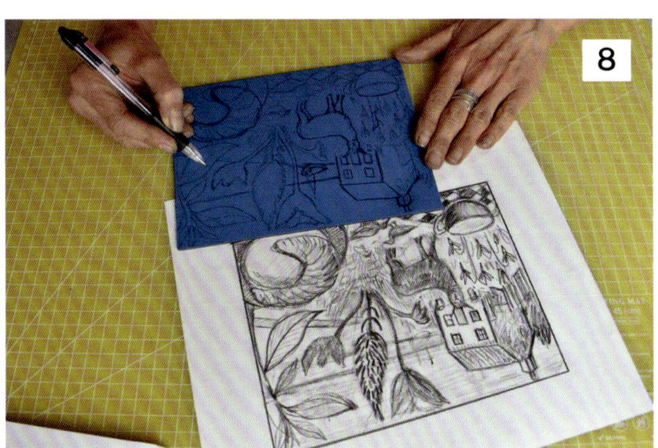

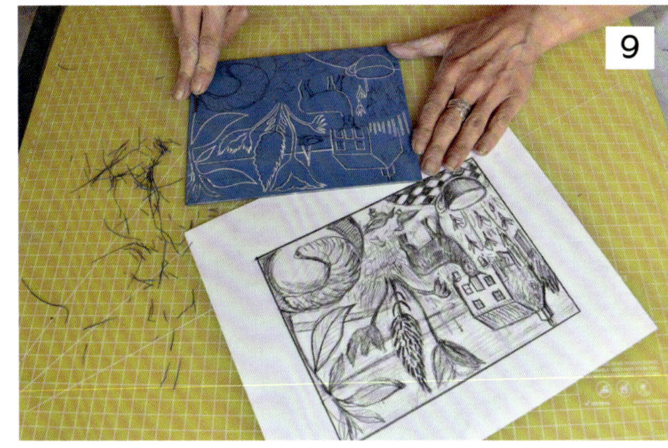

5 Once you are happy with your drawing you can move on to tracing it using your chosen method (see page 29). I often find it helpful when tracing to use masking tape to secure the tracing paper to the drawing, which avoids any slippage.

6 I'm using my preferred technique of using tracing paper to work directly from the drawing (see page 32), meaning that the resulting print will be the reverse of my sketch.

7 If you are using tracing paper, once you are happy with your trace, transfer it to the lino by going over the line with a pencil.

8 Go over the pencil lines with a pen. I'm using biro here as it works nicely on Japanese vinyl. You might want to reinforce your lines with permanent marker pen as remember, if you are proofing as you go, your pencil lines will wipe off.

9 Begin carving with a V tool, going around some of the outlines. I don't always go around everything, as I like to leave certain areas blank to see what the print suggests to me as I proof it. I use talcum powder to help me see what I'm carving (see page 64).

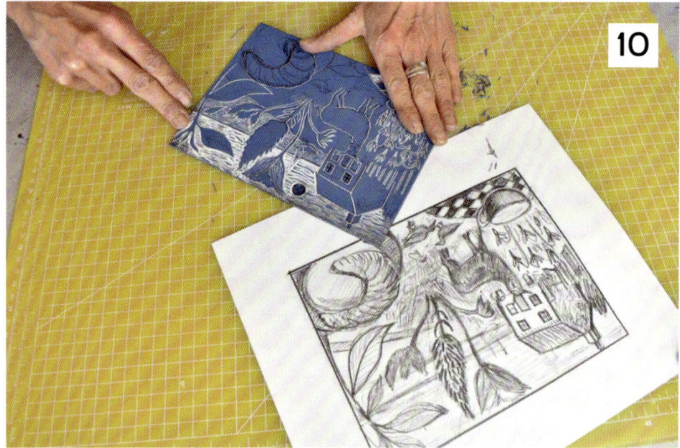

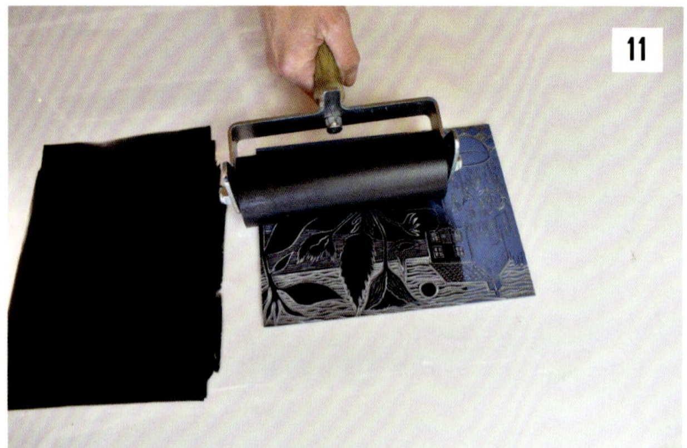

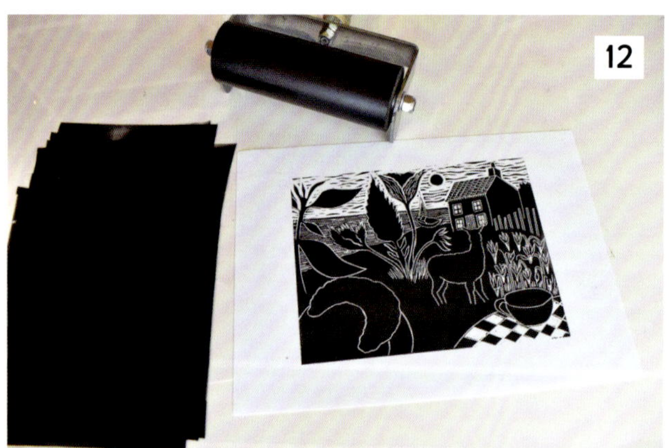

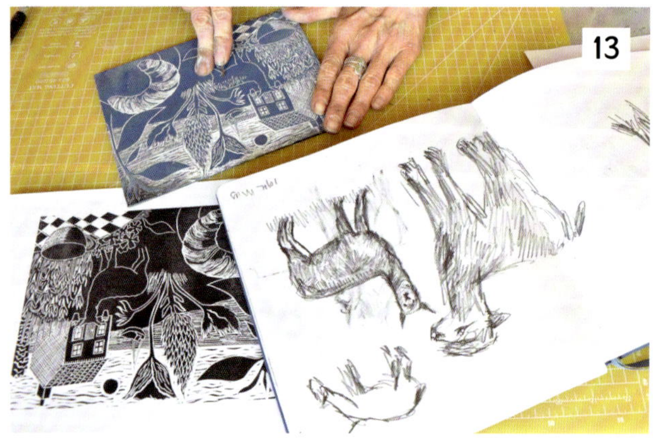

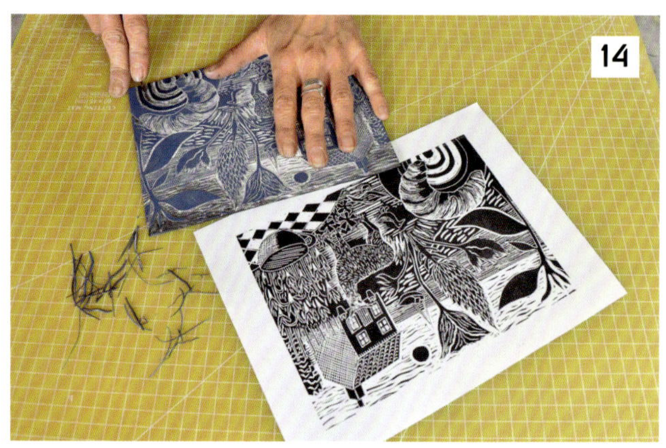

10 Once you have completed most of the outlines, you can work on clearing the large areas you don't want to print – that is, the parts that will be white. Here I'm carving the sky, keeping some noise within it, as I don't want it to be purely white (see page 68).

11 After an hour or so of carving, take a print to see how it's progressing. Ink and print your block in the same way as you did in the mark-making warm-up (see page 39).

12 I tend to use black when I'm proofing as I find it easiest to assess the balance of light and dark areas. Take the time to examine your print to see what needs more work.

13 Keep carving, using both your proof and drawing as a guide. Keep changing your tools to keep your print full of interest.

14 Continue to carve, proof and burnish. Try to ensure that you achieve a good balance of black and white and a variety of different marks.

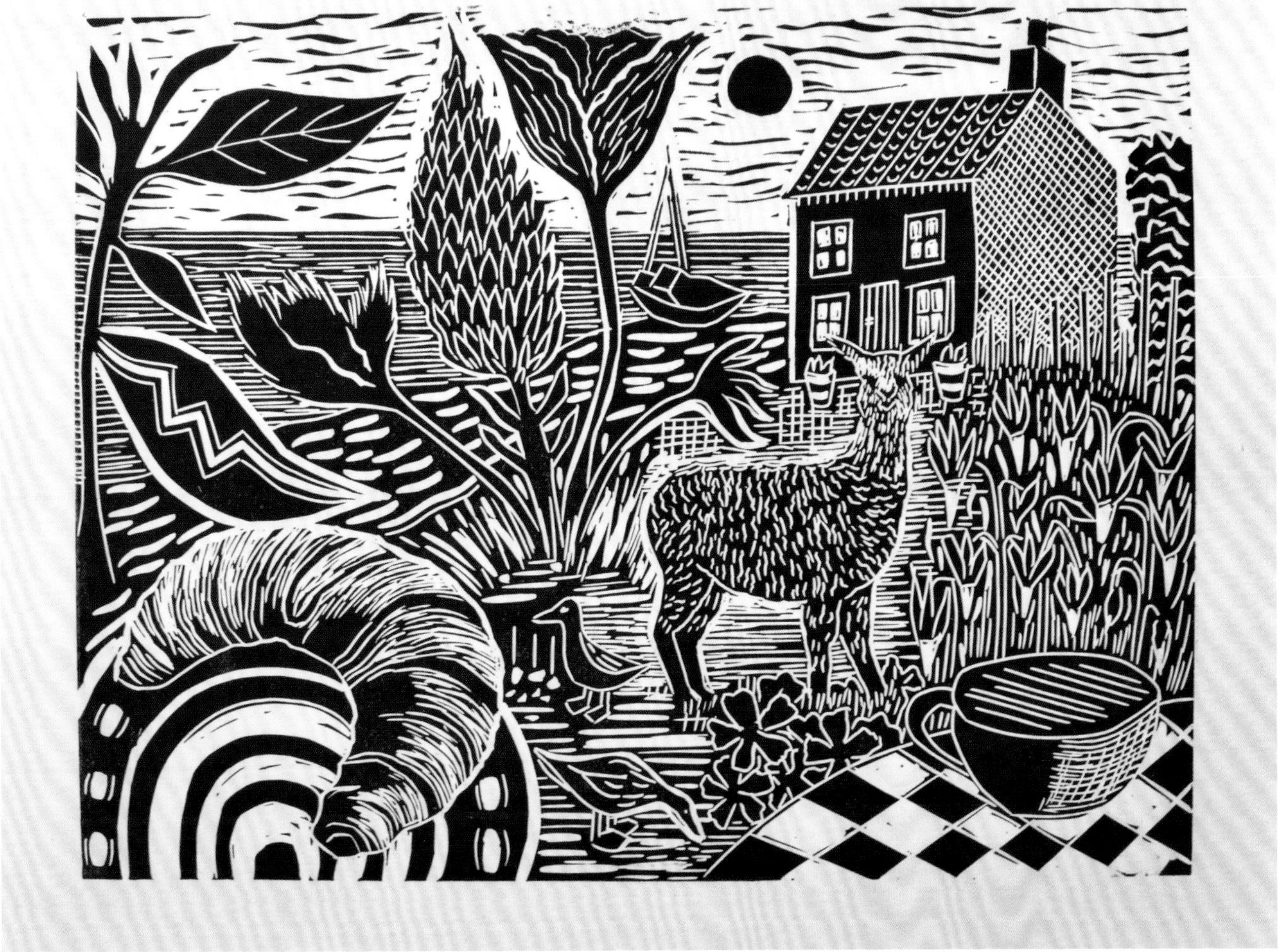

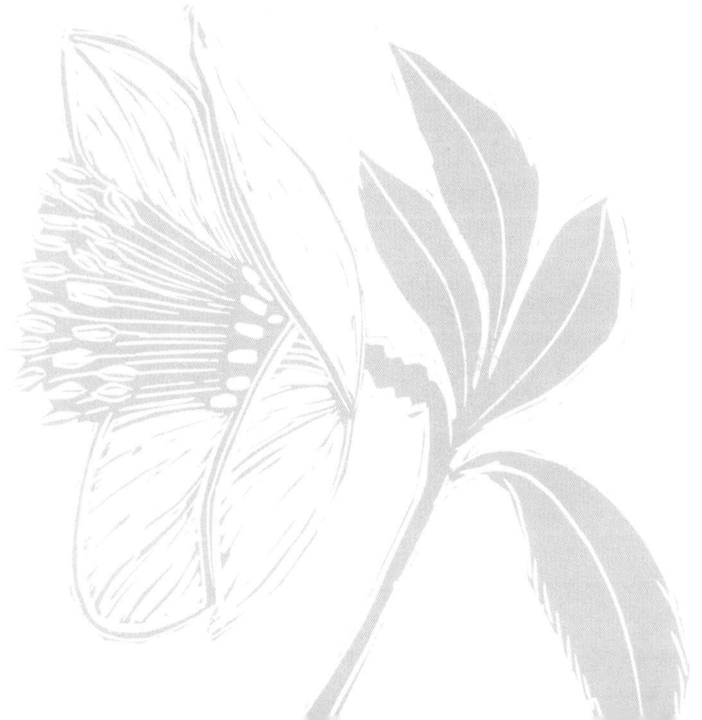

15 Take some time to examine what is successful in your final print and think about what you would change if you did it again. For me, I'm happy with the variety of marks and overall composition, but if I did it again I might make the alpaca slightly larger. I'm generally pleased with the finished result – it's a lovely memory of my time away in Norfolk.

AN INTERVIEW WITH IZZY WILLIAMSON

How do you start a new work?

Each of my prints starts life as a series of sketches. They are usually unrecognisable at first – often small-scale scribbles – while I work out the general compositions and shapes. They gradually become more refined until they are ready to be transferred onto the block using tracing paper.

For more complicated pieces, particularly multi-blocks with lots of layers, I will sometimes jot down little notes and diagrams to help me get my head around the overlays and 'order of service'.

Do you have any particular tools that you like to use or paper preferences for printing on?

I have tried a variety of tools over the years, but my Flexcut gouges are the ones for me! They are great for carving very small details and they feel very natural and comfortable in your hand. I favour traditional grey hessian-backed lino, and Fabriano paper is my go-to.

My favourite inks are vegetable-oil-based inks made by Hawthorn Printmakers, who are a small family business, local to me in York. Many of their pigments are sourced locally and they have a vast amount of colours to peruse. I feel very lucky to have an etching press, also made by Hawthorn Printmakers, which has totally transformed my process over the last couple of years.

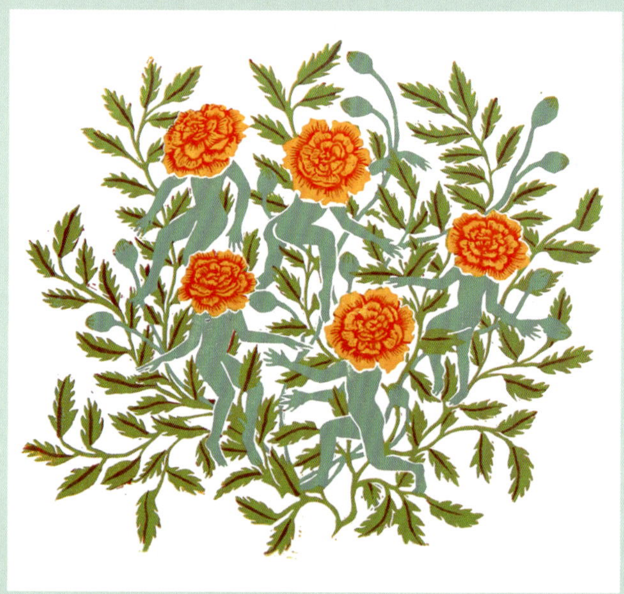

What is your favourite part of the printmaking process?

I have always loved the carving stage the most. Before a big carving session, I have to consciously slow down and really focus on what is in front of me. I think it is a great mindful exercise and can be almost meditative at times. The thrill of pulling the first print from a new block is a very close favourite too!

@izzywilliamsonprints
www.izzywilliamson.com

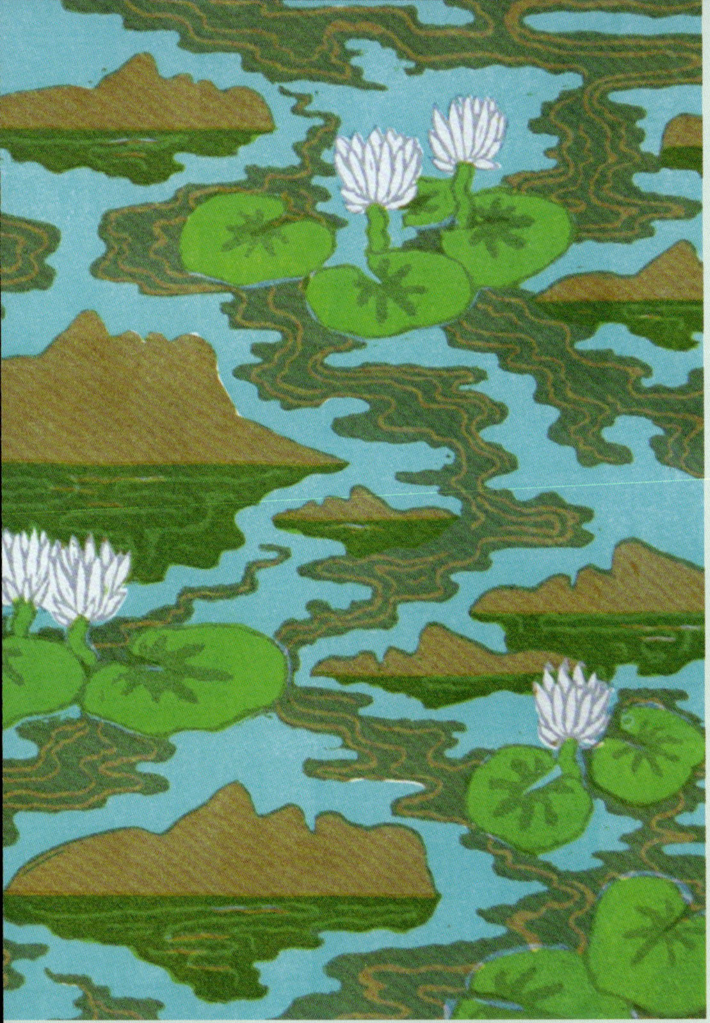

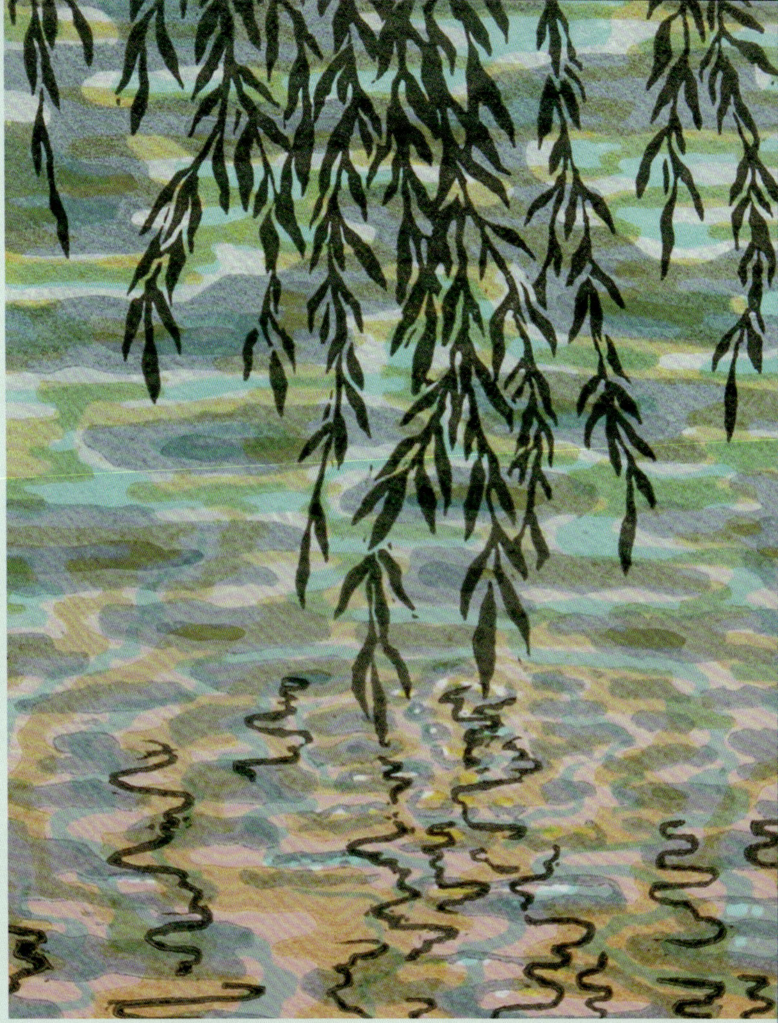

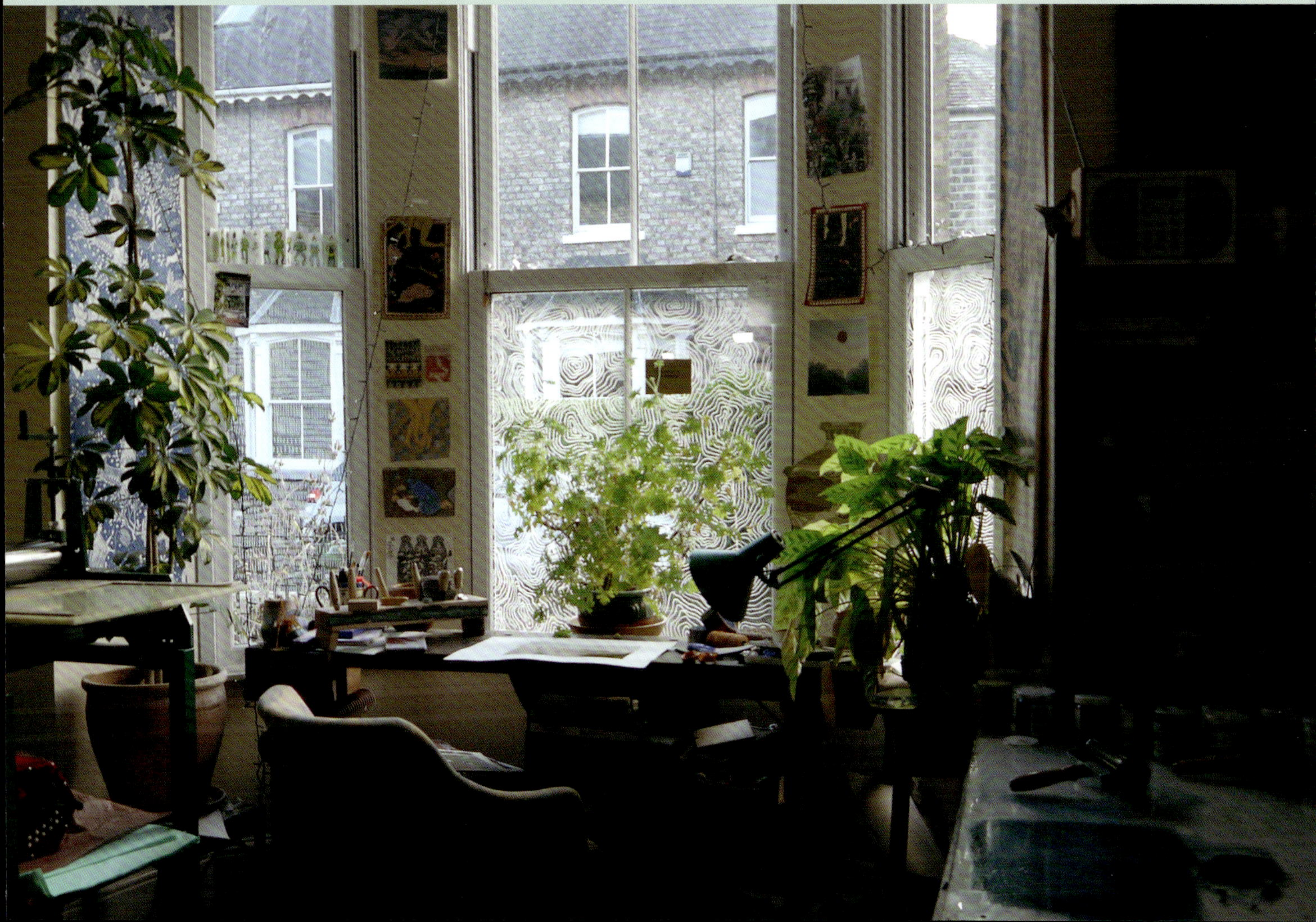

14 REDUCTION LINOCUT

For this project, we will create a multicoloured print using the reduction method. Reduction linocut is a technique of block printing in which each colour layer is taken from the same block. More lino is removed from the block for each layer and each colour is printed on top of the last – for every colour, the block is 'reduced'. It's an economical way of working, as your multicoloured print is produced from just one block. It is also known as 'suicide printing', because once you carve away areas of the block, you can't get them back.

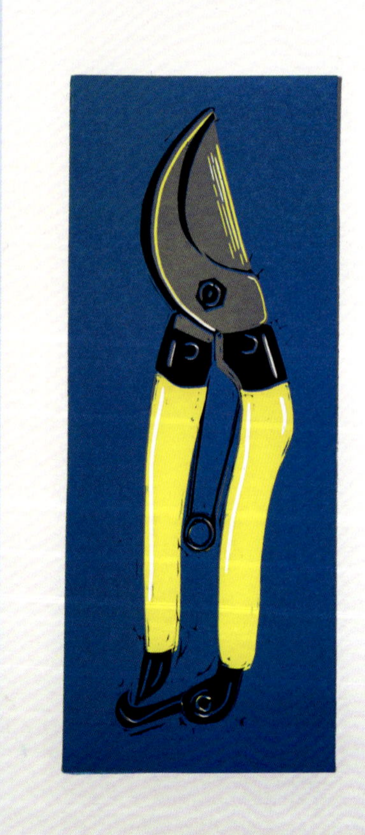

Here are a few pointers that I always give to beginners before embarking on their reduction linocut, as it's one technique that seems to generate a lot of fear!

Keep it simple

Don't overthink it *– it's a process you really only learn by doing*

Start with the lightest colour first. *In this project I start with white, then yellow, grey, blue, and finally black*

With reduction linocuts you have to print all your edition in one go, *so it's always a good idea to print up more than you need. You will inevitably lose prints along the way, as registration can be tricky!*

A PRACTICAL OBJECT

You Will Need

- One piece of lino
- Cutting mat
- Craft knife
- Selection of pencils, e.g. HB/2B
- Rubber/eraser
- Metal ruler
- Paper for drawing/ painting (I used heavyweight cartridge)
- Tracing paper
- Acrylic paints
- Paintbrushes
- Palette (or something to squeeze paint onto)
- Permanent marker
- Cutting tools
- Stiff brush
- Relief printing ink
- Roller
- Inking slab
- Greyboard for registration board
- 15 sheets of smooth printing paper (all the same size)
- Baren or wooden spoon
- Cleaning materials

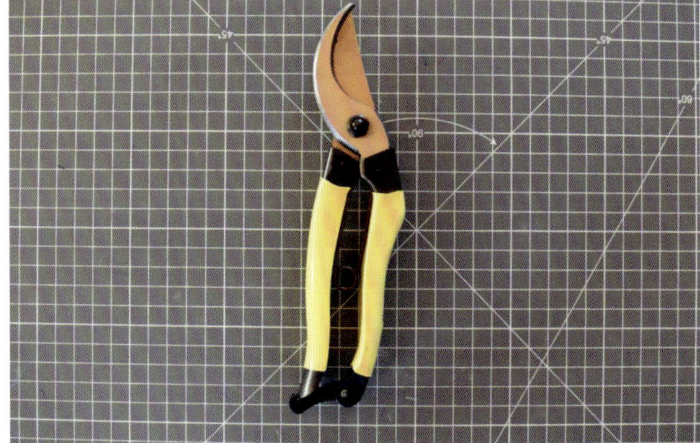

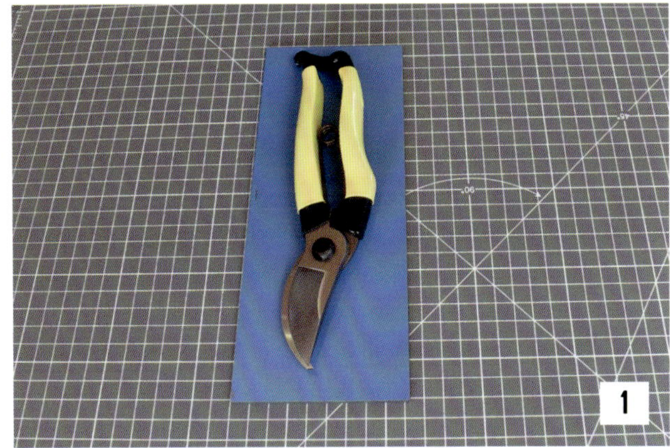

For this project, you should select a practical object from your home that you find visually appealing; ideally something that has only has three to four colours. Here, I have chosen my treasured pair of Japanese secateurs. While I was in Japan, I stayed with a family who used a pair of these all the time in their small garden and, when I returned from my trip, I bought myself a pair to remind me of that magical time. I love the simplicity of the design – the yellow handles are a delight!

1   Cut a piece of lino to a size that would suit the shape of your object.

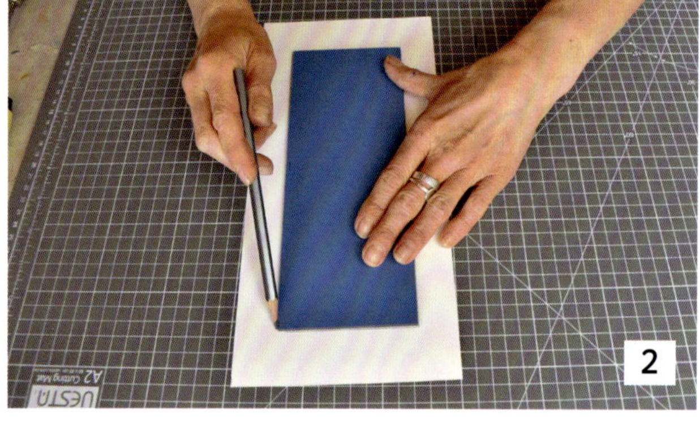

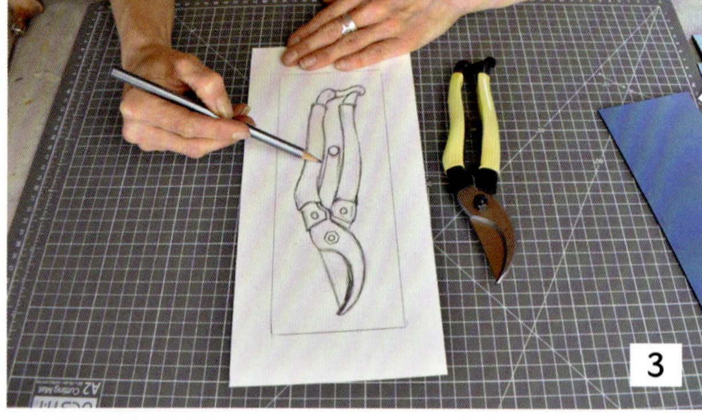

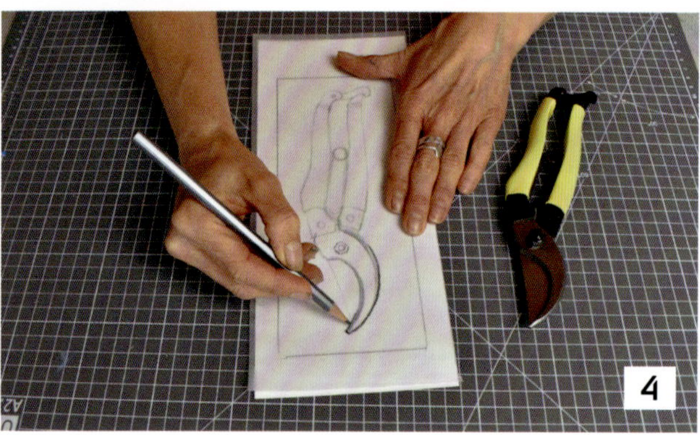

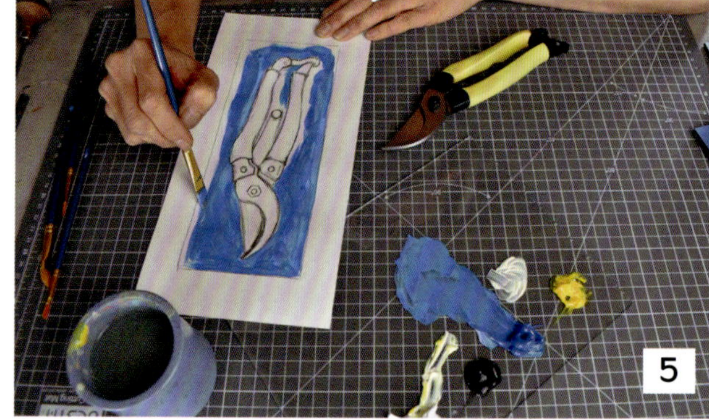

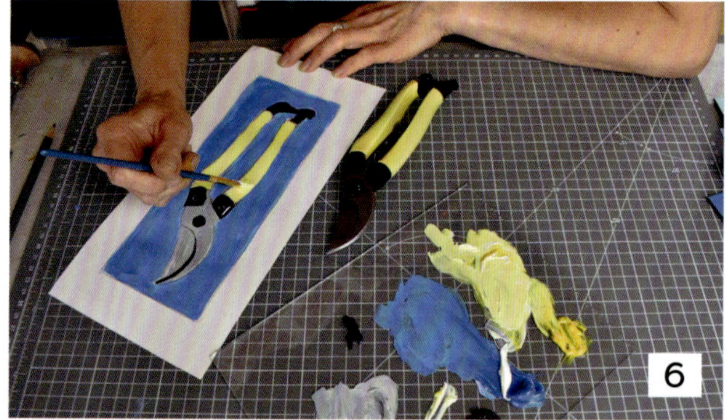

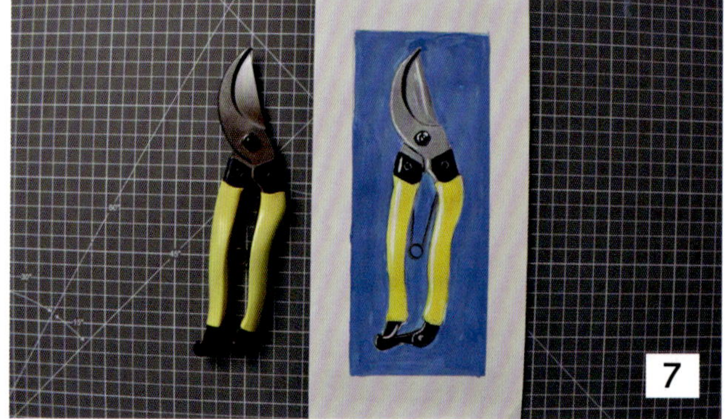

2   Draw around the lino with pencil.

3   Make a detailed line drawing of your object. You don't need to add tone this time, as you will be adding colour to your drawing instead.

4   Trace your drawing then put the trace to one side.

5   It's time to figure out the colours you want to use by painting or colouring in your drawing. I used acrylic paints as they dry quickly and are easy to clean up. I chose a simple blue background as I feel it complemented the yellow of the secateurs.

6   Continue painting until you have all the colours in place.

7   Here is my finished painting. You can see I have used three colours – yellow, grey and blue, as well as black and white – which is more than enough when you are starting off with this technique.

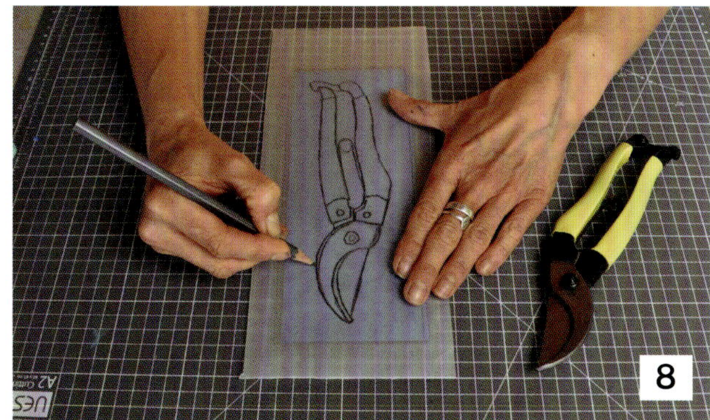

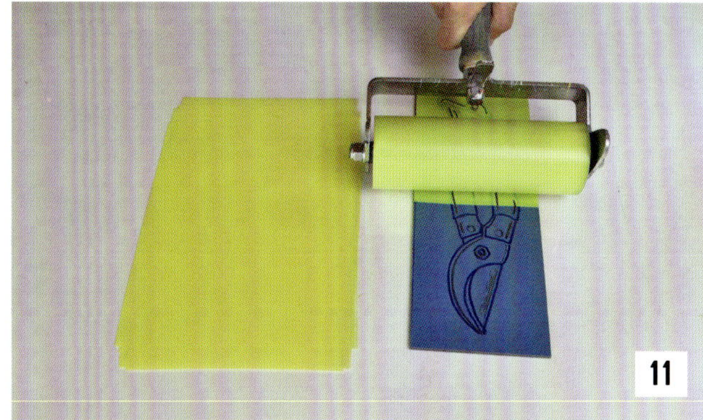

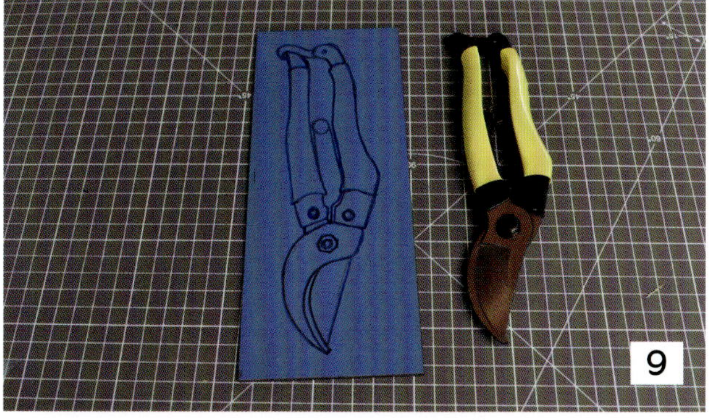

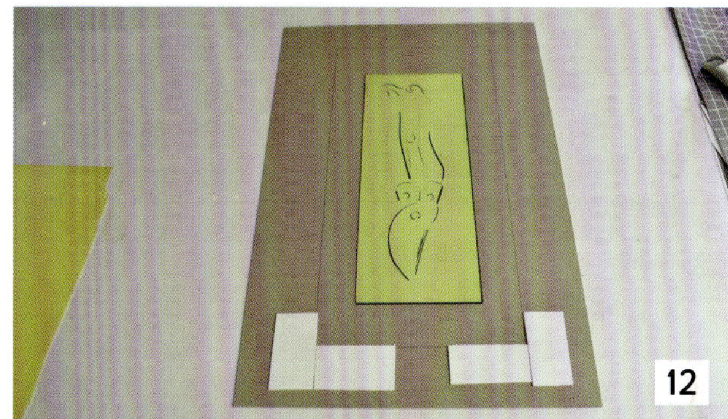

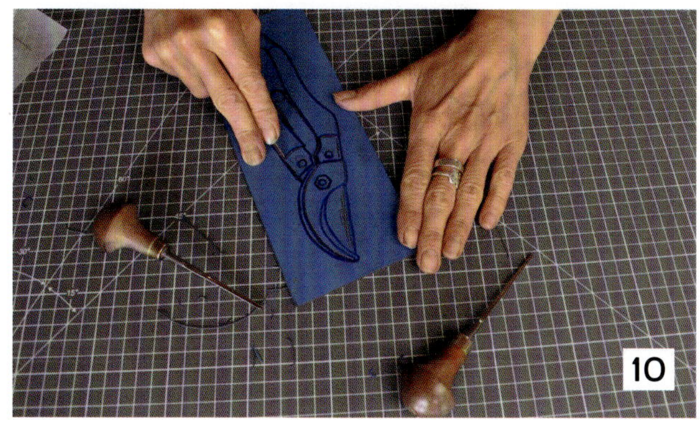

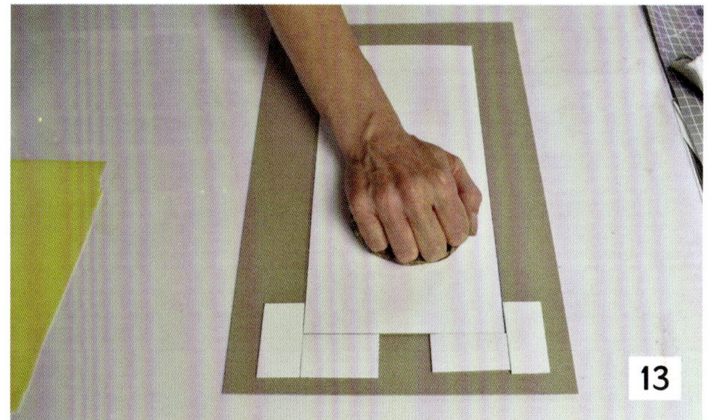

8   Trace your drawing onto your lino block.

9   Go around your pencil line with a permanent marker. This will transfer onto your first few prints, but don't worry as the subsequent colours will cover it.

10 Refer to your painting to see which areas you want to remain white – these will be the lightest part of the print (they act as the highlights on my secateurs). Carve out those areas using a fine V tool.

11 Once you have carved out your white areas, you are now ready to ink and print your lightest colour (in my case, yellow). Ink up and print your block in the same way as you did in the mark-making warm-up (see page 39).

12 Follow the instructions in Chapter 8 to make your registration board (see page 58). Place your block carefully inside the hole.

13 Place your first sheet of paper down into the marked areas and burnish carefully.

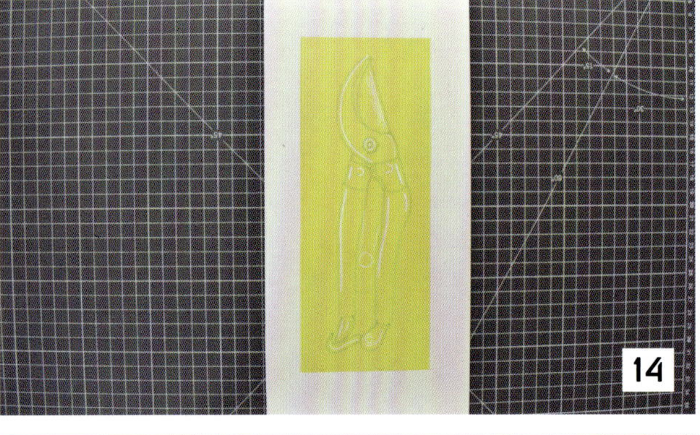

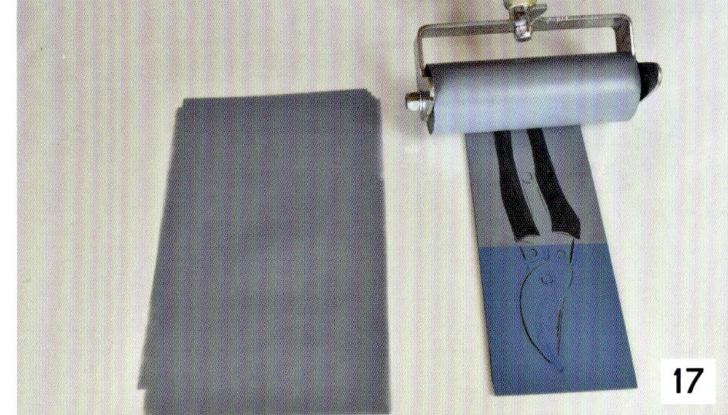

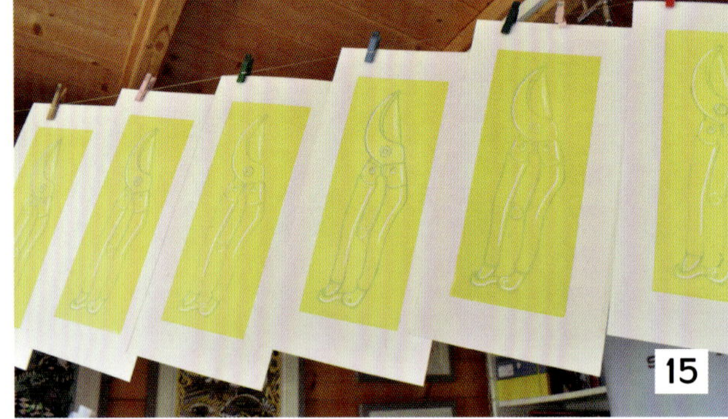

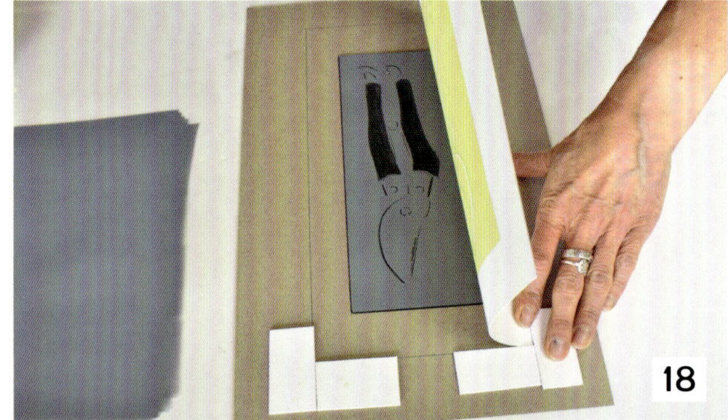

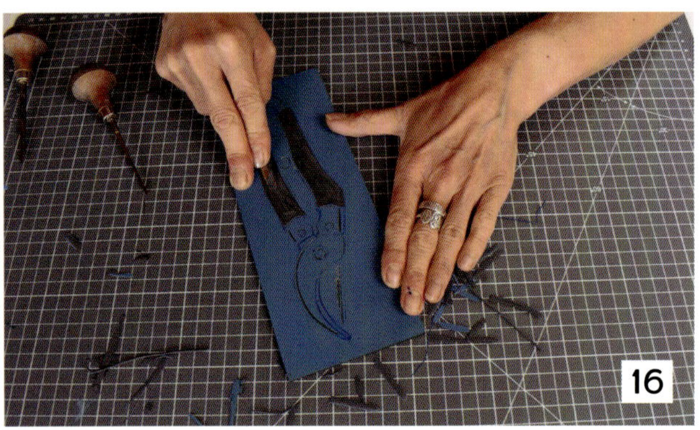

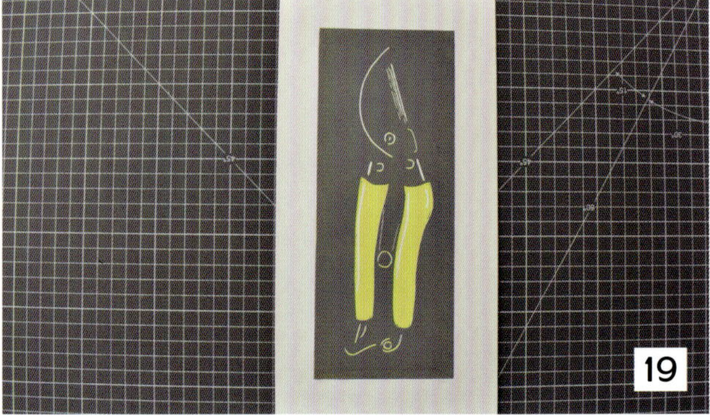

14 Have a good look at your print. You can see here that the permanent marker has transferred across a little.

15 Re-ink your block and print until you have all fifteen copies of your first colour.

16 Clean off your block, ready for your next layer. The areas to carve next are the parts that you want to remain in your first colour (in my case, yellow). The white parts will remain white.

17 Once you are happy with your carving, you are now ready to mix up your second colour (grey for me).

18 Place your inked block in the registration board. Take your first yellow print and place it carefully down. Burnish as before.

19 Take some time to assess your second layer and ensure it is registering properly. You will see here that the grey has covered over all the yellow that I didn't carve away. It's inevitable that some of your prints will be slightly misregistered, but often this can add interest to them, so try not to worry too much about it. Print up the rest of the edition in your second colour, as you did before.

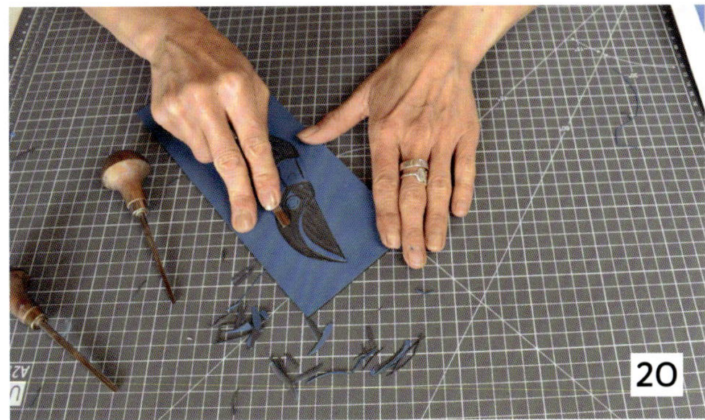

20

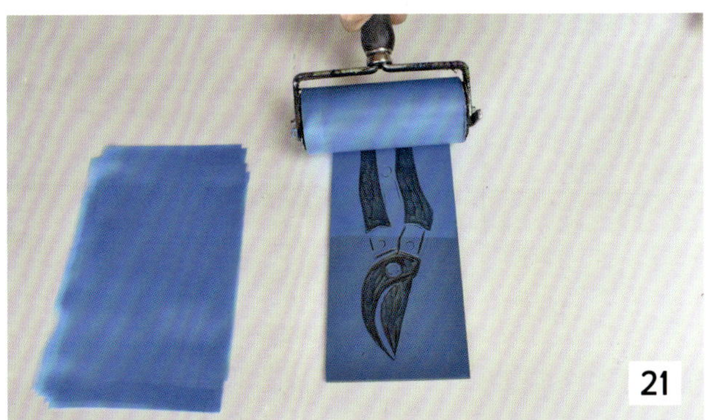

21

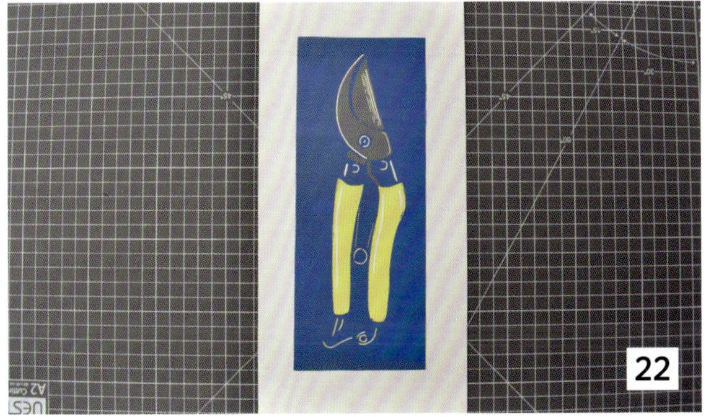

22

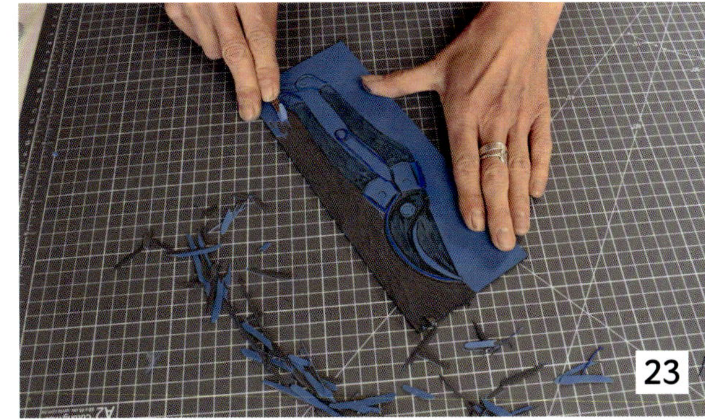

23

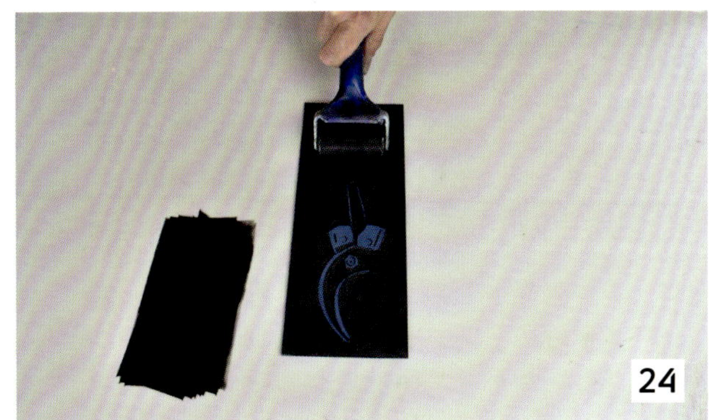

24

22 Assess your print with the three colours. You will see here that the blue has covered all the grey that I didn't carve away. I always like to keep back one of the prints at this stage as a record – and I quite like it like this too. Print the rest of your edition with the third colour.

23 Clean off your block and get ready to carve your final layer. This often means getting rid of a lot of lino. (In my case, I only have a few areas of black, so I must carve away most of the lino and leave the areas I want to remain black in relief.) I use a wide U tool to clear out the large areas.

24 Once you have carved away everything you want to remain in your third colour, you are ready to mix up and print your final layer. I use a small roller here as I don't want to ink up the whole block – I don't want too much noise (see page 68).

20 Once you have printed all your edition with your second colour, clean your block as before and get ready to carve your next layer. Carve away all the areas you want to remain in your second colour (I'm carving away all the parts I want to remain grey).

21 Mix up your third colour (for me, it's blue). Ink up your block and print in the same way, using your registration block.

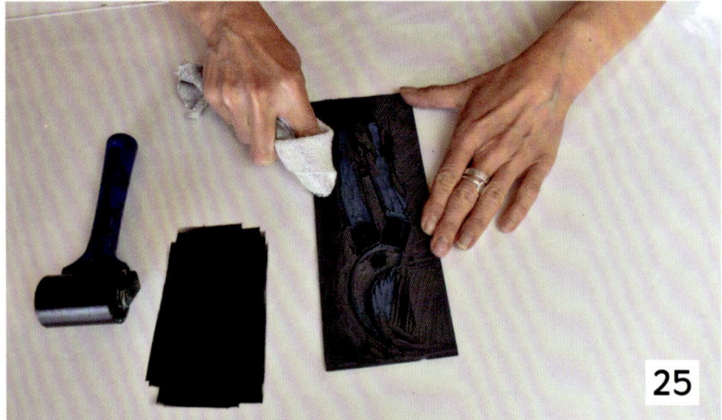

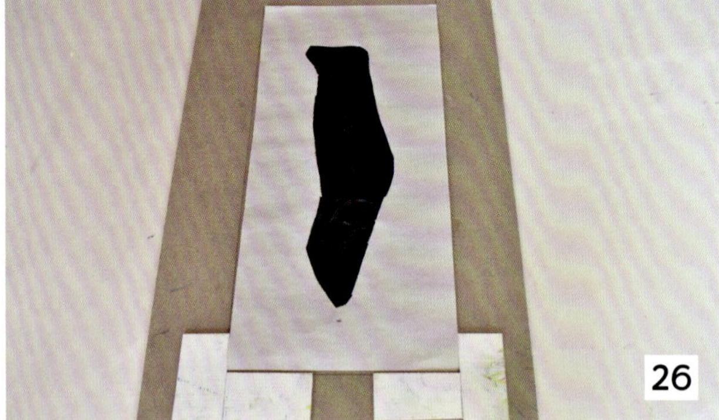

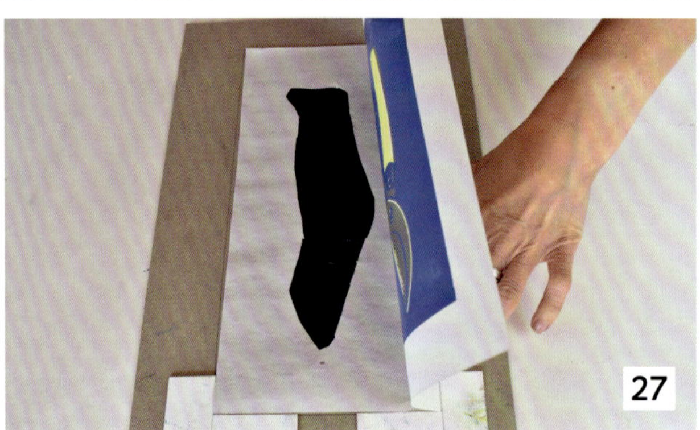

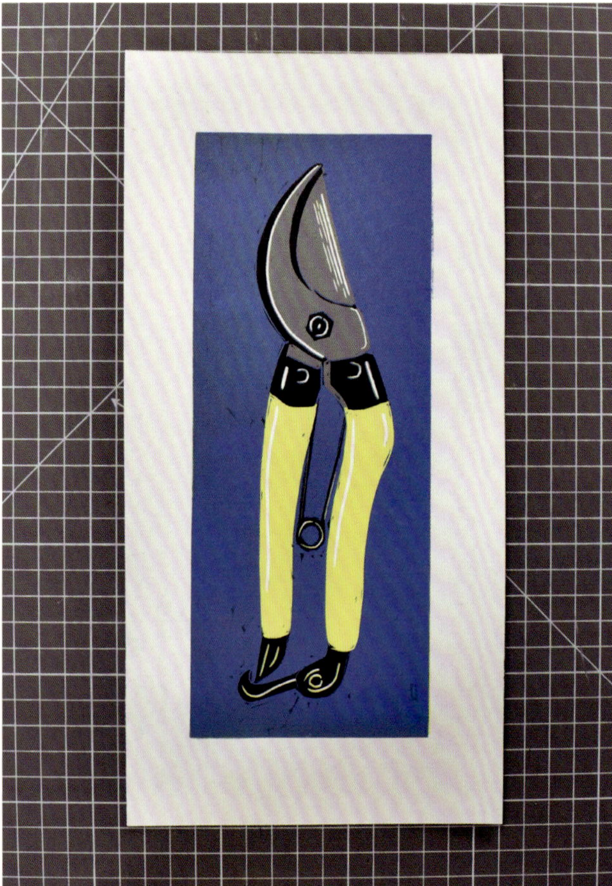

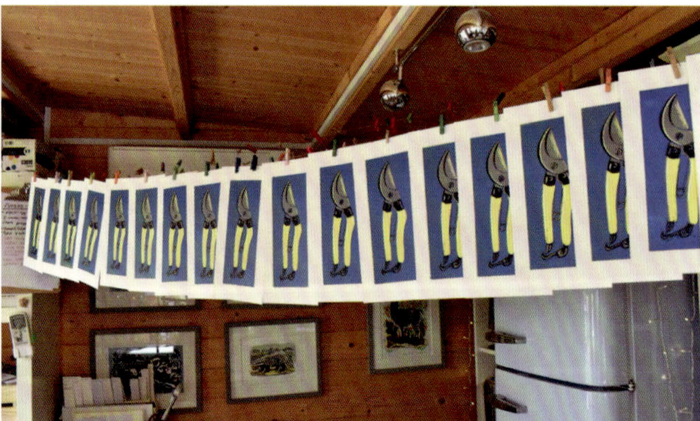

25 Once you have inked up your block, you might want to use a rag to wipe away any raised areas that are holding ink.

26 Alternatively, you can create a mask using newsprint (see page 69) to avoid noise being transferred to your print.

27 Place your paper down onto your block and burnish as before.

28 Take your time to assess your finished print and congratulate yourself on all your hard work! This is a tricky technique to master and one that requires revisiting. I had a few misprints along the way, but I see this as part of the joy of printing.

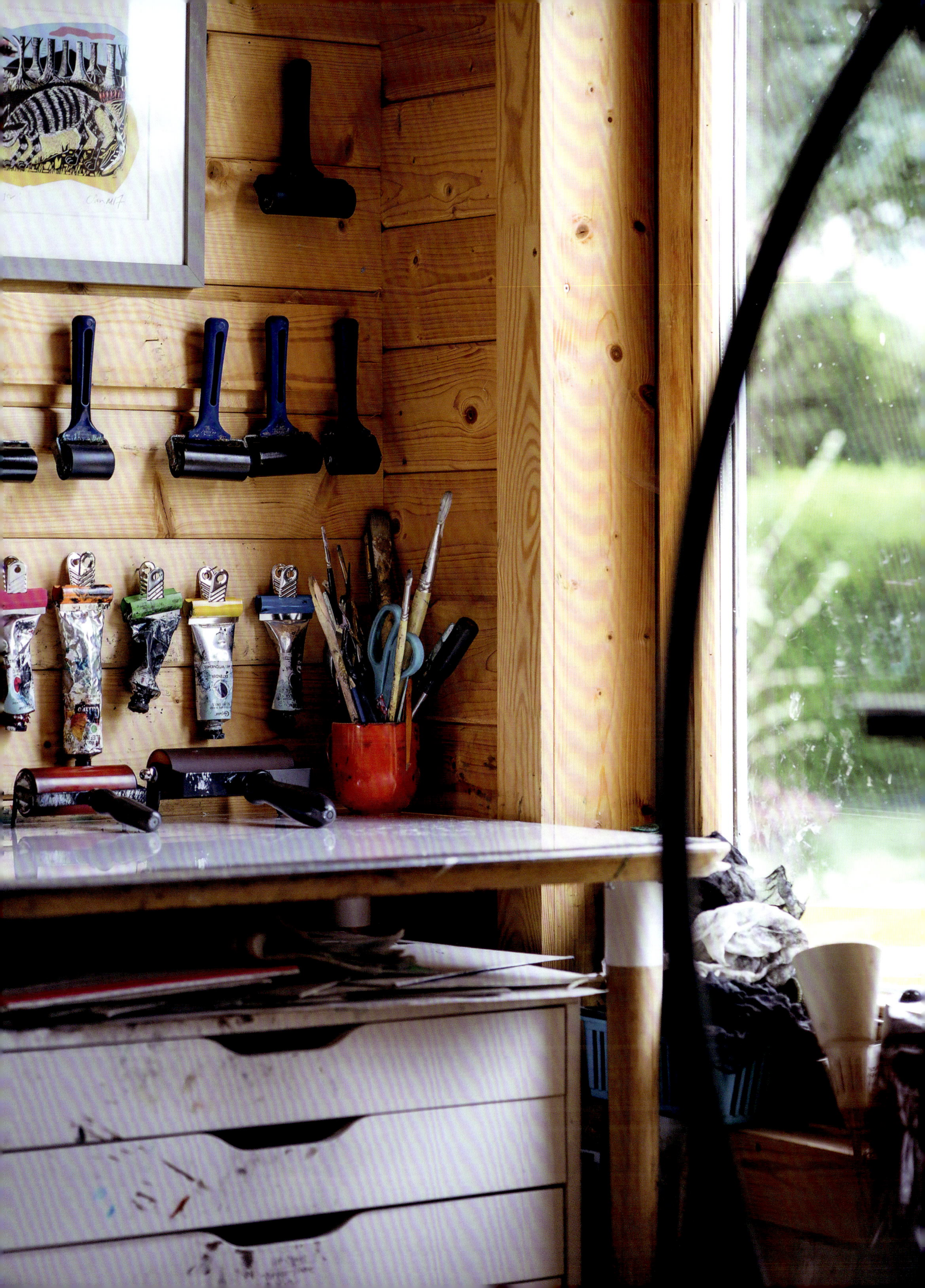

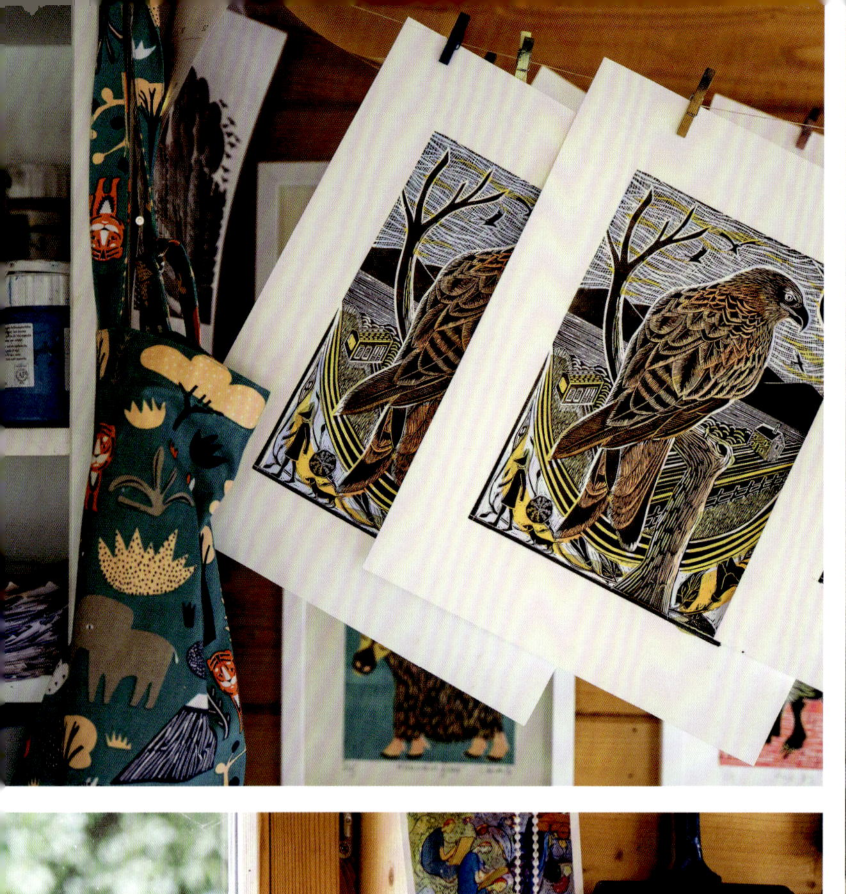

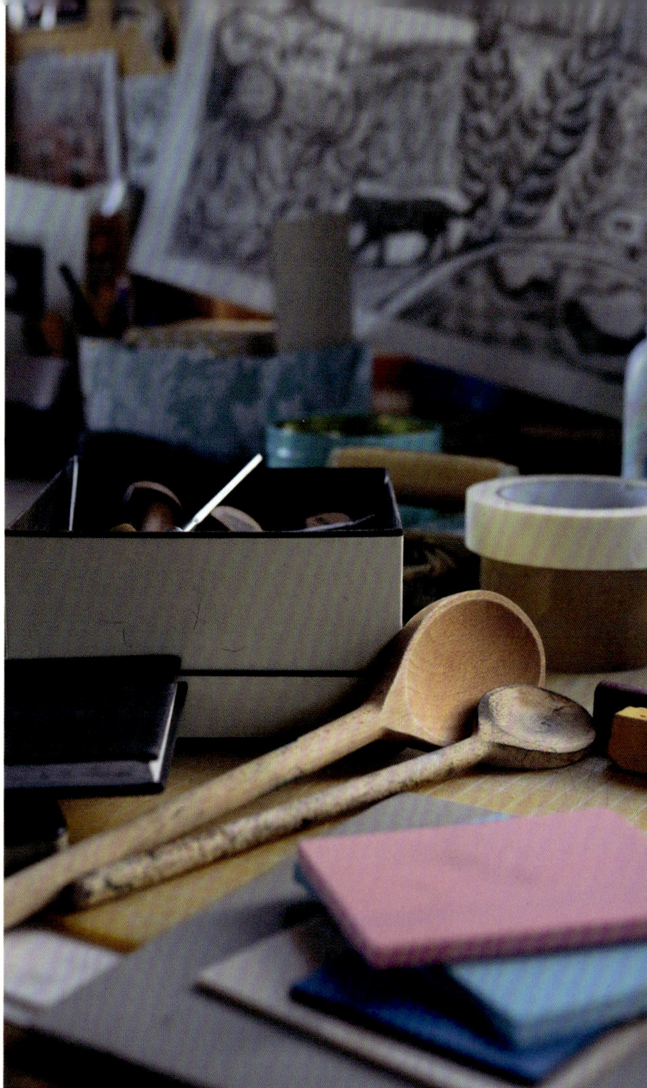

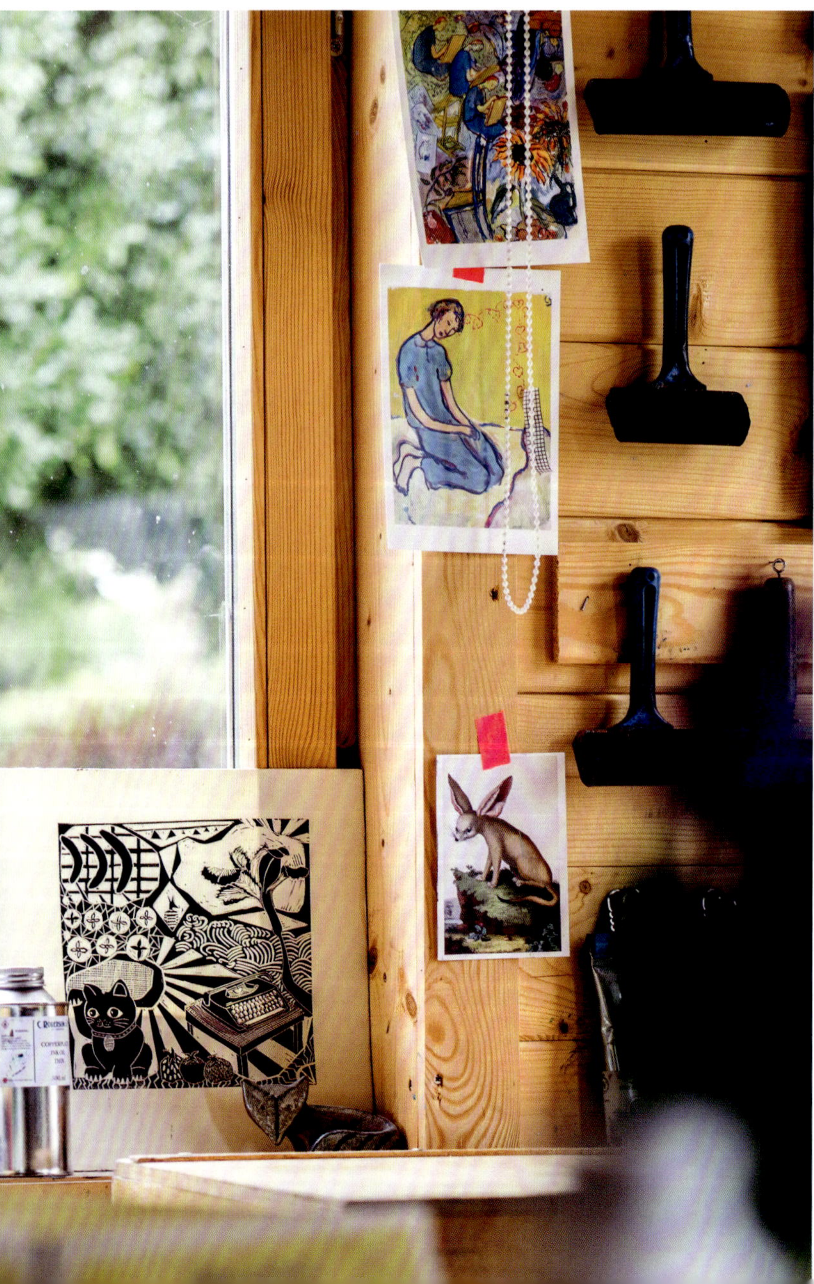

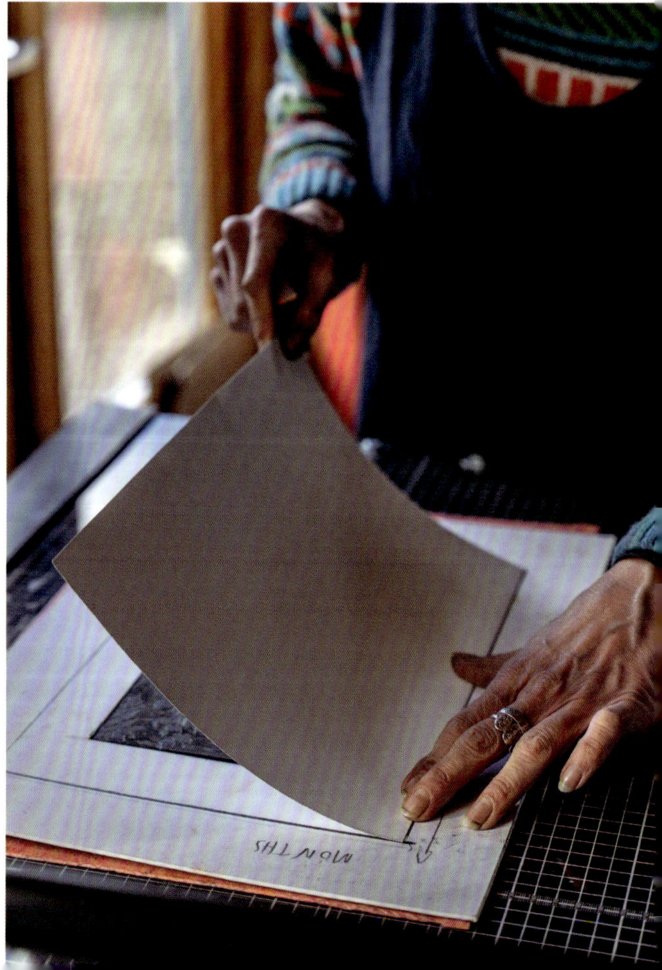

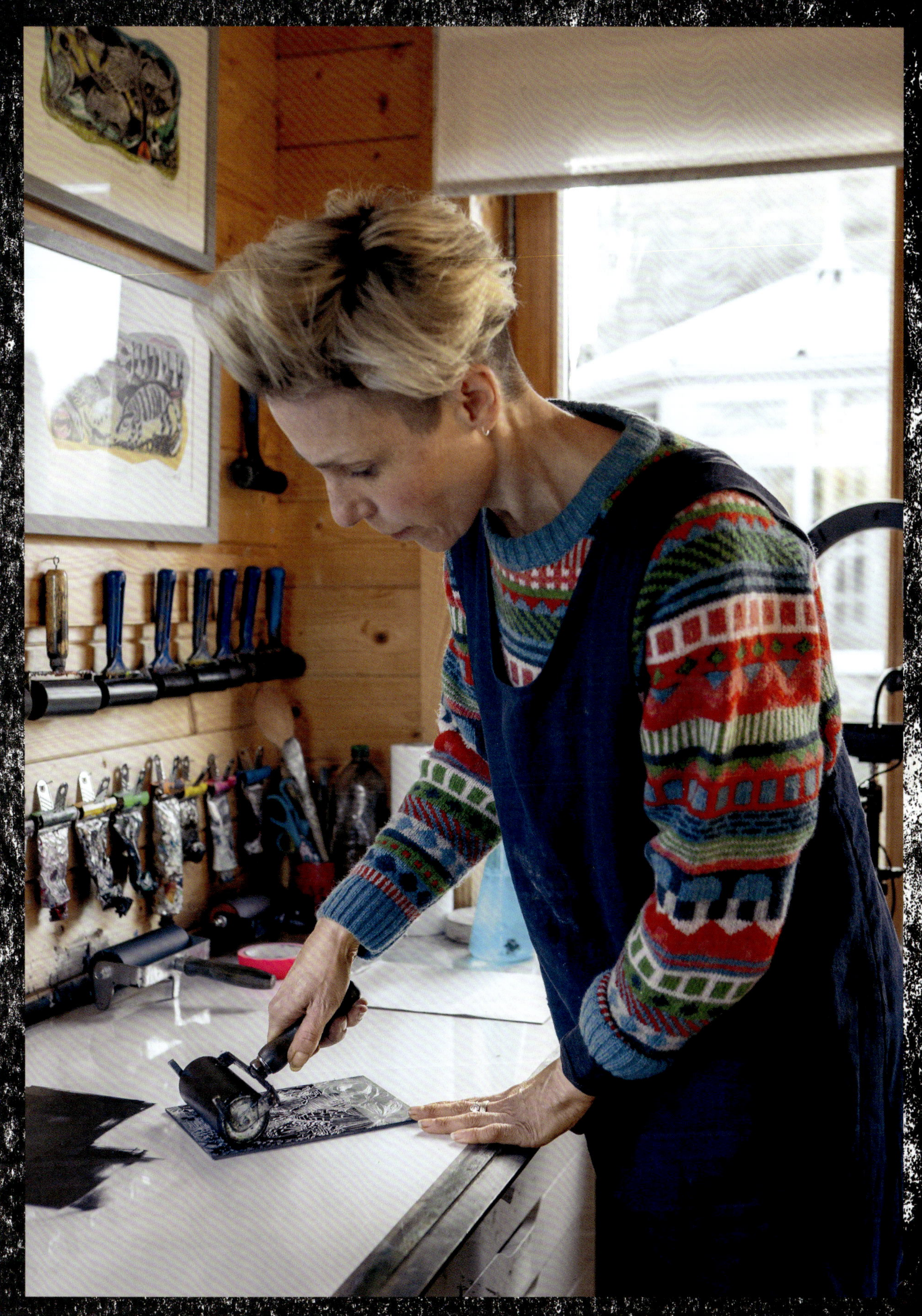

15 MULTI-BLOCK PRINTS

Over the next two projects I will show you how to produce prints using multiple blocks. In contrast to the reduction method technique in the previous chapter that uses just one block, you will be using more than one block for both projects.

KEY BLOCK METHOD

You Will Need

- Two pieces of lino
- Cutting mat
- Craft knife
- Cutting tools
- Metal ruler
- Selection of pencils, e.g. HB/2B
- Printing paper (all the same size)
- Paper for drawing and painting
- Rubber/eraser
- Marker pen or biro
- Tracing paper (cut to the same size as your printing paper)
- Stiff brush
- Relief printing ink
- Roller
- Inking slab
- Acrylic or gouache paints
- Paintbrushes
- Palette (or something to squeeze ink onto)
- Baren or wooden spoon
- Greyboard for your registration board
- Cleaning materials

In this project, you will be using two blocks: one for the detail, known as the 'key block', and the other for the colours. Start by selecting an image that both excites and inspires you. It could be one of your photographs or an image from a second-hand source like a book, magazine or the internet. Unlike the other projects, you won't be drawing from life but from your image. As I'm fascinated by unusual animals, I've chosen a fennec fox as the inspiration for my print.

1   Carefully cut your two pieces of lino to the same size using a craft knife, following the instructions on page 38. Next, start on your drawing – I'm using a combination of two different images as inspiration for my fox.

2   Keep your drawing loose and include as many different marks as you can to help inspire your carving. Don't be too tied to the image at this stage; allow blank spaces in your drawing to enable you to use your creativity as the print progresses.

3   Transfer the drawing to one of your blocks, using your method of choice (see page 29). Once you have transferred your drawing, reinforce the line with marker pen or biro. I'm using biro here as it works well on Japanese vinyl.

4   Begin carving – cutting the key block first gives you the detail of the print from which you can plan where the other colours will be placed. Continue carving until you are curious as to what the print looks like, then pull your first proof.

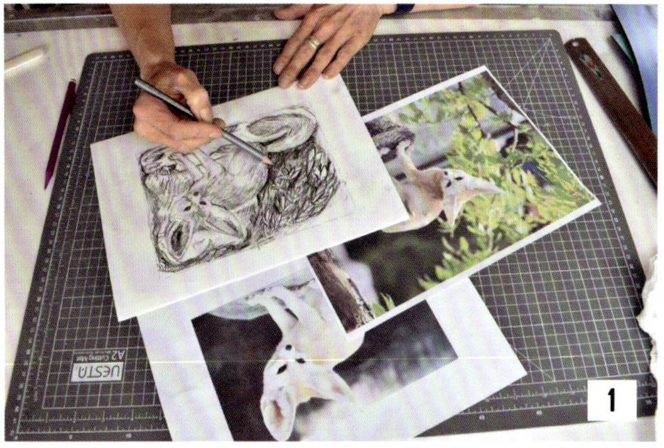

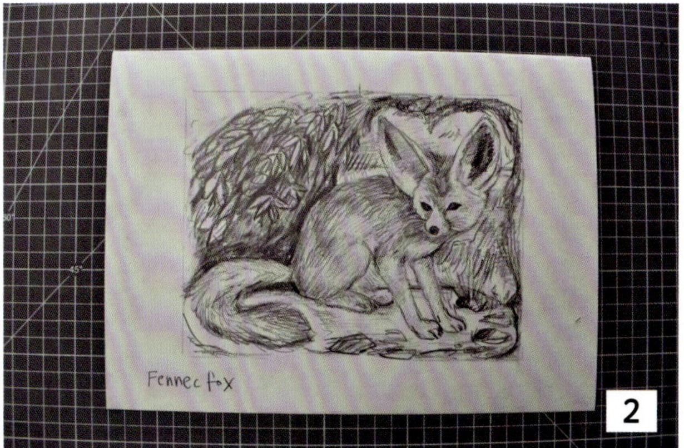

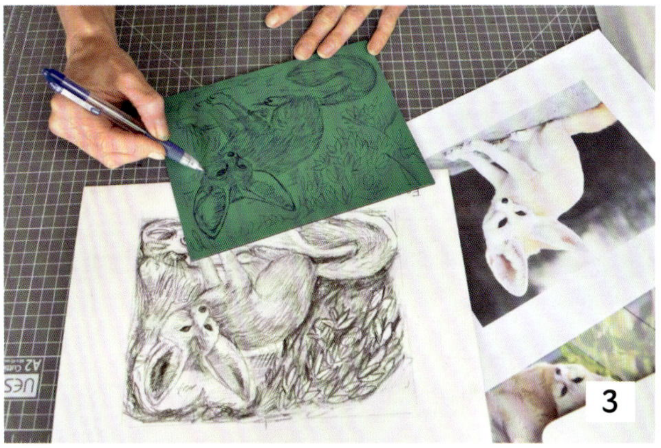

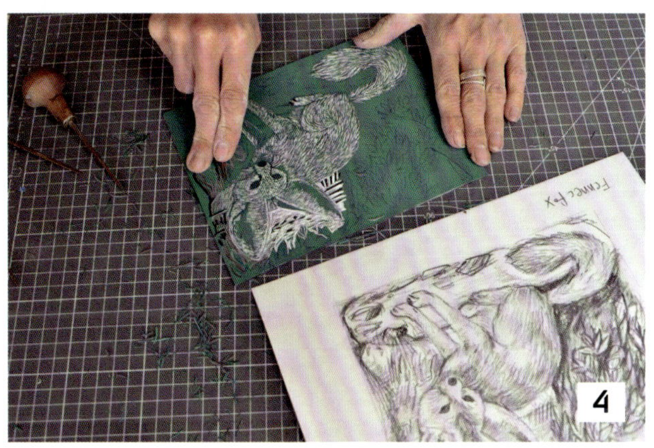

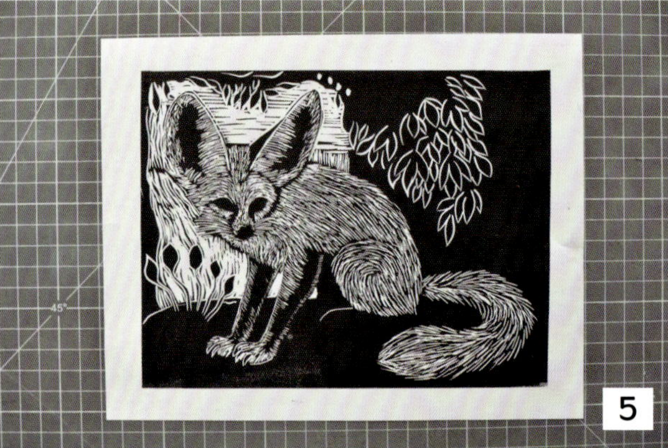

5

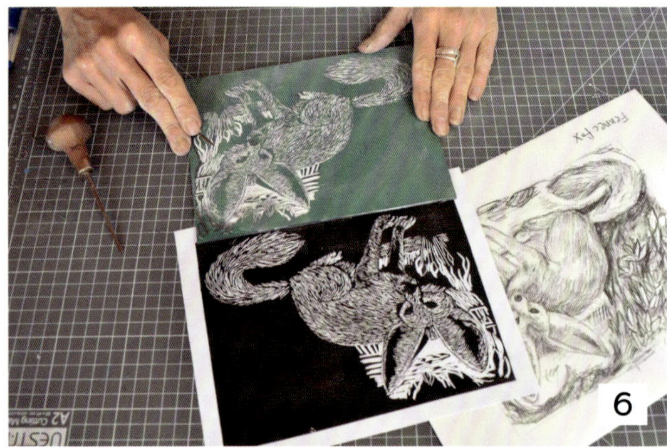

6

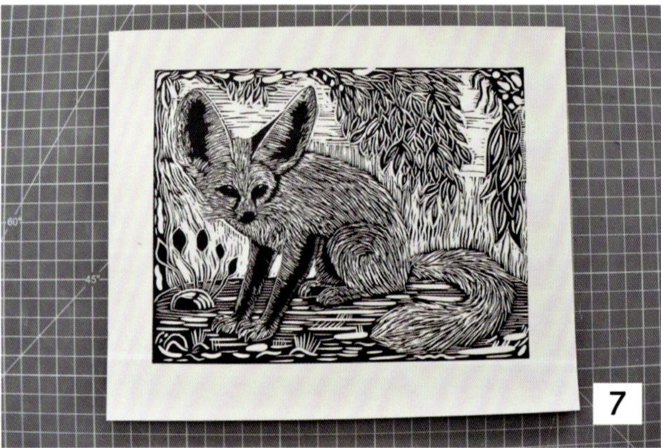

7

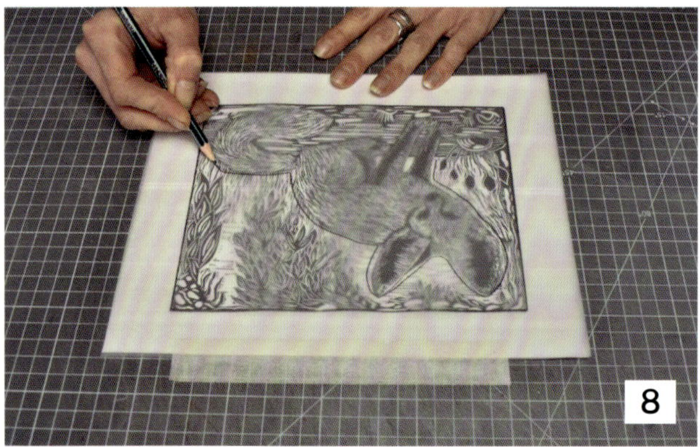

8

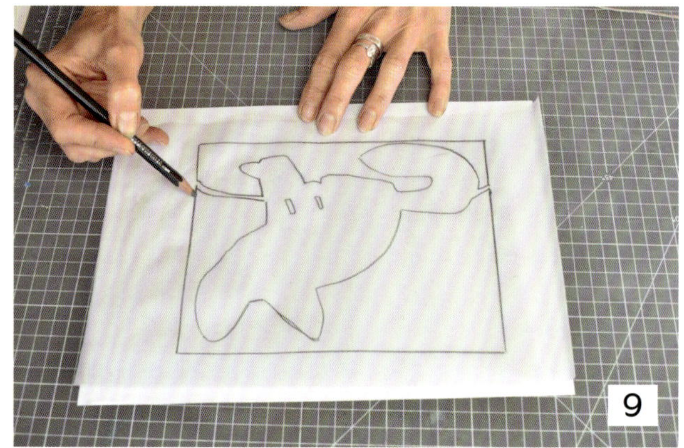

9

5 Here's my first proof. I can see that I need to carve away much more to allow the colours in the second block to come through.

6 Now is the time to veer away from the drawing and let the proof guide you – see how it suggests you move forward with the carving.

7 Once you have finished, print up your linocut onto one of your pre-cut pieces of paper. This is important for registration, as you are going to be using this print to figure out the colours for your second block. I've removed more than I normally do for a black-and-white print as I want the colour to show through, and obviously if you have too many uncarved areas, your colour will be hidden.

8 Let the print dry, then place your pre-cut tracing paper onto your print. Draw the shapes you would like for the colours of the second block.

9 Now trace your shapes onto paper. Repeat on four pieces of paper so you have plenty of options to work your colours out. I have chosen two simple shapes for my blocks of colour and to leave the fox in black and white. You can be more experimental, though.

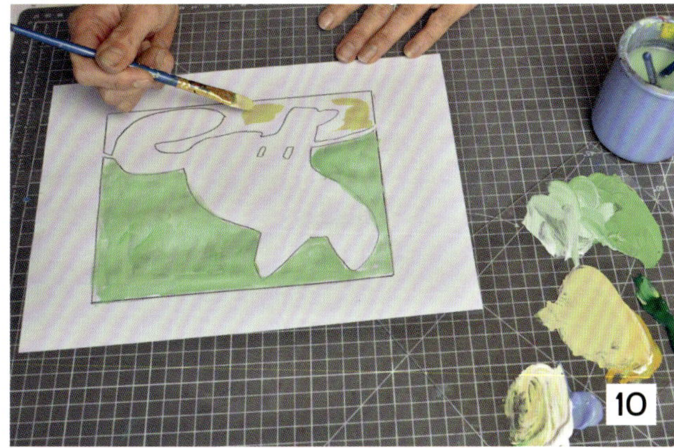

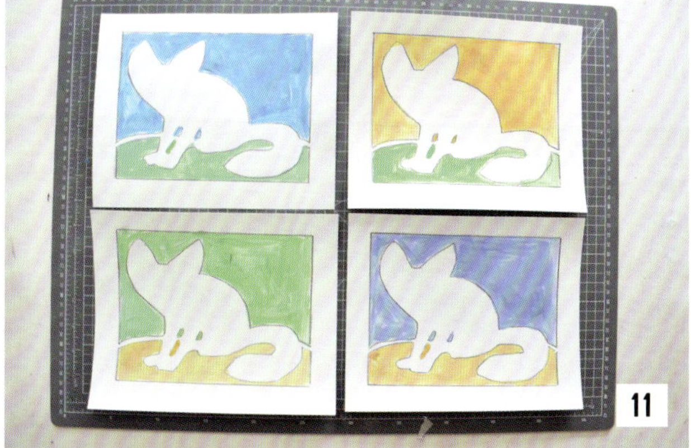

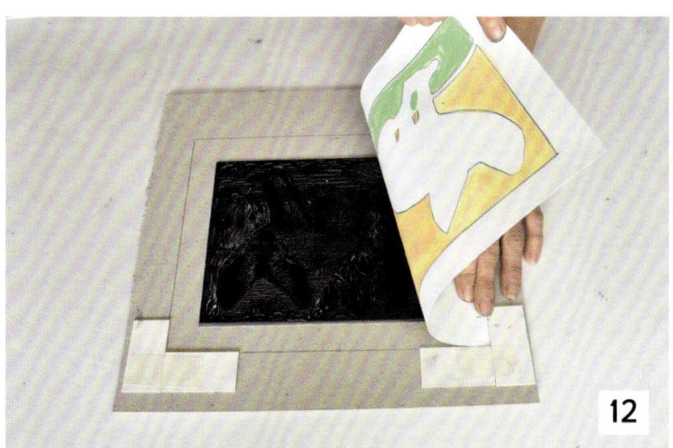

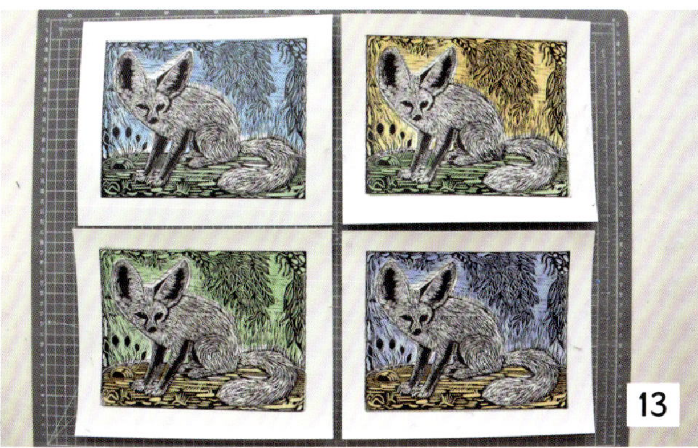

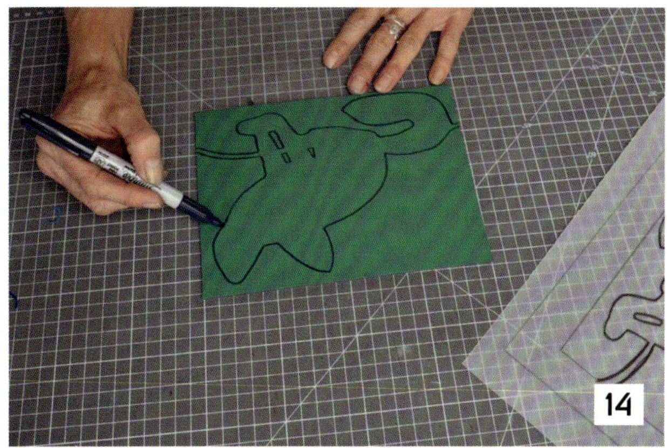

10 Use acrylic or gouache paints to fill in the background in colours that you feel would suit your image.

11 Here you can see that I've tried out a few different colour combinations.

12 Now it's time to see what the colours look like with the key block printed on top. If you haven't done so already, then now is the time to make your registration board following the instructions on page 58. Ink up your block, place one of the coloured sheets onto your registration board and then burnish. Repeat for all the other coloured sheets.

13 Here are my test prints. I decided to go for yellow on top and green on the bottom for my edition as I felt this was the most successful.

14 Now it's time to prepare the second block. Use your earlier tracing paper (or you might want to do another, but again make sure you use the same size paper) and transfer to the block. Reinforce the trace with marker pen.

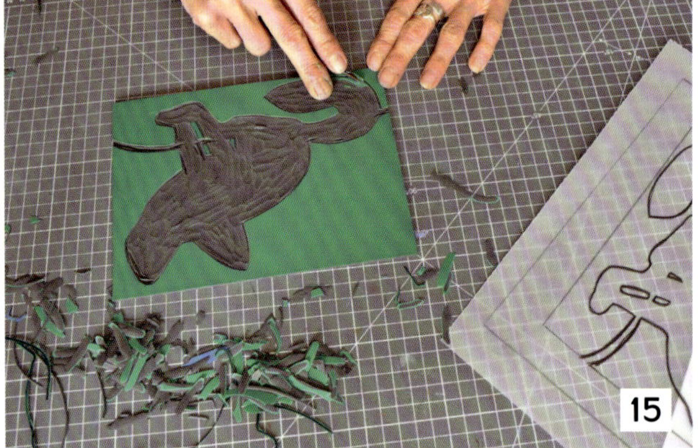

15

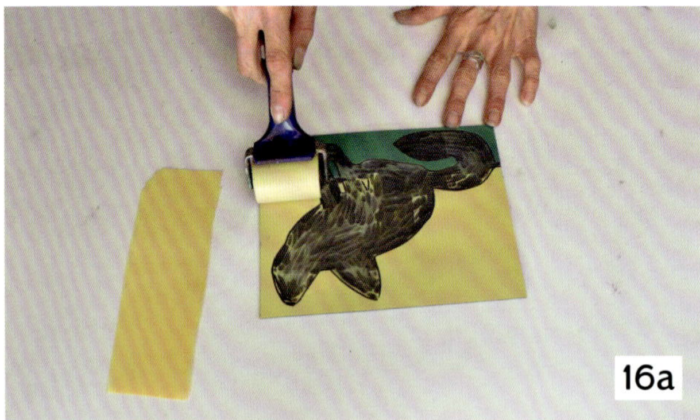

16a

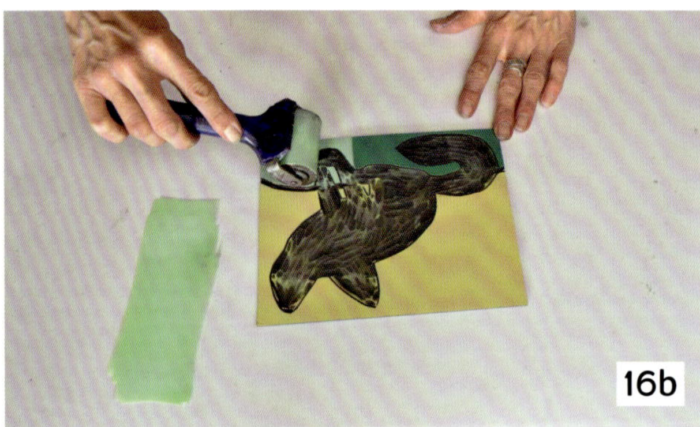

16b

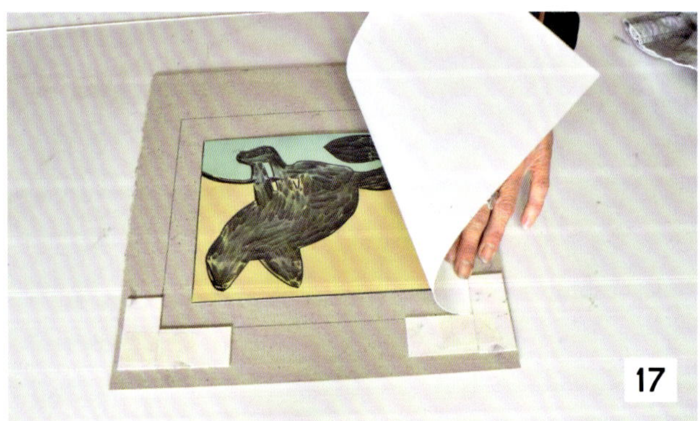

17

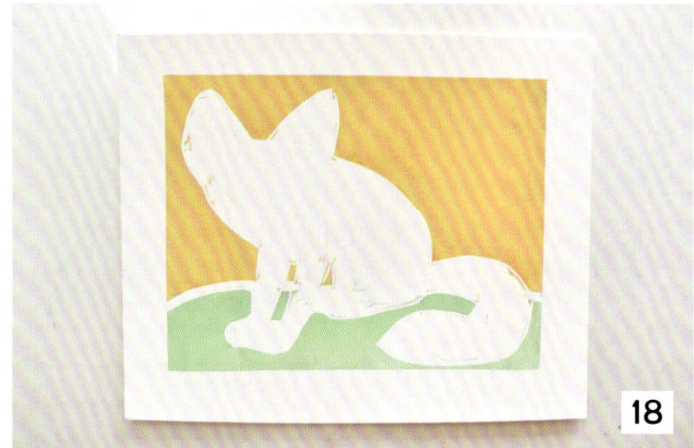

18

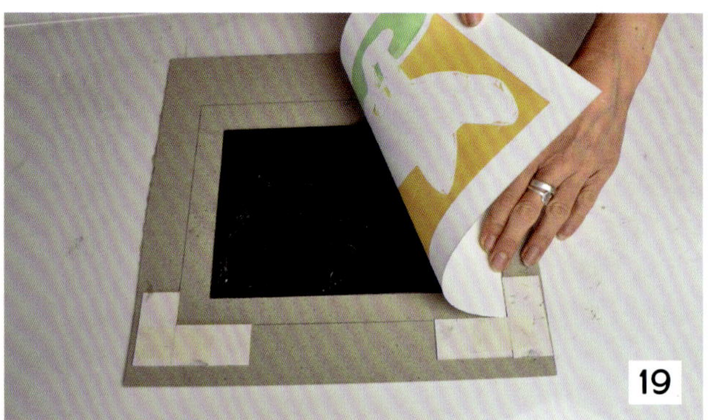

19

15 Carve out the areas that you want to remain in black and white (for me, it's the fox). The areas you leave in relief will be your coloured areas.

16 Mix up your chosen colours and ink up the separate areas – I used a smaller roller for this. I also used a rag to clean up the raised areas in the fox as they will create noise when printed.

17 Place your block in your registration board and print up.

18 Here's the print. You will notice that there is some noise in the white area of the fox, but I'm not worried about this as the key block will cover it up. At this point, make sure you continue to print the rest of the edition, using up all the ink. Let the prints dry overnight, then you will be ready to print the key block on top.

19 When the coloured prints are dry, ink up your key
   block and place it in the registration board. Position
   one of the prints on top, then burnish it and peel
   back the paper. If you are happy with your print,
   repeat for the whole edition.

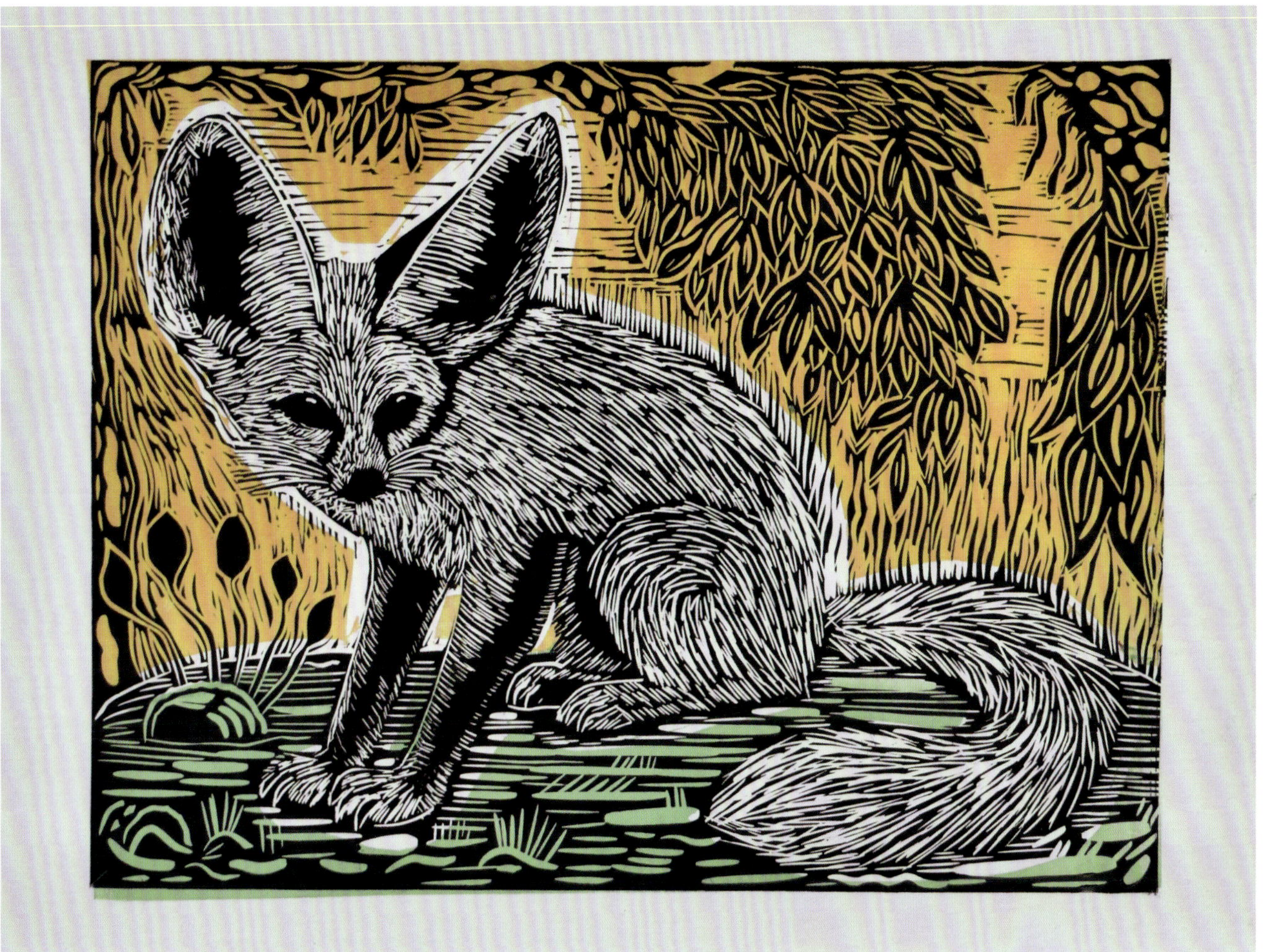

FOUR-BLOCK PRINT

In this project we are going to be using four separate blocks to create a print. Instead of relying on a key block to 'hold it all together', as we did for the fennec fox, we will be using a different block for each colour to build and create the image. This gives you greater flexibility and more scope for experimentation. You can also play around with different colours and reprint more at a later date, if needed.

For this project, source an object that holds a memory for you. It could be an object or photograph from your travels or something that reminds you of a past event or someone special in your life. The most important thing to consider when choosing your object or image is that it can be broken down into four different colours – you will build up the image this way.

I've chosen my Japanese Kokeshi doll, which I bought in Kyoto when I was visiting Japan a few years ago. I love the fact that it is hand painted and that each one is unique. It is also ideal for this project as I can clearly see how the different colour layers will work.

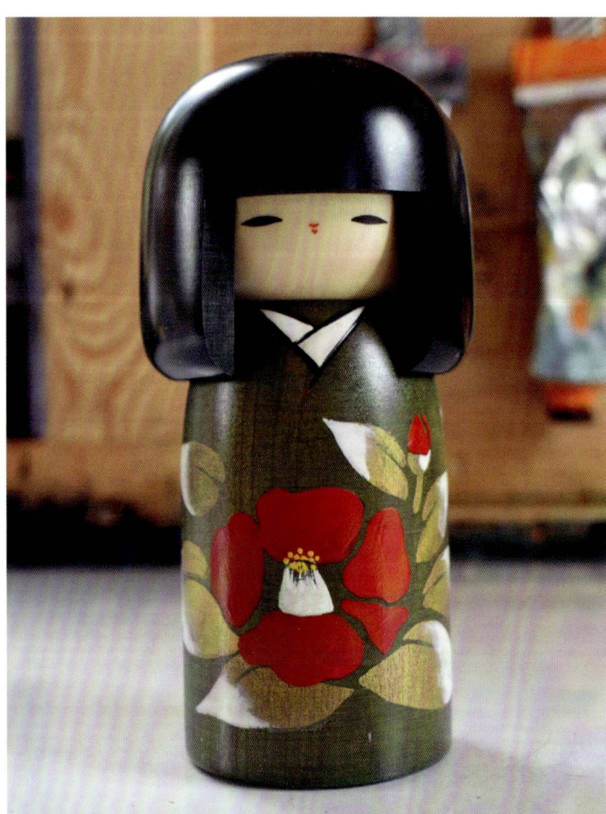

NOTE

As you are printing multiple layers, it's wise to leave the prints to dry before progressing with the next layer, so you might want to work on this project over a few days. I will also be using the Ternes Burton method of registration for this project (see page 60).

You Will Need

- **Four pieces of lino (all the same size)**
- **Cutting mat**
- **Craft knife**
- **Metal ruler**
- **Fifteen sheets of paper (cut to the same size)**
- **Selection of pencils, e.g. HB/2B**
- **Rubber/eraser**
- **Acrylic paints**
- **Paintbrushes**
- **Palette (or something to squeeze ink onto)**
- **Tracing paper**
- **Permanent marker**
- **Cutting tools**
- **Stiff brush**
- **Relief printing ink**
- **Inking slab**
- **Roller**
- **Ternes Burton clips**
- **Newsprint for mask**
- **Baren or wooden spoon**
- **Greyboard for registration board**
- **Cleaning materials**

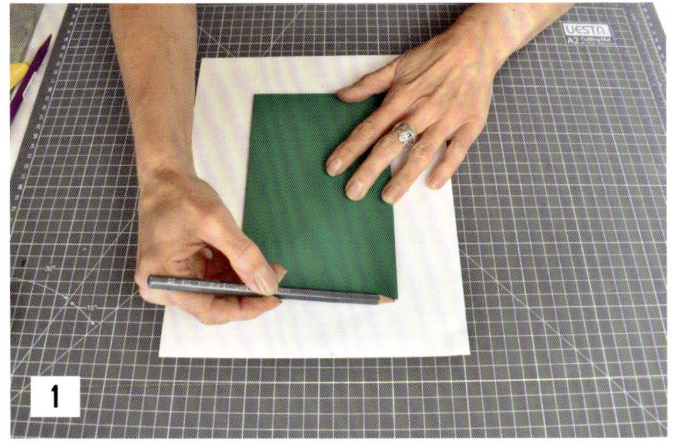

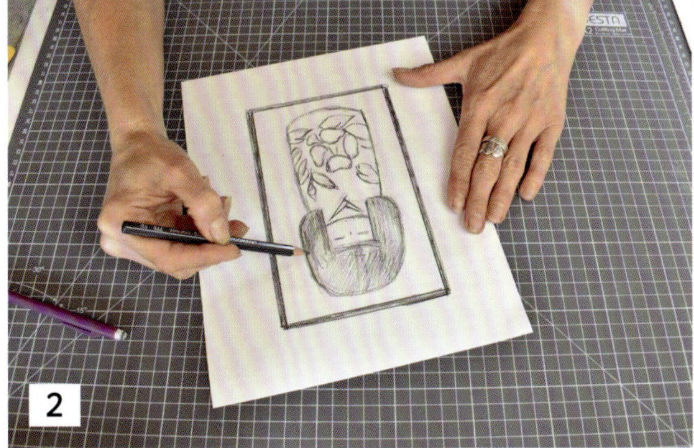

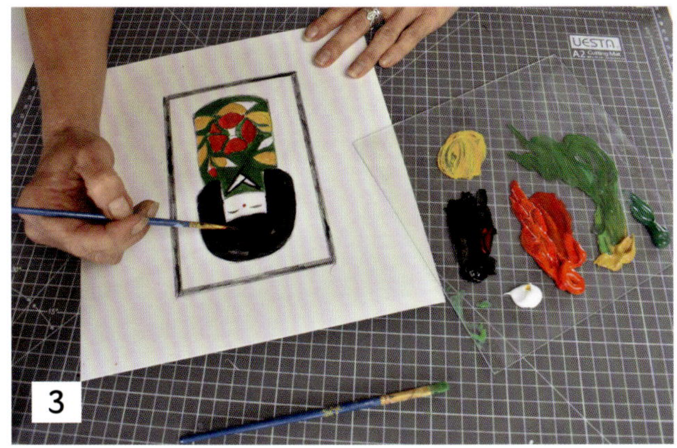

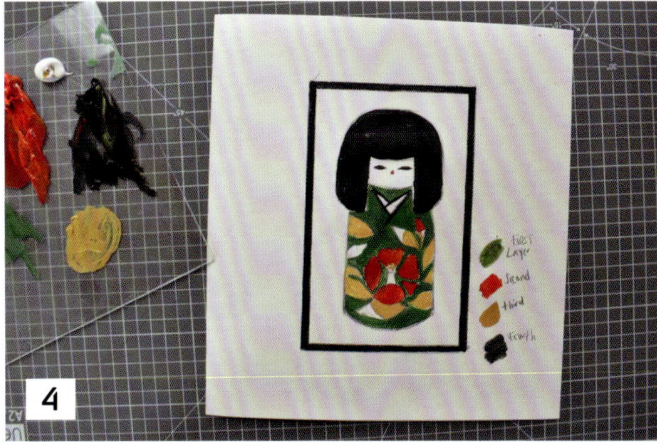

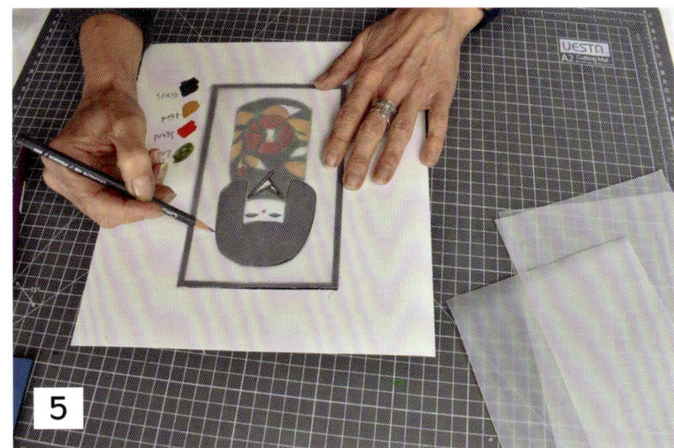

4   While you are painting, you can start to figure out what order you would like to print your colours in. As a rule of thumb, you normally print light to dark, but feel free to experiment with this. For me, it makes sense to print the green first then the red, gold and finally black. Here you can see I have carefully planned out the colours I am going to use.

5   Cut four pieces of tracing paper to match the size of your painting. Place them on top and trace each individual colour layer onto the separate pieces.

1   Carefully cut your four pieces of lino to the same size. It's important to cut them as accurately as you can, as this will aid correct registration. Draw around one of your pieces of lino.

2   Sketch your object or image inside, paying attention to composition.

3   Once you are happy with your drawing, it's time to get your paints out! Use acrylic or gouache paints to carefully paint your design using your chosen four colours.

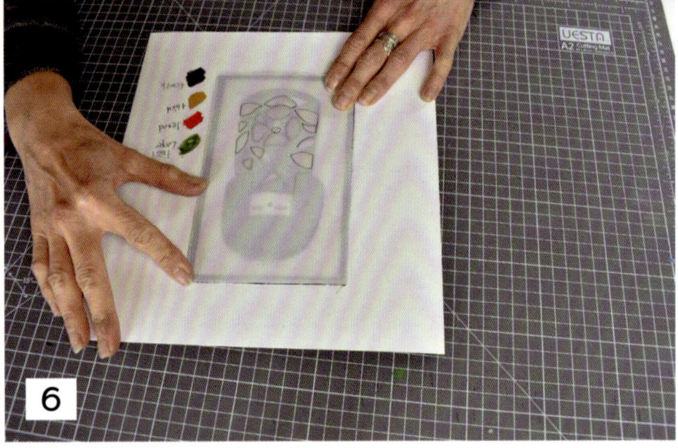

6

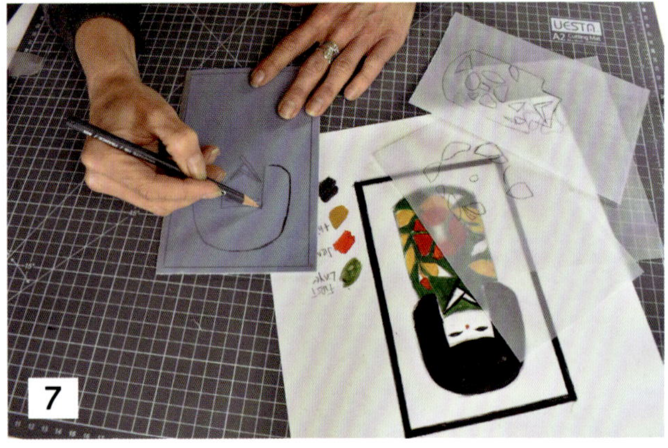

7

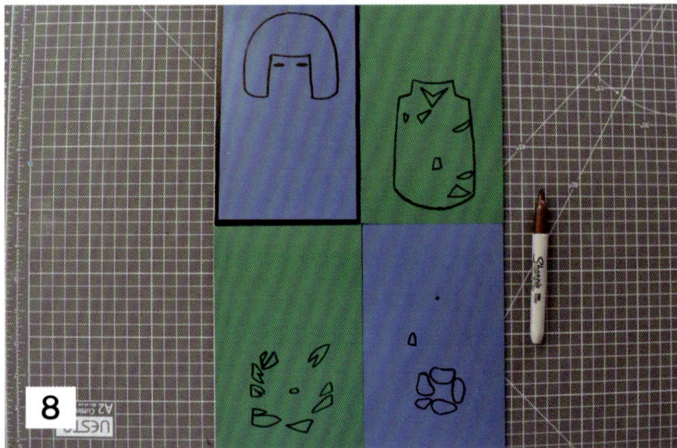

8

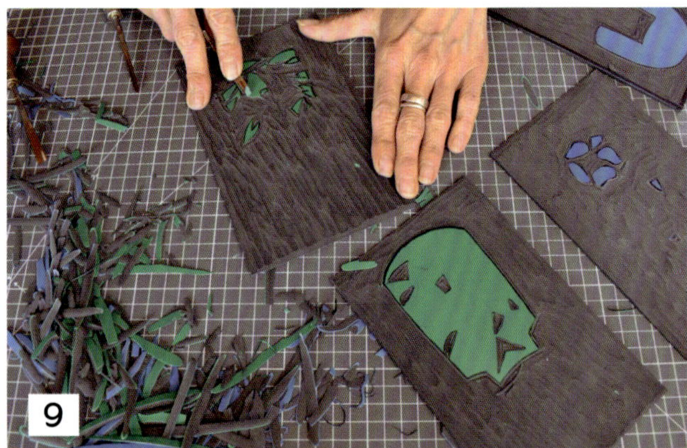

9

6   Repeat until you have four sheets: one for each of
    the colours. Place them all on top of each other to
    check they line up correctly.

7   Place the tracing face down onto the block and
    transfer. Repeat for all four tracings.

8   Repeat for all four blocks and reinforce the pencil
    line with permanent marker. Here I have my black
    block (top left), green block (top right), gold block
    (bottom left) and red block (bottom right).

9   Carve the blocks carefully. I cut around all the
    outlines with a fine V tool and then clear away the
    outside using a large U tool.

10 The finished blocks.

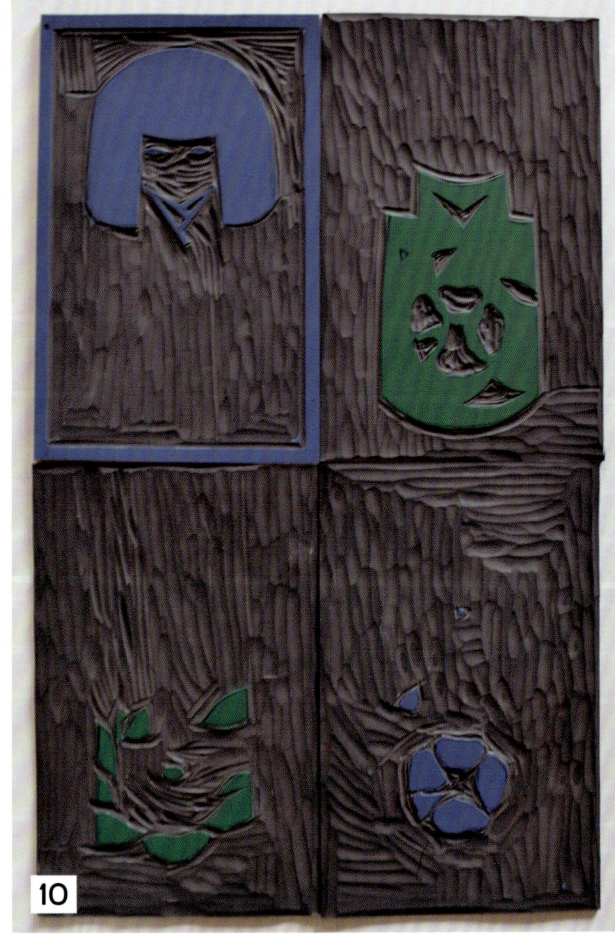

10

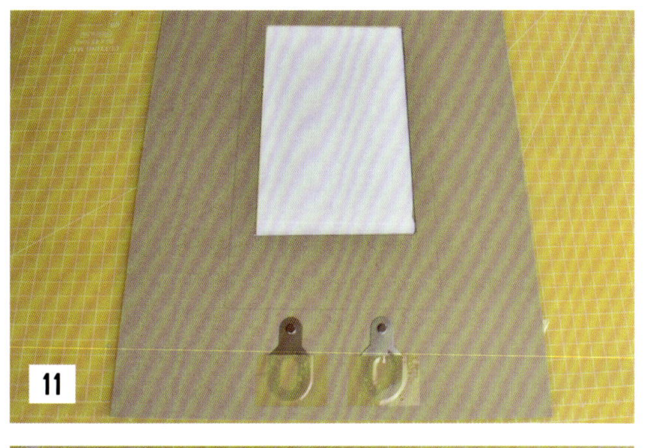

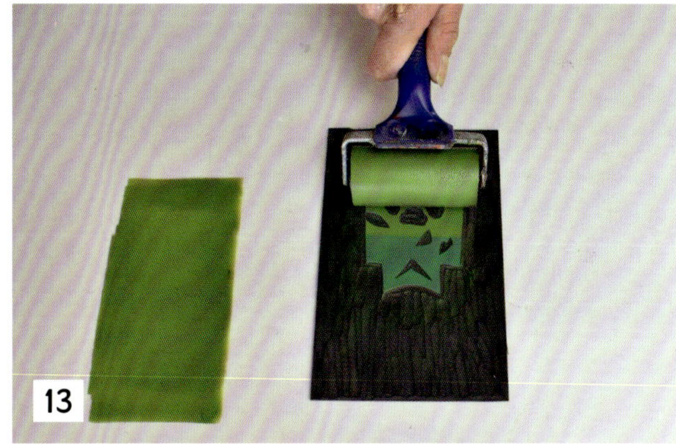

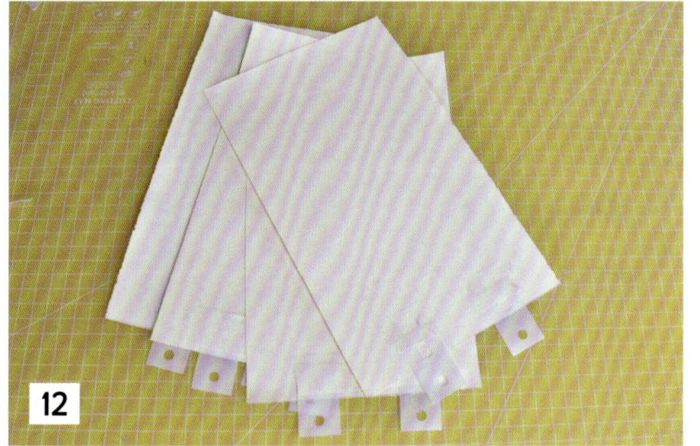

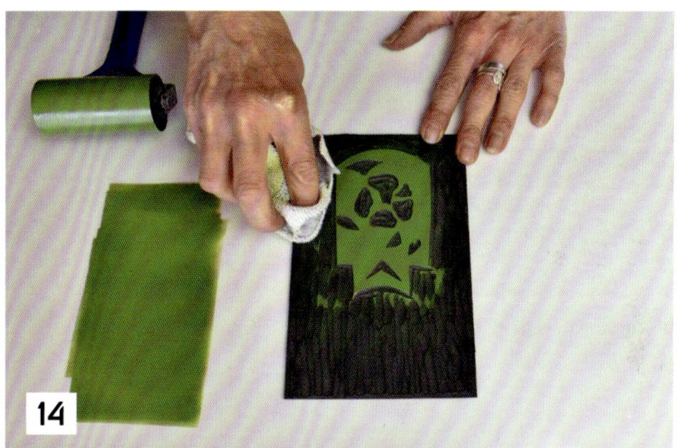

11 Prepare your Ternes Burton registration board, following instructions on page 60.

12 Prepare your papers, adding the tabs.

13 Ink up your first colour (for me, this is green).

14 Carefully wipe up the areas of noise that you don't want to print. Alternatively, you can use a mask (see page 69).

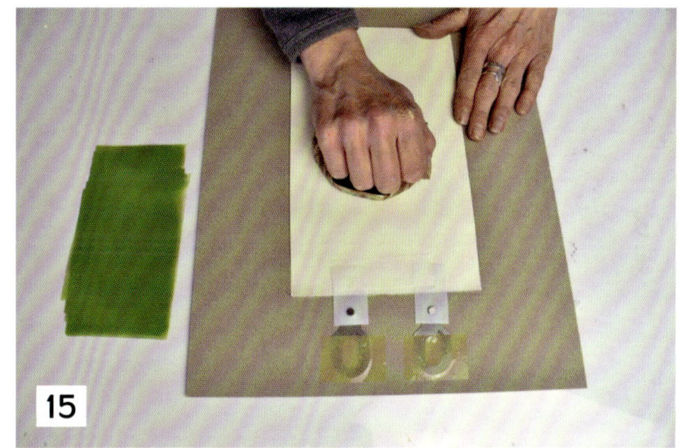

15 Burnish as usual.

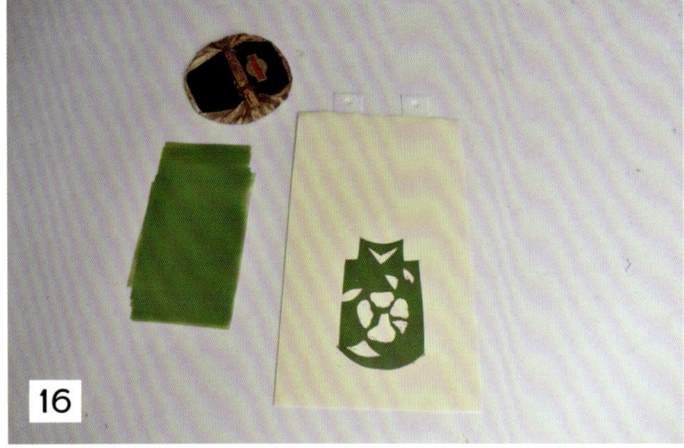

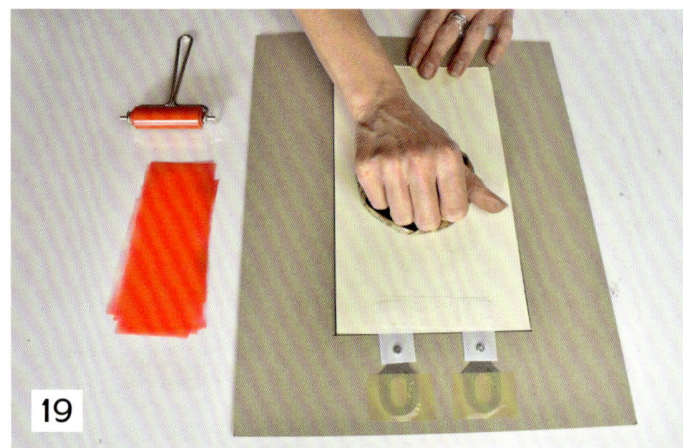

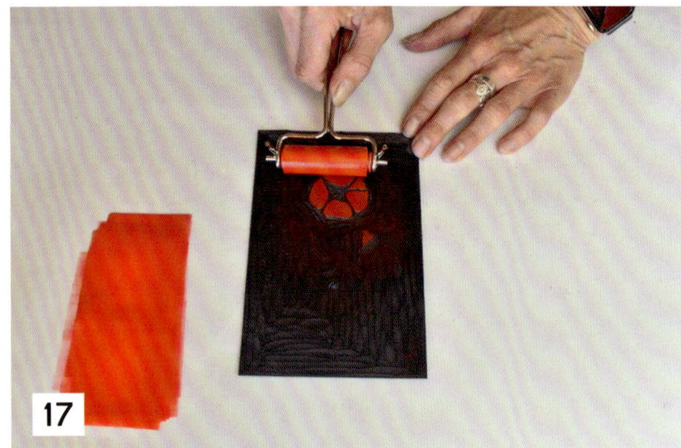

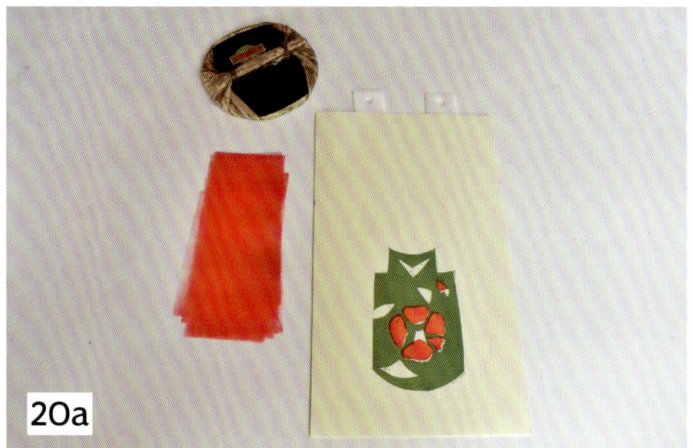

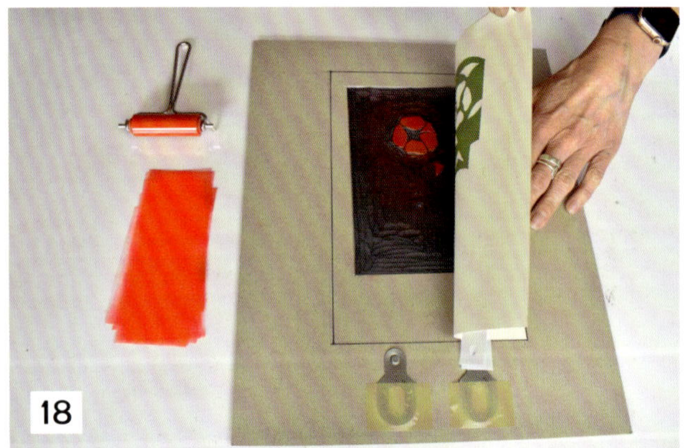

18 Place your second inked-up block into the registration board. Take one of your first layer prints and place it carefully on top.

19 Burnish, then pull back the print.

16 Here is the first layer (in my case, green). Repeat for all your other sheets of paper. If you are using oil-based inks it's wise to leave each layer to dry overnight before printing the next layer on top.

17 Ink up the second layer. I use a small roller here so I can be more precise with my inking.

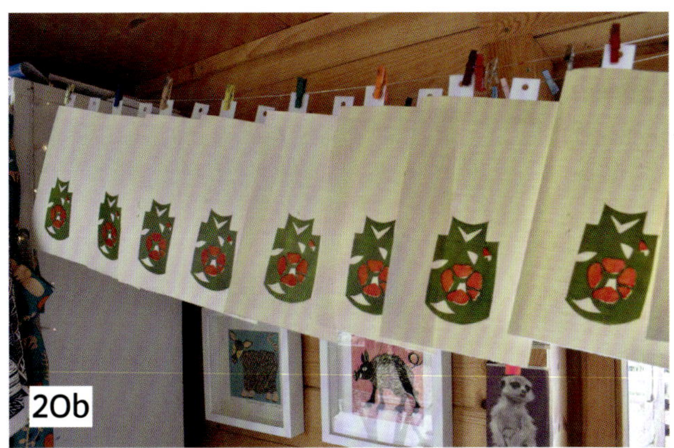

20b

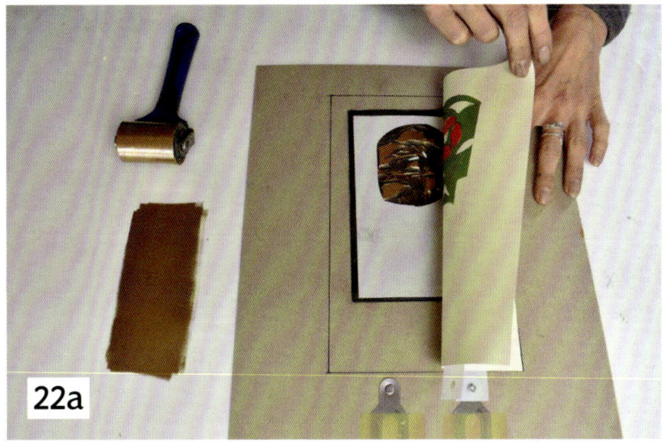

22a

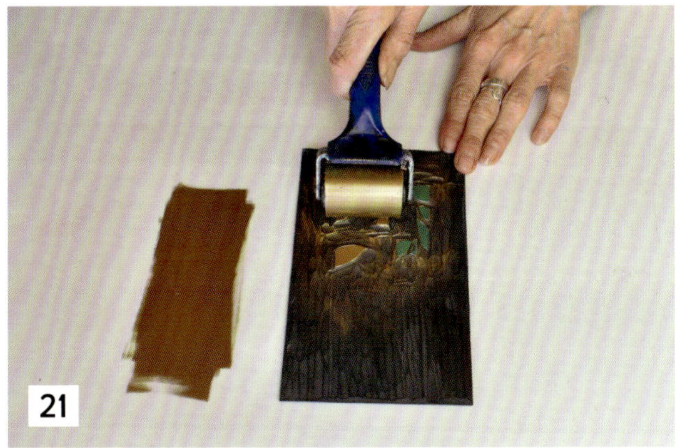

21

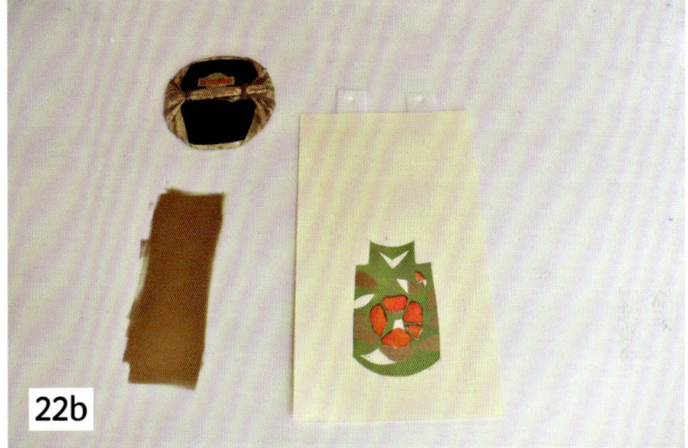

22b

20 Here you can see the first layer (green) with the second layer (red) printed on top. Repeat for all the other first layer prints, then leave them to dry.

21 Once your two-layered prints are dry, you are now ready to ink up your third colour (in my case, gold).

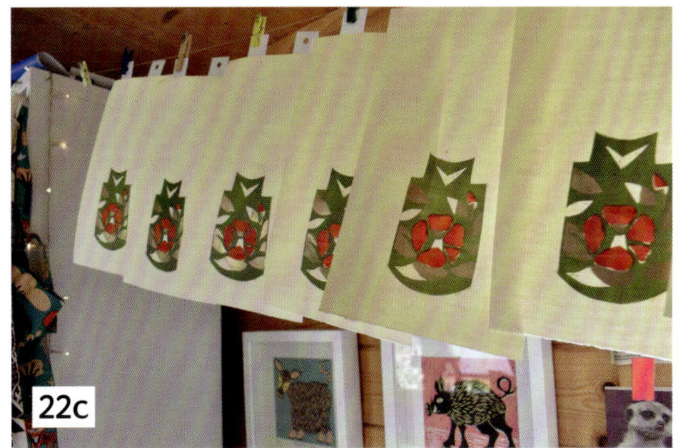

22c

22 For this block, I'm using a newsprint mask to prevent any noise transferring to the block and thus to the paper. Place one of your two-layered prints carefully on top, burnish and pull back the paper. Repeat for all the other prints, then, once again, let them dry.

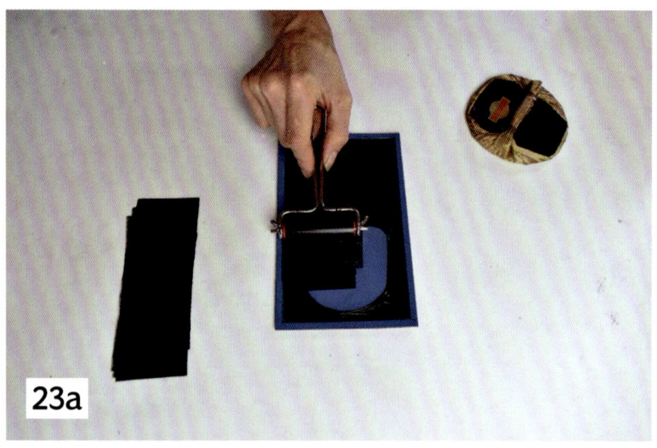

23a

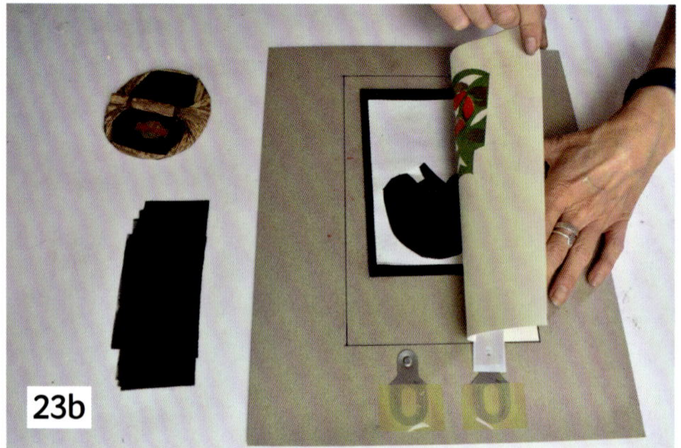

23b

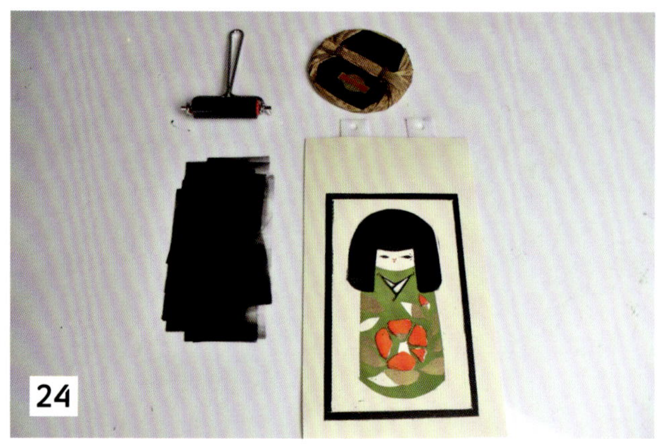

24

23 Once your prints are dry, you can print the final block (in my case, the black block).

24 Repeat step 23 on the rest of the prints.

25 Here's my final print, with all four colours.

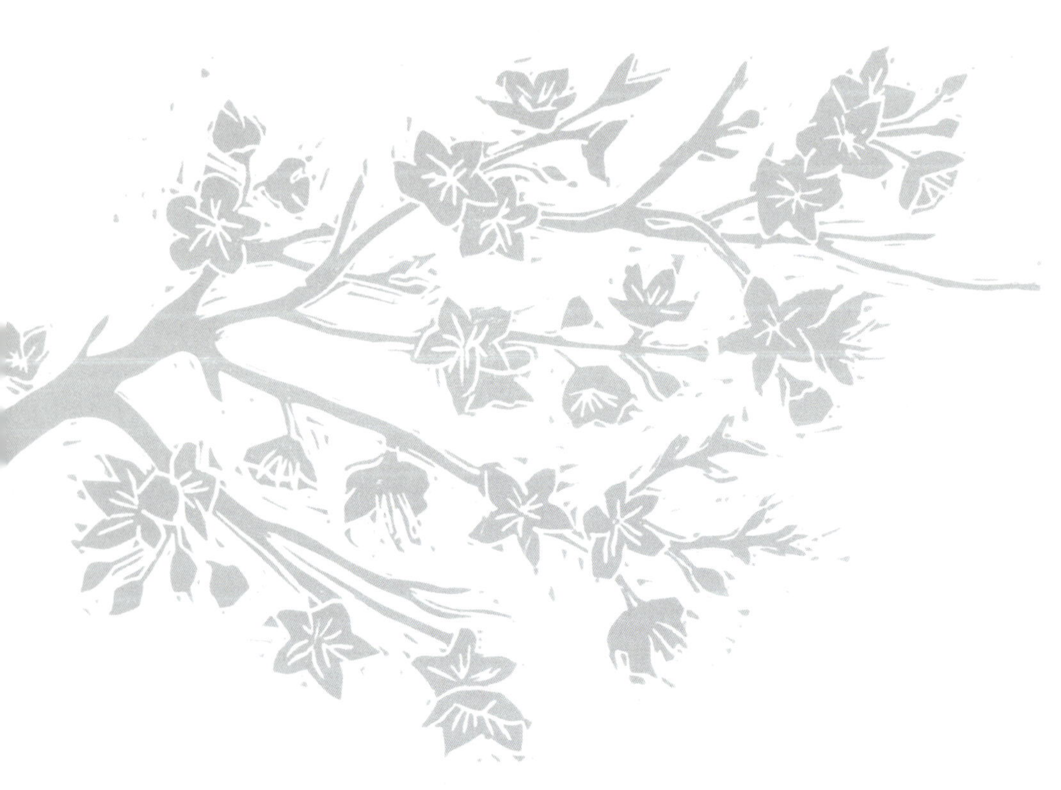

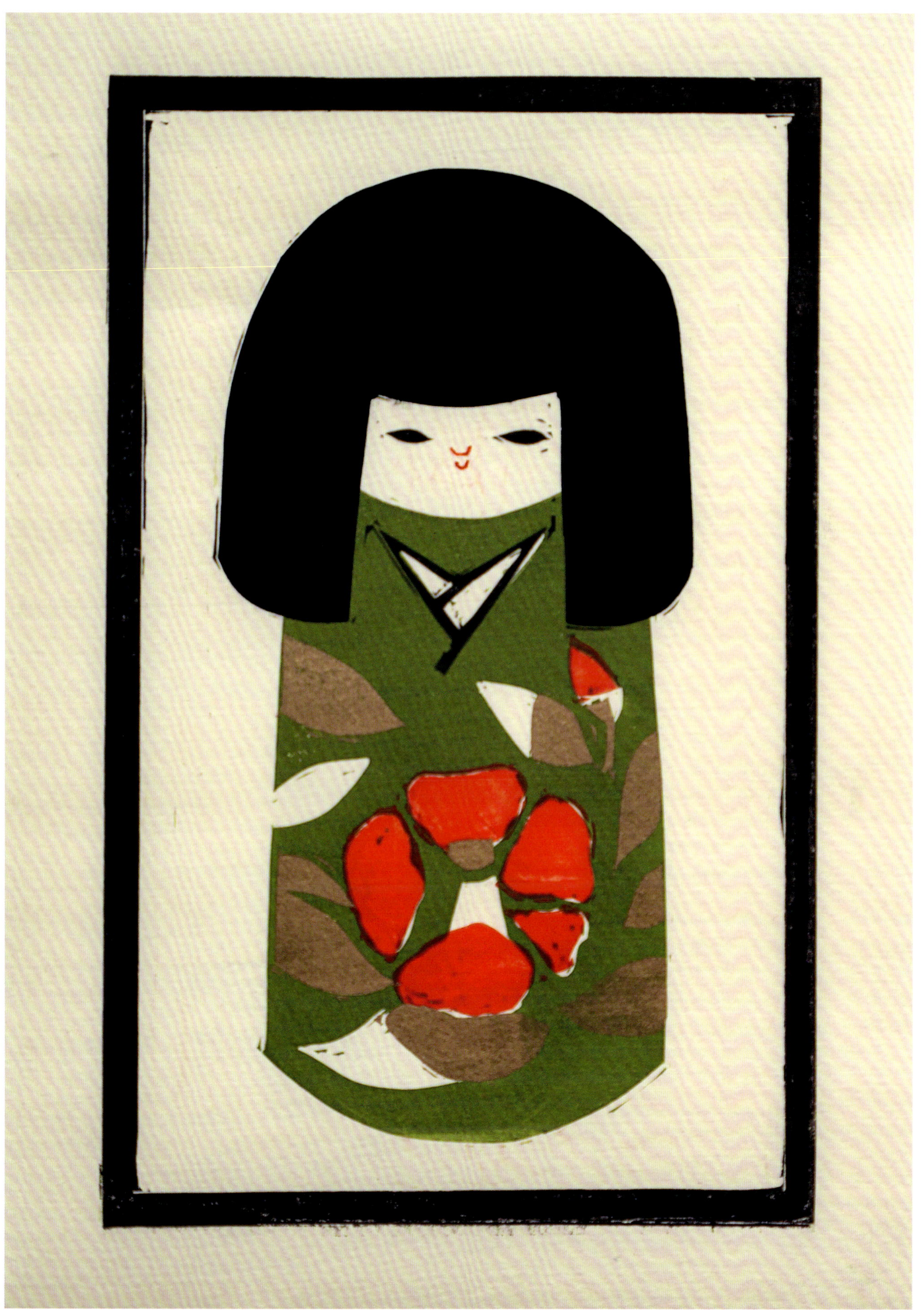

AN INTERVIEW WITH MEG JUSTICE

How did you first get into printmaking?

I took one class on printmaking during my time at Auburn University years ago. I really liked it and still have all the prints I made during that time. My focus, though, was on painting and illustration, and this is what I pursued throughout my art career.

I began printmaking full-time in 2016. I wanted a way to reproduce illustrative art and my designs without having to digitally print them. Printmaking is a perfect medium for this, and I consider each handmade print fine art and one of a kind. I love the whole process of printmaking, from the sketch to the carving to the final printed piece.

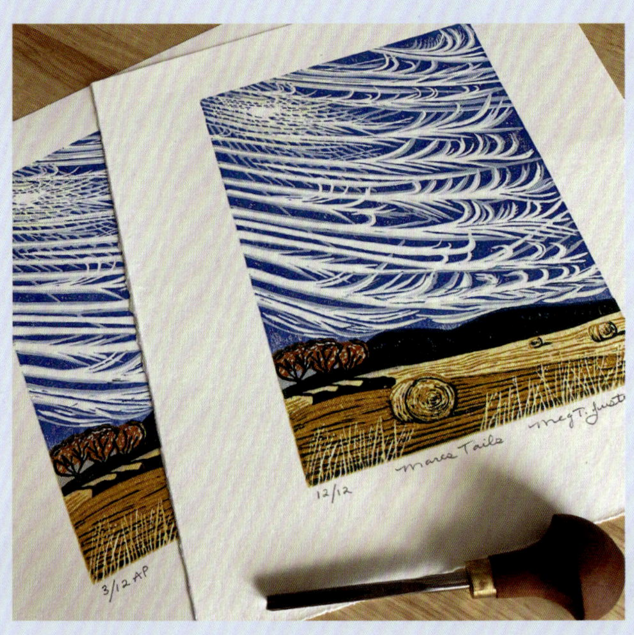

Could you tell us about a specific print and the story behind it?

Most all of my work has a story or memory attached to it. A piece entitled 'The Acrobats' is one that comes to mind. It depicts the swallows that we watch on our property in late summer. They seem so joyful and acrobatic, racing and looping over the Queen Anne's lace growing in the pasture, and through the columns on our porches.

What inspires your work?

The inspiration for my art comes from the beauty in nature and the countryside where I live – the beautiful southern Appalachians and Tennessee River of North Alabama. I'm drawn to our beautiful skies and country landscapes and the wild bird population that thrives here.

@meg_t_justice_art

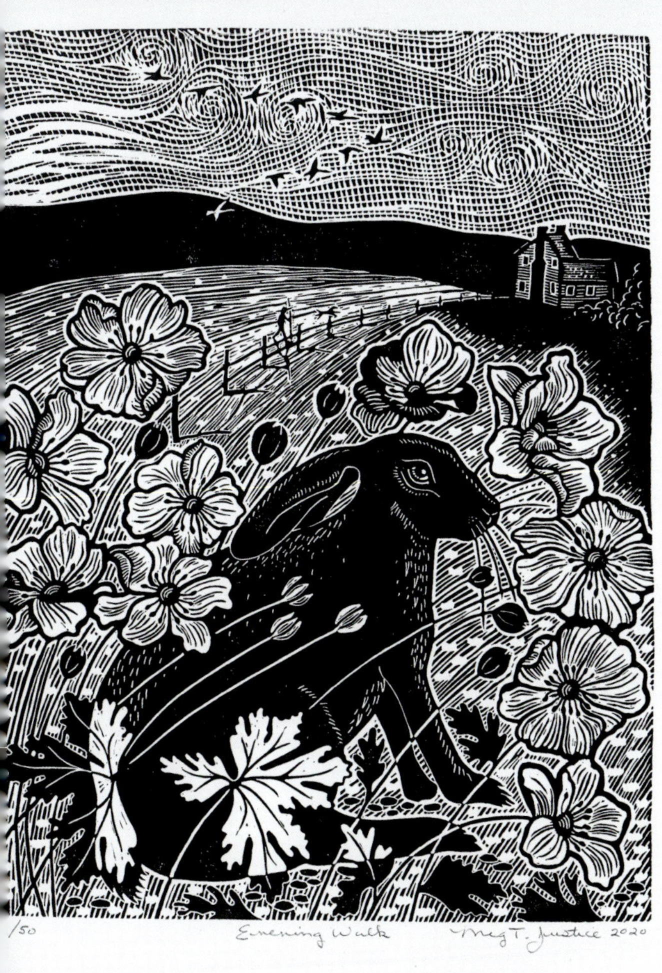
/50
Evening Walk
Meg T. Justice 2020

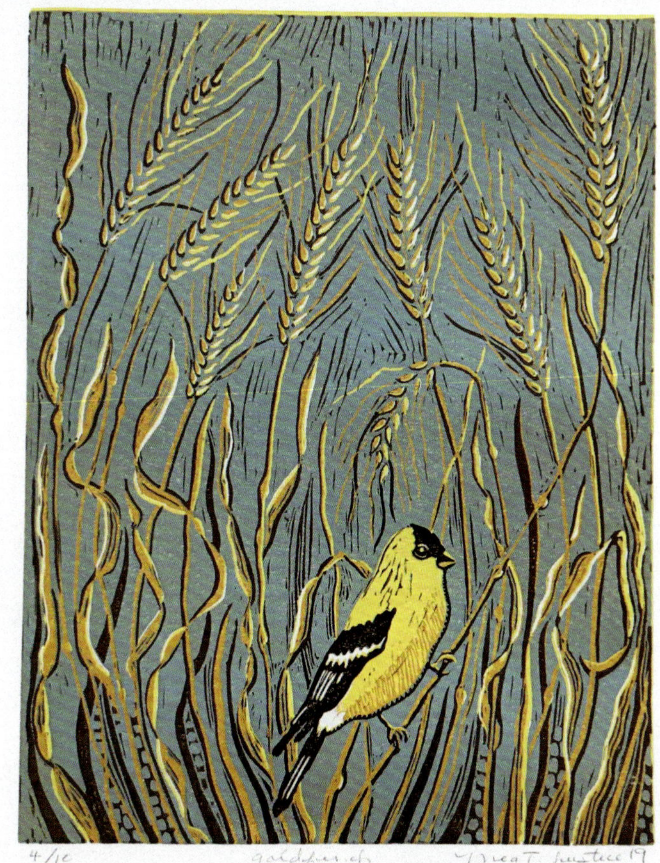
4/10
goldfinch
Meg T. Justice 19

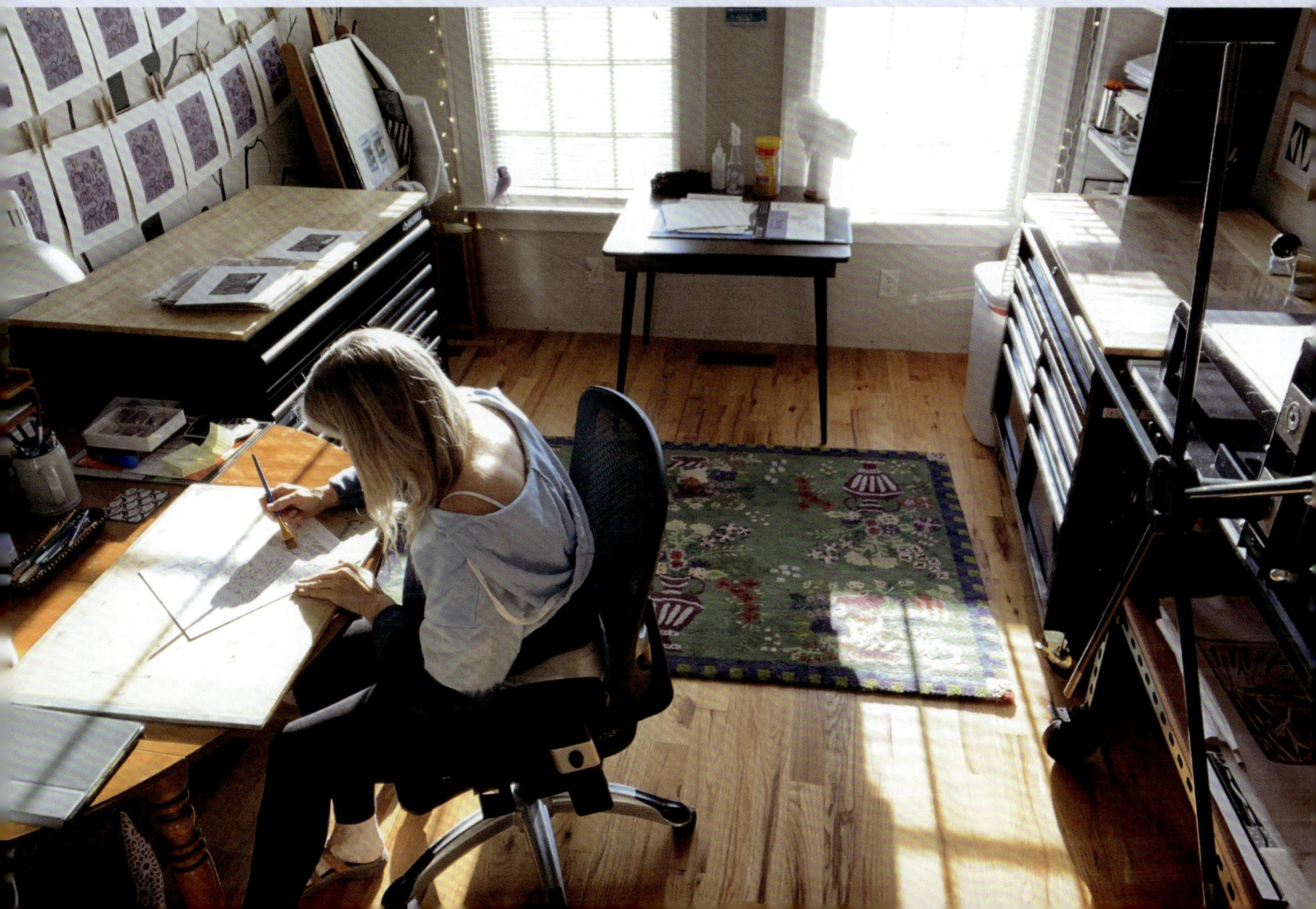

16 DISPLAYING MULTIPLE PRINTS

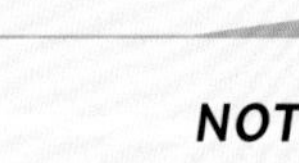

For this project you are going to create a concertina (or zigzag) book. It's a great way to show multiple prints – or a series of prints – in a simple book format. The book will be made from two pieces of paper that are folded one way and then the other to make a zigzag. The pages can be viewed individually, like a traditional book, or opened out to be viewed in full.

As with the previous projects, you are going to start with a sketch, preferably drawn from observation. My sketchbook is full of drawings of the flowers in my garden, and I thought that a selection of them would make a nice series of prints. When you are thinking of ideas for your book, it might help you to think about a collection of images that have some sort of narrative. Play around with your sketches and see what you come up with.

NOTE

A bone folder (or folding bone) is a dull-edged hand tool used to fold and crease material in crafts such as bookbinding, cardmaking, origami and other papercrafts that require a sharp crease or fold. As an alternative, you can use the side or edge of a ruler.

CONCERTINA BOOK

It's a good idea to choose your book cover paper first as this will help you decide on the colours for your prints. The concertina book is such an adaptable project; once you have made one book, you can continue to experiment with different heights and lengths of paper.

You Will Need

- Six pieces of lino, cut to 8 x 8 cm
- Cutting mat
- Craft knife
- Metal ruler
- Long piece of paper for drawing
- Selection of pencils, e.g. HB/2B
- Rubber/eraser
- Tracing/carbon paper
- Biro or marker pen (optional)
- Cutting tools
- Stiff brush
- Talcum powder (optional)
- Relief printing ink
- Inking slab
- Roller
- Photocopy paper for proofing paper
- A3 piece of greyboard
- Piece of paper, measuring 9 x 36 cm
- Piece of paper, measuring 9 x 38 cm
- Baren or wooden spoon
- Six pieces of lightweight patterned paper for end covers, measuring 9 cm x 9 cm
- PVA glue, glue brush and container for glue – I use milk bottle tops
- Bone folder (or alternative)
- Cleaning materials

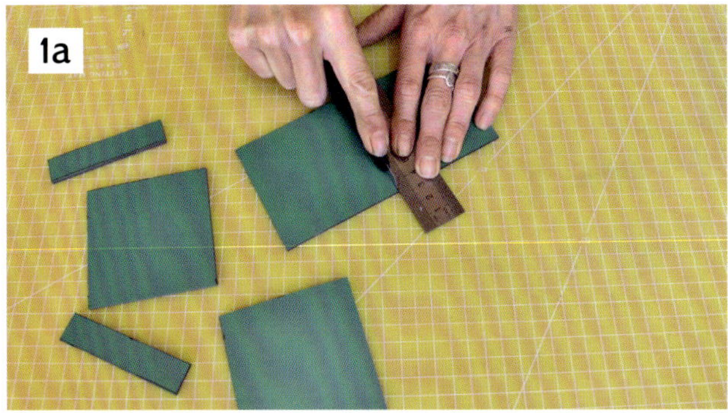

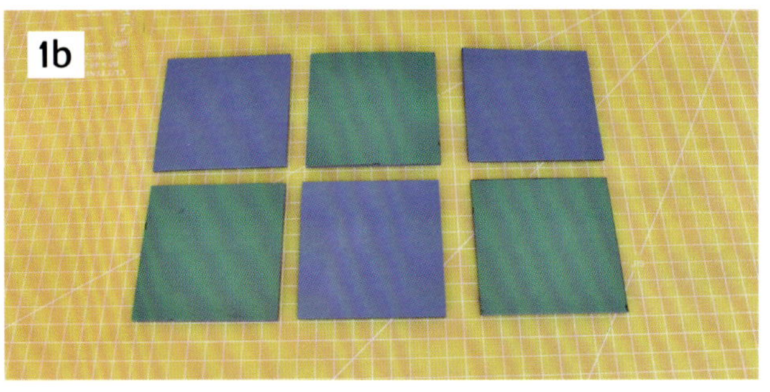

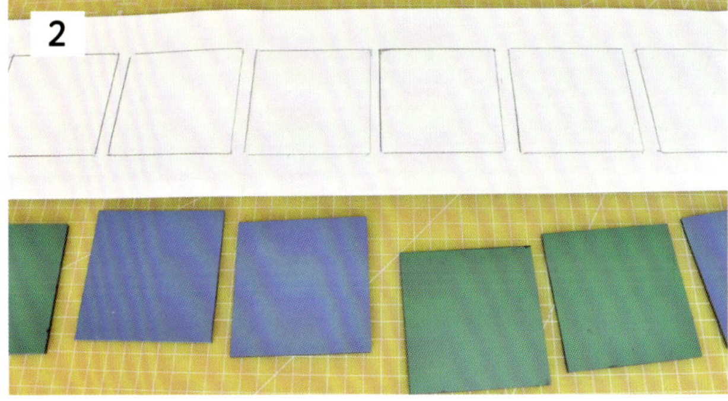

1   Carefully cut up all your pieces of lino to the same size using a metal ruler and cutting knife.

2   Draw around each of the blocks onto your long piece of drawing paper.

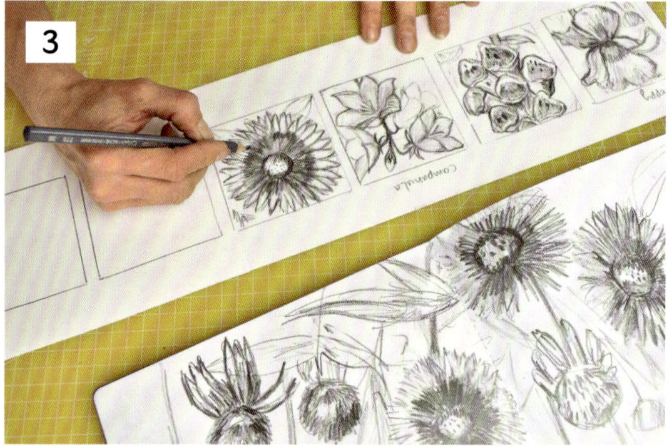

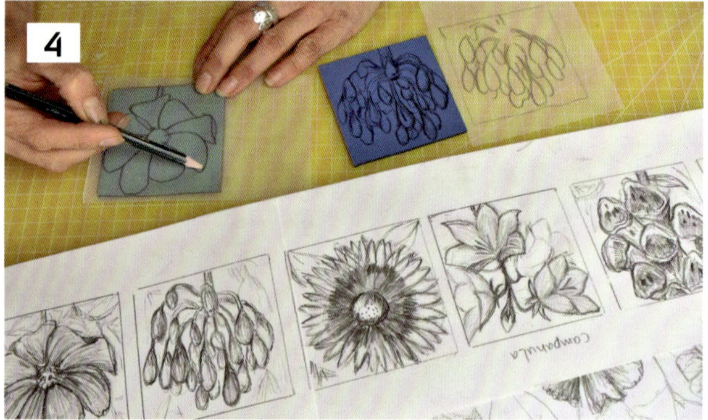

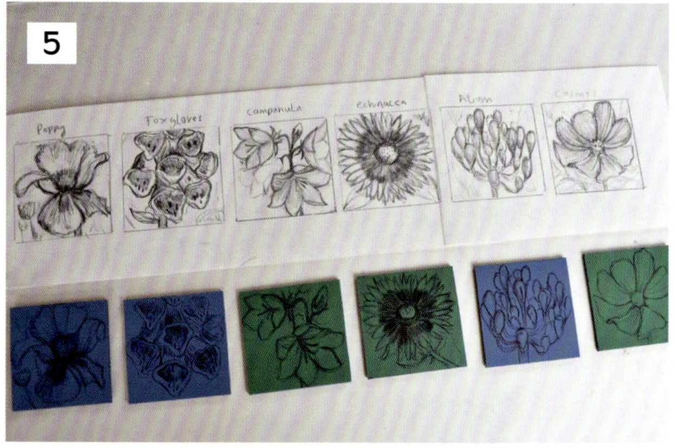

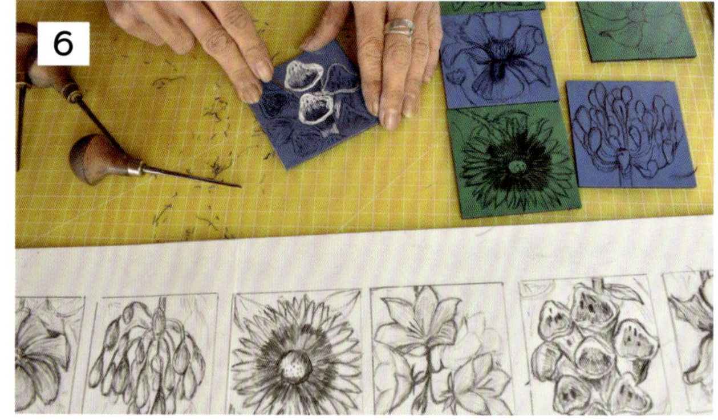

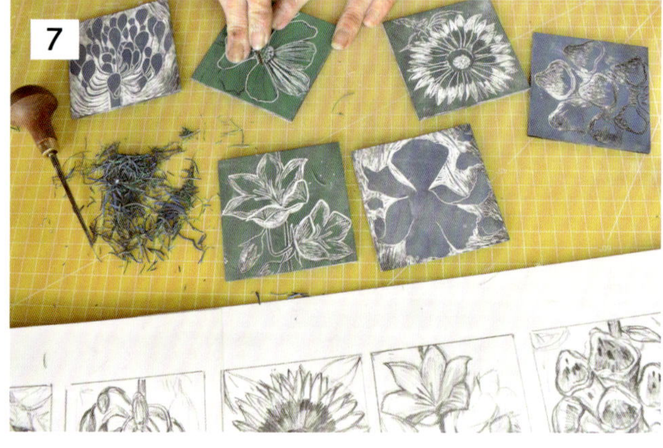

3 Using the drawings from your sketchbook, start working on all six of your designs. Try to fill the space as much as you can, adding detail and points of interest. While you are drawing, think about how you might be able to transfer the drawn lines onto linocut.

4 Once you have finished your drawings, transfer them to all six of your linocut blocks using your transfer method of choice (see page 29).

5 Here you will see that I have used biro to draw further onto the blocks (when drawing onto Japanese vinyl, biro works better than pencil). I decided not to go over with marker pen this time, but feel free to use it if you prefer. Don't feel obligated to stick to the order in which you have drawn your designs; as you will see later, I change the layout to suit the colours I'm using.

6 Start carving using your drawings as a reference. I'm using my trusty talcum powder method (see page 64) to enable me to see what I'm carving.

7 Continue carving until you are ready to take your first proof.

8 Here's my first proof – I used A4 paper, which I divided in half lengthways. It's always exciting to see the first proof and it's so important to check your progress. I could see from mine that there was still a lot of work to be done and it helped me to decide to alternate a printed background with a white one. Remember, proofs don't have to be perfect – they just need to serve as a guide to enable you to see how you are getting on.

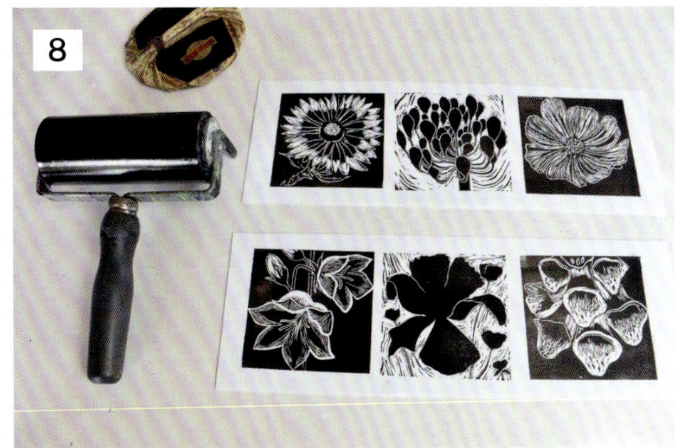

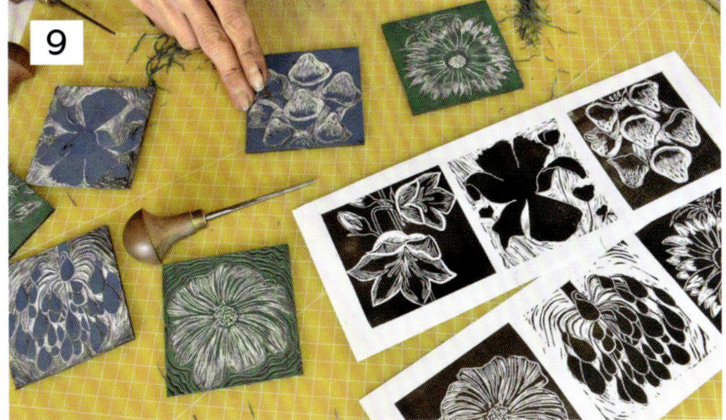

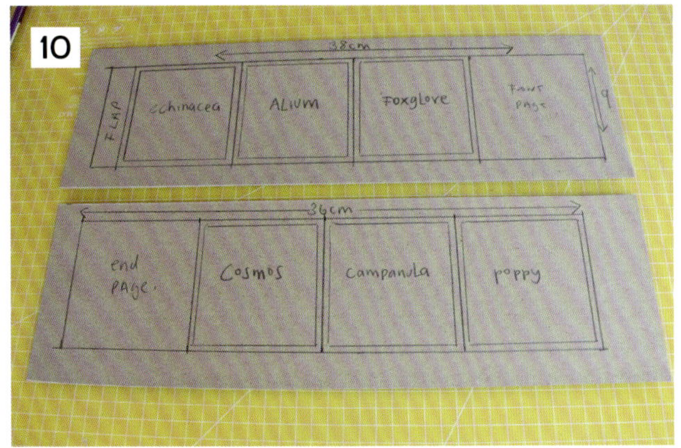

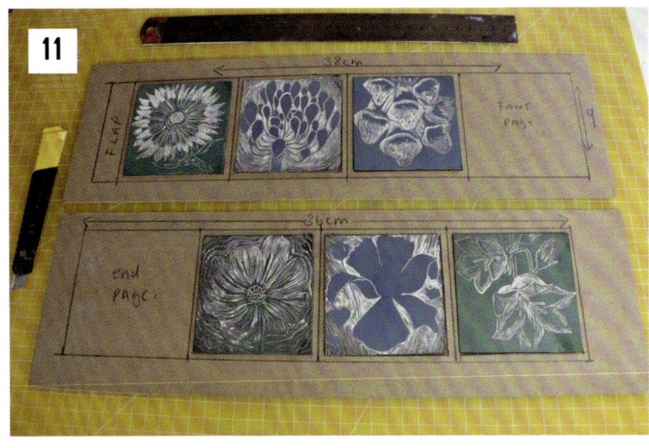

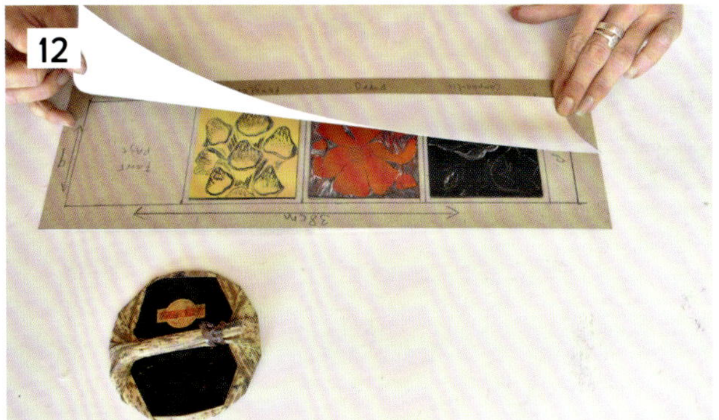

Measure 9 cm across and draw a line down until you have all four sections marked out on both pieces of board (again, you will have space at the end of the first page for your flap).

Draw around your linocut blocks inside each square – there should be a small gap at either side. Notice you are printing from right to left so that when you pull the print it will be the correct way around. (I have changed the layout of my linocuts – they don't match the drawing.)

9   Continue carving, using your proof prints as a reference.

10   Now it's time to make your registration boards. Cut your A3 greyboard widthways into two sections. Draw around both sheets of paper onto each board. The longer piece of paper is the first page; the extra centimetres are for a flap that will attach to the second page. Divide each of the strips into eight sections where you are to place your linocuts (and two for the front and back page).

11   Use your cutting knife to cut out the squares, then place your blocks inside the gaps and make sure they fit snugly. This is important for correct registration.

12   Next, choose the colours that you want for your prints then ink up and print your blocks as usual. I've chosen to ink up my six blocks in three colours that complement the book cover.

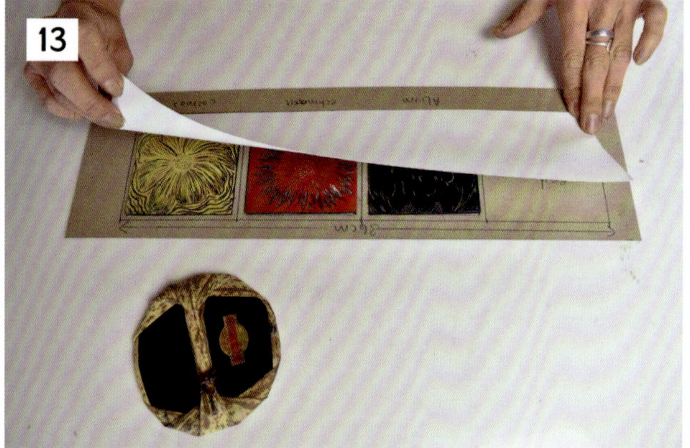

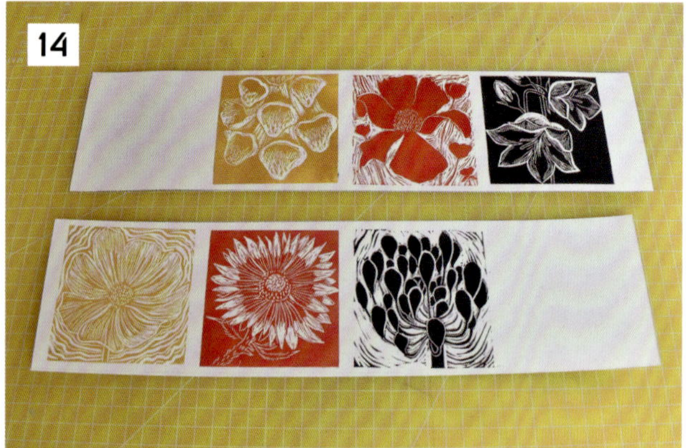

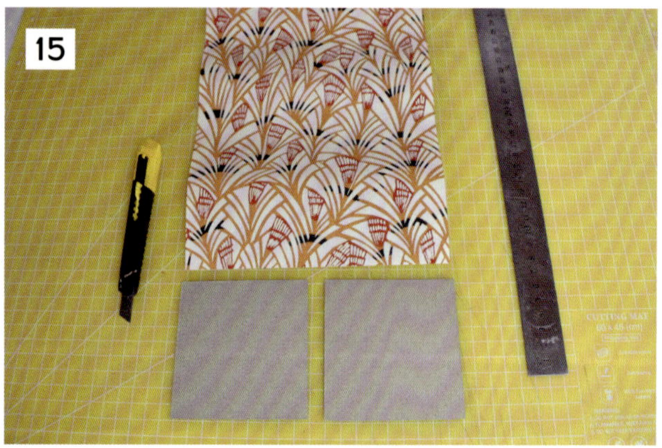

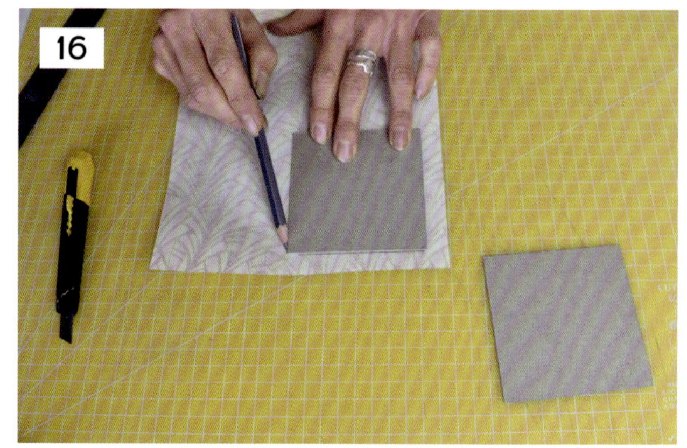

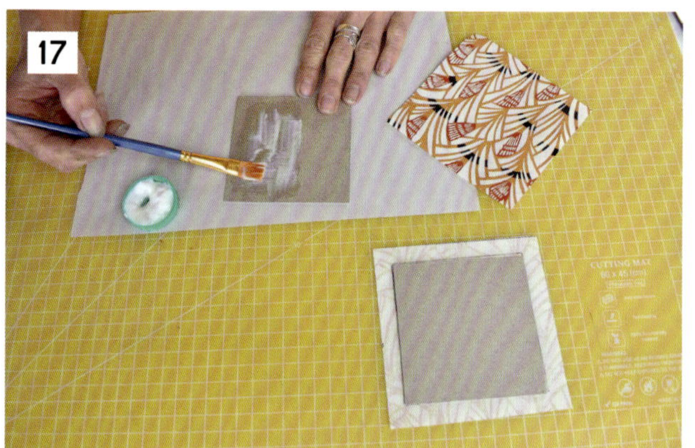

13 Print up the next strip and burnish carefully.

14 It might take a few attempts to get all linocuts to print out consistently (it did for me!) but no print need ever go to waste – you can always cut them up and use them individually as notecards. I use mine as thank you cards for my customers. Place your print strips aside and leave to dry.

15 Now it's time to make the end covers for your concertina book. Before I started printing, I chose a light handmade paper from a specialist paper store, which helped me decide on the colours for my prints.

16 Take your paper and place your boards on top. Leave a 1 cm gap around the edge of the board so that each piece of paper measures 9 x 9 cm. They need to have a border, as you are going to fold them over. Draw around the greyboard so you know where to place the board when gluing them down.

17 Place a piece of newsprint underneath your board to protect your surface from the glue. Coat the board with glue, ensuring that you cover the whole surface, right to the edges. Repeat for the second board.

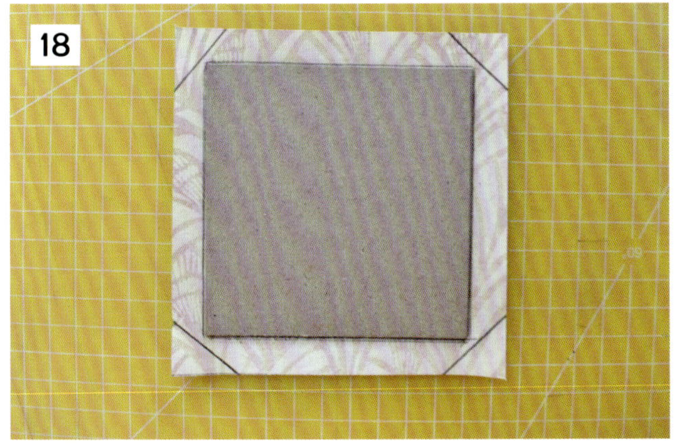

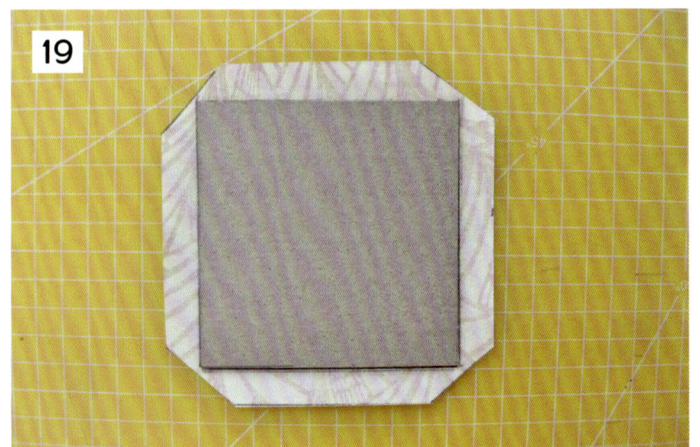

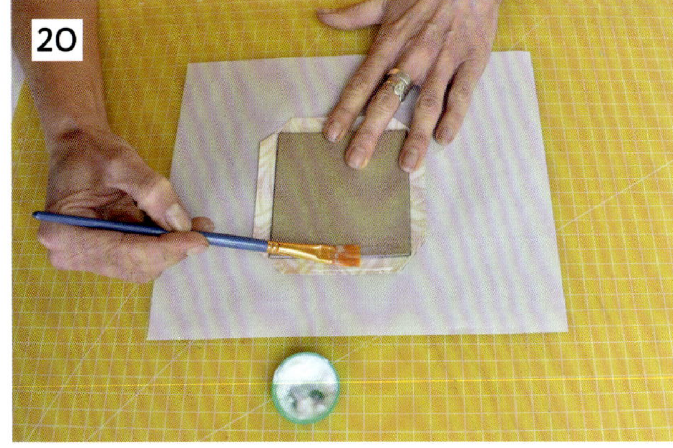

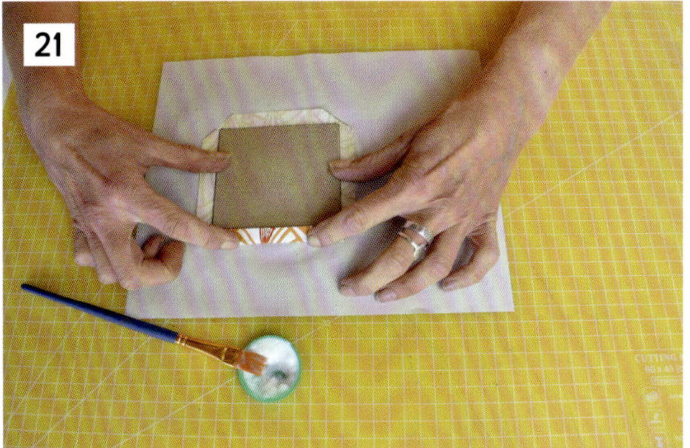

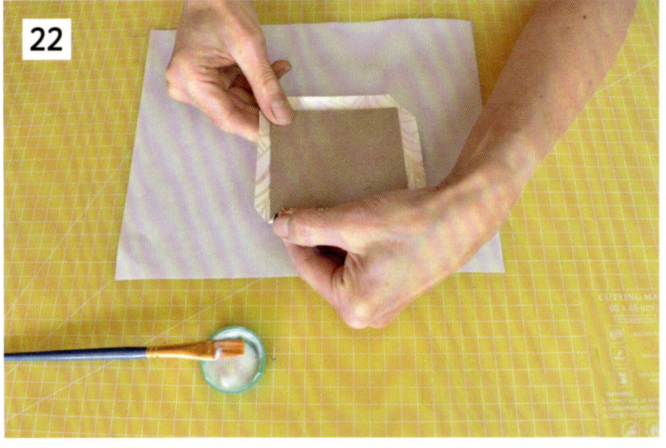

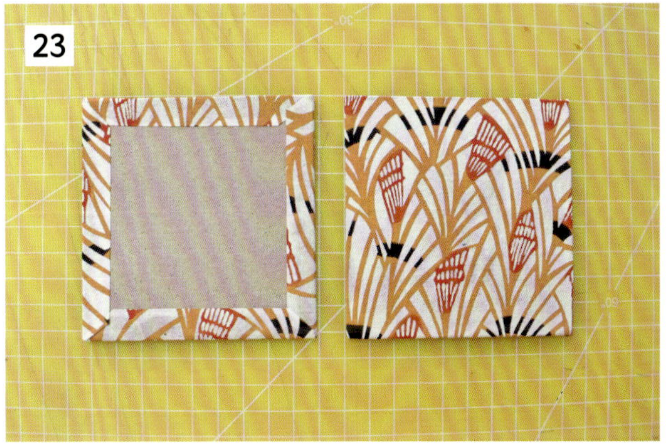

18 Carefully place the glued board onto the paper and press down firmly. Next, draw diagonal lines at each edge, leaving a few millimetres from the corner. This is important to ensure you don't see the board at the corner when you fold the cover paper over.

19 Using your cutting knife, carefully trim off the diagonals.

20 Take your glue brush and spread glue across the top flap.

21 Gently fold over the flap and press down firmly onto the board.

22 At the corners, gently push your nail in towards the board to make sure the edge of the board is covered.

23 Complete for all corners and flaps. Place the end covers under something heavy to allow the glue to stick and for the paper to flatten out.

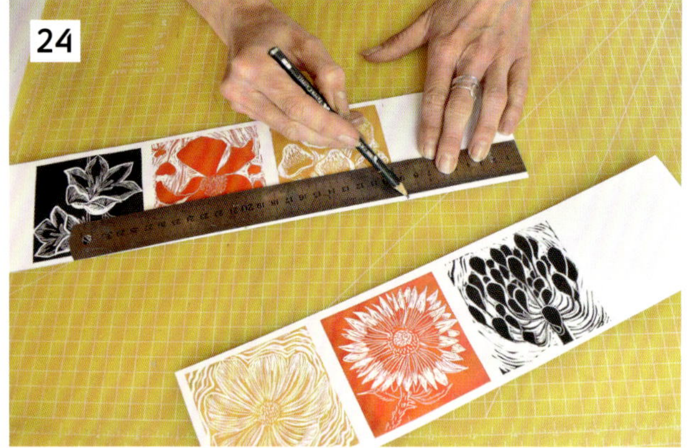

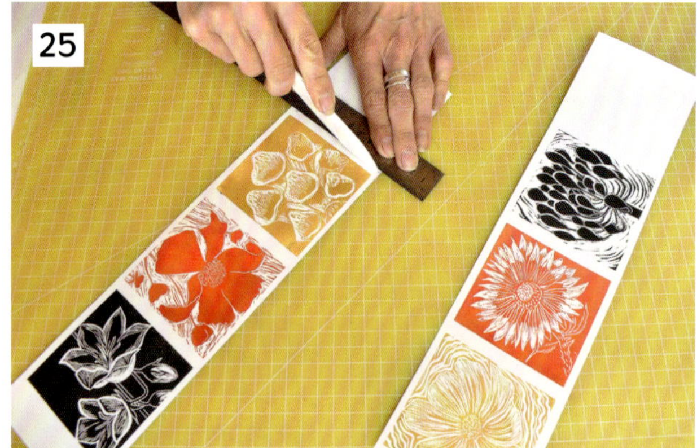

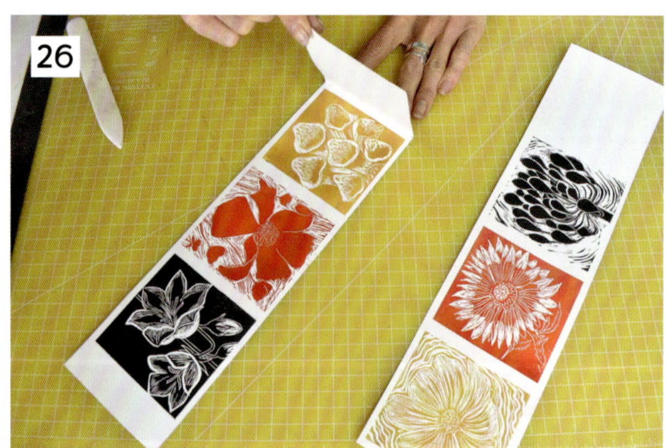

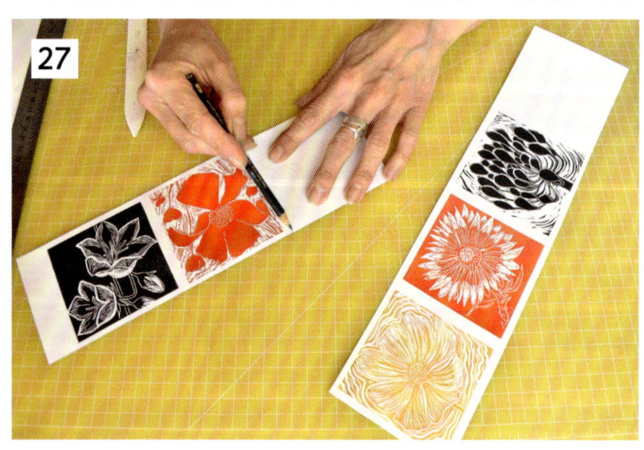

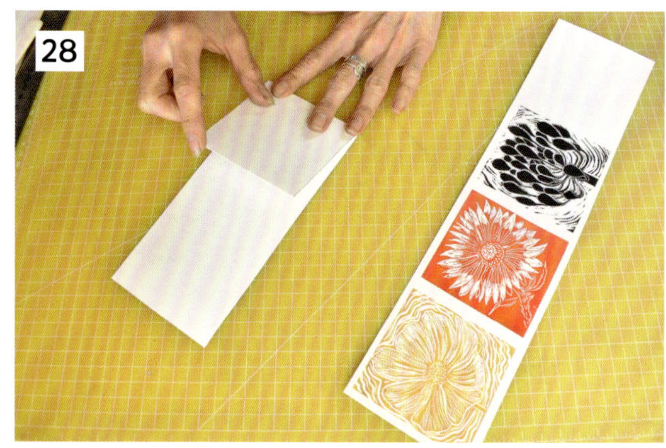

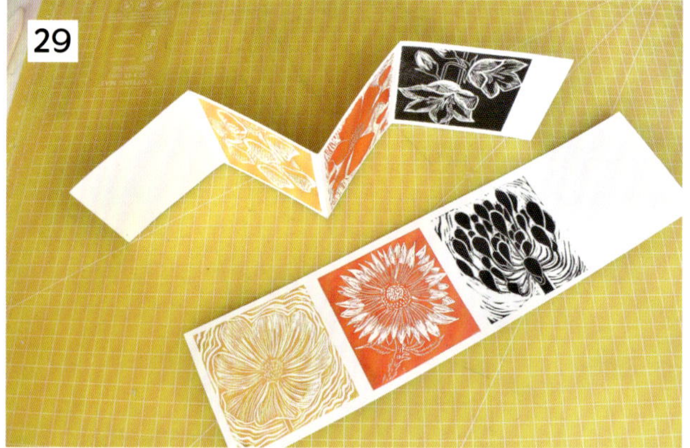

24 Once your prints have dried, it's time to fold them into a zigzag format. Take your first print strip and mark 9 cm from the left, both on the bottom and top.

25 Take your bone folder and make a crease from the top mark to the bottom mark.

26 Fold this flap inwards.

27 Mark the top of and bottom of the folded flap with a pencil, this will give you the next fold line – use your bone folder to make the crease using the pencil lines at the top and bottom as a guide.

28 This time, turn the page over and fold inwards. Repeat for the final page – take your pencil, make a mark at the top and the bottom, use your bone folder to create a crease and fold inwards.

29 Once you have folded it three times it should look like this. Repeat the process for the second print strip.

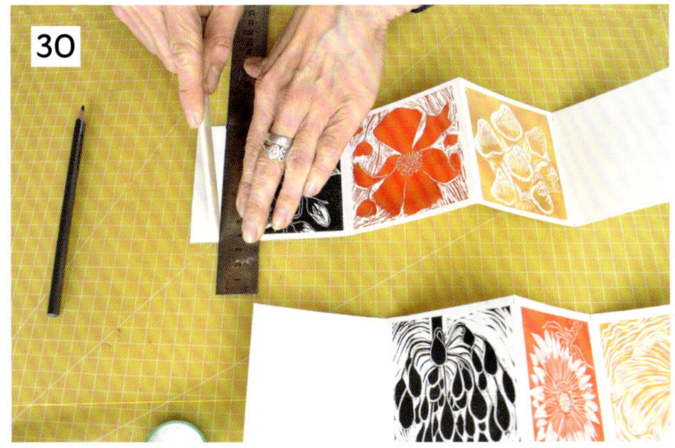

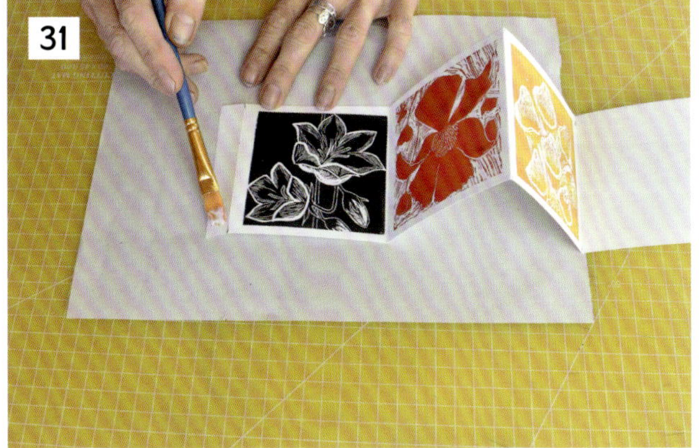

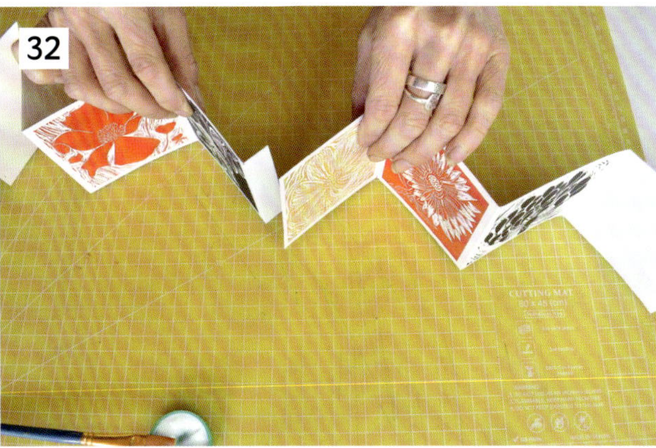

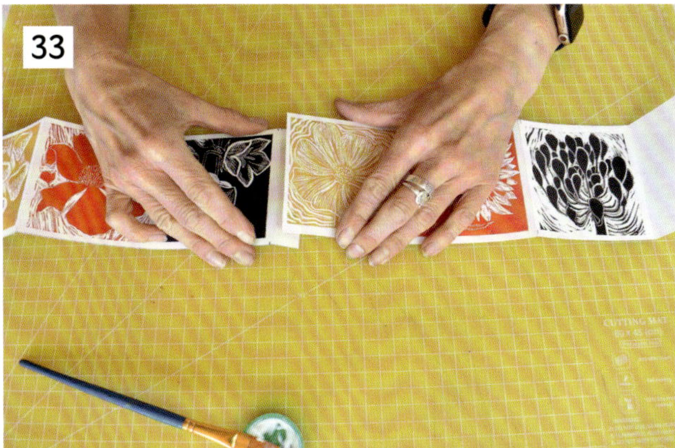

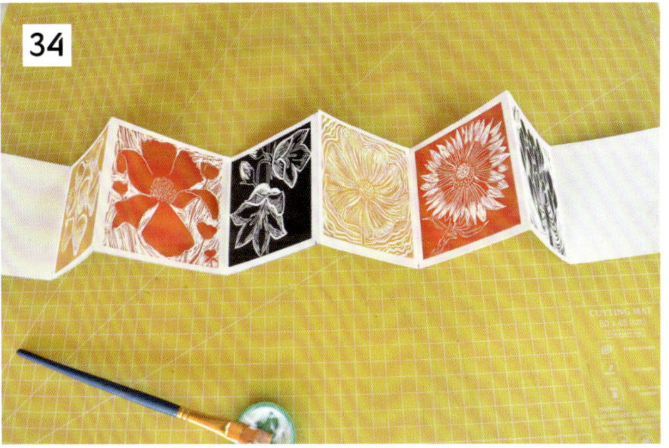

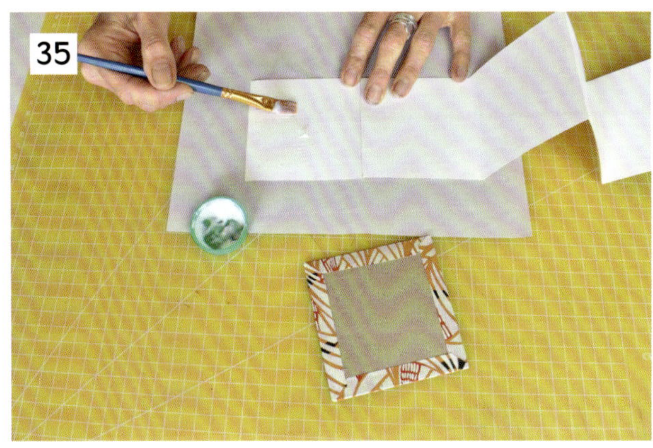

30 Once you have folded both papers, you can glue them together. Take the first print strip, which has an extra 2 cm at the end. This is your flap. Mark 9 cm at the top and bottom from the last fold and, like before, use your bone folder to create a crease. Fold, and you should now have a flap ready to glue.

31 Glue the flap carefully.

32 Press the glued flap onto the back of the second print strip.

33 Press it firmly together to make sure it sticks.

34 Your concertina book should now look like this.

35 Now we need to attach the end covers to the print strip. Turn the strip over and glue the end page.

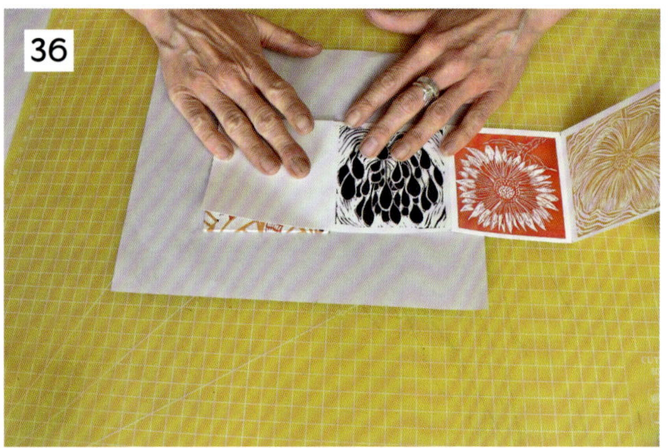

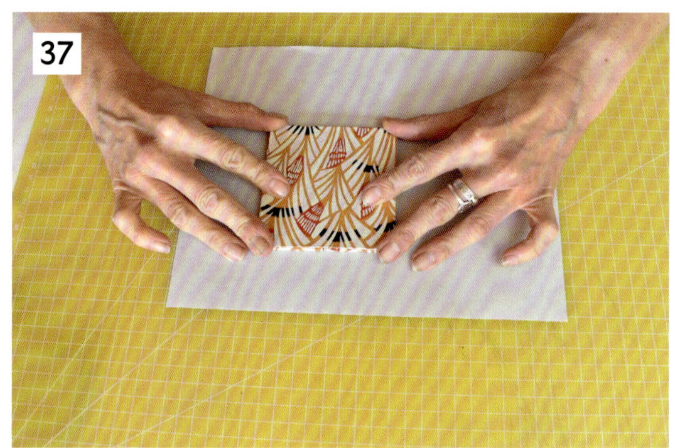

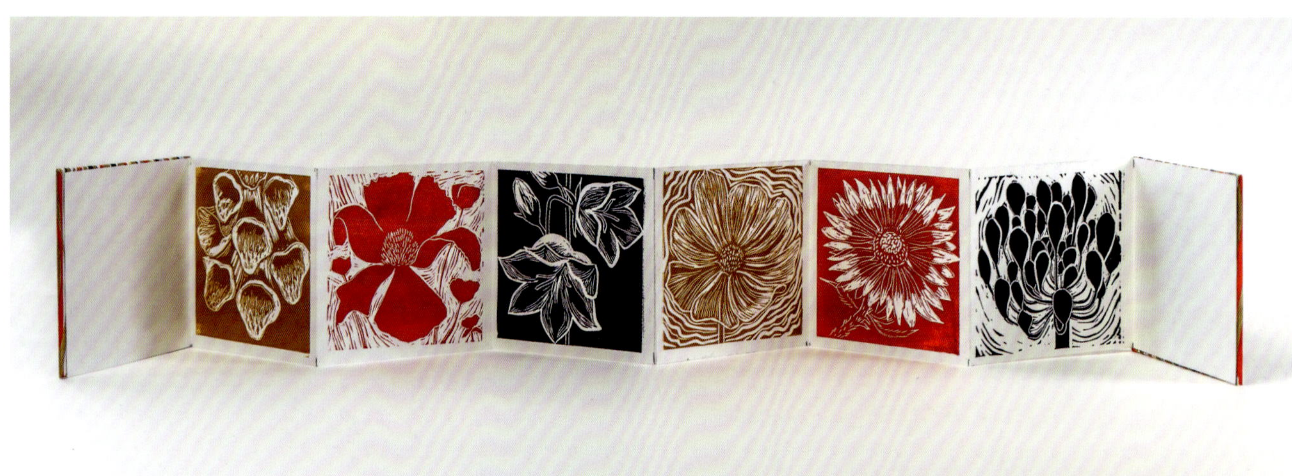

36 Carefully place the glued page onto the book cover, making sure it is central.

37 Repeat for the second book cover. Place your book under something heavy until the glue has dried and the pages are flat.

38 Once the pages are dry, open the book out and admire your efforts. Experiment with printing your linocut blocks in a different order and in various colours. You can also change your cover or make your prints separately.

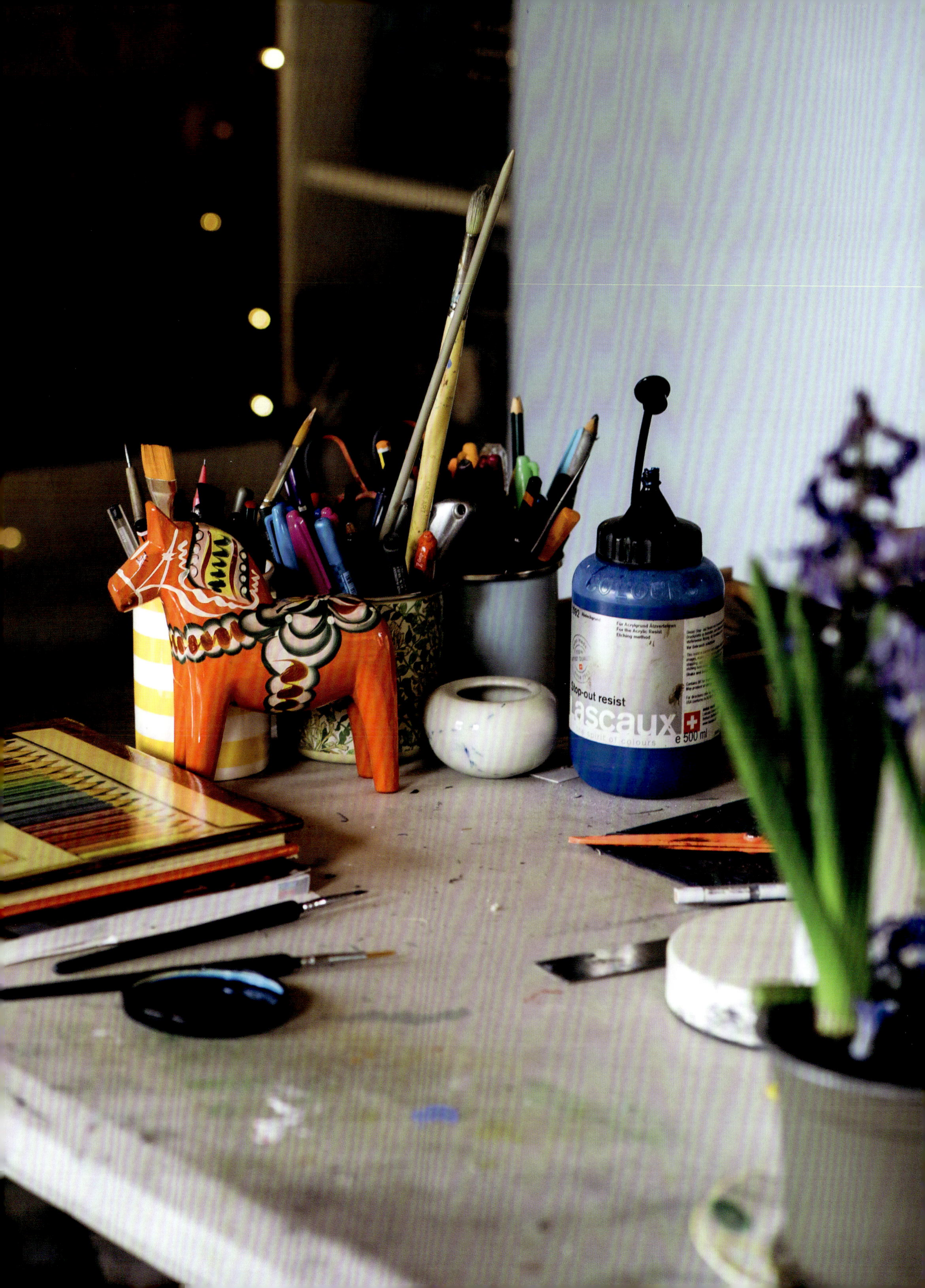

Stop-out resist
ascaux
e 500 ml

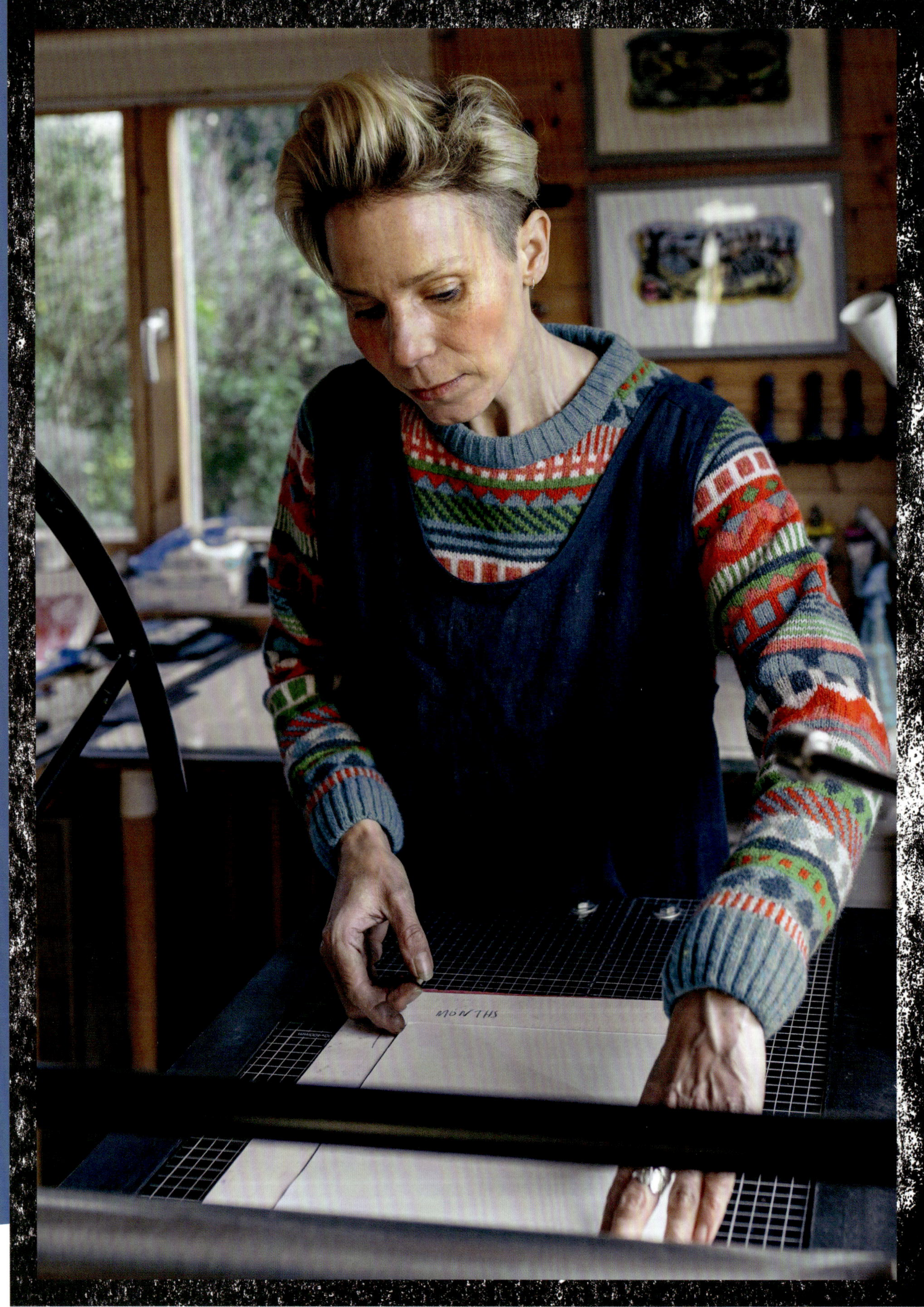
MONTHS

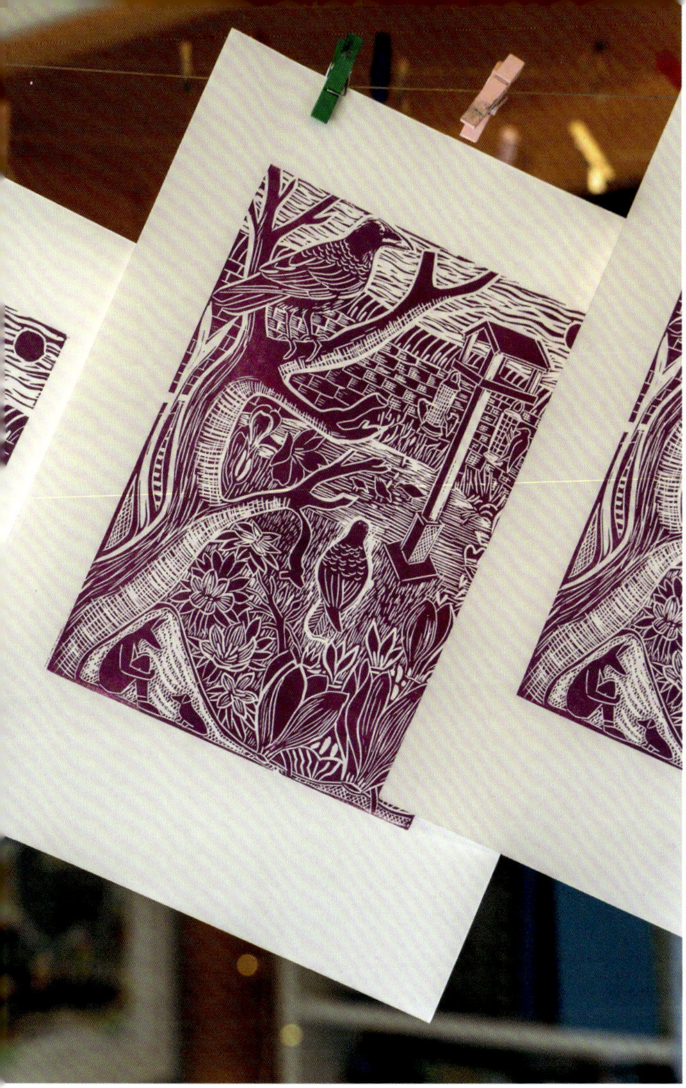

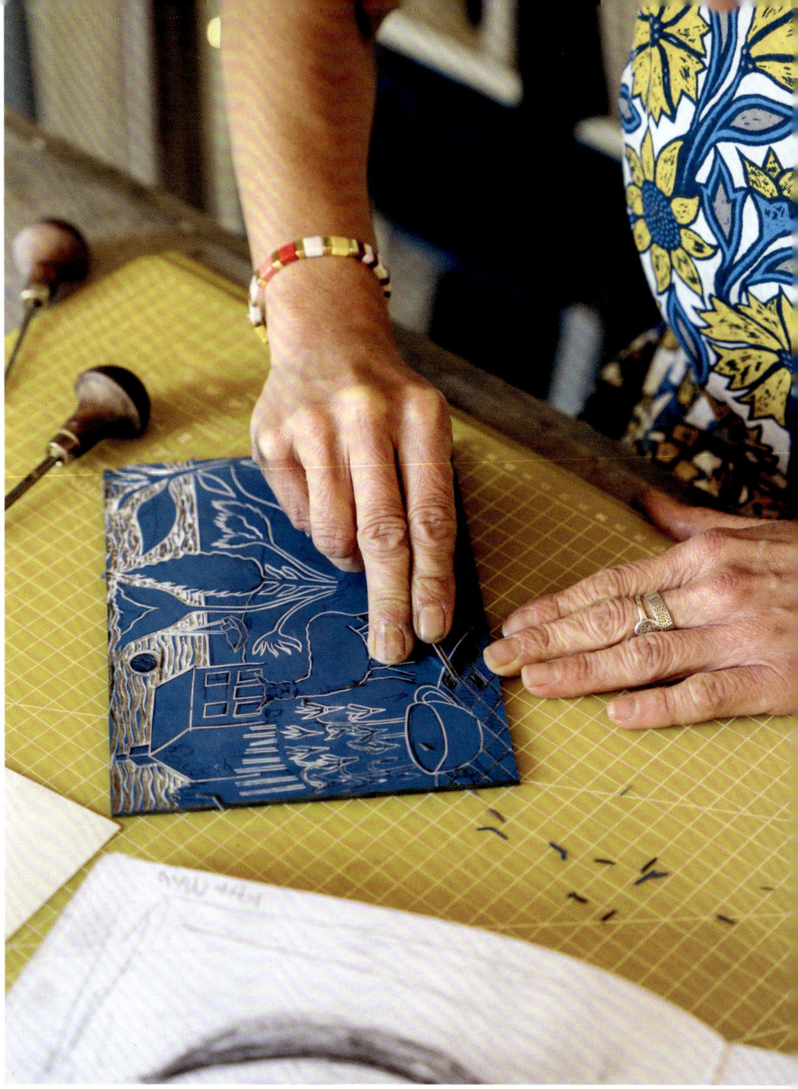

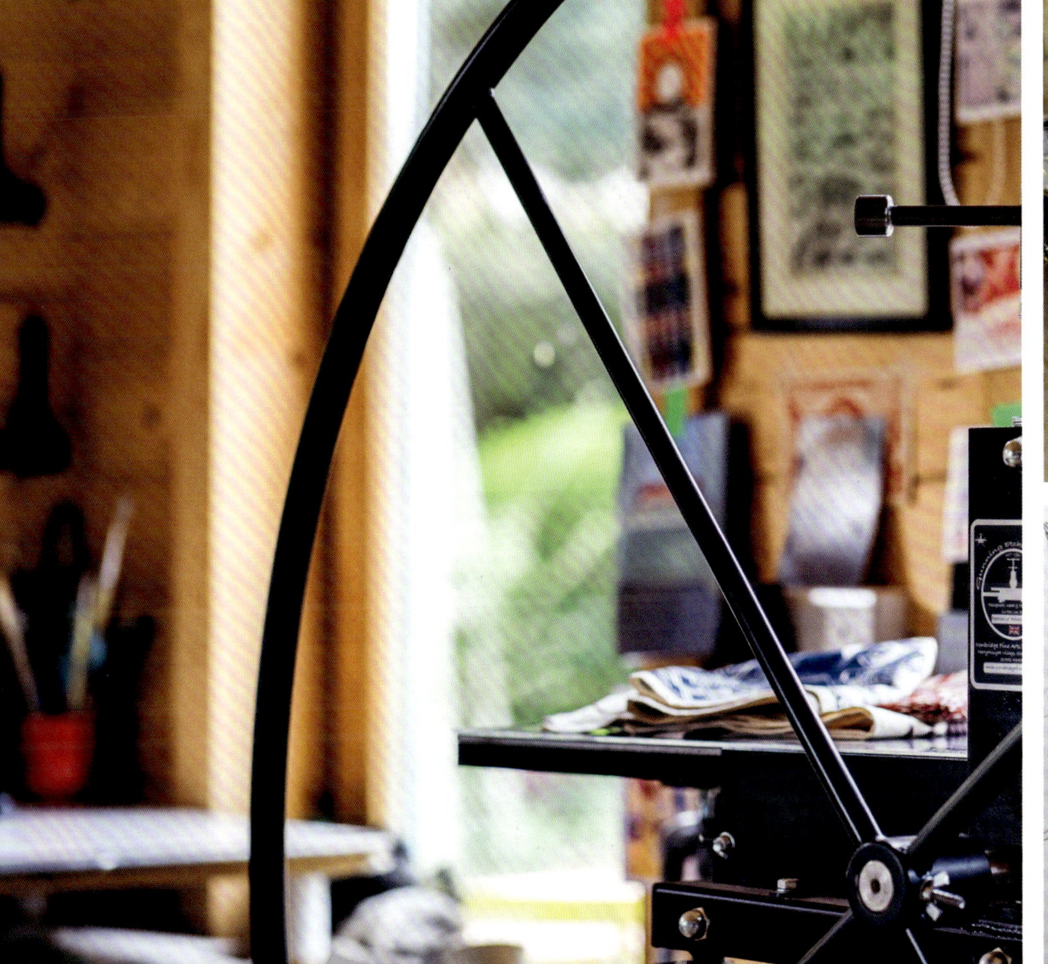
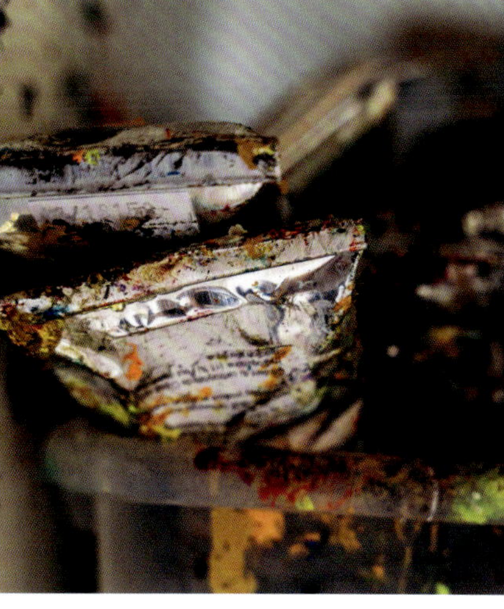
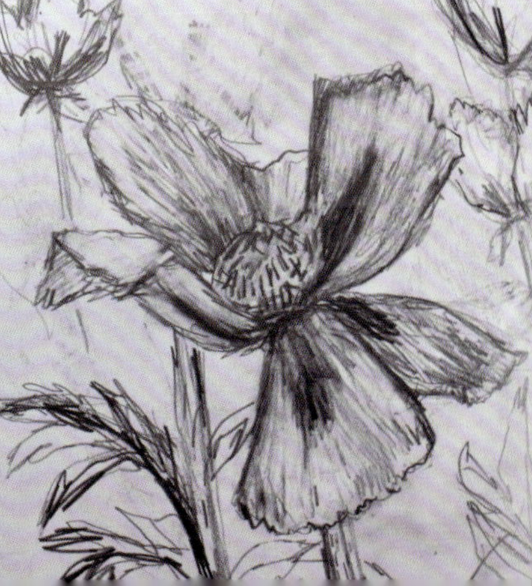

17 EXPERIMENTAL PRINTMAKING

In this chapter we are going to be getting more experimental, moving away from straightforward carving and printing to work with a whole range of different materials and methods. This is the joy of printmaking; it's so adaptable and playful – the possibilities are endless! I hope that these projects will help you to see your work in a new way so that you are able to take some risks and see where your imagination carries you.

First, we will work with combining linocut and monoprint. Monoprint is a form of printmaking where the image can only be used once – they are one-offs, hence 'mono'. It is a very painterly and spontaneous technique, and is a lovely way to add a colour to your work without the need to carve another block. Ink can be applied in a variety of ways – with a paintbrush, roller or rag. Here, I am just going to use a roller, but feel free to experiment with other tools. For this first section, we will use a pre-carved linocut and use monoprint to act as a background to enhance and complement the print.

COMBINING MONOPRINT AND LINOCUT

You Will Need

- Lino, already completed and carved
- Relief printing inks
- Rollers
- Inking slab
- Paper – double the size of your completed linocut
- Baren or wooden spoon
- Paper for printing
- Piece of Perspex/plexiglass or glass – roughly the same size as your linocut
- Tracing paper
- Cutting mat
- Craft knife
- Metal ruler
- Selection of pencils, e.g. HB/2B
- Rubber/eraser
- Stiff brush
- Cleaning materials

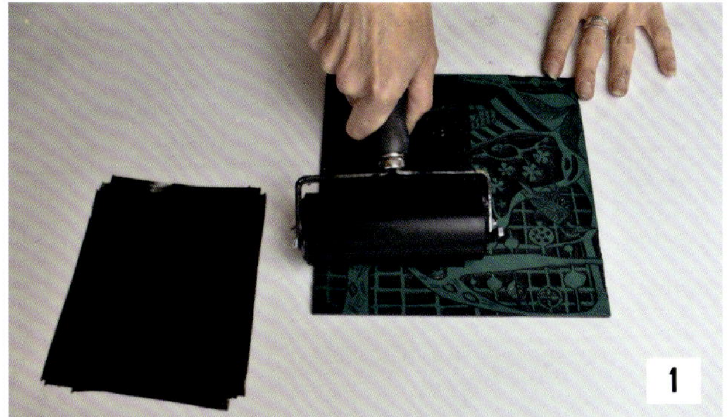

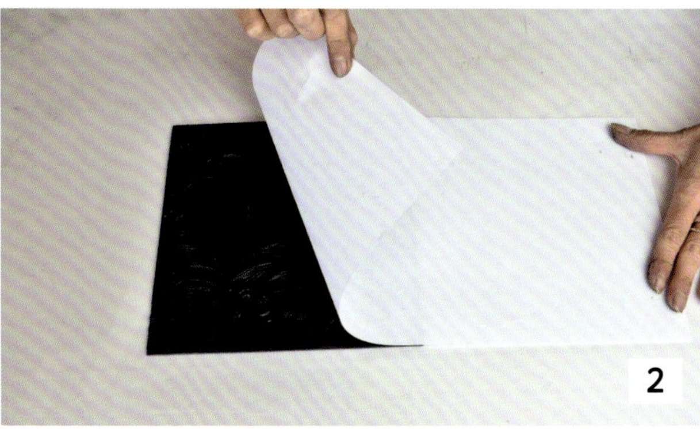

1 Take your carved block and ink it up in black. You can use other colours, of course, but I recommend starting with black as it adds a bold contrast to the monoprint.

2 Take a piece of paper that is double the size of your linocut and carefully lay it down onto your inked-up lino. It doesn't matter which side you print onto.

3 Burnish using your wooden spoon or baren.

4 Peel back your print, then fold your paper in half so the plain side is lying on top of your print.

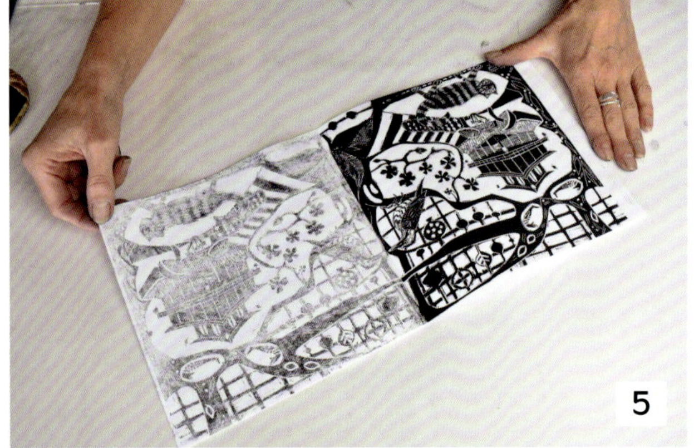

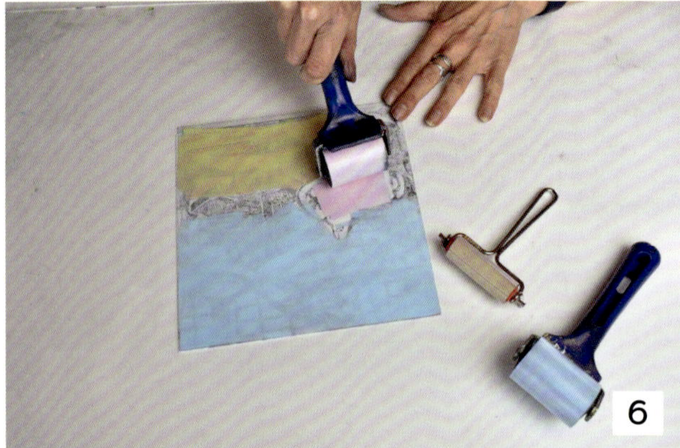

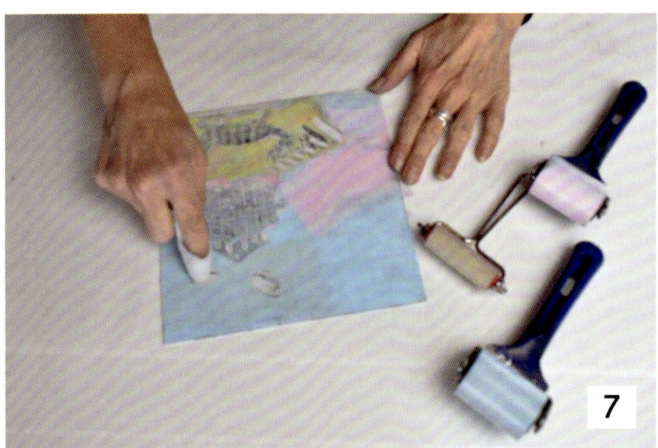

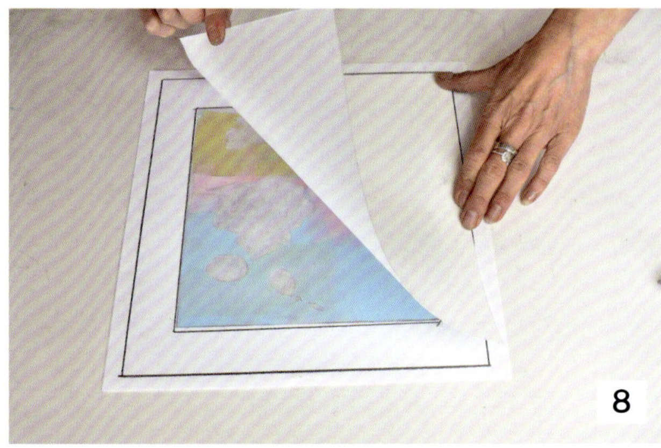

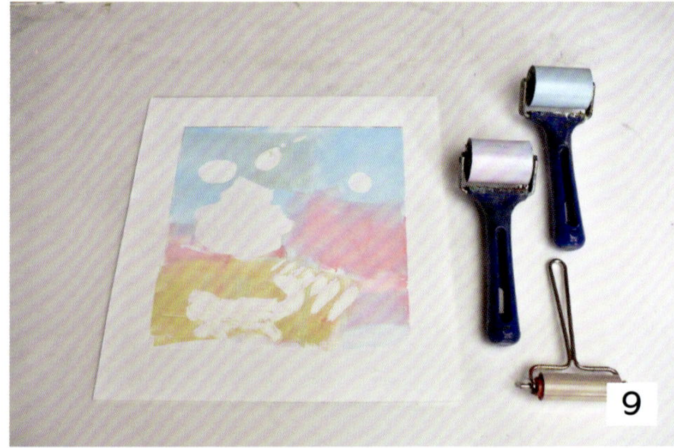

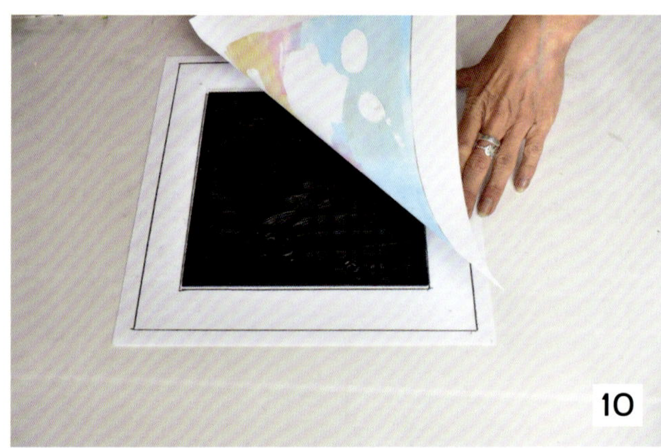

5 Burnish and peel back the paper. You will have a reverse print of your linocut, which we are going to use as our guide for the monoprint.

6 Take the reverse print and place your piece of Perspex, plexiglass or glass on top. Decide on what colour inks you would like and mix them up (it's best to keep it simple at this point, while you are getting the hang of the process). I used three colours, which I thought would complement my linocut. Using your rollers, roll the inks out on the Perspex, paying attention to the image underneath.

7 Use a rag to wipe away any areas you want to remain white. Try to keep it loose and intuitive, if you can.

8 Use the paper template registration method (see page 57) to create a registration sheet. Then position your monoprint in the centre, place your paper on top and burnish.

9 Peel back the paper to reveal your monoprint.

10 Take your inked-up block and place it in your registration sheet. Place your monoprint on top and burnish.

11 Peel back to reveal the print. You will see that the monoprint just gives the print an extra bit of interest. I deliberately kept the colours quite muted, but do feel free to experiment with bolder colours. You will also see that the monoprint bleeds down underneath the linocut – I like this effect as I feel it loosens up the whole image.

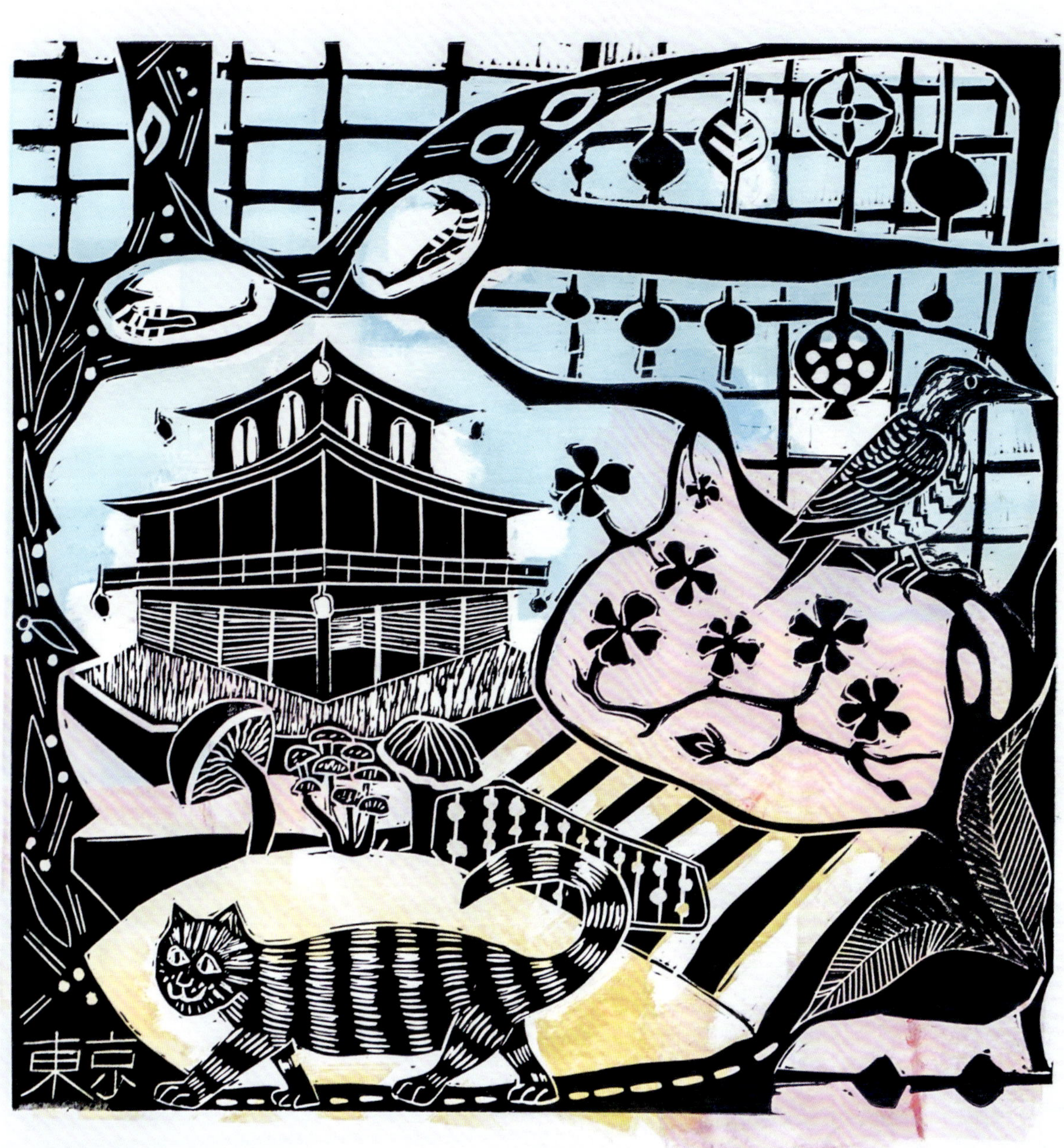

REPURPOSING OLD BLOCKS

This project is a great way to breathe new life into old linocuts – ones that perhaps you felt didn't work out in the way you wanted them to. When I first started linocutting, I was so critical of my work that I often discarded and abandoned pieces halfway through the printing process. I always kept them, though, and one day when I was having a clear out, I decided to have an afternoon of playing around with them – cutting them up and printing them in random ways. I found it really inspiring, and it enabled me to see my work in a different way. It also provided many new ideas for future prints. I hope you find this too.

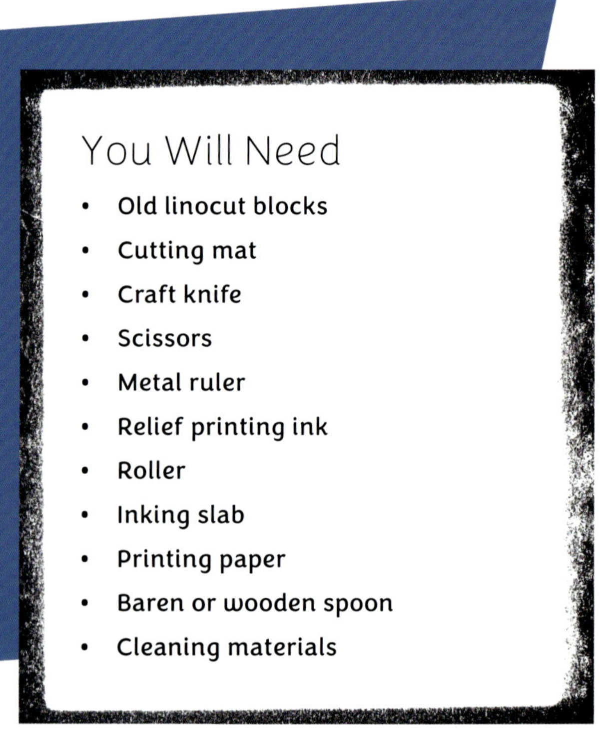

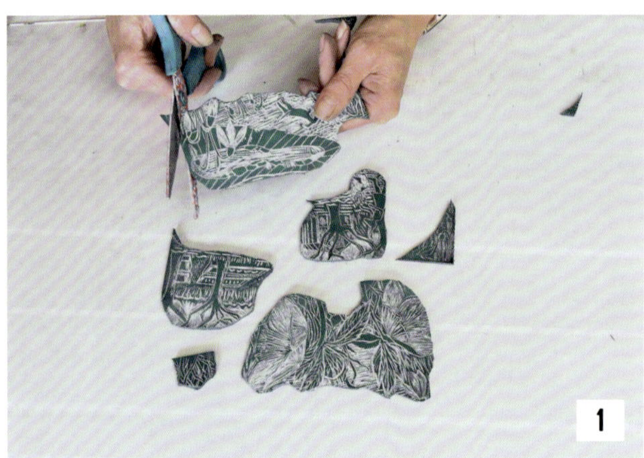

1

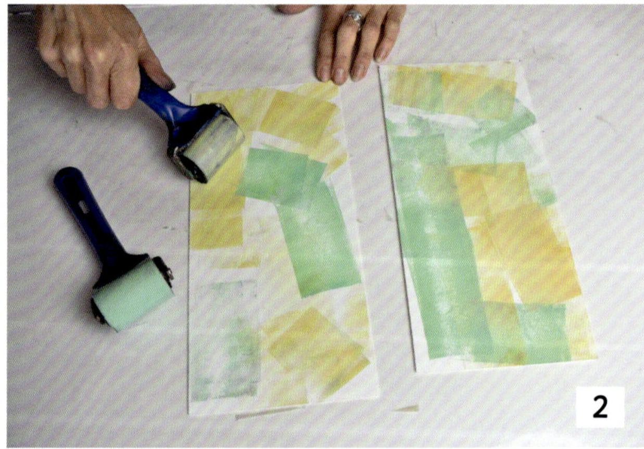

2

1 Cut up your linocut into pieces. Vary the sizes, so you have smaller and larger pieces.

2 Select the inks you would like to use as background colours. Using your rollers, roll colours onto some pieces of paper, keeping it random and loose. Do keep some areas white as this adds interest and gives a sense of space to the print.

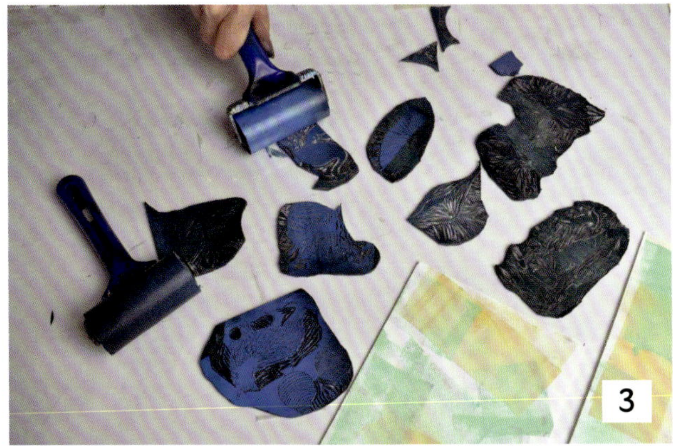

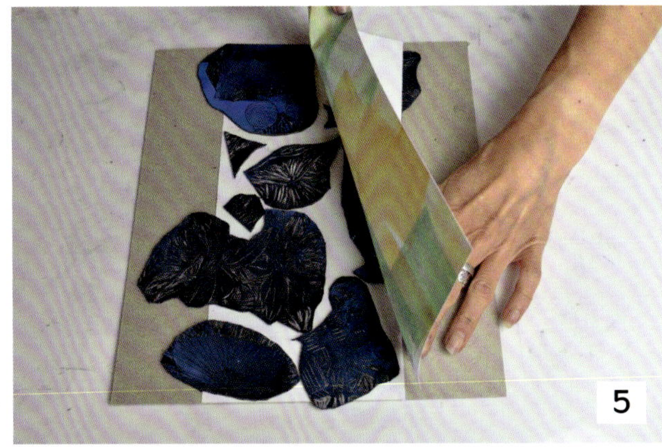

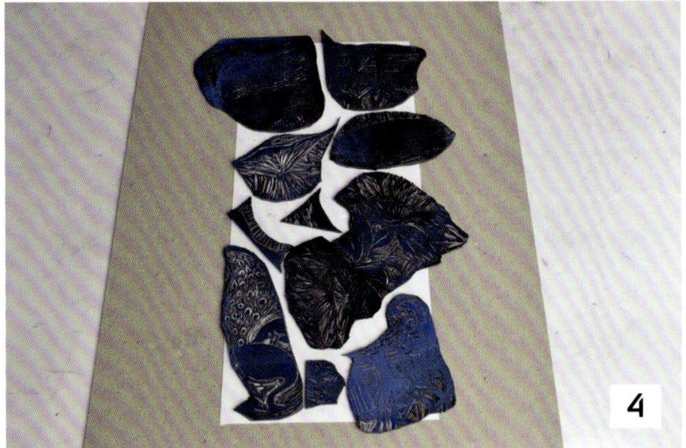

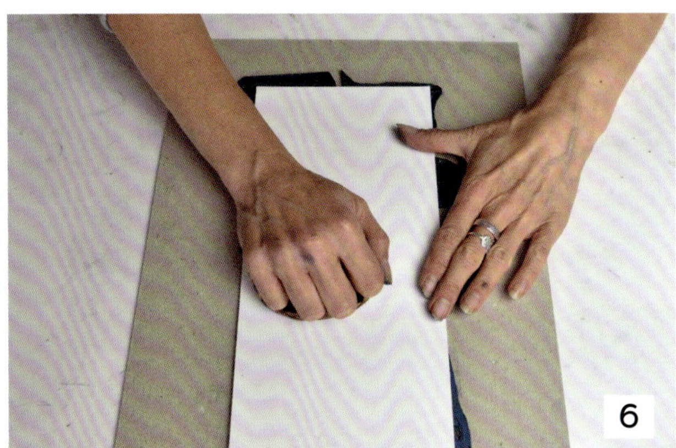

3   Ink up your linocut pieces. It's easiest to use a
    small roller for this.

4   Place a piece of paper, the same size as your other
    papers, on your surface to act as a guide. Place your
    inked-up linocuts on top. Don't worry if they go
    over the edges – this makes for interesting prints.

5   Place your prepared paper carefully on top.

6   Burnish carefully.

7   Carefully peel back and assess your print. Continue
    to experiment using different background colours,
    sizes of paper, placement of blocks, etc.

I also printed some of my cut-up linocuts onto plain
paper, which I think works well, too (see overleaf).
These strips remind me of wallpaper and have already
inspired some ideas for wallpaper designs in the
future. That's what I love about this project – it can
fire up lots of new and exciting ideas and ways to
approach your work.

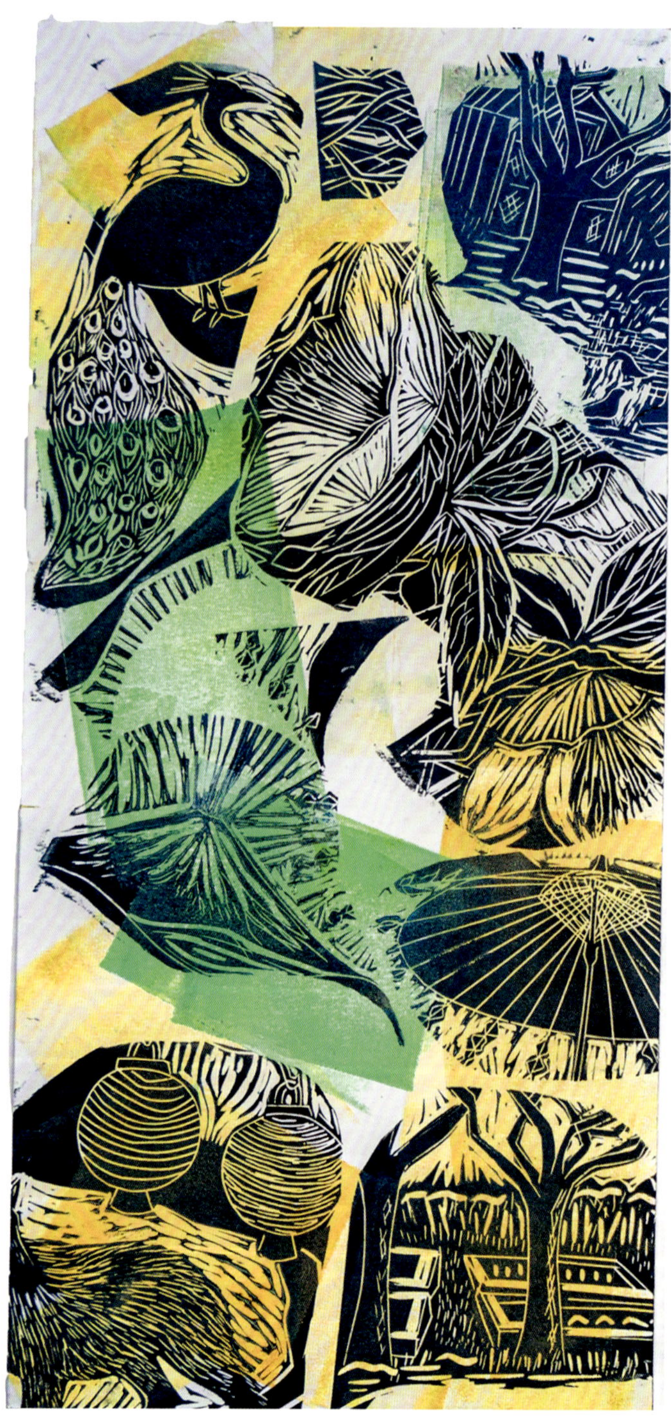

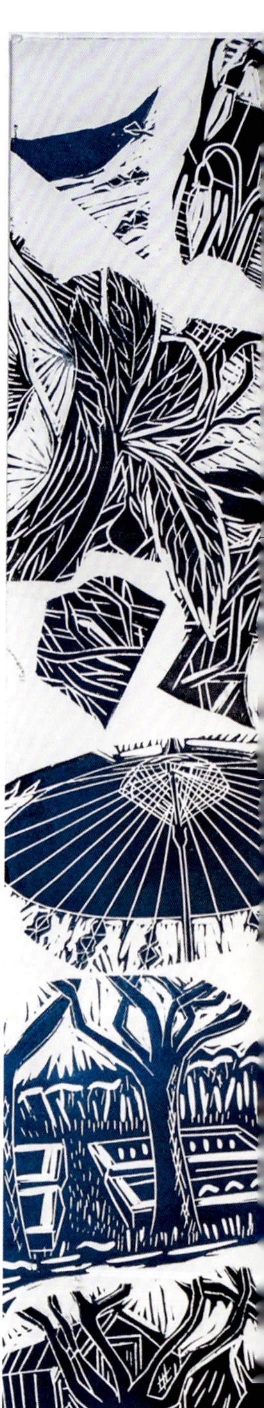

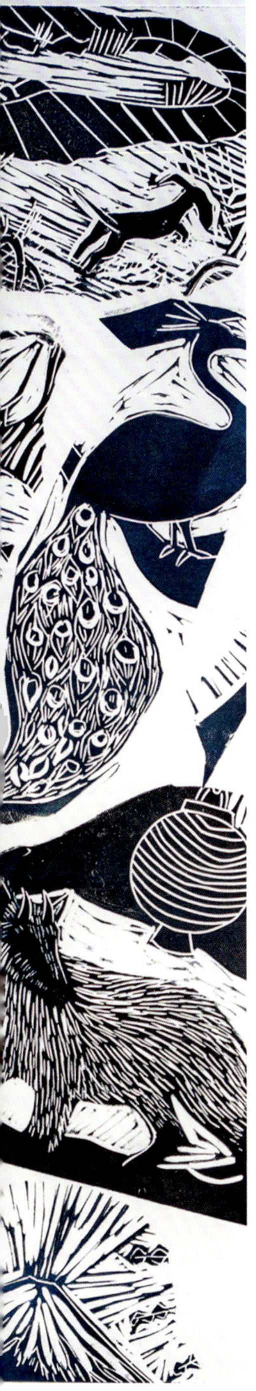

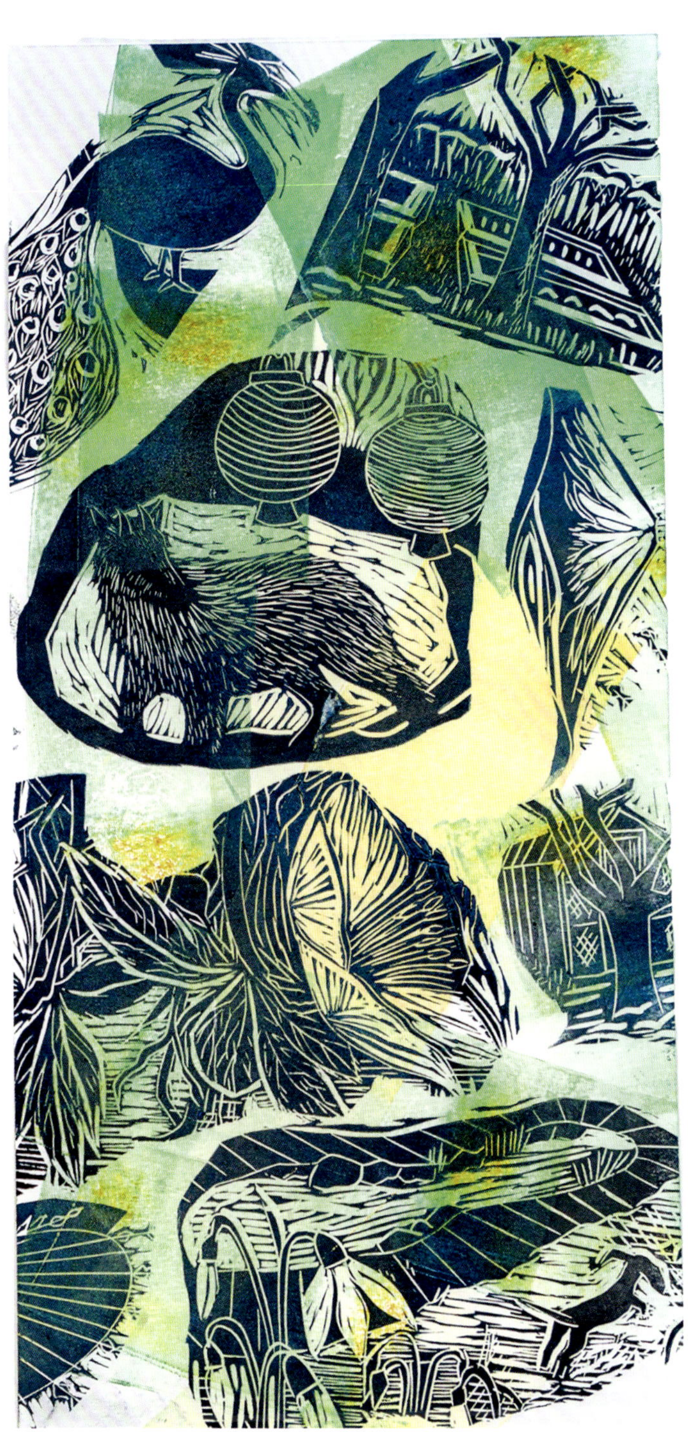

LINOCUT AND CHINE COLLÉ

In this project we are going to explore a technique known as chine collé; a special method in which paper of a different colour or texture is adhered to the print, allowing you to add colour without making another block. The paper – usually thin, coloured and in pre-cut shapes – is sandwiched between the printing paper and the printed image. It is bonded to the printing paper during the printing process and is integral to the print.

Chine collé roughly translates from French as tissue (chine) and glue or paste (collé). The word chine is used because the thin paper used was traditionally imported to Europe from China, India and Japan.

You can experiment with many different types of paper. Japanese papers are often used, but you can experiment with any type of lightweight papers – wrapping paper, craft paper – anything thin, fairly strong and with an absorbent surface is worth a try. We are going to use tissue paper in the second part of this project – this is not usually lightfast, so if you are planning to sell or frame your work then try another paper type.

I am going to demonstrate two different methods of using chine collé: the first acts as a background to your linocut and the second adds splashes of colour using small torn pieces of tissue paper.

> ### NOTE
> *Japanese rice paste is a starch paste made from natural materials. It works especially well with delicate fine papers that are often used in chine collé. You can buy it from most printmaking suppliers.*

USING CHINE COLLÉ AS A BACKGROUND

You Will Need

- Greyboard for registration board
- Pre-carved linocut block
- Printing paper
- Craft knife or scissors

- Relief printing ink
- Roller
- Inking slab
- Lightweight paper (tissue, newspaper, thin wrapping paper, etc.)

- PVA glue/white glue/ Japanese rice paste
- Glue brush
- Baren or wooden spoon
- Cleaning materials

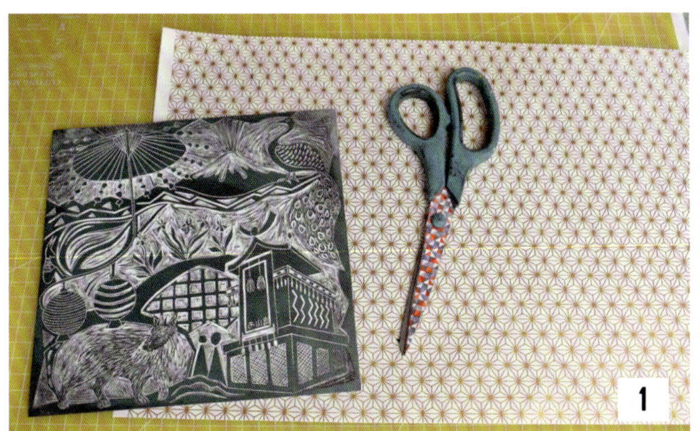

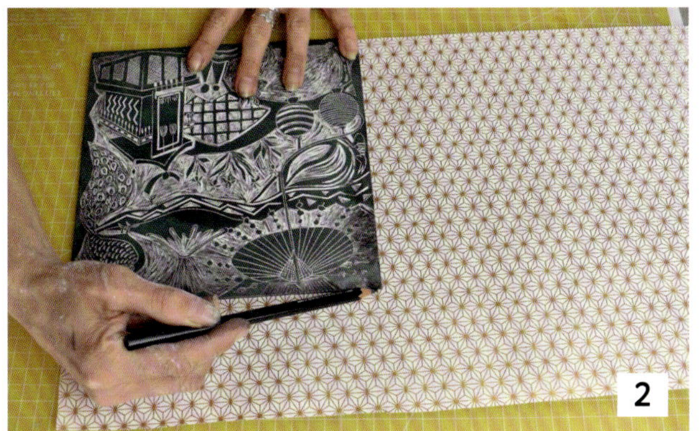

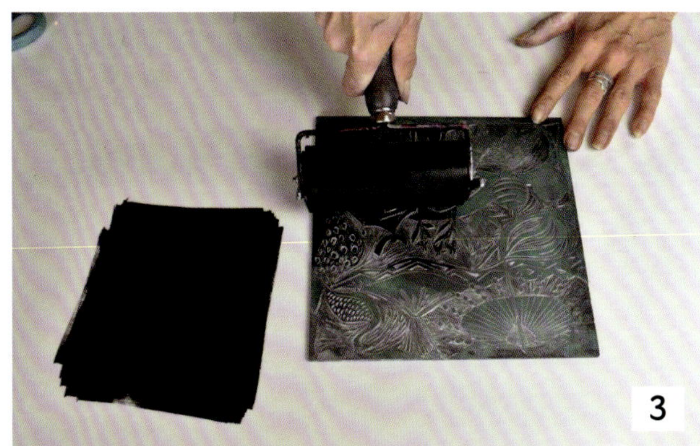

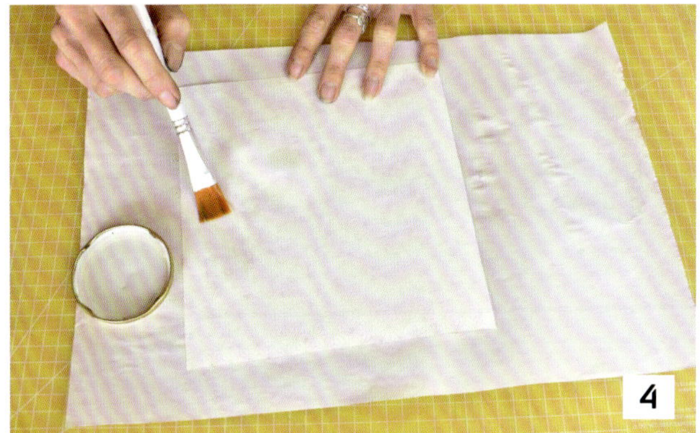

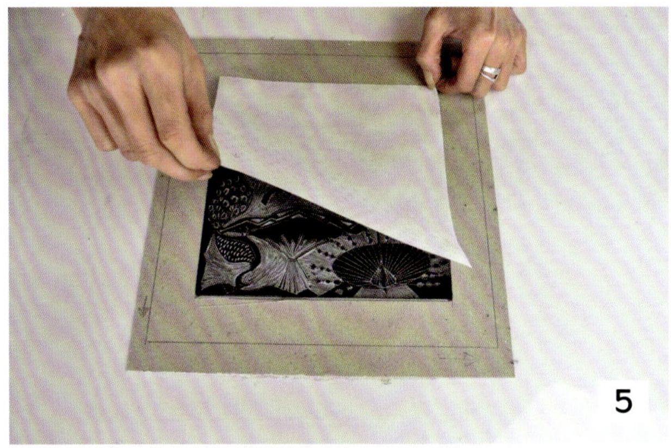

1   Make a registration board for your print following
    the instructions on page 58. I've chosen to use
    greyboard for my print, but a paper registration
    would work well too. Select the pre-carved linocut
    and paper you would like to use. I've chosen to work
    with one of my Japanese linocuts and a lightweight
    Japanese paper, which I feel will work well.

2   Place your linocut on top of your paper and cut
    around it.

3   Ink up your block as usual.

4   Turn your chine collé paper over and coat a thin
    layer of either PVA glue, white glue or Japanese
    rice paste over the entire surface, making sure you
    coat right up to the edge. You only need a small

amount of glue – don't drench the paper! If you
are using Japanese rice paste, add a little water to
make a thick syrupy paste.

5   Place your linocut in your registration block (see
    page 58). Carefully place your paper – glue side up
    – on top of your inked block.

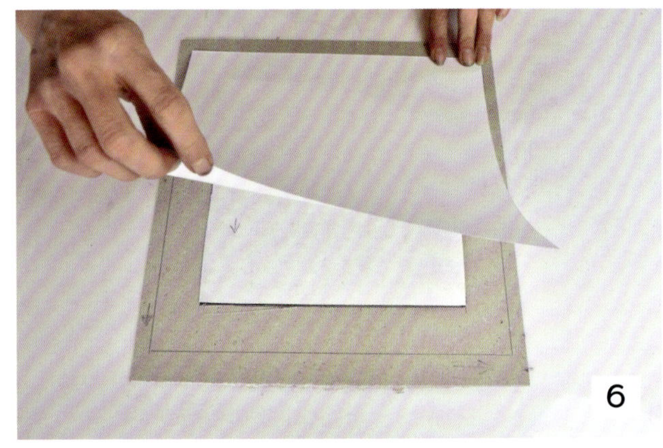

6 Place your printing paper on top and burnish as usual.

7 Peel back to reveal your print. The paper will have bonded to the surface, with your linocut printed on top.

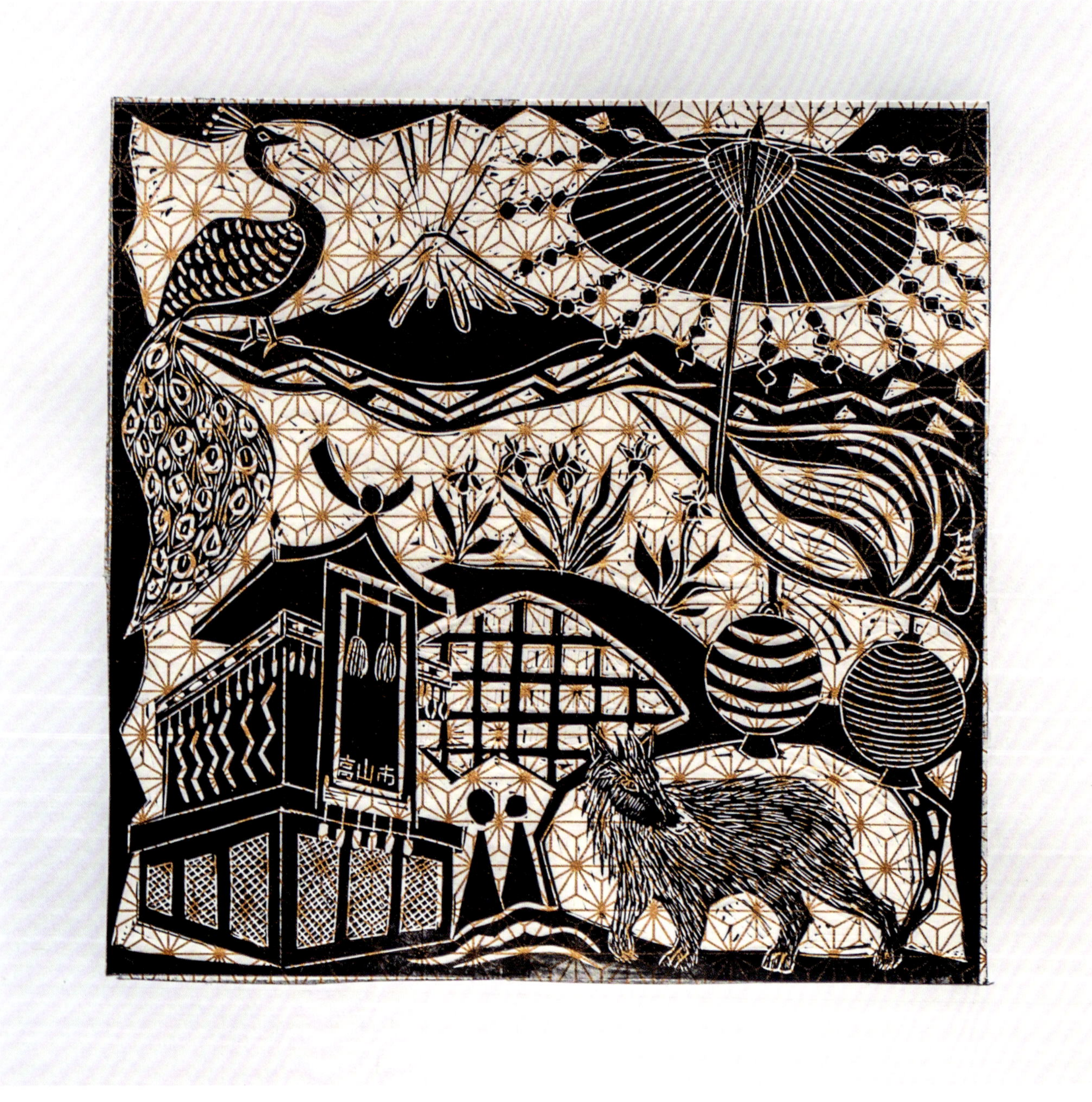

CHINE COLLÉ USING TISSUE PAPER

Next, we are going to use tissue paper to add a splash of colour to your linocut. This is a fun technique; it can be fiddly and a bit messy, though, so you might find you have plenty of prints that don't work out (keep them in a folder, as you can always use them later for collage, etc.). If you find the tissue paper too delicate to handle, you could prepare your own paper by using acrylic or gouache paints to paint photocopy paper.

You Will Need

- **Tissue paper**
- **Scissors**
- **Pre-carved linocut block**
- **Relief printing ink**
- **Roller**
- **Inking slab**
- **Printing paper**
- **PVA glue/white glue/Japanese rice paste**
- **Glue brush**
- **Greyboard**
- **Tweezers (optional)**
- **Cleaning materials**

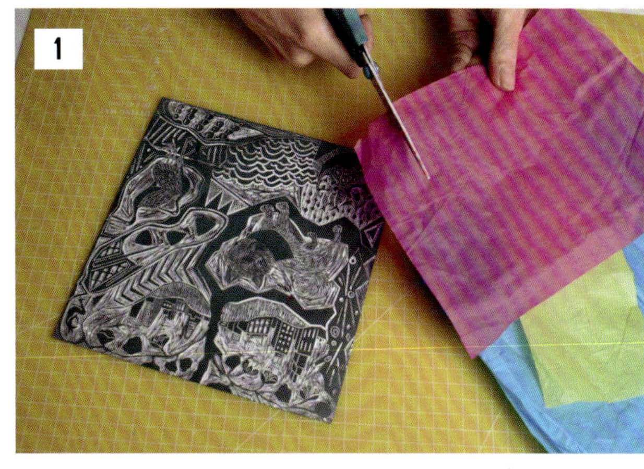

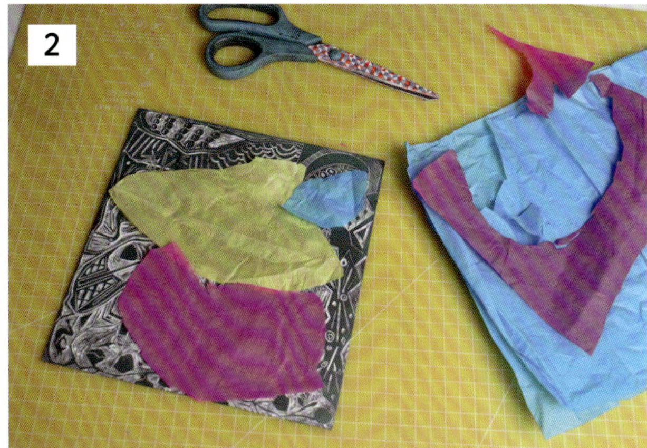

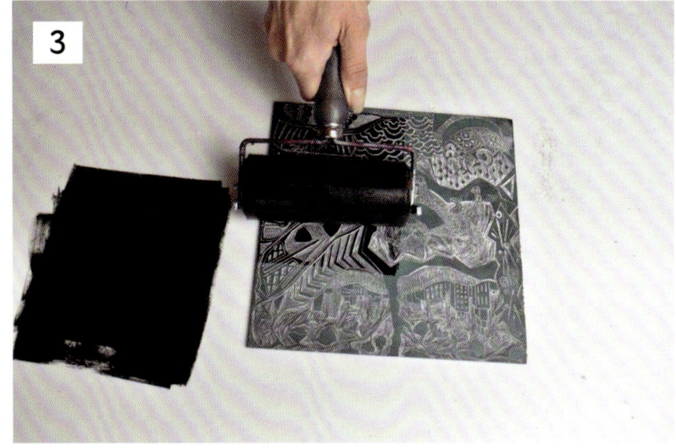

1   Cut up or tear pieces of tissue paper in various colours.

2   Experiment with placing the tissue paper onto your linocut, considering where the colours will complement the images. Alternatively, you can just place the pieces down randomly and enjoy the surprise, as I did here.

3   Ink up your linocut, as usual.

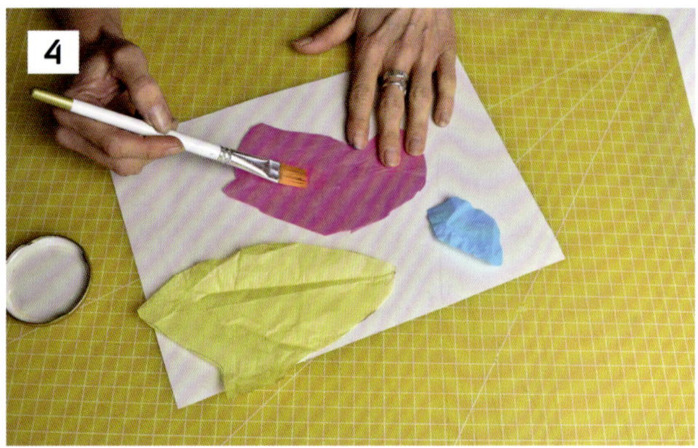

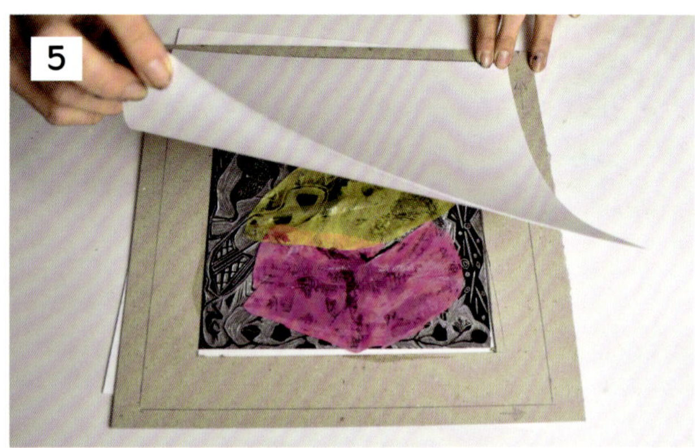

4   Carefully apply a light coating of glue to your pieces of tissue paper, ensuring you cover the whole surface.

5   Place your linocut in your registration board (see page 58) and place your tissue paper – glued side up – on top of the inked-up linocut. This can be fiddly, so it can help to use tweezers to hold the tissue paper. Place your paper down on top of the linocut and tissue paper.

6   Peel back the paper to reveal your print. The tissue paper should have bonded onto the printing paper with your print on top. Keep experimenting with different colours and sizes.

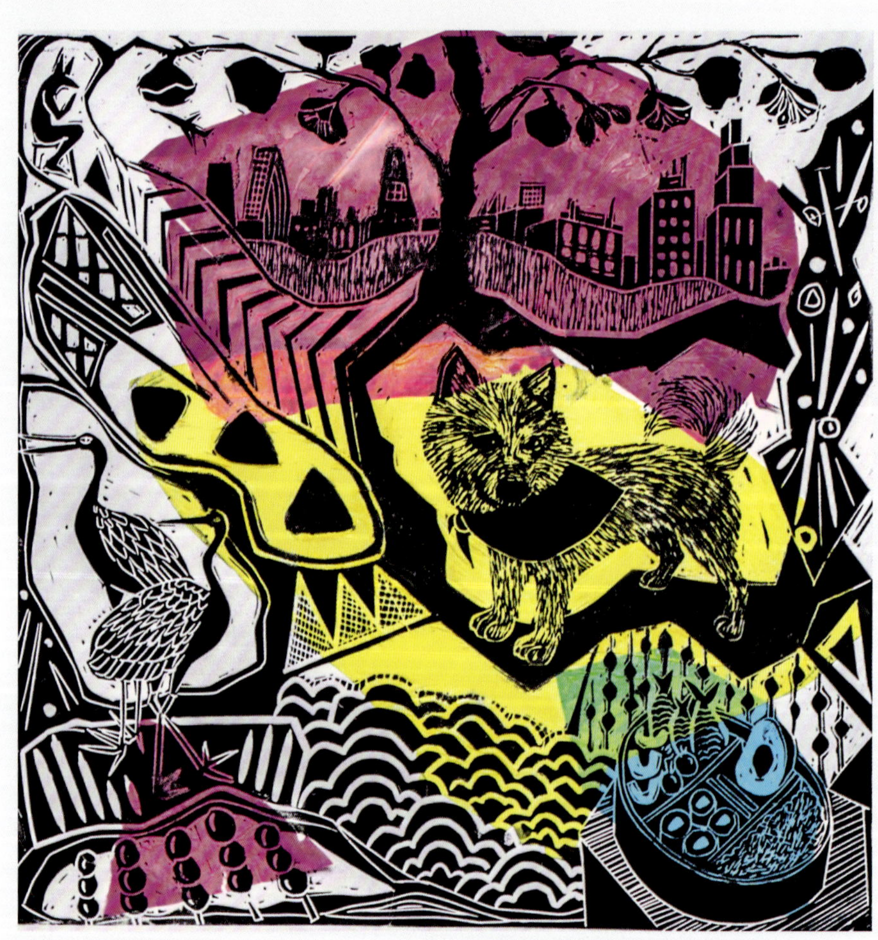

JIGSAW LINOCUT

BISHOP OF CANTERBURY DAHLIAS

You Will Need

- **Four pieces of lino (all the same size)**
- **Cutting mat**
- **Craft knife**
- **Metal ruler**
- **Selection of pencils, e.g. HB/2B**
- **Rubber/eraser**
- **Printing paper**
- **Tracing/carbon paper**
- **Masking tape**
- **Permanent marker or biro**
- **Cutting tools**
- **Stiff brush**
- **Scissors**
- **Relief printing ink**
- **Roller**
- **Inking slab**
- **Baren or wooden spoon**
- **Cleaning materials**

The jigsaw linocut method involves carving the design from one lino block, which is then cut up into sections for inking in different colours. The lino pieces are brought together like a jigsaw to complete the design. The paper is then placed on top and burnished to transfer the design onto paper.

It's autumn when I'm writing this, and I still have a few of my favourite Bishop of Canterbury dahlias left in the garden. I picked a few and realised they would be a perfect subject matter for this jigsaw project as they have a clear division of colours with their dark purple stems and vivid cerise flowers.

So, your task for this project is to source something which can easily be divided into different sections. Have a look around your house for something suitable; there is bound to be inspiration lurking in the cupboards! It's up to you how many different sections of colour you want to include – for this demonstration I've chosen to keep it simple with just two colours.

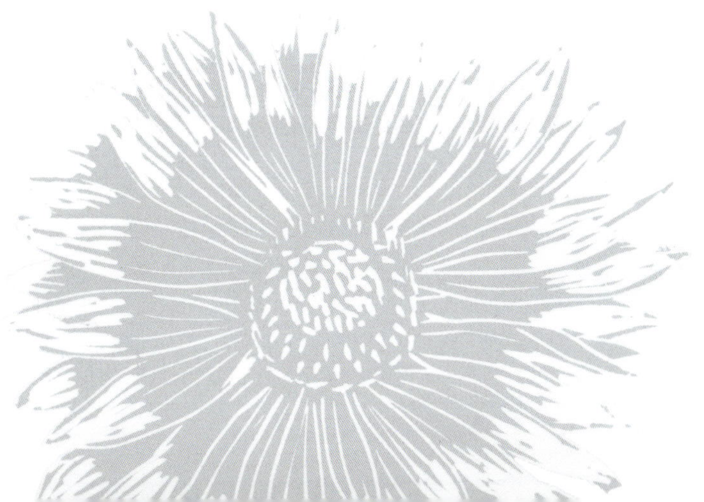

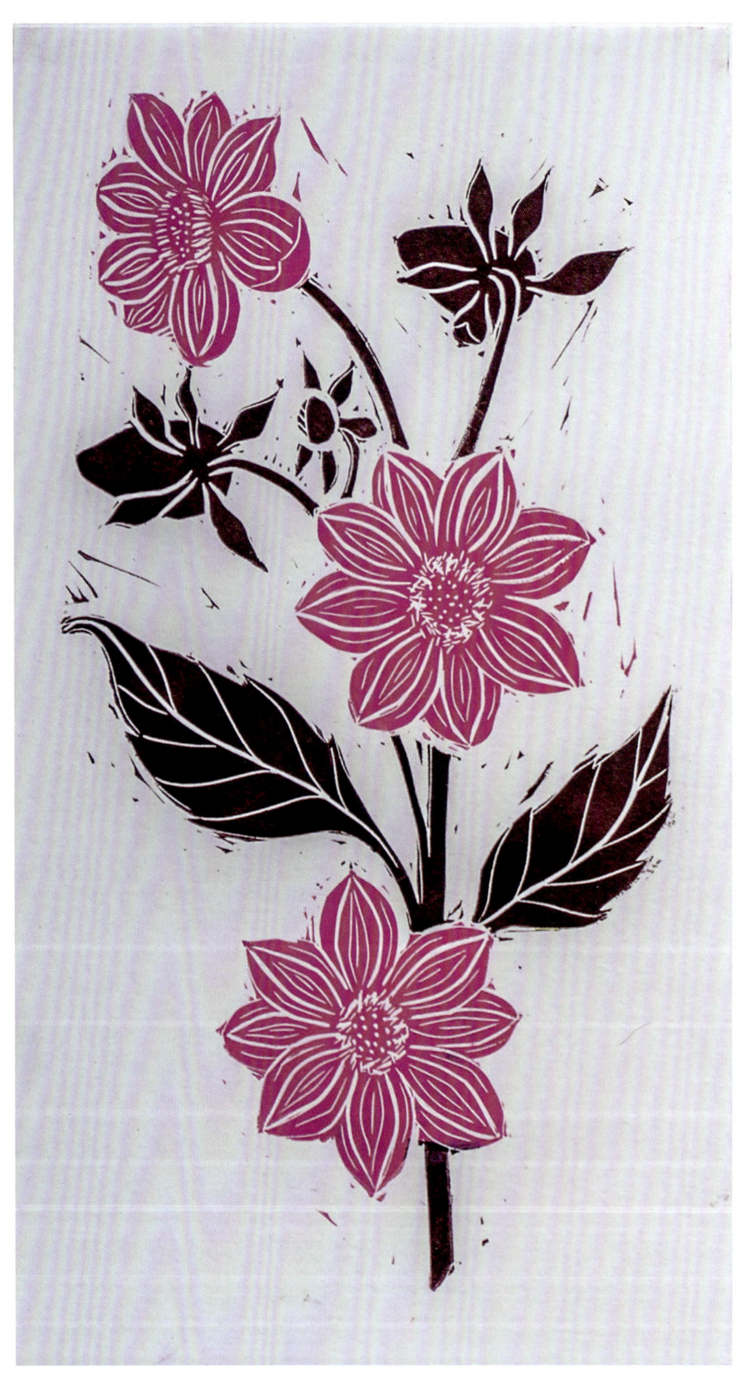

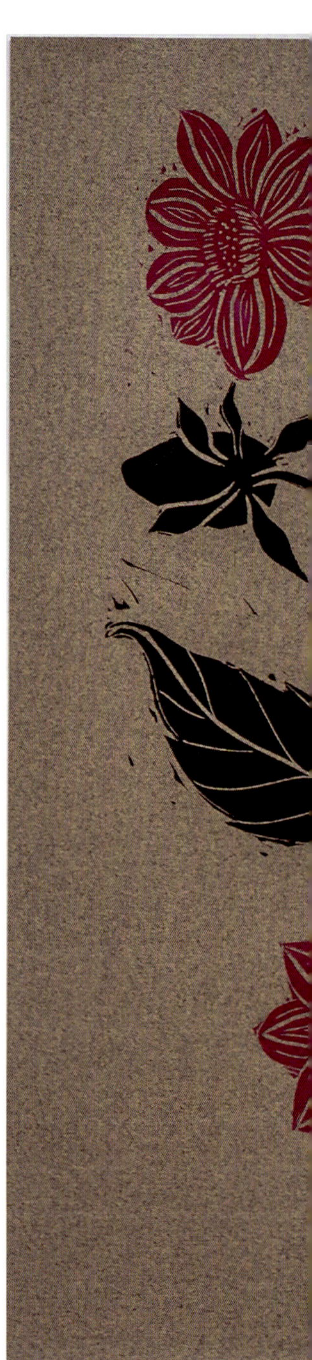

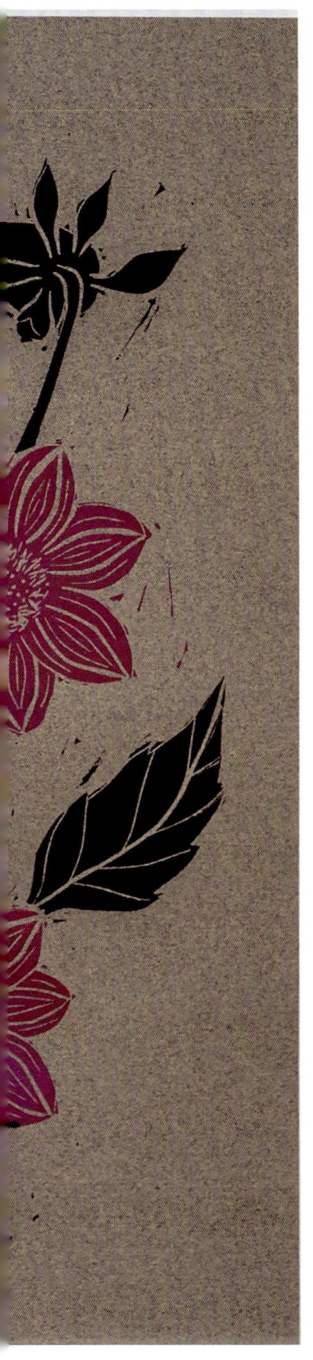

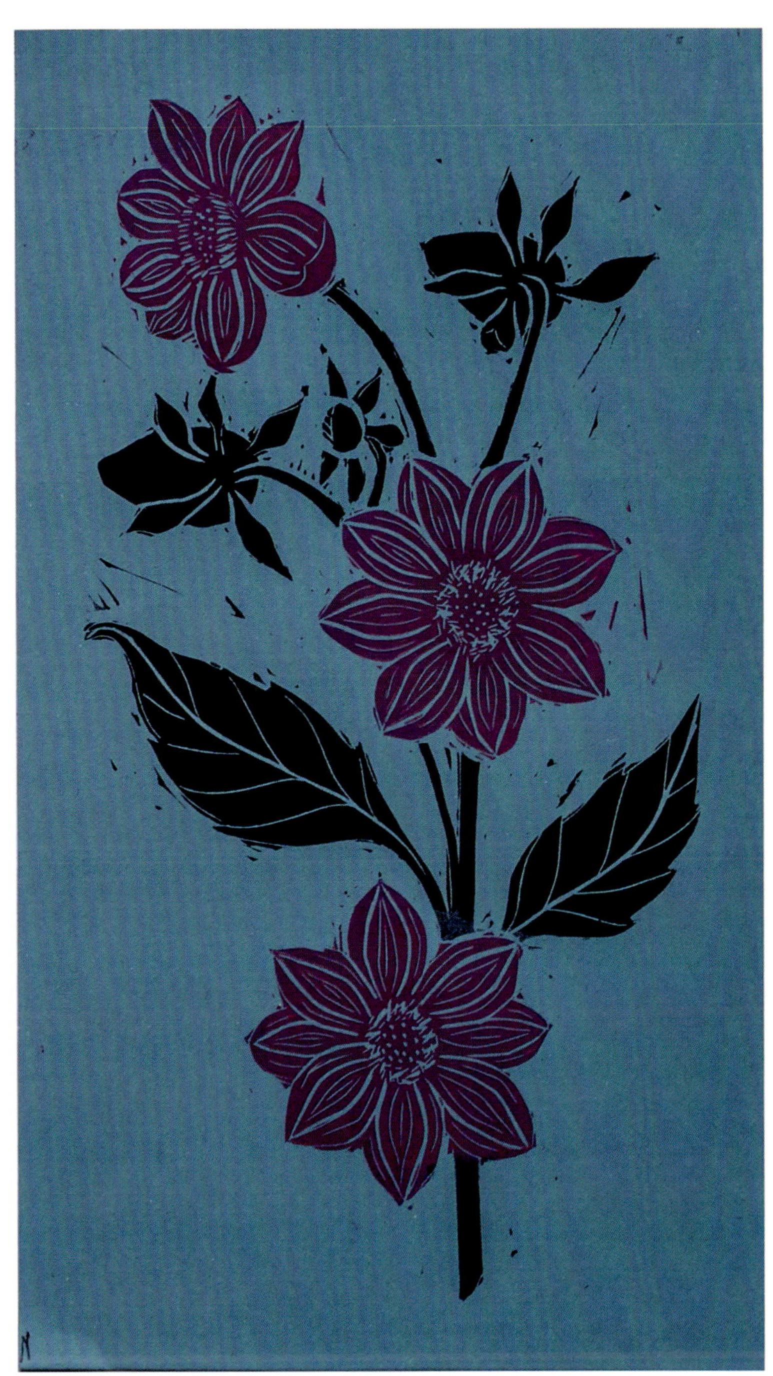

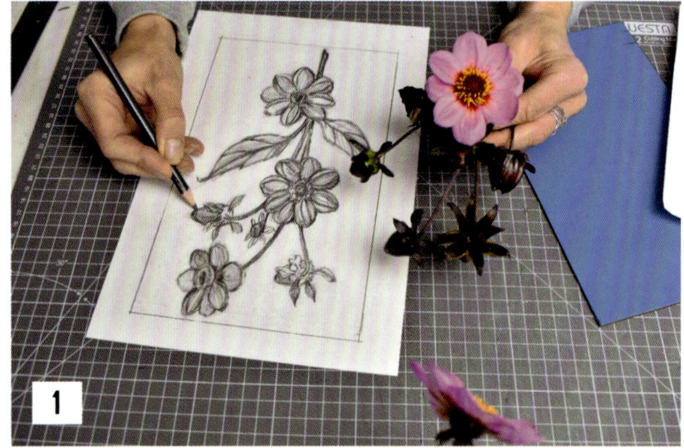

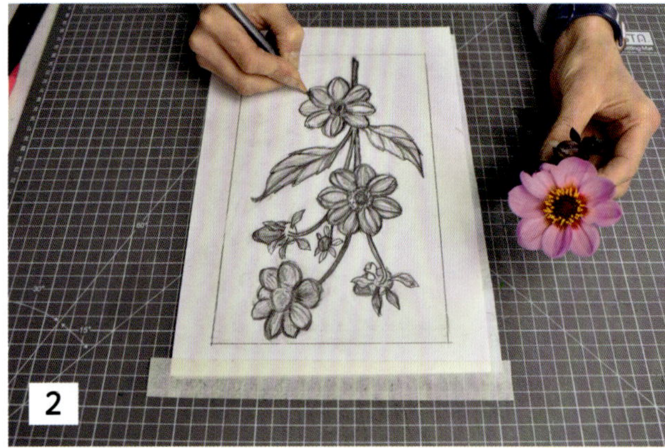

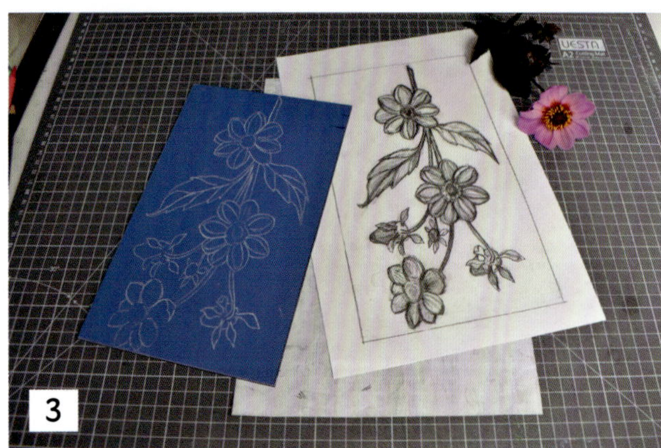

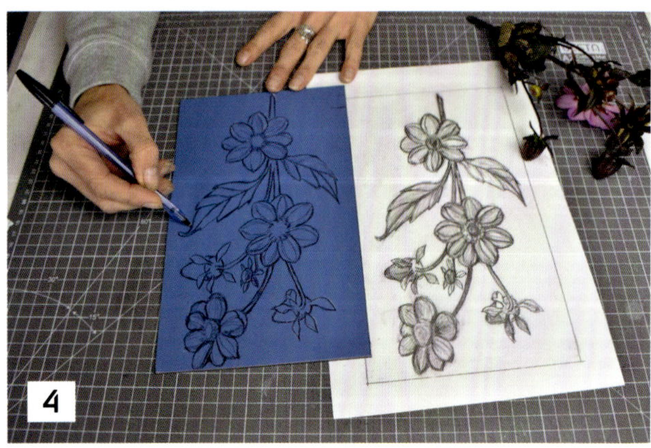

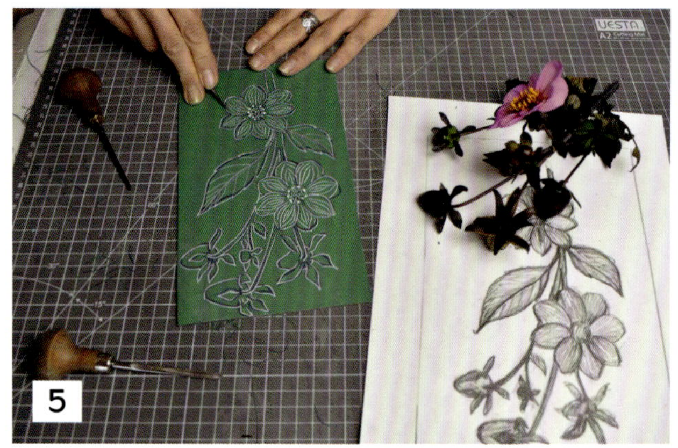

1   Cut the size of your lino blocks in relation to your chosen subject. Draw around the block and sketch your design in the box. As you are drawing, decide which areas you are going to divide.

2   Transfer your drawing – for this print, I'm using white carbon paper (see page 33). I have placed the carbon paper on top of my lino block and then positioned my drawing on top of the carbon paper. Always make sure you use masking tape to secure your drawing.

3   Carefully check the transfer to make sure you have all the details you need.

4   Reinforce the transfer line with permanent marker or biro.

5   Start by outlining your image with a fine V or U tool.

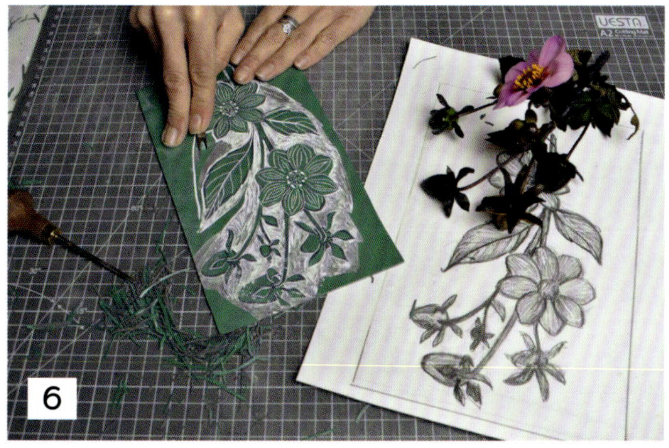

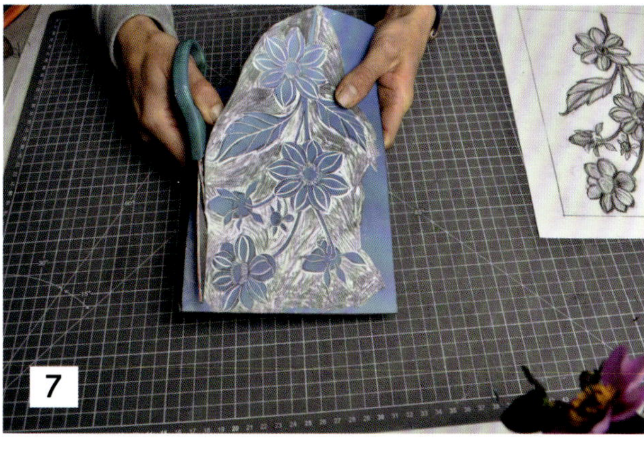

6   Use a wide U tool to start clearing away the background. You don't have to clear it all away here, as you can cut the excess away with scissors in the next step.

7   Use a sharp pair of scissors to cut the excess around the edges.

8   Decide which parts you want to divide. Carefully cut the lino up into sections using a craft knife.

9   Create a template using the paper template registration method (see page 57). Draw around each block.

10 Reinforce your drawing with marker pen, making sure each piece of the jigsaw fits together.

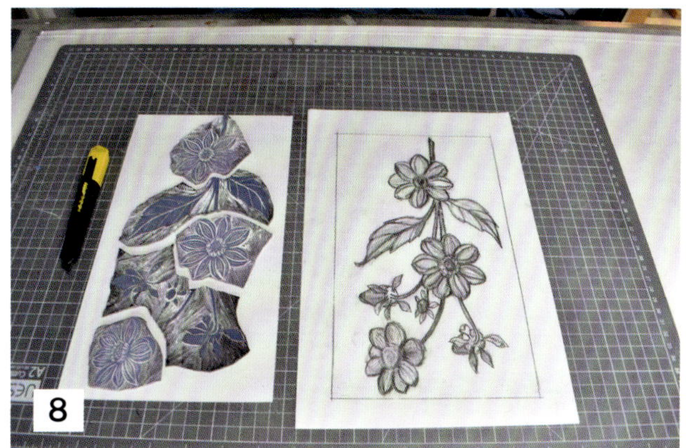

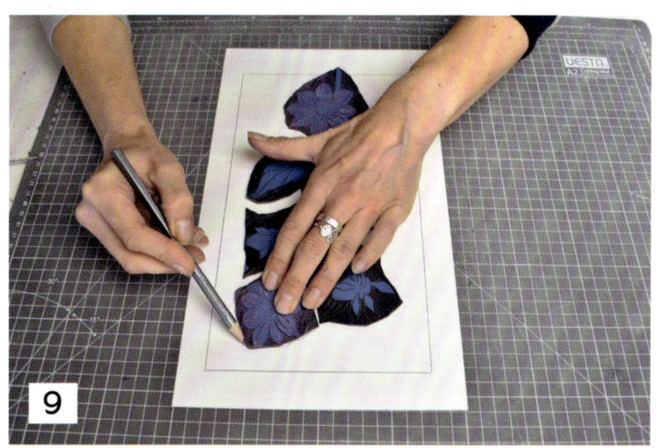

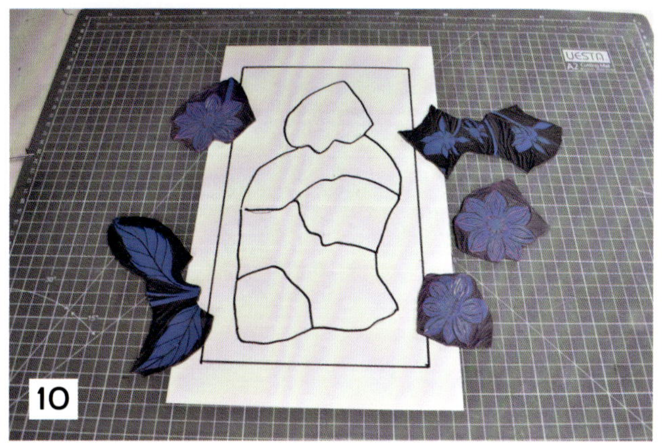

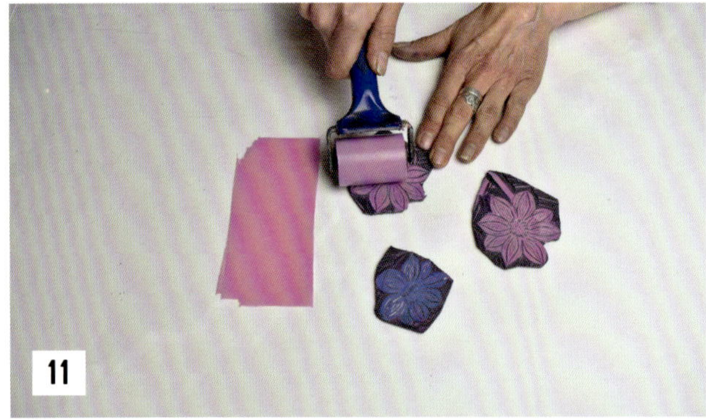

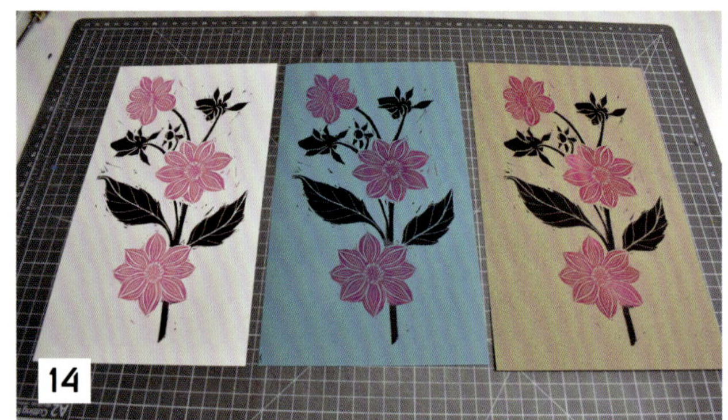

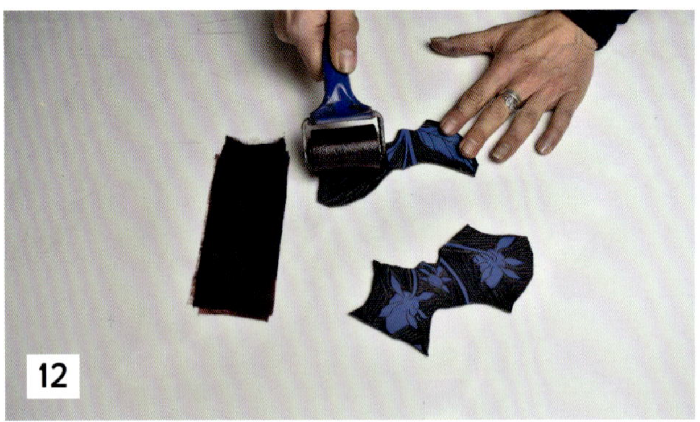

11 Ink up the separate blocks using your first colour.

12 Ink up the remaining blocks using your second colour.

13 Place the inked-up lino blocks carefully in your registration sheet, making sure they fit together nicely. Place your paper down and burnish.

14 Here are my finished prints (see also pages 144–5). Try printing on various paper types or inking up with different colours – you will be surprised just how making one small change can affect the whole look of a print.

RAINBOW ROLL

For the final project in this chapter, I'm going to show you how to create a rainbow roll. A rainbow roll is a lovely way to add a range of colours to a linocut, whereby two or more colours are rolled out and blended on the roller, creating a graduated colour effect.

In the first demonstration, I am going to work with two primary colours to achieve a secondary colour on just one linocut block. In the second, I will show you how to use three colours on a two-block print.

It's important that your roller is slightly larger than your linocut block, to ensure a nice even coverage of colour. With this in mind, I've chosen to use a small linocut for this project.

You Will Need
- Roller
- Relief printing ink
- Inking slab
- Pre-carved linocut block
- Printing paper
- Baren or wooden spoon
- Cleaning materials

USING TWO COLOURS ON ONE LINOCUT BLOCK

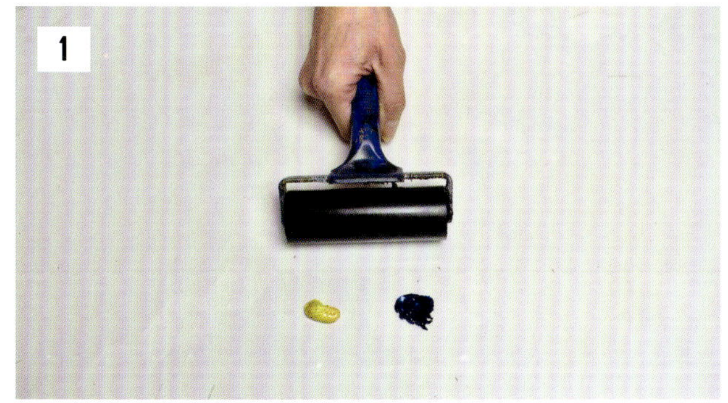

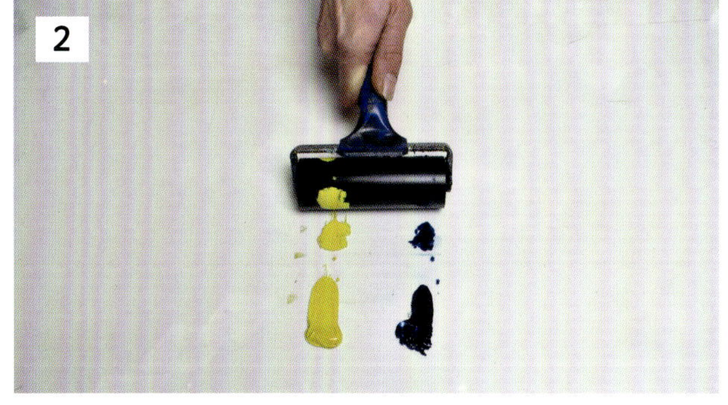

1   Squeeze out two blobs of ink in different colours, spacing them just within the width of the roller.

2   Gently pull the roller down, working in strokes. Make sure you keep the roller in one orientation.

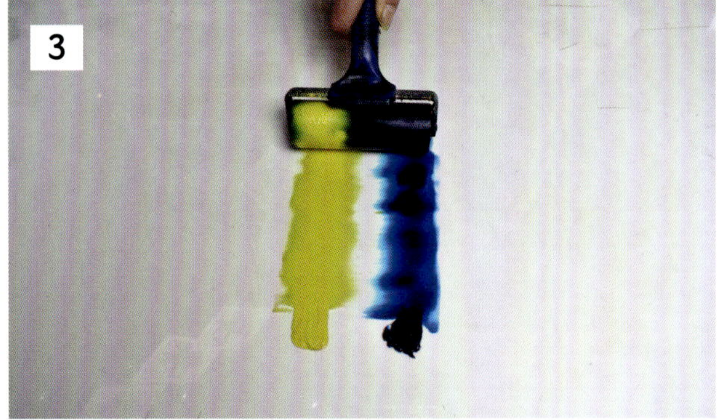

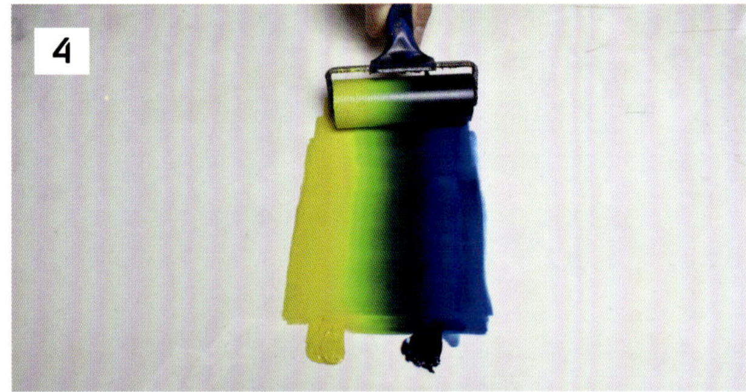

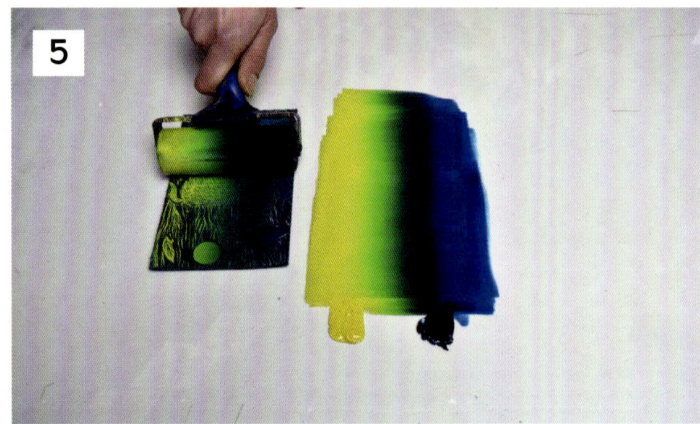

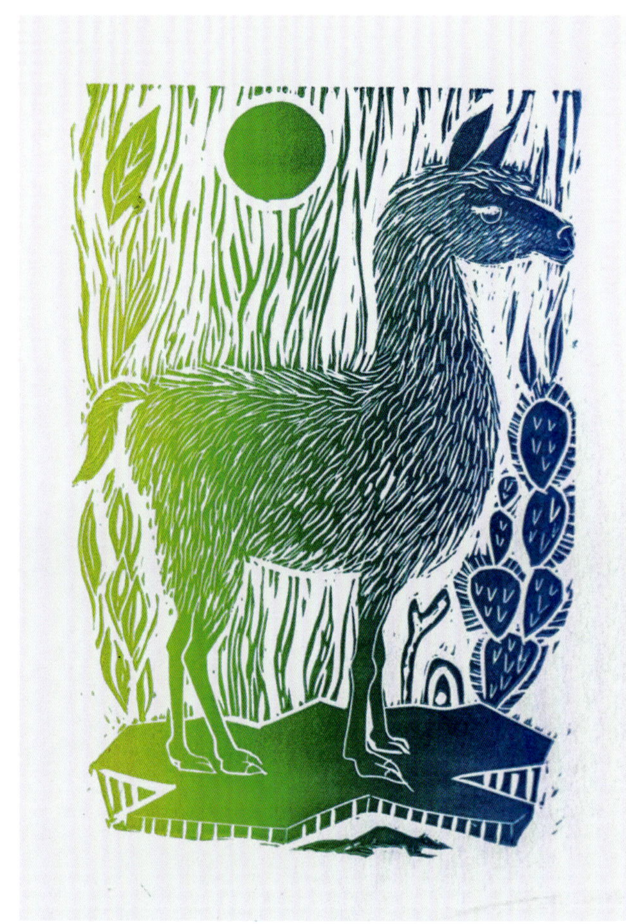

3 Once you have rolled down the colours, you should now have a gap in the middle, which is where your blend will be.

4 To achieve the blend, gently move your roller from left to right; the colours will start to meet in the middle and mix. The more you move the roller from side to side, the more of the blended colour will fill the centre. You can see here that the blue and yellow have mixed together to form a green.

5 Once you are happy with your blend, take your carved linocut and ink and print up as usual.

6 Here is my finished print. You will notice the change from yellow to green to blue. This technique has so many possibilities – you could try rainbow rolling your jigsaw prints so that you create different colour blends on the separate blocks.

USING THREE COLOURS ON A TWO-BLOCK PRINT

Next, I'm going to show you how to create a rainbow blend for a two-block print. For this, you will need an uncarved linocut block the same size as the carved linocut you used in the exercise above. You will also need to make a registration board for this project (see page 58).

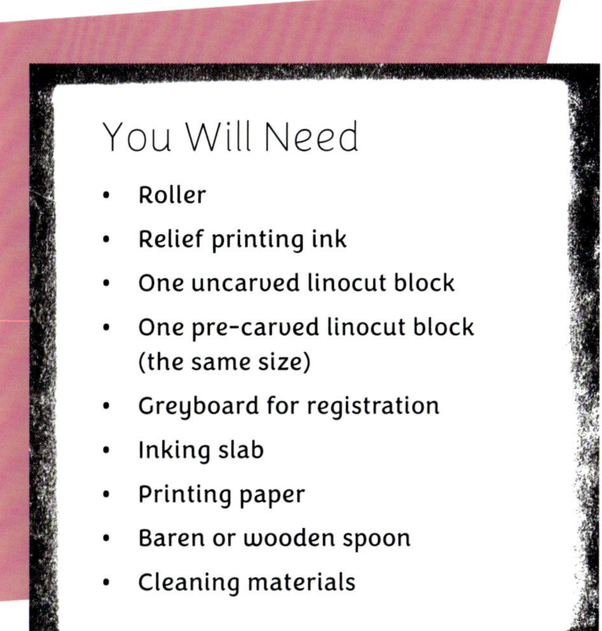

You Will Need

- Roller
- Relief printing ink
- One uncarved linocut block
- One pre-carved linocut block (the same size)
- Greyboard for registration
- Inking slab
- Printing paper
- Baren or wooden spoon
- Cleaning materials

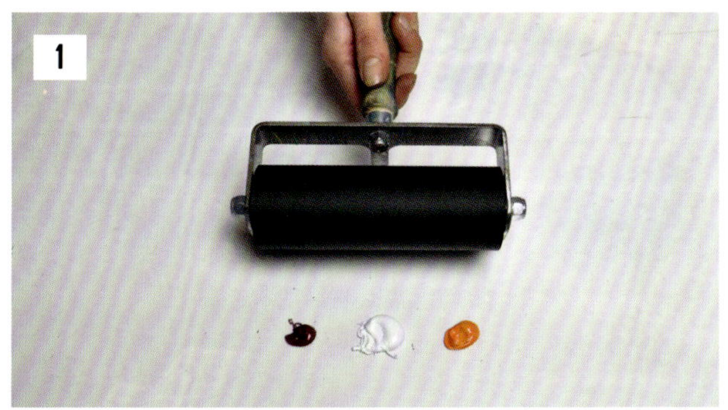

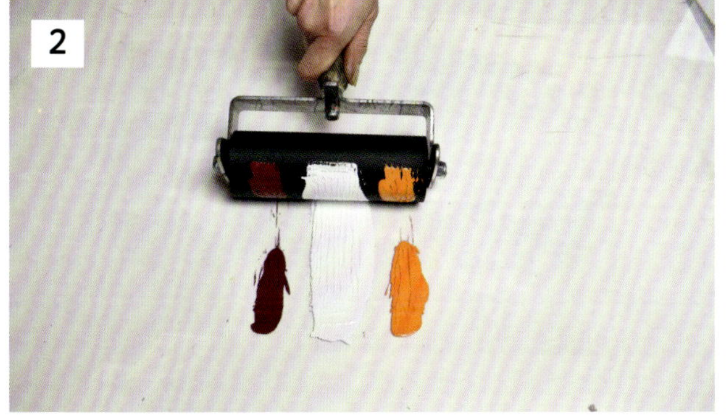

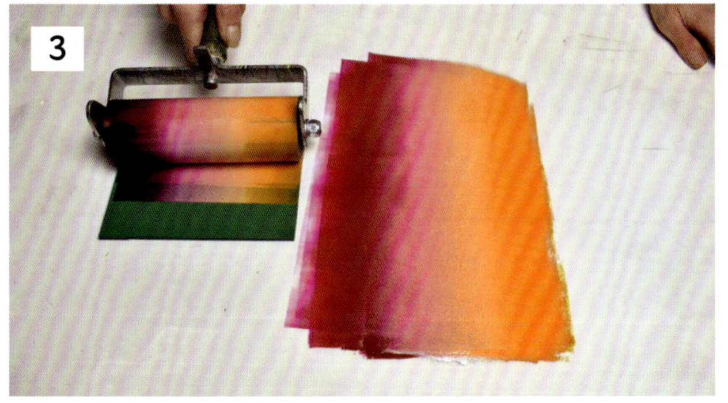

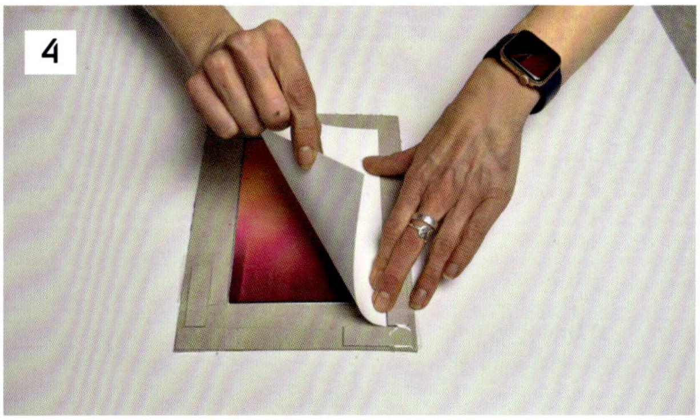

1   This time, I'm using three colours: magenta, white and light orange. I have squeezed out more white than magenta and orange, as I want to lighten both the orange and the red.

2   Roll down the colours and spread them, as in steps 2–4 of the previous project, gently moving the roller from left to right.

3   Once you have achieved your blend, take your uncarved block and ink it up. I'm inking up widthways, as I want the orange to be at the bottom and the red at the top.

4   Place your inked-up block in your registration board and print as usual.

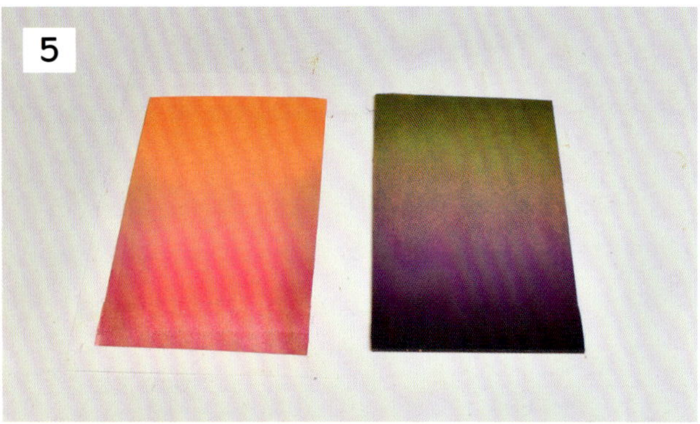

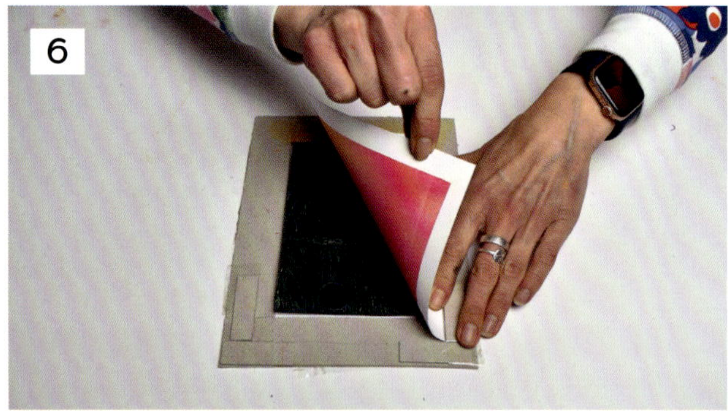

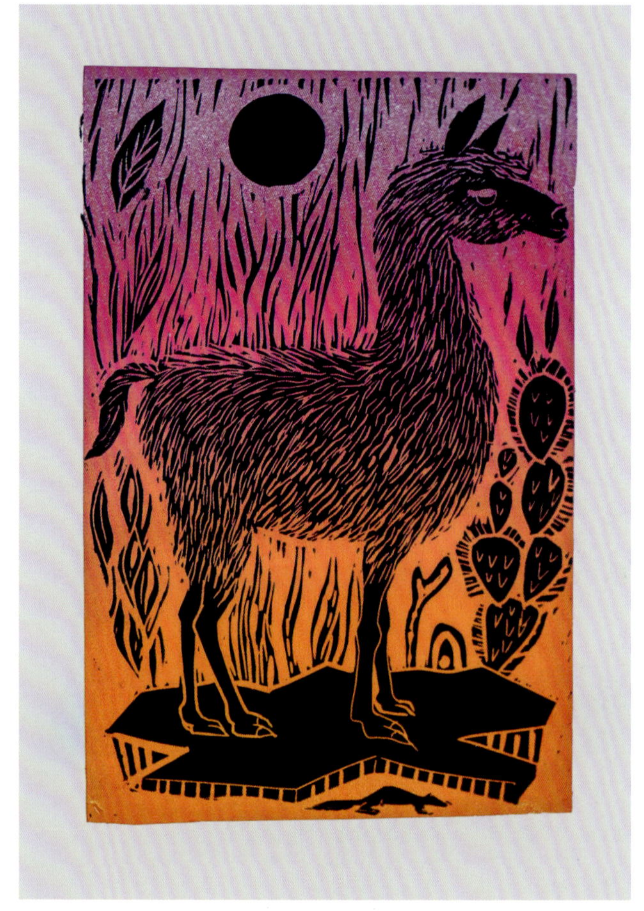

5   Here you can see the print and the block that has just been printed. If you are using water-based inks, you can print your other block on top straight away. With oil-based inks, I tend to leave the prints to dry for a day so that the second block sits better on top.

6   Once your coloured prints are dry, ink up your other linocut block and place in the registration board. Take your coloured print, place on top and burnish.

7   Here is the finished print, with the rainbow roll in the background. This is such a fun technique with the possibility for some really interesting results.

18 MAKING LINOCUT CARDS

Linocuts are really suited to making cards as they are usually smaller, quick to create and can be less intimidating than producing a larger print. They are also a great way to showcase your work and share it with others. My cards have proven to be some of the most popular items in my shop – people love to receive a handprinted card.

In this chapter I'm going to show you how to create two different linocut cards: one uses a simple block and the other is a more complicated two-block linocut design like the fennec fox (see page 103) – but this time in card form.

For the cards themselves, you will need something a little more robust than the lightweight papers you have used in previous projects. There are many card blanks available and you might find it easier to use these than to cut your own – experiment with a few and see what works for you. Remember, though, if you are hand burnishing it's best not to choose card that is too heavy or textured.

SINGLE-BLOCK CARD

You Will Need

- Card or greeting card blanks (with envelopes to fit)
- One piece of lino
- Cutting mat
- Craft knife
- Metal ruler
- Printing paper

- Selection of pencils, e.g. HB/2B
- Rubber/eraser
- Tracing/carbon paper
- Relief printing ink
- Roller
- Inking slab
- Cutting tools

- Stiff brush
- Scissors
- Greyboard for registration
- Sellotape
- Baren or wooden spoon
- Bone folder or alternative
- Cleaning materials

1 Cut your lino to the required size for your card and draw around it onto paper. I'm using pre-cut card stock as I find it more convenient to use.

2 Plan and draw out your design. I wanted to create a simple linocut of my dachshund, Miss Marple, so here I am carefully drawing a photo that I took myself. I've made sure the dimensions of my photo will fit the square size of my card.

3 Once you have finished your design, trace around it carefully.

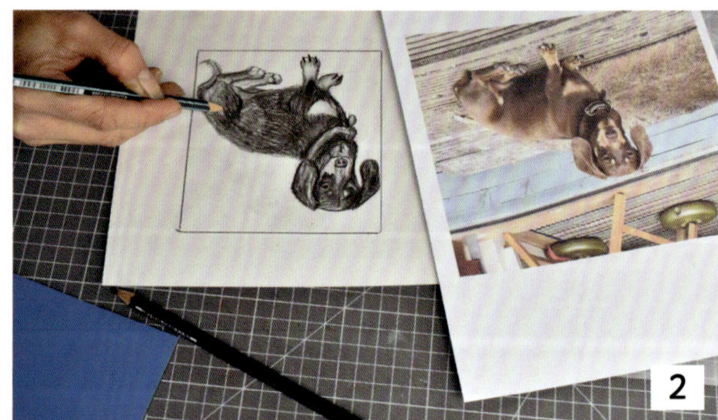

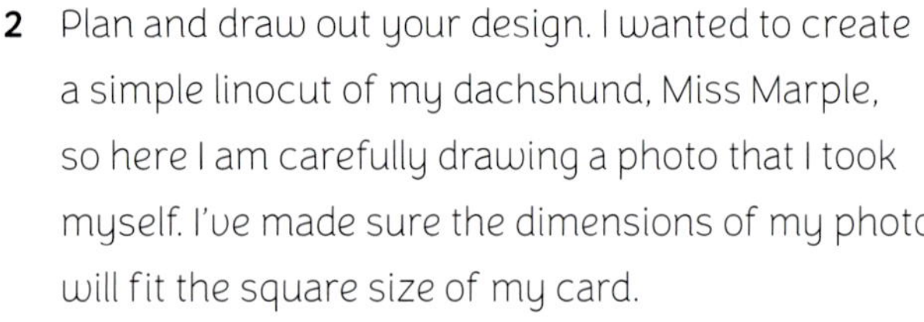

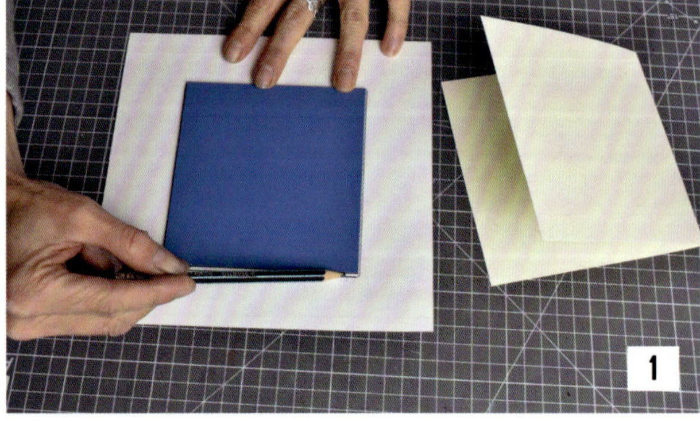

4 Transfer your drawing to your lino block (see page 29) and start carving, proofing as you go as we have done in all of the previous projects.

5 For this card print, I decided I didn't want any noise in the background. One of the simplest ways to achieve this is to cut out the design using sharp scissors, so you end up with a standalone block.

6 Here you can see the areas I cut away. Keep any remnants as you can always use them for experimental projects.

7 Here I have created a normal registration board (see page 58). On the back of the board, I've attached a piece of paper to support the block. I then taped small pieces of board around my block to make sure it is held securely in place when printing (this means that, when printing, the image will always be in the same place).

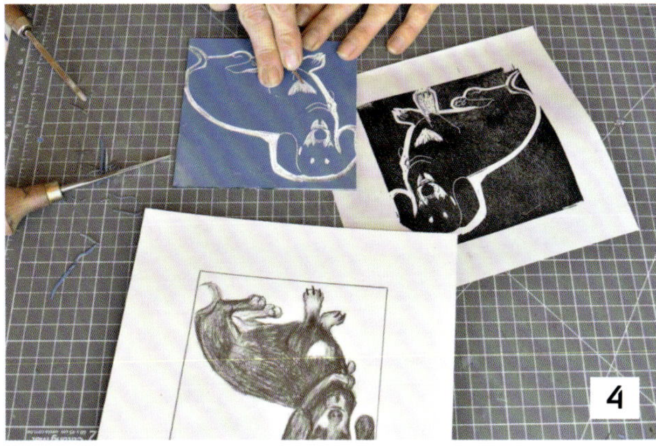

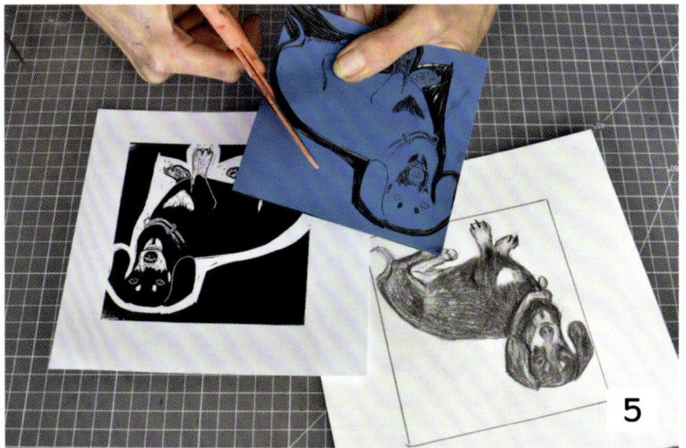

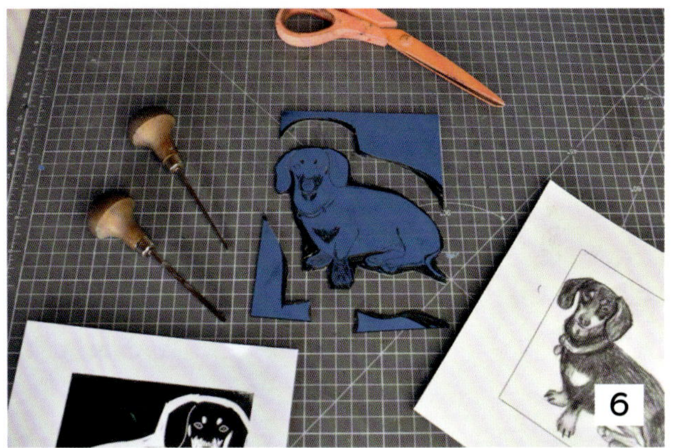

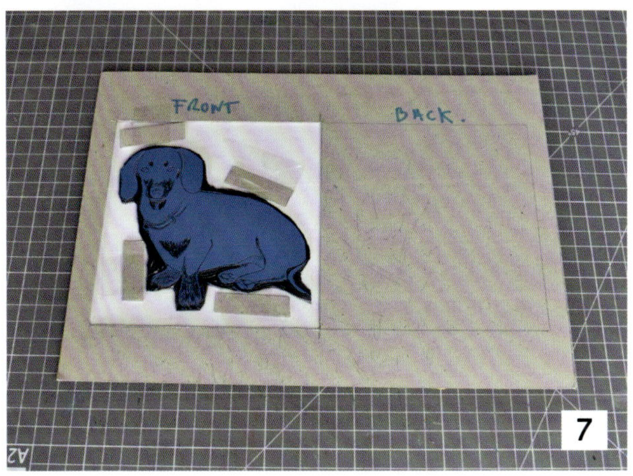

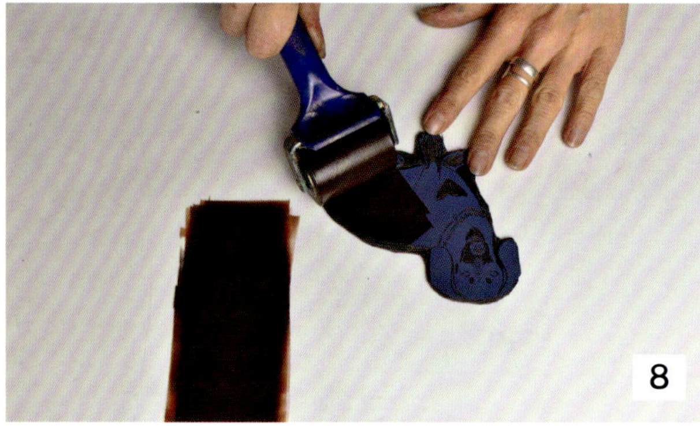

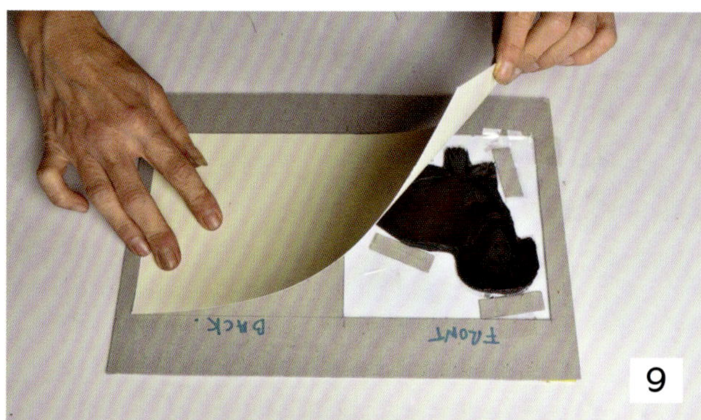

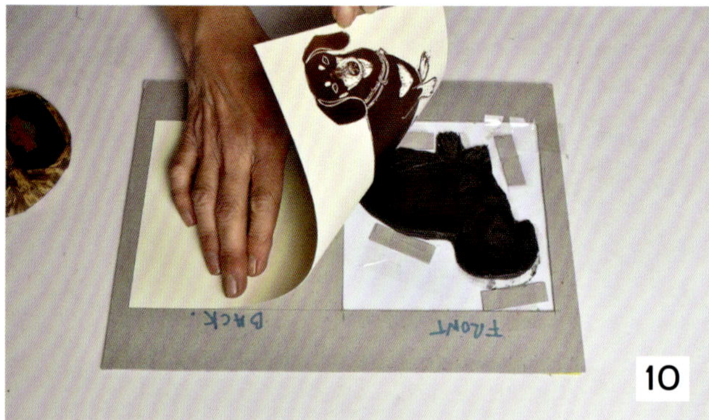

8 Ink up your linocut in your chosen colour.

9 Make sure you have noted the front and back of the card, so that the print will appear on the front – it's easy to get this confused! Place the block carefully into the registration board and place your card down.

10 Burnish the back of the print carefully, then lift the card to reveal your print.

11 Once the prints have dried, use a bone folder to reinforce the crease, then they are ready to be popped into an envelope and sent out.

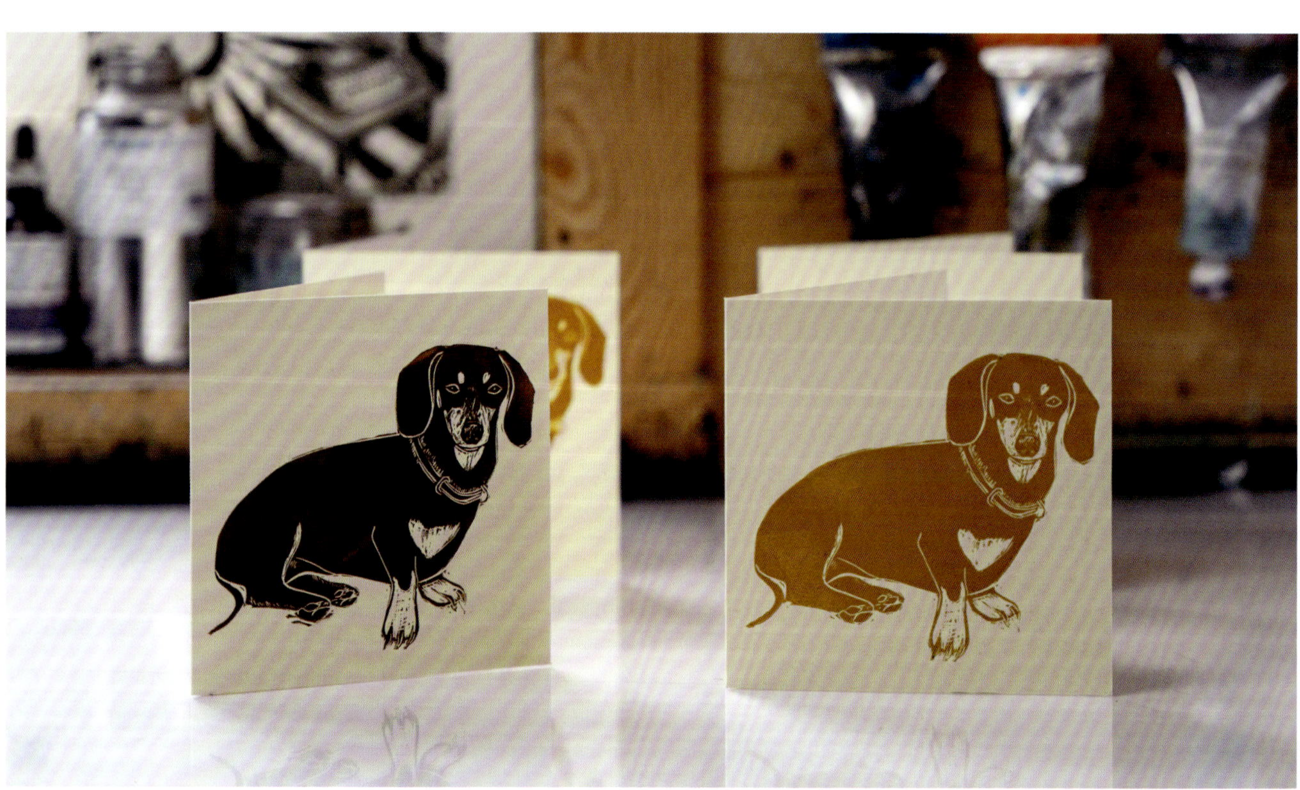

TWO-BLOCK CARD

You Will Need

- Two pieces of lino (the same size)
- Rubber/eraser
- Printing paper
- Coloured pencils
- Tracing/carbon paper
- Cutting mat
- Cutting tools
- Selection of pencils, e.g. HB/2B
- Stiff brush
- Relief printing ink
- Roller
- Inking slab
- Craft knife
- Metal ruler
- Greyboard for registration
- Card or greeting card blanks (with envelopes to fit)
- Baren or wooden spoon
- Bone folder or alternative
- Cleaning materials

For this project we are going to use the same two-block technique that we used for the fennec fox in Chapter 15, but this time on a smaller scale. The fact that you must print each block onto one card creates extra work, but this makes the cards that extra bit special.

As it's Halloween at the time I'm writing this, I decided to create a Halloween-inspired card, and it was just fortuitous that the previous week I had spent an afternoon at my friend's house drawing her black cat, Flump. Making linocut cards for special occasions is really rewarding; I like to add new cards to my stock every year.

1   Draw around your lino and plan out your design. Here, I am using the sketches I made of Flump, but combining elements of the drawings to make up my own cat design that I think will translate well to print.

2   Add colour to your drawing with coloured pencils to help you to figure out which colours to use. As mine is a Halloween-themed card, I've chosen orange and black.

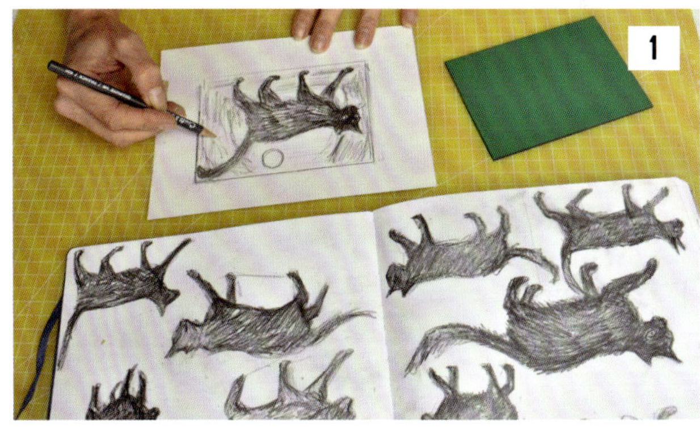

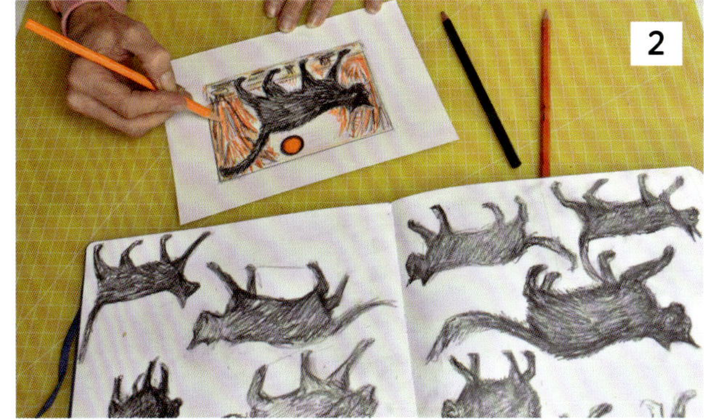

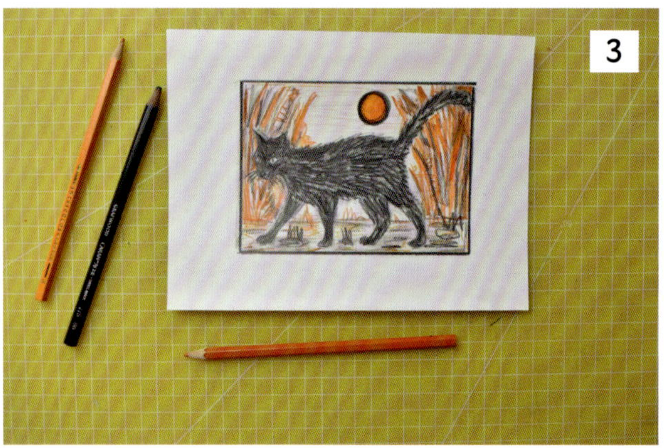

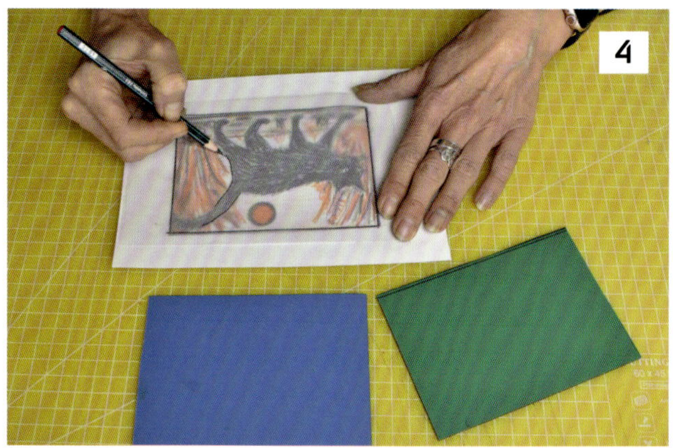

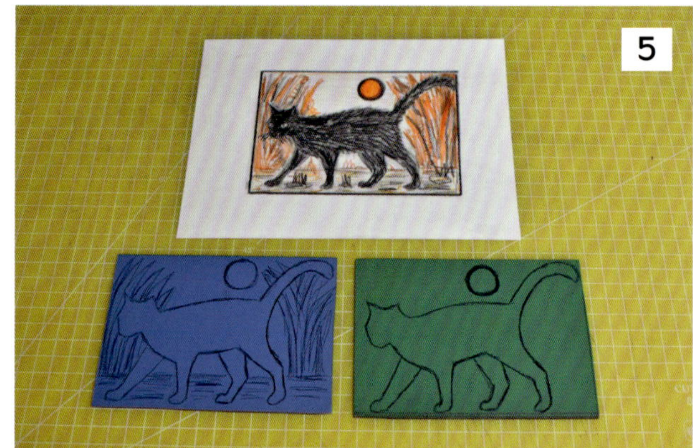

3   I've deliberately left my design rough and loose as I plan to use a lot of expressive marks in the background.

4   Use separate pieces of tracing paper for your two colours and transfer to your two pieces of linocut.

5   Here you can see both blocks – the blue lino is for the orange colour and the green lino is for the black. Again, I've traced my design so that it appears the same way as my drawing, but use your transfer method of choice (see page 29).

6   Carve out both blocks.

7   Ink up your coloured block as this will be printed first.

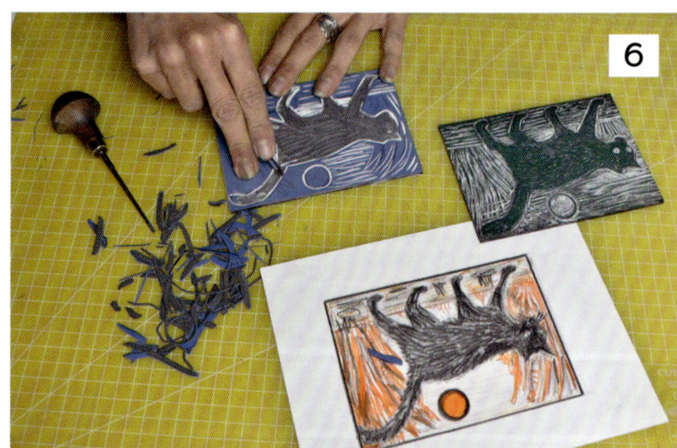

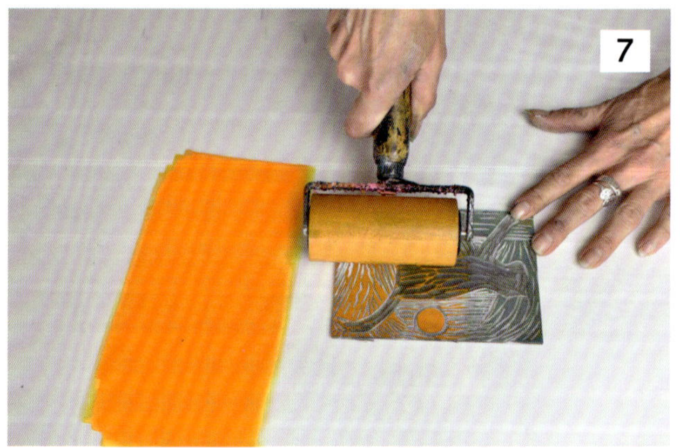

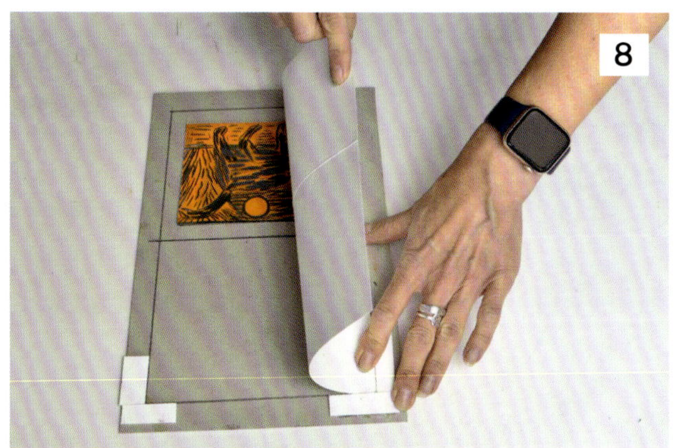

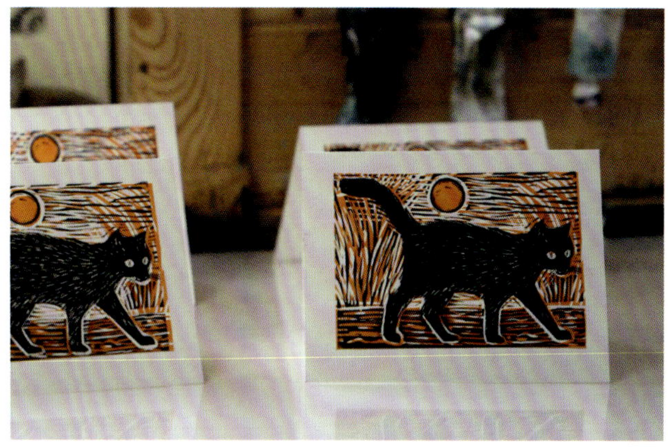

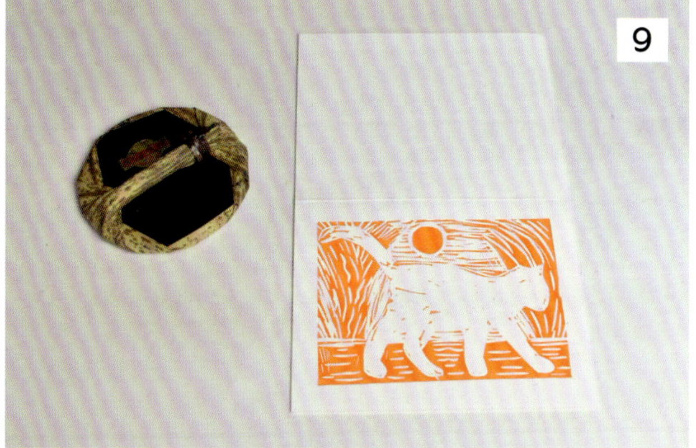

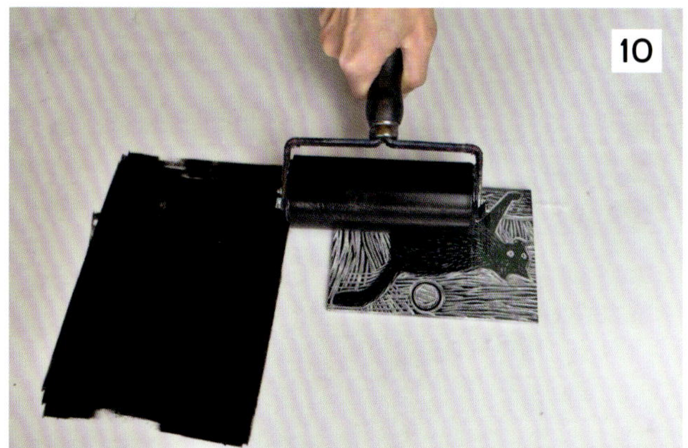

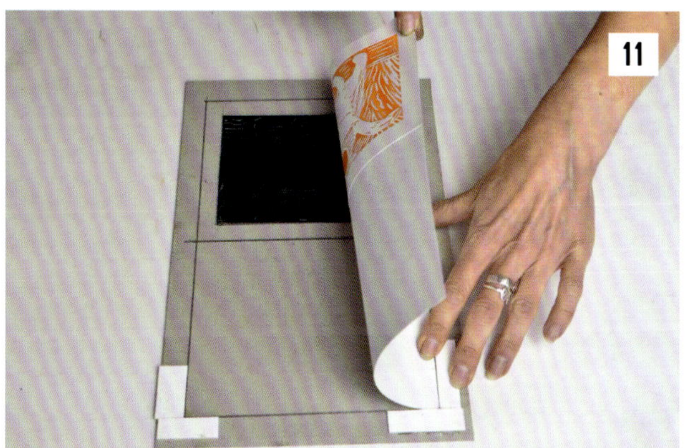

8 Make your registration board as usual (see page 58), ensuring you have cut the hole for the linocut correctly so it will appear on the front of the card. As I'm using a landscape format, my linocut sits at the bottom of the board. Place your inked-up block inside your registration board.

9 Here is my coloured block. There is a lot of orange noise on the cat's body, but I'm not concerned about this as the black linocut will cover it. Keep printing your first colour onto your card stock, letting them dry before moving onto the next step.

10 When your first layer is dry, you can print the second block on top. Ink up as usual.

11 Place the second block into your registration board. Take one of your cards with your first colour, carefully lay it down and burnish.

12 Peel back to reveal your print and use a bone folder to reinforce the crease. It took me some time to get the print to where I wanted it – I had to work hard to achieve the correct balance of orange, black and white. I say this to reassure you that it's not as easy as it looks – to be honest, at times, I felt like giving up! I'm pleased I persisted, though, as I'm happy with my cat now and I know my friend will really appreciate it.

AN INTERVIEW WITH TRISTAN SHERWOOD

What are your main sources of inspiration?

Visiting museums and galleries has always been important to me, but I can also be found snooping around bric-a-brac and antique shops, looking for decorative ceramics and patterned objects that tell the stories of everyday folk from times gone by.

Some of the printmakers I really admire are Enid Marx, Barron and Larcher, Sheila Robinson, Rena Gardiner and Peggy Angus. A top tip is to spend lots of time looking at prints that bring you pleasure; you can learn so much by studying them and, by really looking, you are able to learn from a lifetime's experience!

Many of your prints are reduction prints. Could you tell us what you like about this method?

The reductive technique is a pretty straightforward way to create a lino print with lots of layers and colours. You only need one piece of lino, which means you don't need to try to register multiple blocks. In fact, you just keep cutting away from the original block until you have all of the colours you want printed. Although it's pretty straightforward, there is an element of danger with this process, so you have to be brave.

I would recommend starting with a really well thought-out design. I always have a master drawing, but I never plan the colours that carefully. I tend to make some rough notes about the number of layers and colours I think I will use, then I tend to improvise. I really enjoy responding with colour mixing as I lay down each new colour relationship.

You are a very successful and much-loved teacher. Could you tell us how this influences your printmaking?

I feel very privileged to work with young, enthusiastic, imaginative students every day. Responding to their artistic needs and finding creative solutions to help them problem-solve ideas keeps my own practice fresh. I support students in producing work I would never be able to dream up myself; the great thing is that they have no fear and will attempt anything, so I end up stretching my own technical expertise to help them realise their ambitions.

Teaching printmaking definitely keeps my passion alive. It's such a joy to share something you love with others, and because I am continually demonstrating and supporting students in the process, I get lots of practice, which is so beneficial. If you feel you have a creative block, I would definitely recommend working collaboratively or demonstrating your practice – it's very invigorating!

@tristan_sherwood_printmaker

trisso76.wixsite.com/printmaker

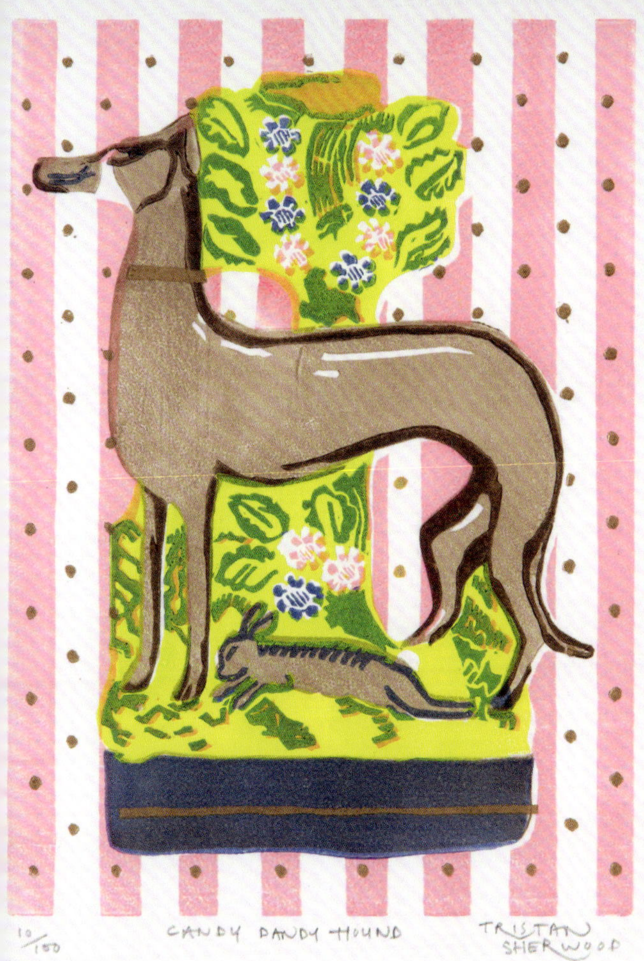

10/150
CANDY DANDY HOUND
TRISTAN SHERWOOD

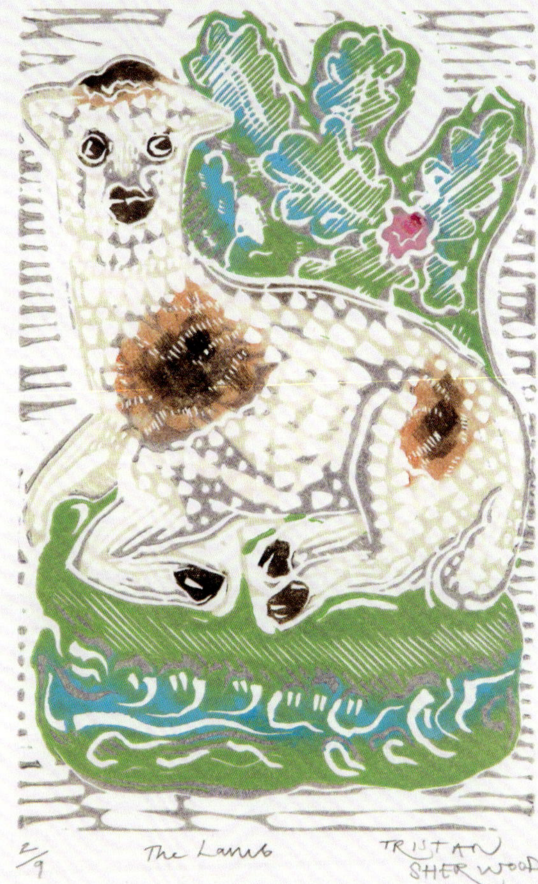

2/9
The Lamb
TRISTAN SHERWOOD

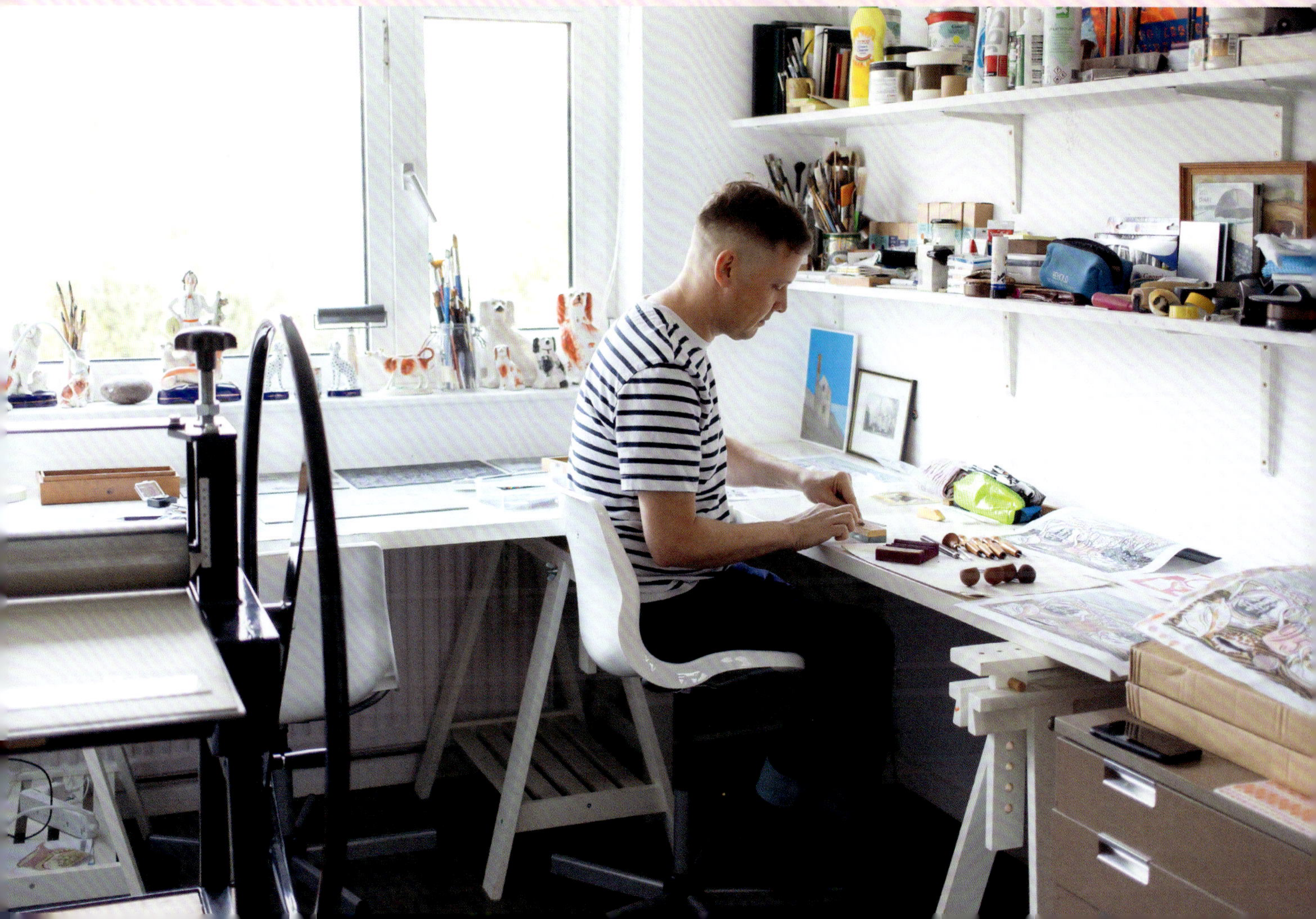

19 BRINGING IT ALL TOGETHER

For our final project, we are going to work on a large linocut – preferably A3 size. The aim of this exercise is to incorporate many of the drawings you have done throughout the book and combine them in one large print. In a similar way to how we worked in the Weekend Away project (see page 84), you will create a sketch that plays around with scale and composition – redrawing and rearranging your sketchbook drawings into one scene. It's a chance to celebrate all of the hard work that you have put in throughout the projects in this book.

A LARGE LINOCUT

You Will Need

- Large piece of lino (preferably A3 size)
- Printing paper (I'm using Japanese Kozo paper)
- Selection of pencils, e.g. HB/2B

- Rubber/eraser
- Tracing/carbon paper
- Biro
- Cutting tools
- Stiff brush

- Relief printing ink
- Roller
- Inking slab
- Baren or wooden spoon
- Cleaning materials

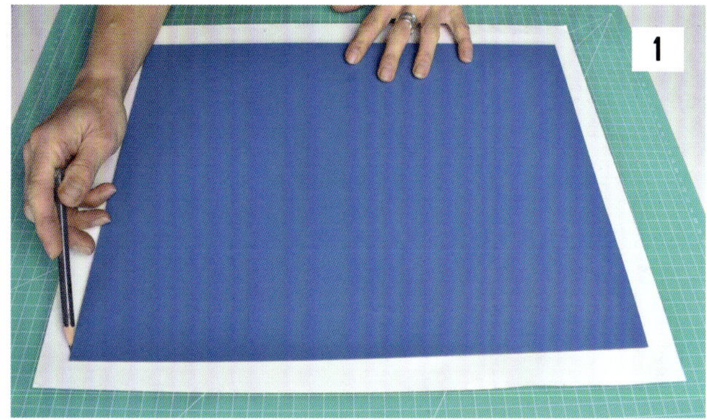

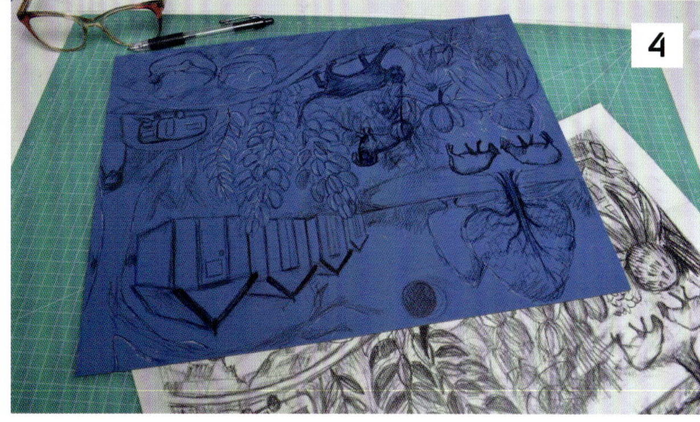

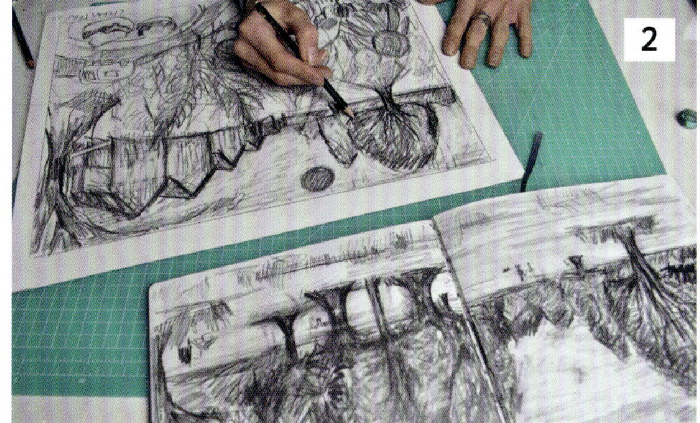

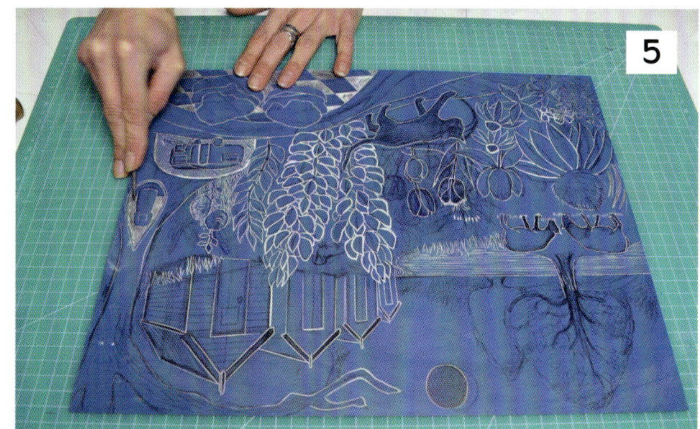

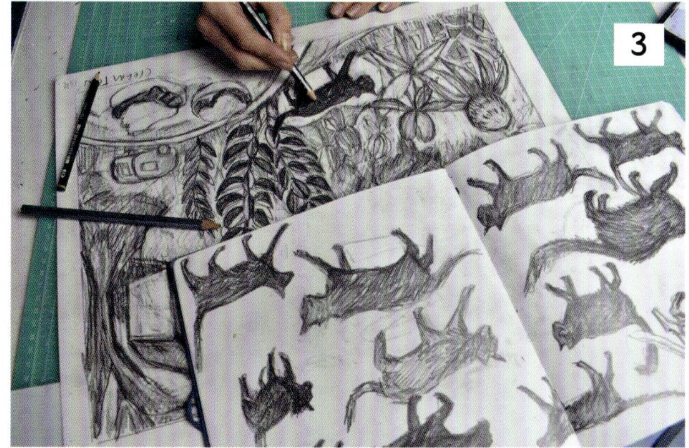

1   As we have done in previous projects, take your large piece of linocut and draw around it onto a piece of paper that you will use for drawing.

2   Begin by loosely sketching in some of the drawings you have completed in your sketchbook.

3   Continue drawing, editing and rubbing away until you are happy with the overall composition of your work.

4   Once you are happy with your sketch, transfer it to lino using your method of choice (see page 29). Here I used white carbon paper and reinforced the line with biro.

5   Begin carving. For this piece I started outlining the main elements using a fine V tool and then began working on different areas. I don't really have a method when I'm working on a large linocut – I tend to do the easiest sections first, leaving the trickier bits until last!

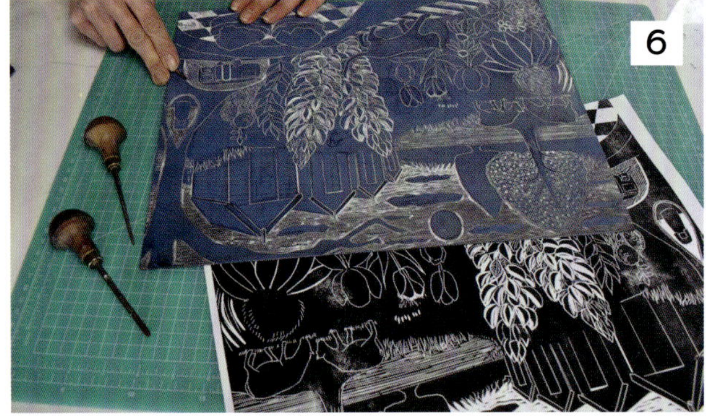

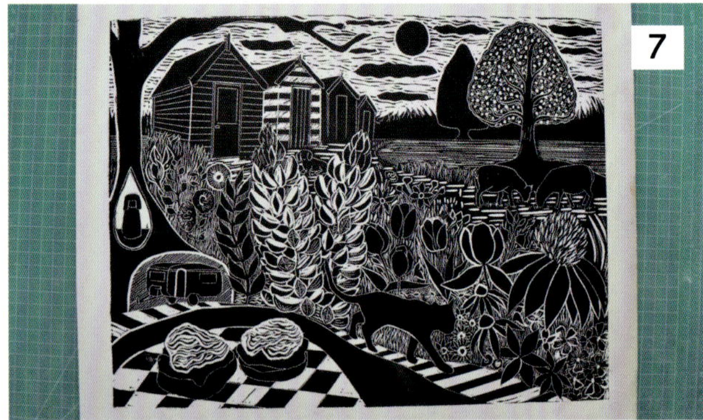

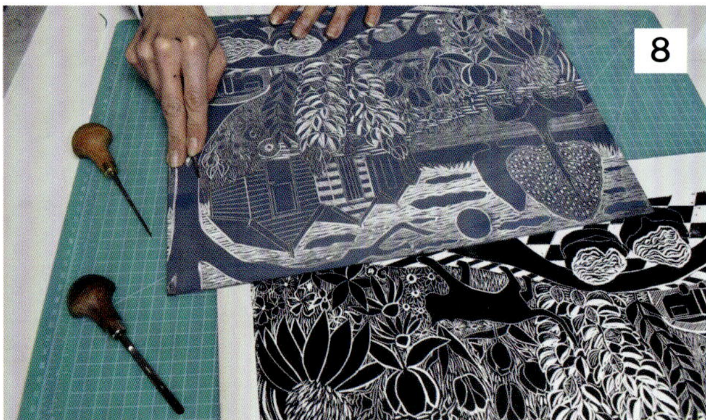

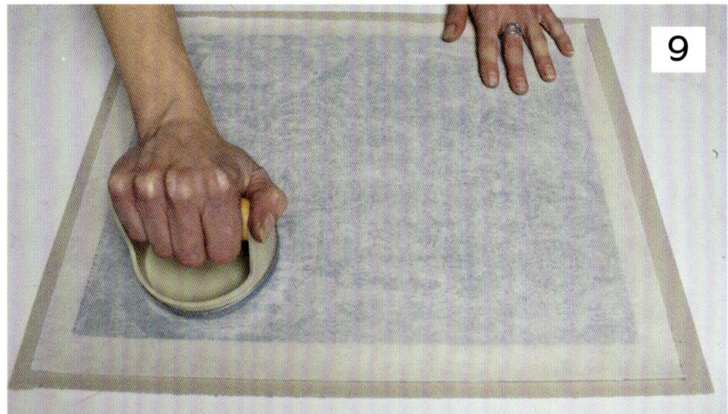

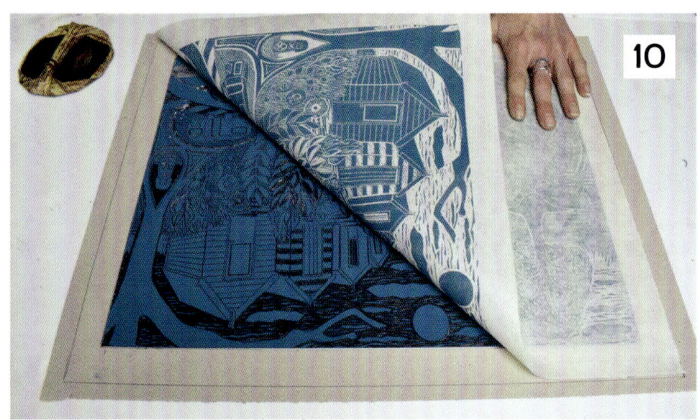

6   Take a first proof when you are curious to see how your work is progressing (see page 42). Start to let your proof guide you now, more than your drawing.

7   This is my second proof. I always make sure I assess my proofs from a distance as this helps me to see the balance between black and white. If it's possible, I leave it a day or so before I start work again, so that I can view my work less critically.

8   Continue carving and proofing until you are happy with your print.

9   Choose your colour and ink up as normal. As it's a large linocut and I'm burnishing by hand I'm using Japanese Kozo paper – a lovely, strong but lightweight paper that consistently prints well.

10 Peel back the paper carefully.

11 Here is my finished print. I chose a nice teal colour,
which I mixed from process blue, yellow ochre and
phthalo green.

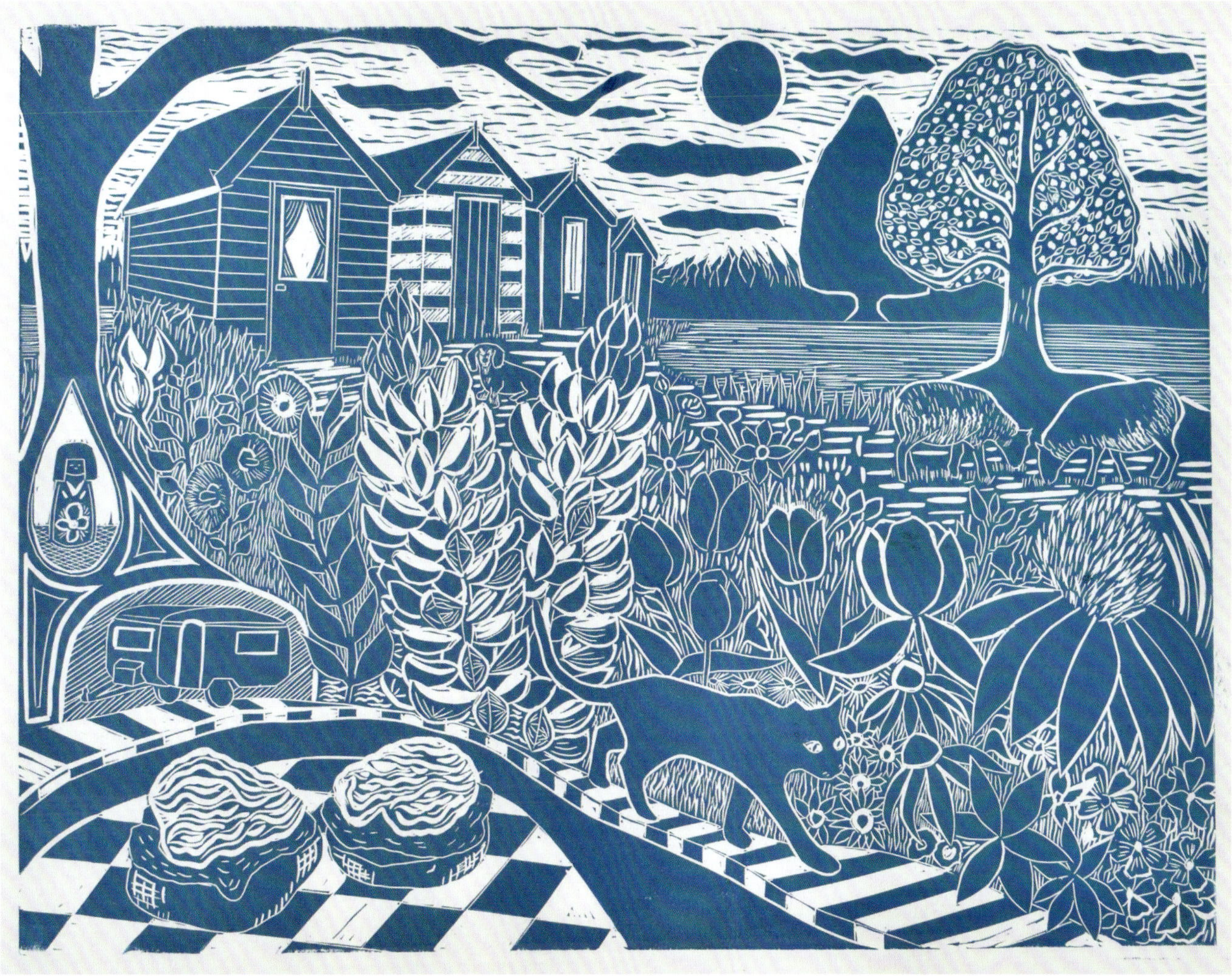

20 NEXT STEPS IN PRINTMAKING

As we are now at the end of the book, I want to give you some further ideas on how to expand your printmaking practice. After all, linocut is just one part of the printmaking family. You can try out many of the techniques below for yourself, but some of them require a press and, ideally, a printmaking studio. Have a search around your local area – if you are lucky, you might find a studio near you that runs classes and workshops.

RELIEF TECHNIQUES

As we have explored with linocut, relief printmaking is the technique of carving away the areas that are not to be printed, leaving the raised areas – the areas in relief – to be printed, forming your image. Here are some other forms of relief printmaking.

WOODCUT

Woodcut is the oldest form of printmaking. Similar to linocut, it is a relief process in which tools are used to carve a design into the surface, but this time from a wooden block. When printed, the carved areas remain white and the remaining area receives the ink. In a woodcut print, the piece of wood is carved along the grain to produce an image. As with linocut, you can do this at home.

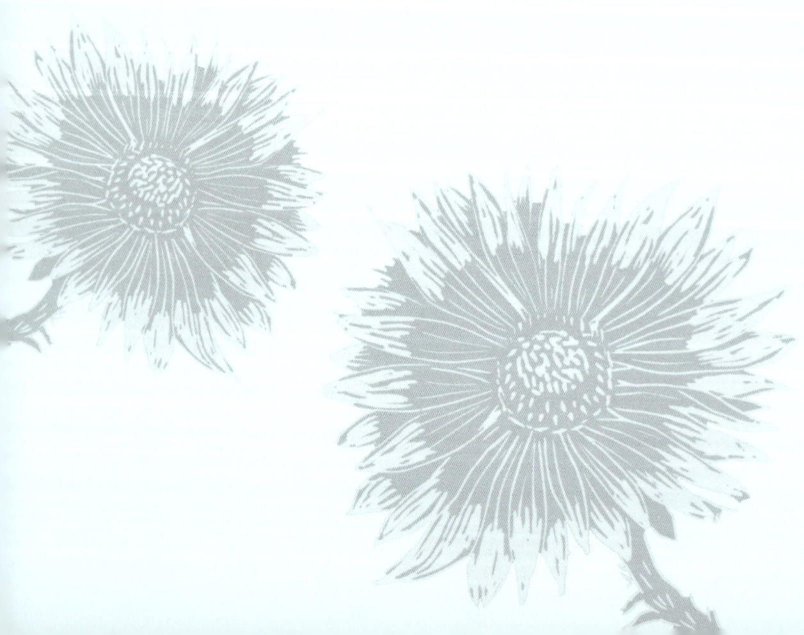

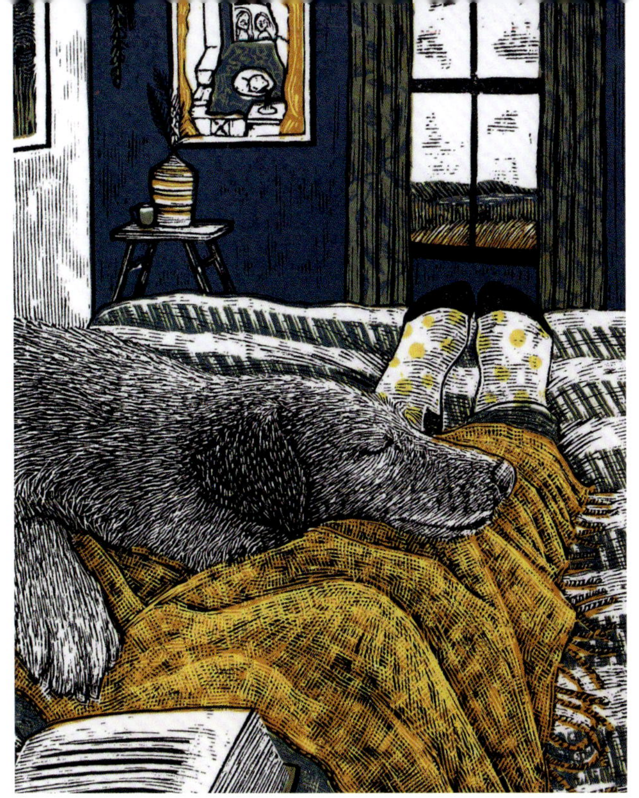

WOOD ENGRAVING

Wood engraving is a much newer process. It differs from woodcut in that the line is incised into the woodblock, rather than the background being cut away to leave a line in relief. Wood engraving tools can achieve very fine detail but only on the hard, dense surface of wood, such as box, which has been cut across the grain. Because box is so slow-growing only small blocks are available, which has led to wood engravings often being done on an intimate scale. Again, you can carry out wood engraving at home.

Credit: Molly Lemon

INTAGLIO PRINTMAKING

Intaglio printmaking is the opposite to relief printmaking in that the incised areas are printed, rather than areas in relief. Therefore, the ink goes into the line, rather than remaining on the surface, as it does with relief. This makes intaglio printmaking much more akin to drawing.

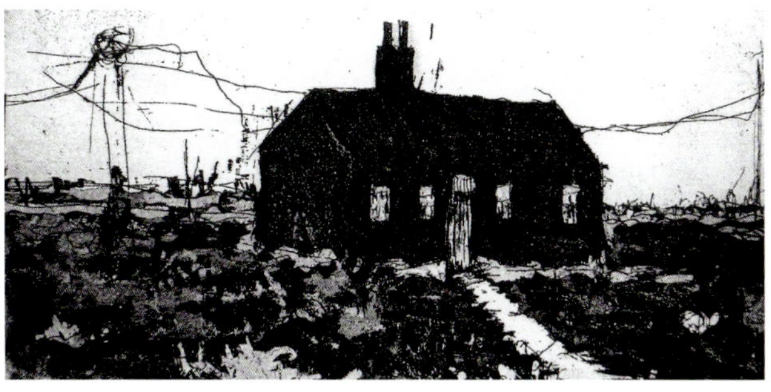

DRYPOINT

In drypoint, an image is drawn onto a plate using a hard, sharp, pointed needle-like tool. The process of scratching into the surface with the tool creates a slightly raised, ragged and rough edge to the lines, known as the burr. The burr, when printed, has a lovely velvety quality – a real characteristic of drypoint.

Owing to the delicate nature of the burr, drypoint is usually made in small editions, as the action of inking and printing through the press flattens and crushes the burr. Drypoint is often referred to as etching – this is incorrect, as etching involves acid or salts – drypoint is a form of engraving.

ETCHING

In etching, the metal plate (usually copper, zinc or steel) is coated with an acid-resistant ground. This is then used as your surface upon which to draw into, using a sharp etching needle, which then exposes the metal. The plate is then immersed in acid and the exposed metal from your drawing is bitten and 'etched'. The resulting incised lines are then inked up and printed.

Etching is a wonderfully addictive technique with so many possibilities. I can guarantee that, if you find a good place to learn etching, you will be hooked. Etching is difficult to do at home due to the chemicals involved.

OTHER PRINTING TECHNIQUES

Alongside relief and intaglio printmaking, here are some other printmaking techniques that you might find interesting and want to try out.

SCREEN PRINTING

Screen printing is the process of transferring a stencilled design onto a flat surface using a mesh screen, ink and a squeegee. The basic method involves creating a stencil on a fine mesh screen and then pushing ink or paint through the mesh to create an imprint of your design on the surface beneath.

Stencils can be created simply with paper, paint, glue or lacquer, or by using a light-sensitive emulsion to create a stencil, which is then developed in a similar way to a photograph. The process is sometimes called serigraphy or silk screen printing, but all of these names refer to the same basic method.

I have a very basic screen printing set-up at home where I use stencils made of newsprint. I use the screen-printed colours as a background to some of my linocuts.

MONOPRINT

A fabulous way to explore printmaking is through monoprint – a technique we have dabbled with a little in this book. A monoprint is essentially a one-off print, hence the use of 'mono', which in Greek means alone.

One of my favourite forms of monoprint is the 'transfer' monoprint technique. This is when you ink up a surface, place a piece of paper on top and then draw onto the paper with a wide variety of tools. This creates a mirror image transfer on the other side of the paper. The resulting marks are smudgy, rich and unique to this technique.

Other forms of monoprint are the additive and subtractive methods – additive when you add ink to a blank plate, and subtractive when you remove ink. All of these can be done at home.

COLLAGRAPH

A collagraph is a print made from a collage of textured materials. A whole range of diverse materials such as cardboard, leaves, string, tape, sandpaper, seeds, fabric and so on can be glued onto a flat surface to make a printing plate. Once the materials have stuck to the plate and dried, they are then coated with shellac, which seals in the materials, enabling you to ink up the plate. The different materials absorb and release ink in different ways to make exciting – and often surprising – prints.

LITHOGRAPHY

Lithography is a printing process that is based on the fact that oil and water don't mix. It uses a flat stone or metal plate onto which the image areas are worked using a greasy substance that the ink will adhere to, while the non-image areas are made ink-repellent. Lithography is a technique that requires special equipment, and finding places that offer courses can be tricky.

CONCLUSION
PRACTICAL TIPS WHEN THINGS AREN'T GOING 'RIGHT'

After spending hours on a print – drawing, carving and printing – the realisation hits you that you just aren't happy with it. No matter how hard you try, you don't feel that sense of accomplishment and satisfaction you hoped for. Rest assured, I've been there many times, and over the years I have developed strategies to help me reframe and find practical ways to move forward.

The first thing to remember is that we are our own worst critics. We have such high expectations of what we want to achieve that we can quickly feel deflated if the print doesn't look exactly as we had anticipated. But ask yourself: Does it really matter if your print doesn't look as you had hoped? After all, we would have been working from and looking at a drawing, which, due to its nature, looks very different to the print. It might just mean we need a little time for our eyes to adjust to the final piece and to let go.

1 MOVE AWAY FROM THE PRINT

When you have been working intensely on a piece, you are so tuned into it that you become hypersensitive to imperfections – any little perceived errors are magnified in your eyes.

I have learnt my lesson the hard way with this. I once printed a whole edition of fifty prints involving six screen-printed colours with the key block printed on top – it took days to print and was a huge amount of work. When I finished, I decided I wasn't happy with it for the smallest reason, so I impulsively reprinted the whole edition, which also took days and, again, was a huge amount of work. I looked back at both sets of prints a couple of weeks later and struggled to see the difference!

Therefore, I always recommend putting the print away for a few days – you will become less attached to it and gain some helpful distance – you might even come back to it and decide you like it after all.

2 USE IT AS A WARM-UP BLOCK

Let's say you are halfway through a linocut when it becomes obvious that it just isn't working. Instead of abandoning it and starting on another, my advice would be to keep going with it and use it as a test block.

I often find that I can become too tight when carving – it's almost like I become scared of the block. Then when I decide to use it as a warm-up, the pressure is off, and I become much looser and more experimental. Inevitably, some of the marks I make on the warm-up block will find their way onto the next (and hopefully final) block.

3 REPURPOSE

If you take the advice above and end up with lots of test or warm-up blocks, a great way to reuse them is to cut them up and experiment with them, as we did in Chapter 17. This can be a great way to spark new ideas and find new directions for your work.

Test prints and proofs can be used as cards or cut up and used in collages. I also cut up my test prints and use them as thank you notes when someone buys an editioned print.

4 TOUCH UP

I get asked a lot about correcting mistakes in linocut – the most common question is: If you have mistakenly carved something away, can you stick it back on? The answer is: You can try, but you might not be that successful. If you are using traditional battleship grey lino, then you can apply a tiny amount of wood glue – this can work as wood glue dries very hard.

It's inevitable that, at some point, a rogue bit of carved lino will get into your ink (see page 45 to see what this looks like). This can be easily remedied by taking a cotton bud with a small amount of printing ink and gently dabbing the white area.

Again, give yourself some distance from the work – what you perceive as a glaring mistake at the time might not be visible to you in a few weeks.

SETTING UP A REGULAR PRACTICE

So, you have bought all the kit, completed the projects and been printing like a demon. You have told all your friends you are going to quit your job and become a full-time printmaker, as that seems the most sensible option. Then you suddenly lose momentum and enthusiasm. The voice in your head starts telling you that you aren't that good and you are just wasting your time. So, you put down your tools, pack away your inks and feel deflated – another flash in the pan – thus reinforcing your belief that you aren't creative, you can't draw and you certainly can't print. The best way to avoid this scenario is to build up a regular practice, and the following tips should help you to achieve this.

1 PACE YOURSELF

I truly believe that to build up a regular practice it's important to pace yourself. Instead of bingeing, do it in small regular chunks.

In the studio with my own practice, I hardly ever work past five in the afternoon and the most I carve for is three hours a day.

I've learnt that small chunks of work time keep you from burning out and losing interest. The important thing is to be consistent and to keep chipping away. Stopping helps strengthen the muscle of patience that permits you to keep coming back, sustaining your creativity and productivity over time.

2 SET REALISTIC GOALS

It's important to be realistic about your goals. When you first start out, aim to complete and edition a few sets of prints, getting to grips with the basics. Over time, you might want to start turning your smaller prints into cards and sending them to friends and family. Similarly, giving away prints as presents is a lovely way to share your work. Eventually, you may decide to open an online shop to sell your work or hire a stall to sell your prints at a local craft market. The key is to start small and build up your confidence over time. There is nothing more deflating than trying to sell your work before you are ready.

3 BE PATIENT

When I first started out, I sold nothing for months on end; sometimes years went by and I only sold a handful of prints. It's only now, after twenty-five years of doing a huge range of very diverse jobs, that I'm able to support myself by selling my work, giving tutorials and running workshops.

Having a job that pays the bills takes the pressure off your creative work and enables you to make the work you want to make. One of the best books I've ever read about the creative process, and one I recommend all the time, is Elizabeth Gilbert's *Big Magic* – do read it; I think you will enjoy it.

4 HAVE YOUR MATERIALS TO HAND

Having all your tools ready and accessible is so important when building up a regular practice. Keeping them clean and organised is vital, too – there's nothing more dispiriting than wanting to start work, only to find that your rollers are caked in ink and some of your tools have gone missing. With everything ready to go, there can be no excuses for not cracking on.

Similarly, if it's feasible, it can be a good idea to keep a block and some tools out so you can have a quick carve whenever you get the chance. One of my students is a really busy teacher with a hectic family life. Trying to find time to do any creative work was tricky, so we came up with a plan that he would leave a block and some tools on the kitchen table so whenever he sat down for a coffee break he would carve a little more on his block. It was amazing what he achieved in just five or ten minutes a day.

By now you will know how passionate I am about drawing. Therefore, in the same vein, I have a prepared drawing bag with all my materials in it so that I can just grab it and head off when I feel like it. It contains my sketchbook, pencil case, stool, water and snacks. I leave it by the door so I see it every time I go out, and if I think I can squeeze in a bit of drawing, I take it with me.

ADVICE FOR WHEN YOU ARE LACKING IN MOTIVATION

It's inevitable that there will be times when you feel unmotivated and a little unsure how to proceed with your work. Here are some suggestions that will hopefully get you going again.

1 PRACTICAL THINGS TO DO

When I'm stuck and feeling unmotivated, one of the things I do is tidy my studio. The process of sorting, clearing and cleaning is helpful in allowing my thoughts and concerns to float around – reordering my studio helps me to reorder my mind. I know many of you won't have a studio or allocated workspace, but even just cleaning your rollers, inks and inking stations or organising your prints and papers can help unstick a sticky mind. I firmly believe that no time in the studio, or at your workspace, is ever wasted time.

Looking through art books is another great way to find inspiration. I often recommend choosing a painting that you are interested in and spending some time drawing it. It's a wonderful way to learn about painting, and to improve your art history and drawing skills. Plus, the pressure is off as the subject matter is already sorted.

If possible, go and visit an exhibition. Seeing artwork first-hand is beneficial in so many ways – just spending time looking and observing can help to calm the mind, forcing you to think about something else. It can also help to improve your critical thinking skills. Ask yourself: How does it make you feel? Does the art help you to feel calm? Does it irritate you or excite you? Does it trigger any memories? If you don't like it, can you say why? When you look at a new piece of art, your brain starts looking for patterns, shapes and anything else that is familiar to help you feel more connected to the piece. Even if you don't 'get it', your brain is still going to work, trying to find meaning in what you're looking at. One study found that a single hour in a museum changed the way people thought and felt. The subjects of the study exhibited improved critical thinking skills, increased empathy for how people lived in the past, and improved tolerance for people different from themselves. The next time you've got a brain-block, looking at art just might help to clear it up!

Finally, organise a creative afternoon with a friend. You could use the time to show each other your work so you can help and advise one another – or why not work quietly together, having a natter? When I lived in London, eight of my other artist friends and I would get together once a month at my friends' studio, where we would chat, drink tea, eat and make work – we called it 'the Imaginarium'. Those afternoons are some of the happiest and most creative times from my thirties.

2 LOOK FOR INSPIRATION IN THE ORDINARY

One of the reasons I have set most of the projects in this book around the house and garden is to prove that you don't have to travel far to find inspiration. During the pandemic, travelling anywhere was difficult and many of us looked to our surrounding area for ideas.

For one of my beginners' drawing projects, I ask my students to create a still life from the items under their kitchen sink. It might not sound like the most exciting of subjects, but they always draw happily for three hours and are amazed at how interesting they find the relationship between a bottle of detergent and a cleaning sponge!

3 SHARE YOUR WORK

Sharing your work with others and getting positive feedback can be such a motivator. If you are feeling unconfident about your work, I always suggest showing it to someone who you know will appreciate it and encourage you. Similarly, if you are feeling more robust and want to be challenged, show your work to someone who you feel will offer you constructive and helpful feedback.

Sharing on social media can be very beneficial too. The more you share, the easier it gets, and you will become much stronger and more resilient.

4 ZOOM OUT AND GET THE BIGGER PICTURE

Often, when I'm stuck or struggling for motivation, it's because I've become self-conscious and too much in my own head. I find one of the best remedies for this is to get some perspective. I remind myself that no-one is as concerned or bothered about my work as I am, and instead of finding that thought demotivating, I find it really liberating. It enables me to get on with my work while feeling much less self-conscious.

5 REMINDING YOURSELF IT DOESN'T HAVE TO BE PERFECT

Being a perfectionist can be crippling when it comes to making artwork. At the core of perfectionism is fear: fear of failing, being rejected and not measuring up to others' expectations. This vulnerability has the ability to stop us in our tracks and prevent us from making artwork.

One student of mine was busy working on a Christmas card design. When we met for a tutorial, she had been working on her print all week and was clearly dispirited. I asked her what she didn't like about the print, and she said she disliked all of it and

that it wasn't 'perfect'. Now, to me, the print was fun, full of interesting marks and shaping up to a be truly fabulous Christmas card. She had already come up with another design that was so different from the original one and was about to embark on carving it, even though she was running out of time and was clearly in a panic – not the best conditions for carving! I encouraged her to put her work aside, put the print away and review it in a few days to see how she felt. The week after, I received an email with a photo of the original card, looking wonderful. She said she was so happy she persevered, and that she was pleased with the print now. It's so good to remind yourself that people aren't going to see the imperfections you see and looking for them is only holding you back.

6 CELEBRATE

Another great way to get yourself out of a creative rut is to review your progress. Whenever I feel a bit glum and stuck, I get a pen and paper out and list everything I've achieved in the past two weeks; things that I haven't found easy but have done anyway. It doesn't have to relate to your artwork, (although that, of course, would be great), it could just be making a dentist appointment or cleaning out the garage. I find when I have a list of things that I have accomplished, it motivates and inspires me to get going on work that I'm avoiding starting.

7 REMIND YOURSELF WHY YOU DO IT

And finally, most importantly, remind yourself what you love about printmaking. What is it that drew you towards it? What makes you want to keep coming back for more? For me, it's the pure joy of peeling back the print for the first time – that magical moment of the first reveal. And, of course, the process of drawing – the physical act of making marks on paper – which brings me so much pleasure. To be honest, I love it all, but when you are feeling deflated and unmotivated, it's easy to lose sight of the fundamentals.

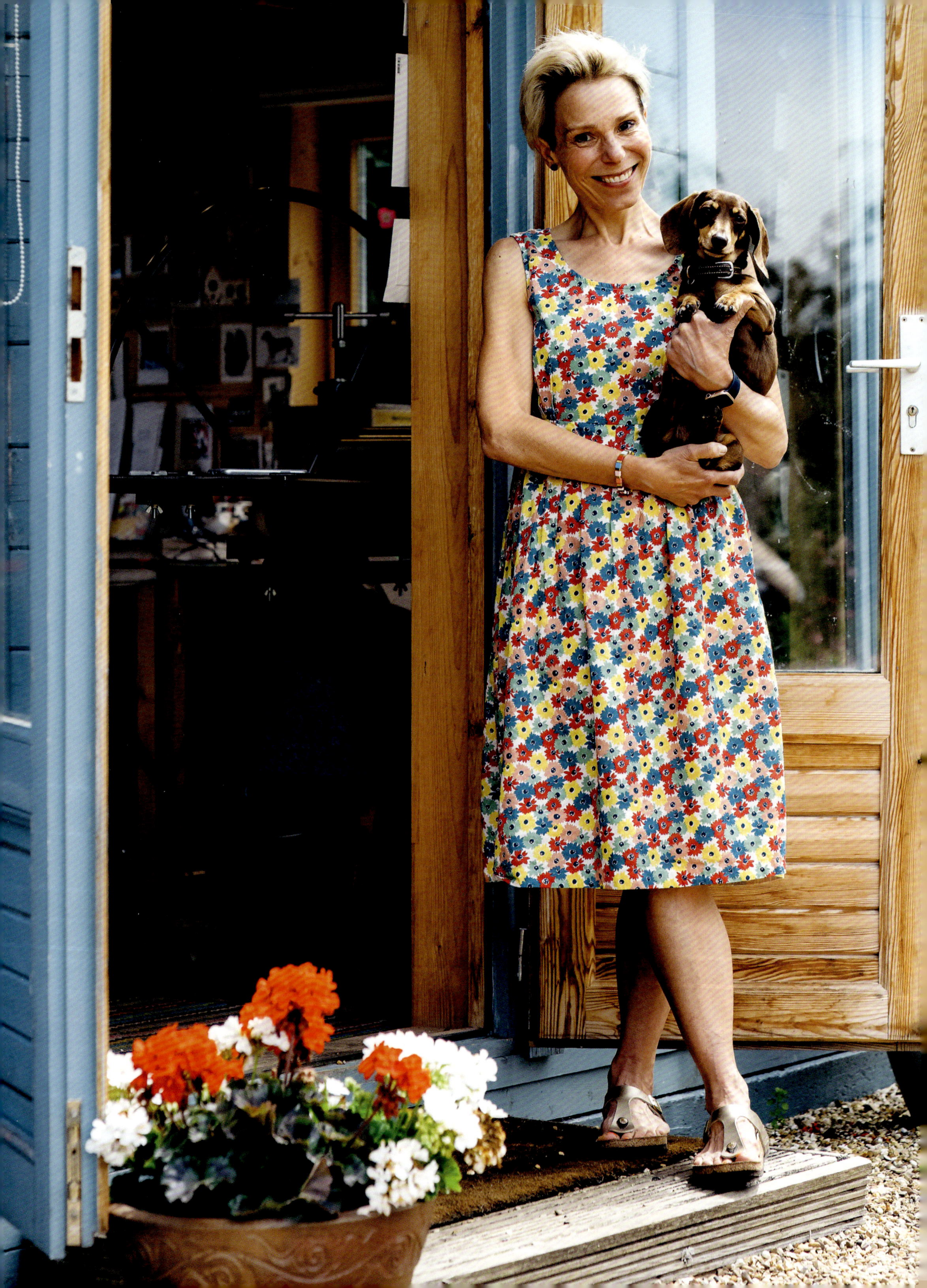

CALL YOURSELF AN ARTIST

One last thing before I go: If you have done some or all of the exercises in the book and you are continuing with printmaking on a regular basis – which I hope you are – then I would like you to call yourself a 'printmaker', or an 'artist', or both. So many people are afraid to call themselves artists or printmakers as they don't feel they are good enough or don't believe they have the 'right' to do so.

In this fabulous quote, 'Every child is an artist. The problem is how to remain an artist once he grows up', Picasso implies his belief that we are all born artists, we just lose our belief in ourselves as we grow up.

The dictionary definition of a printmaker is: 'A person who makes pictures or designs by printing them from specially prepared plates or blocks.' So, if you do this – and I believe you all do – then you are a printmaker.

And here is the dictionary definition of an artist: 'A person who creates art (such as painting, sculpture, music or writing) using conscious skill and creative imagination.' So, this means if you create something with creative imagination, you can call yourself an artist.

It doesn't matter if you earn money from your work or whether you attended art school – you can still call yourself an artist. Try to practise not caring about other people's opinions of whether they think your art is 'good enough' for you to call yourself an artist. Believe me, you will always find people who either like or dislike your work!

I hear you, though; it might sound a bit grandiose and pompous, and indeed just the thought of calling yourself a printmaker or an artist might make you squirm, but just try it out and see how you feel. It's all about confidence and believing in yourself. Try to forget about what other people might think and say it with pride – even if you don't quite believe it yourself. Over time, you will.

I love this quote from Andy Warhol (I have it printed out on the wall in my studio): 'Don't think about making art, just get it done. Let everyone else decide if it's good or bad, whether they love it or hate it. While they are deciding, make even more art.'

And on that note, I will say goodbye. Thank you for printing along with me. I wish you all the best with your continuing printmaking practice.

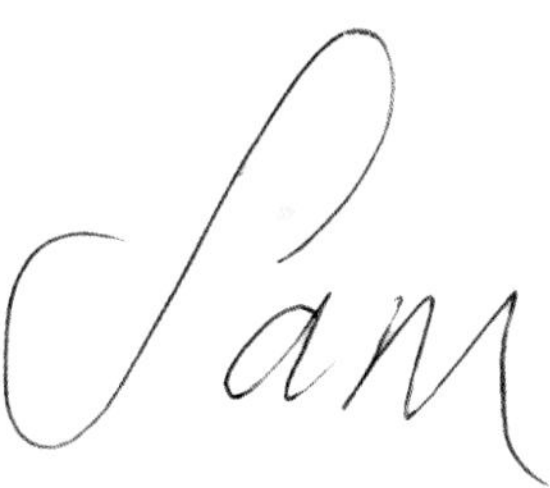

SUPPLIERS

UK

HANDPRINTED
Bognor Regis, West Sussex
www.handprinted.co.uk

HAWTHORN PRINTMAKING SUPPLIES
Murton, North Yorkshire
www.hawthornprintmaker.com

INTAGLIO PRINTMAKER
Southwark, London
www.intaglioprintmaker.com

IRONBRIDGE PRINTMAKERS
Ironbridge, Shropshire
www.ironbridgeframing.co.uk

JACKSON'S ART SUPPLIES
Stoke Newington, London
www.jacksonsart.com

LAWRENCE ART SUPPLIES
Hove, East Sussex
www.lawrence.co.uk

USA

BLICK ART MATERIALS
Stores throughout the USA
www.dickblick.com

MCCLAIN'S
(Online only)
www.imcclains.com

FRANCE

JOOP STOOP
Paris
www.joopstoop.fr/en

GERMANY

GERSTAECKER
(Online only)
www.gerstaecker.de

MODULOR GMBH
Berlin
www.modulor.de/en

SPAIN

GRABAD ONLINE
(Online only)
www.grabadonline.com

AUSTRALIA

ART TO ART
Adelaide
www.arttoart.net

UNION ST PRINTMAKERS
Hindmarsh, Adelaide
www.unionstprintmakers.com